The Complete and Utter 'My Word!' Collection

A strange feature of the English language is the way in which many of our well-known phrases and sayings started out as something quite different. For instance, it is believed that the conjuror's phrase 'Hocus-pocus' is a travesty of the words which opened the consecration of the Mass 'Hoc est corpus'.

But it remained for Frank Muir and Denis Norden to reveal to the listeners of the 'My Word!' radio programme the full extent of the damage to our oral culture. Who would have dreamed, until Mr Muir opened our eyes, that the hollow cliché 'You can't have your cake and eat it' was a corruption of the wise old Eskimo saying 'You can't have your Kayak and heat it'?

Who would have suspected – until Mr Norden blew the gaff – that the dull rhetoric of the bard's 'Dress'd in a little brief authority' in fact derived from the vivid description of a daringly sparse costume at a north London fancy dress party – 'Dressed in a little brie for Thora T'?

Over the past twenty-five years Messrs Muir and Norden, maestros of hocus pocus, have developed their perverse art of elucidation into a unique literary genre. Four volumes of their stories – originally elaborated over the air – have captured in print the intricate lunacies of the human spirit of which they have become such celebrated exponents. *The Complete and Utter 'My Word!' Collection* brings these outrageously tall stories together within the compass of a single volume for the first time.

METHUEN HUMOUR CLASSICS

Chas Addams
ADDAMS AND EVIL

Alphonse Allais
A WOLF IN FROG'S CLOTHING
Selected, translated and introduced
by Miles Kington

H. M. Bateman
THE MAN WHO . . . AND OTHER DRAWINGS

Noël Coward
THE LYRICS OF NOËL COWARD
A WITHERED NOSEGAY

A. P. Herbert
UNCOMMON LAW
MORE UNCOMMON LAW

Paul Jennings
GOLDEN ODDLIES

Jerome K. Jerome
THREE MEN IN AN OMNIBUS
Edited and introduced by Martin Green

Osbert Lancaster
THE LITTLEHAMPTON SAGA

Tom Lehrer
TOO MANY SONGS BY TOM LEHRER

S. J. Perelman
THE LAST LAUGH
THE MOST OF S. J. PERELMAN

W. C. Sellar and R. J. Yeatman
1066 AND ALL THAT
AND NOW ALL THIS

James Thurber
LET YOUR MIND ALONE!
THE MIDDLE-AGED MAN ON THE FLYING
   TRAPEZE

FRANK MUIR & DENIS NORDEN

The Complete and Utter 'My Word!' Collection

Stories from the panel game devised by
Edward J. Mason and Tony Shryane

A METHUEN HUMOUR CLASSIC

A METHUEN PAPERBACK
This collection first published in 1983
This paperback edition first published in 1984
by Methuen London Ltd
11 New Fetter Lane, London EC4 4EE
Reprinted 1985

You Can't Have Your Kayak and Heat It first published in 1973
Upon My Word! first published in 1974
Take My Word For It first published in 1978
Oh, My Word! first published in 1980
by Eyre Methuen Ltd
The 'My Word!' Stories (incorporating *You Can't Have Your Kayak and Heat It* and *Upon My Word!*) with a new introduction reproduced on page ix first published 1976 by Methuen Paperbacks Ltd

Copyright © 1973, 1974, 1980 and 1983
by Frank Muir and Denis Norden

Printed in Great Britain
by Richard Clay (The Chaucer Press) Ltd
Bungay, Suffolk

ISBN 0 413 56420 7

Contents

Upon My Word!

Take My Word For It

Oh, My Word!

Introduction

Readers who have never heard the radio programme in which these stories were first brought forth are due a word of explanation.

'My Word!' was devised by Tony Shryane and Edward J. Mason in 1956. It is a literary quiz in which the contestants, instead of treating the subject with the usual po-faced reverence, are encouraged to indulge in what Robert Frost called 'perhapsing around'.

For one of the questions on the first show the two male contestants were each given a quotation and asked to explain when, where and by whom the phrase was first used. The quotations were 'Let not poor Nellie starve', and 'Dead, dead and never called me Mother!'. As the first one was too easy, and the second one was a bit difficult to identify as to names and dates, we each invented our answers: (1) 'It was first said by the chef at the Savoy when, late at night and short of puddings, he poured things over a peach, hastily christened it "Peach Melba", and sent it out to a famished Dame Nellie Melba'; (2) 'It was first said by a lad reeling away from a vandalised phone-box after failing to telephone his parent.'

This round became a permanent part of the show and, as the years rolled by, the short explanations grew longer, wilder and more wide-ranging, while the puns at the end – apart from giving pleasure to those listeners who guessed them before we came to them – became less important and more desperate.

And so for a great many years now we have been faced each week with the agony of having to knock out a reasonably coherent story based upon a given quotation – however unpromising the quotation's syllables appeared at first sight.

This volume is a final medley of the squeaks produced by the pips being thus squeezed.

F.M. and D.N.

You Can't Have Your Kayak and Heat It

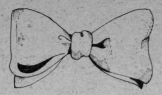

NOW that I am in my fifties, and looking forward to the first glimmerings of the approach of the beginning of the first foothills of early middle-age, I can look back, in my tweedy, pipe-smoking way, to the searingly painful process of growing up and be glad that it is at last almost over.

I suppose my most traumatic period was when I was fourteen. A lot of significant things happened to me that year: my nickname was changed from 'Flossie' to 'Raker', I became aware of my personal appearance, and I discovered Women – or, to be more precise, Maudie Thwaites.

Up until this hinge in my life I had been a happy enough little lad. We lived at Broadstairs and I enjoyed a healthy, open-air life, losing one sandal every day on the beach and riding my bike; I had one of the first dynamos, a great thing the size of a teapot which clamped to the front wheel with such force that I had to stand on the pedals to get the bike to go faster than 2 mph. And I was a short, chubby fellow, addicted to candy-floss – hence my nickname, Flossie.

On or about my fourteenth birthday a number of dramatic changes occurred. Almost overnight I shot up from being five foot one and a half inches to being six foot three inches, and my teeth started to splay out – hence my new nickname of The Rake, or Raker. Bets were laid at my school on whether I could eat an apple through a tennis racquet.

And I fell madly in love with Maudie Thwaites. With the wisdom of hindsight I can't think why I did this, apart from the undeniable truth that she was there. She was very short indeed, and dumpy with it. She wore spectacles, which she was in the habit of pushing back up her nose with a forefinger about every third second, and she preferred sniffing to having a good blow. And she always seemed to be leaning up against a wall. She would spend whole evenings leaning up against

3

a wall, pushing her spectacles back up and sniffing. I don't think I have ever met anybody since, with the possible exception of the late Mr Maurice Winnick, so devoted to leaning up against a wall. She also kept saying "I'm bored".

It was a period of the most acute agony for me. I had become extremely self-conscious about my appearance, which meant that I was overcome with shyness if anybody even looked in my direction, let alone spoke to me.

I tried to improve my appearance. I went at my hair with fistfuls of solidified brilliantine. To make myself look spotty like the older boys I stuck little round bits of cut-up inner-tube on my chin and neck with fish glue. I persuaded my parents to let me have a brace on my teeth – a device made of gold wire which went round the front of the teeth with two little screws at the back which, when tightened a quarter of a turn every other day, dragged the teeth, squealing, back into the skull. But all to little avail.

Whenever I joined Maud at a wall, all six foot three of me, with my rubber spots and my hair sticking out like a sweep's brush dipped in sump oil, she would just sniff and say "I'm bored". And I couldn't think of anything to say back.

This was partly because I didn't know what 'bored' meant. It wasn't a word which had crossed my path before. I thought it meant something like "I'm Belgian". So I would just lean with her in miserable silence for an hour or so and go home. What, I asked myself desperately, does one DO with a woman?

The whole affair might have ended there had not a friend lent me a book. I was quite interested in moths and butterflies at the time and when my friend slipped this book to me and whispered its name in class I accepted it gratefully; I thought he had whispered "Lady Chatterley's Larva". On the way home in the tram I started reading it and it wasn't about larva at all. It was about a gamekeeper and a lady in a wood and he was chewing her ear. But what interested me was that the lady liked it. It had never occurred to me that what ladies wanted was not being talked to but something much easier to do – having an ear chewed.

Elated, I sought out Maud and found her leaning up against the Public Library wall.

"I'm bored," she said.

With quiet confidence I leaned down and gave her ear a thorough gnawing.

Now one thing I omitted to mention was that Maud was an ear-ring girl. Some girls are ear-ring girls and some are celluloid slide girls and some are slave-bangle girls. But Maud was an ear-ring girl and that night she was sporting a large, complicated pair made of bent wire in the shape of gladioli.

And as I tried to straighten up – my back was beginning to give – I found that I couldn't. It was as though we were welded together. A moment's panic, a brief exploration, and the ghastly truth was apparent: her ear-ring and my tooth-brace had somehow got twisted round each other and we were fast-lodged.

It was during the ensuing two hours, before we got to Margate General Hospital and the Casualty Officer disconnected us, that I left childish things behind me and became a man. My emergence from the chrysalis was somewhat accelerated by the language Maud used; a string of words entirely new to me – I tried one out on my mother when I got home and she caught me such a cracker with her ring-finger hand that I ricocheted off three walls.

But more than that, Maud's behaviour during that arduous journey opened my eyes to the danger of giving one's affection to a woman before she has proved herself worthy of it. She repeatedly tried to pretend that it was all my fault. My fault! As if *I* had made her wear the fatal ear-rings! And she did nothing but grizzle and complain – and, of course, sniff. She complained when, with a new authority I had somehow acquired, I persuaded old Mr Toddy to cart us part of the way in his wheelbarrow. She moaned at me when cars refused to give us a hitch-hike into Margate – it wasn't my fault, it was the fault of the stuff we had to lie on in the bottom of the wheelbarrow.

And she even carried on when I finally got Mr Parkinson to drive us all the way to the hospital, even though we could lie down comfortably in the back of his vehicle, bracing ourselves against the coffin.

I used to see Maud from time to time after that day and we would chat civilly enough but my passion was spent; I had grown up.

Sometimes, as I was strolling through the town with a younger, more impressionable friend, he would spot Maud leaning up against the wall and ask eagerly, "Hey, who's that leaning up against the wall?"

"That?" I would say, a light, sophisticated smile playing about the corners of my mouth:

"Maud, bored, and dangerous to gnaw."

A nod is as good as a wink to a blind horse

R. H. Barham
'*The Ingoldsby Legends*'

IN 1942, I was a Wop. Before I get either a reproachful letter from the Race Relations people or a Welcome Home card from the Mafia, let me explain that term. In 1942, a 'Wop' was the RAF abbreviation for 'Wireless Operator', and that was what Daddy did in World War Two. (Oh, come on, child, you've heard of World War Two, it starred Leslie Banks.) I was 1615358, Wireless Operator U/T: U/T being another ingenious RAF abbreviation. It stood for 'Under Training'.

About that training. The RAF had calculated that the maximum period necessary to transform even the most irresolute of civilians into a red-hot Wireless Operator was three months. At the time we are considering, I had been Under Training for a year and a half.

That, again, needs some explanation. You see, before the RAF would allow you to Operate a Wireless for them, you had to pass two completely different examinations. They were both designed to test your skill at reading Morse Code signals.

The first one tested whether you could read them aurally. That, if I've spelt the word right, does not mean through your mouth – but through your ears. What happened was, you put on a wireless headset and translated any Morse bleeps you heard into letters of the alphabet.

Of the two tests, that was the one I had no trouble with. In fact, I can still do it. To this day, I find myself 'hearing' Morse in all sorts of things. Remember the 'Dragnet' theme – "Dum . . . di-*dum*-dum!"? To my ears, that still comes out as "Dah . . . di-*dah*-dit", which is Morse Code for 'T.R.' Useful facility, isn't it?

No, it was the second test which, as far as Wireless Operating was concerned, turned me into what we now call a late developer. In this test you had to prove that you could read Morse 'visually'.

Let me describe what that entailed. They stood you on top of a hill, from which you gazed across a valley at another hill. On top of that hill stood the Senior NCO we called 'Fanny', for reasons which memory has blurred.

He operated what was known as an Aldis lamp, a sort of lantern with movable shutters in front. He blinked this on and off at you. The alternations of long blinks of light and short blinks of light formed the Morse Code letters which the RAF expected you, at that distance, to distinguish, translate and write down.

I couldn't even see them. To me, the whole operation was just a vaguely luminous, slightly shimmering, blur.

There was good reason for this. A reason immediately apparent to any of you who've ever seen me in that temple of peculiar pleasure, the flesh. The most dominant feature is the glasses with the thick black frames. I wear them nowadays not, as some have supposed, to de-emphasise the deep eye-sockets but to stop me bumping into things. Like office blocks.

In *those* days, however . . . in 1942! Well, I was only going on for twenty, wasn't I? There were girls! I mean, did anyone ever see Robert Taylor wearing *glasses*? Not even when he was playing a scientist.

So that was why, long before the Beatles were even born, I was known to Fanny as 'the fool on the hill'. Never mind not being able to distinguish the blinks of his Aldis lamp – I could barely make out the intervening valley.

I could well have remained Under Training until the Yalta Conference. The reason why I didn't can be summed up in the words of another Beatles' song: 'I get by with a little help from my friends'. Specifically, the other trainees on that 1942 course.

Mind you, it wasn't easy for them to help me. Regulations demanded that the rest of the class stood at least ten yards behind the trainee taking the test – so that no Hawkeye among them could *whisper* the letters to him as they were being blinked out.

So what they did was this. They put themselves in possession of a very long stick of bamboo. 'Liberated' it, as we then used to say. Then, as each letter was flashed at me, they prodded that stick into the small of my back. Soft-prod for a short blink of the lamp, hard-prod for a long blink.

If we return to that Dragnet example, in bamboo-stick terms it becomes "HARD . . . Soft-*HARD*-soft". Are you with me? So was good fortune. I passed out top of the entry.

Admittedly, I still have to see the osteopath once a week. And, what's more, paying for the visit out of my own pocket. Although I could well present the damaged spinal column to authority as an authentic war wound, to do so might spoil someone else's chances. Because, so I've been told, the ploy is still operating in the RAF.

Even today, RAF trainees who have trouble making out what visual signals are being shone into their short-sighted eyes, are being rescued by that same system of dig-in-the-back simultaneous translation. The lads have even adapted a proverb to cover the situation:

A prod is as good as a blink to a shined Morse.

So he passed over, and all the trumpets sounded for him on the other side

John Bunyan
'Pilgrim's Progress'

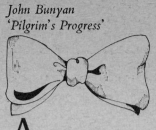

A FEW weeks ago the publisher, Mark Bonham Carter, was walking in Hyde Park when he heard somebody calling his name, "Mark! Mark!" He turned and there was nobody there. He walked on a little and again he heard a small rather querulous voice call, "Mark! Mark! Mark!" Then he looked downwards and there at his ankles was a small dog with a hare lip.

I mention the incident as a demonstration of the peculiar quality which names have for being other things.

I mean, did you know that the Victoria and Albert Museum was named after two people? Well, it was. It was named after the men who founded it, Frank Mu and Alastair Seum.

And take Strip-Tease. Were you aware that Strip-Tease was named after the man who imported it into this country at the fag-end of the last century, Phineas Stripp? Well, it was. It had no name in France but when Phineas imported the idea he hired a theatre in London in between the matinee and the evening performance and served tea while the ladies divested. These became known as Stripp Teas, and the name stuck.

The story of how Phineas, a poor boy with dreams, beat the great impresarios at their own game is gripping. Not very funny, but gripping. Well, not very gripping really; say, semi-gripping.

He had heard tell from travellers that a new form of entertainment was sweeping the halls of Calais and Dieppe. A number of girls were engaged – chiefly from the ranks of unemployed clog-chisellers – and each was provided with a pair of stout, iron button-hooks. Then, to the inflammatory music of Offenbach, the girls stood on stage and proceeded to unbutton their dresses. As at that time the dresses were done up with over three hundred buttons the process took about an hour and a half. The girls then posed for an intoxicating moment in an undershift of bullet-proof mauve bombazine reaching from shin to neck and the customers reeled out into the night air with steam coming out of their ears.

Phineas set to work. He persuaded a theatre manager to lend him a theatre in exchange for two pounds in cash, a second-hand overcoat with a fur collar and first crack at the lady clog-chisellers. Next Phineas had suitable music written for him, on tick, by the composer Hubert Seldom-Byte. His name is not remembered much now but in those days Seldom-Byte was the English equivalent of Offenbach.

It was at that point that young Phineas came up against a snag. His next move was to travel across the channel to Calais and audition a batch of unbuttoners. Although of tender years Phineas had been through the School of Hard Knocks and he had no illusions about the girls: he was fully aware that any unemployed clog-chisellers prepared to parade themselves stark-naked from the shin down and the neck up were No Better Than They Ought To Be, and would need to be carefully selected if he was to get them past Customs.

But he had no money for the fare to Calais.

A lesser man might have given up at this point. For a moment Phineas did contemplate returning to his old job of sprinkling tinsel on coloured picture-postcards of Lord Palmerston but British grit won through. He decided to swim. Or rather, as he could not swim, to float.

It was bitterly cold on Broadstairs beach that morning when, watched by a small group of weeping creditors, Phineas prepared to take to the waves. He had provided himself with twenty yards of string upon which he had threaded eight hundred medicine-bottle corks. With a creditor holding one end of the string, Phineas tied the other end just below his knee then spun round like a tee-to-tum until he had wound himself up in the corks and string. He sang out a cheery farewell, hopped to the water's edge and fell in.

He floated rather well. In a moment the tide had caught him and along the coast he went, his brave figure getting smaller and smaller to the tense watchers on the beach.

Half an hour later his brave figure began to get larger and larger. Just when he was approaching Dover the tide had changed and swept him back to Broadstairs.

The following morning he tried again: the same thing happened. Forty-eight attempts he made that long, hot summer and never once got beyond Dover before being returned by the changing tide.

Then came the breakthrough. One day he was standing next to the plate-glass window of a toy-shop – just reflecting – when he glanced within. There, in the window, a tiny boat was being demonstrated. It skeetered busily around a plateful of water propelled by a tiny chip of camphor at its rear end.

"Europa!" cried Phineas (who had little Greek). "That's my answer!"

In a trice he had purchased from a ladies' outfitters a voluminous undergarment pioneered by Mrs Amelia Bloomer for the use of lady bicyclists. He put double-strength elastic in where the garment gripped below the knees, climbed in, and poured half a hundredweight of fresh camphor balls in at the rear. It was but the work of a moment to wind himself up in the string and corks and totter into the briny.

What a difference this time. There was a fizzing and a bubbling behind him and he found himself zig-zagging erratically round Broadstairs harbour. Fortunately all the Stripp family were noted for their enormous, spatula-like feet and Phineas found that by moving his feet this way and that they made a pair of fine rudders, giving him perfect steering control. He straightened up and, to a muffled cheer from the beach, settled down to a steady eight knots on a course of roughly SE by S.

The rest is show-biz history (see *Decline and Fall of the Holborn Empire*, Eddy Gibbon, vol. 4, chap. 8).

So he passed Dover, and all the strumpets undid for him on the other side.

Charity shall cover the multitude of sins

The New Testament
First Epistle General of Peter

I happened to drop into my club last week – it's
the Odeon Saturday Morning Club, I try to get in there about once a
month – and, while the adverts were on, I got chatting to the fellow
sitting next to me. He made a disconcerting observation about the way
I tell these stories on the 'My Word!' radio programmes. "Do you
realise," he said, "you have a very . . . slow . . . delivery."

Now that's a strangely uncomfortable thing to have pointed out
about yourself, that you've got a very slow delivery. It makes you
feel like a delinquent laundryman. Or an inexperienced gynaecologist.
Although this chap went on to explain that all he meant was that my
mode of utterance seems inordinately deliberate and emphatic, that
only made me feel worse. You see, I know the reason *why* I talk like
that when on the wireless. And there is no way of making that reason
sound like an achievement.

It's because, on these broadcasting occasions, I am invariably drunk.
Oh, not "I'll fight any man in the room" drunk, not even "I've brought
nothing but unhappiness to everybody who's ever had anything to do
with me" drunk. Just "unless I say this word slowly it won't come out
right" drunk.

It's all a result of something that happened to me about the time I
reached forty. Some kind of chemical change took place in my – it's
all right, you can do these four-letter words now – body. I don't know
exactly what happened but, almost overnight, the absolute minimum
of alcohol suddenly became sufficient to start me yodelling. Isn't it
terrible to be struck down like that in the prime of life? Without any
prior warning, I became a secret non-drinker.

What made that almost a professional disaster, however, was that
the alteration in my metabolism coincided almost exactly with the
tenth year of the 'My Word!' series. Let me explain the significance of
that anniversary: when a radio programme has been on the air for ten

12

years, it thereafter becomes eligible for what the BBC calls 'hospitality'; henceforth, the Corporation provides drinks for the cast before the programme. Mind you, when I say 'drinks', perhaps I should be more precise. Five slim-line tonic-waters, and a bottle of gin which you are allowed to drink down as far as the pencil-mark. So there I was, invited at last to drink at the BBC's expense – but, at the same time, rendered physically incapable of accepting the invitation.

Why couldn't I simply stick to tonic-water, you may ask. To answer that, one has to understand the workings of a public corporation. If they were to discover that their bottle of gin was not being drunk down to the pencilled-level indicated, Accounts Department would then embark on what's called 'revising the estimate'. The following week, we'd find the pencil-mark an inch higher up the bottle. And, in Show-Business, status is all. The first question any member of one BBC programme asks a representative of another programme is, "How far down the bottle is your pencil-mark?"

"All right," you might acknowledge, "then why don't you just give your gins to one of the other people in the show?" Answer: it would only create worse problems. I mean, which one could I give them to? Certainly not Dilys Powell or Anne Scott-James. Look, you know from films what lady newspaper-columnists are like. Think of Glenda Farrell, Eve Arden, Rosalind Russell – tough, cynical, suspicious. Way their minds work, any man who starts offering them buckshee gins, he's only after one thing.

Jack Longland, then? No, it just wouldn't be right. You can't offer additional gins to a man who has to drive his wife all the way back to Derbyshire after every programme. It's already difficult enough for him to negotiate those motorways with someone sitting on his cross-bar.

Frank Muir? Oh, come on...! I know Frank's alcoholic reactions as well as I know my own. When he goes on to perform, he is already at the very frontier of his capacity. One more gin and he'd be rolling up his trouser-legs and putting on Dilys's hat.

No, for the welfare of the team, for the sake of the programme, I cannot do other than swallow those gins myself. Even though it results in my performing every show with my upper lip gone numb and my tongue feeling like it's got too large to fit my mouth.

That's the reason for my slow delivery. The only way I can disguise the fact that I have consumed more alcohol than my body can now deal with is to articulate very slowly and ... very ... CLEARLY. In the hope that, as the Good Book almost has it:

"Clarity shall cover the multitude of gins."

And so to bed

Samuel Pepys
'Diary'

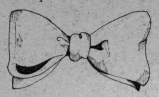

"OH, botheration!" exclaimed Drusilla Kennington-Oval, her gamine face puckering at the corners in a tiny moue of vexation. She had come to the end of her novel, *Heartsease*, by Monica Liphook (Olympia Press), and it was time for her to get out of bed and face another mad, jolly, gorgeous day.

She widened her slim, artistic fingers, and a thumb, and the book slipped to the cottage floor with an unaccustomed plonk. In a trice she was out of bed, long limbs flashing, and down on her knees mopping up the plonk – a bottle of agreeable but cheap Yugoslav Chablis which she was trying out.

It was nearly half-past ten and already she could hear her farmer neighbours beginning to stir; the slam of a shooting-brake door as one set off for a round of golf; the cheerful clatter of helicopter blades as another was whisked away to some dreary old business meeting in Brussels.

Not wanting to miss a minute of glorious sunshine Dru flung on an old pair of patched jeans, thrust her feet into an old pair of patched moccasins and ran down to her front gate.

"Hello, Mr Helicopter Pilot!" she cried gaily, waving both her arms high in the air. "Bon voyage!"

The helicopter hit a tree.

Biting her lip at her silly forgetfulness she ran back into the cottage and flung on an old patched bra and an old patched sweater.

Dru never was much of a one for breakfast. Just a spoonful or two of game pâté flung onto an old Bath Oliver biscuit and she was running like a deer over the familiar hillocks and meadows of Platt's Bottom, breathing in the pure country air – she loved breathing – stopping only for a quick draw on a fag or a chat with a cow.

And then ... suddenly, there was Derwent Hilliton. A moment before, the lane had been empty. But, now. There was Derwent Hilliton in his new Maserati, forty feet long and nine inches high. Derwent ...

"Hi, you!" said Derwent, in his usual laconic fashion. He was wiping a speck of dust from the steering-wheel with a ten pound note. Once again Dru was conscious of the sheer animal magnetism which exuded from his every pore. As ever, she caught her breath at his fabulous profile, which he was holding so that she could admire it. There was something almost feminine in his grace of movement as he folded the banknote and put it back into his handbag.

"This is good-bye, Dru." He said, all of a sudden.

"But ..." gasped Dru, "Why ...? What ...? Who ...? When ...? If ...? Could ...? Is ...? How ...? Can ...?"

"Father has just given me a million pounds to make good on my own. I'm off to Tibet tomorrow to build a luxury hotel; the Shangri-La-Hilliton."

"I see. At least, I think I see."

"But it doesn't have to be good-bye. Will you come, Dru? As Mrs Hilliton. Think it over. I'll ring you tonight."

With a muffled roar from the gold-plated twin-exhausts, he was gone.

Dru's heart was in a turmoil; lickety-spit, lickety-spit, it went. Did she really love him? Did he really love her? What to do?

As ever when she was troubled she found that her feet had taken her to Blair Tremayne's cottage, at the back of the 'Dog and Duck'.

And as ever her heart skipped a beat at the simple, bachelor scene inside. An old tennis racquet lying just where he had used it for draining the chips. An old army boot full of cold porridge ready for an early breakfast. The old-fashioned wooden mangle he used for getting the last scrap of toothpaste out of the tube.

For Blair had no father to give him a million pounds. He was just a humble, dedicated writer, hard at work translating a French/English dictionary into English/French. But so kind. And reliable. And ...

A muffled grunt made her turn, and there was Blair towering over her. He folded her in his arms twice – he had rather long arms – and hugged her tightly to him.

His tweed jacket smelled deliciously of old spaniel dog.

"Dru," he gasped, throatily. "Dru. Oh, Dru ..."

Releasing one hand, he removed an old spaniel dog from beneath his jacket.

"Oh, Dru. Dru."

Blair was a man of few words and had to work those he knew rather hard.

"Dru. Me. And you, Dru. Marry? Eh, Dru? May I be Mr Drusilla Kennington-Oval?"

With a half-cry, Dru freed herself from his dear arms. She had to have time to think. So she walked, and walked. All that day she walked. Through fields, along roads; she knew not where. At one time she thought she recognised the Manchester Ship Canal. Another time she was hailed by a friend in the foyer of the Royal Albion Hotel, Bognor Regis. But she walked on.

When she arrived back at her little cottage there were two bunches of flowers waiting for her. Five hundred orchids tied with satin ribbon bore a card, "Say yes. Derwent." Three daisies tied together with fuse-wire bore a piece of tissue paper, "Be mine. Blair."

Which to choose? When she opened the curtains on the morning of the honeymoon was she to see the massive glaciers of far-off Tibet? Or an army boot full of cold porridge and a view of the Gents at the back of the 'Dog and Duck?'

Gentle reader, can you doubt her choice?

Dru made her decision. She was wedded and bedded. And on the first morning she flung back the curtains of her bedroom window . . .

And saw Tibet.

It is better to be envied than pitied

Ancient Greek Proverb

ONE of the more depressing of middle-life experiences, not that most of them aren't, is trying on your old RAF uniform and finding that the only part of it that still fits you is the tie. That's why my attention perked up at one of the adverts in my local cinema.

"Men!" it said, the exclamation-mark blinking on and off, "Are you finding yourself with more waist, less speed? Then join our Health Club." The accompanying visuals displayed a variety of narrow-hipped prematurely-greys vaulting easily over wooden horses, exchanging pleasantries in Our Organic Juice Bar and roaring off in open cars with droopy girls running fingertips up their forearm.

I joined the following day. The name of the Club escapes me now, but it was something out of mythology – 'Priam', or 'Priapus', the kind of allusion that's been popularised by all those classical scholars now on a retainer to advertising agencies for the naming of male deodorants. What I do recall is that the place was a former slaughter-house and that the young man who greeted me wore one of those thick rollneck sweaters I still associate with U-Boat captains. He also had the kind of handshake that ought never to be used except as a tourniquet. It took me a good four minutes to get my knuckles back in line.

His first move was to sell me, for a price I would normally expect to pay for a winter overcoat, a pair of gym shorts and a cotton singlet. After I'd changed into them, I presented myself before him for inspection. All right, admittedly not an impressive sight but, for heaven's sake, hardly deserving the performance he put on.

"Oh dear, oh lor," he kept repeating. He was walking round me slowly and respectfully, as one does at Hadrian's Villa or Pompeii, any of the places where the guidebooks use the phrase 'ruined grandeur' "Oh, you have let yourself go, haven't you," he said finally.

"I have," I said. "And I enjoyed it. Both times."

"Not to worry, old-timer. We'll soon have you leaping about again. Be the fittest sixty-year-old down your street."

"I'm forty-six," I said. But by this time he had me in among the rest of the class.

Well, I don't like to appear condescending, but honestly, repulsive really is the only word. Not one of them could have been a day under forty-eight or fifty. Watching all of them wheezing about in those baggy shorts and the singlets with 'I Am The Greatest' across the chest, I couldn't help but give the U-Boat captain a rueful wink, which he affected not to notice.

No one can say that, over the next hour, I didn't co-operate fully in all that bend, stretch, lift, pull, lie flat, run on the spot, up-up-up-up, everybody jump on everybody else's back. Nor did I fail to pull my weight during all the succeeding Wednesdays and Fridays that I joined the old crocks there at what I soon came privately to refer to as 'Hernia's Hideaway'.

I even did, twice a day in the privacy of my office, the special P.T. homework which the Club asked of me. As instructed, I bent forward, grasped the ends of my two feet firmly and, without letting go, did pull-pull-pull for a full quarter of an hour. As far as I could tell, the only noticeable result was that, two months later, I'd gone from a size ten shoe to a size twelve.

It was not till he got me on to weight-lifting that breaking-point was reached. Holding between his thumb and forefinger a thick iron bar with two enormous discs at either end, he said, "Righto then, your turn."

I looked behind me. "It's you I'm talking to," he said. "The Phyllo-san Kid. Let's see a standing snatch. Take your time."

I won't have anyone accuse me of not trying. I spat on my hands, bent down, took a firm grip, jammed my back-teeth together, tightened my stomach muscles, bore down on my heels, and did a sharp, powerful snatch. For eight minutes. At which point he said, "Not bad for first time. Friday we'll see if you can lift it as far as your ankles. Go and have a shower now."

I put a question to him. "Have you got the kind of shower that has its nozzle in the ground, so that the water squirts vertically upwards?"

"What do you want one of them for?"

"Because I can't straighten up."

No more could I. Well into the autumn I was still moving around in a kind of Groucho Marx lope. If Physical Training is the price you have to pay for Physical Fitness, I'll settle for pooped. Those Ancient Greeks knew what they were talking about:

It is better to be unfit than P.T.'d.

The lamps are going out all over Europe

Edward, Viscount Grey of Fallodon
3 Aug. 1914

THE Most Unforgettable Character I ever met was
– well, he's dead now and I don't remember much about him. On the
other hand, the Most Forgettable Character I ever met is most memorable. He was elected Most Forgettable Character by our form at school.
The craze for electing the Most Something-or-other had hit our form
heavily that year – I was, I recall elected the Most Smelly, an injustice
which has rankled ever since. But the application of the word 'forgettable' to Oliver Sinclair Yarrop was only too appropriate. I can see
him now, a veal-faced lad with no colour about him anywhere; his
hair was the same colour as his skin, which was colourless; he had
almost transparent ears. He took no interest at all in the normal pursuits
of healthy schoolboys, like boasting loudly, spitting, eating, punching
girls: his sole passion in life was the love, and care, of animals.

It is a melancholy fact, which as schoolboys we but dimly perceived,
that Dame Fate is a cruel Jade; and one of her little caprices is to allow
a growing lad to work up a lifetime ambition whilst at the same time
making sure that he is totally unequipped to achieve it. Thus my best
friend, Nigel Leatherbarrow, wanted to be the Pope: he was Jewish.
And my second-best-friend, Tarquin Wilson, wanted to be a girl. And
I wanted to be rich. But the worst example was poor little, Forgettable
Oliver; he desperately wanted to be a vet, and as much as he loved
animals, they loathed him.

I, interested in people but indifferent to furred and feathered beasts,
was beloved by the animal kingdom. Even now I cannot walk very
far before dogs appear from nowhere and sniff my socks. When I
return home I find a nest of field mice in my turn-ups. I have only to
pause a moment to lean up against a tree and ladybirds settle on me in
such numbers that I look as if I have galloping chicken pox.

But all animal life viewed Oliver with implacable hatred. Full of love for them, he would hold out his left hand for every dog to sniff. When he left school the fingers of his left hand were an inch shorter than those of his right hand. Every pullover he possessed was lacerated by kittens' claws. One of his jackets had lost a shoulder where a cow had taken a bite at him. His right shin bore the scar where a chicken had driven her beak in. Animals had bitten him so much that when I saw him, for the last time, stripped for gym, he looked deckle-edged.

I did not see Oliver again until after the war. I was at an RAF hospital in the country being treated for shock – brought on by the real-isation that I was about to be demobilised and would have to work for a living – and on a country walk I suddenly came upon Oliver. He had his back to a brick wall and was being attacked by a duckling. Unclamping the bird's beak from Oliver's ankle I fell to talking. He had changed considerably since we had last met. He no longer wore his school cap and long trousers covered his bony, unmemorable knees. He seemed middle-aged before his time. His hair was very thin; almost emaciated. And he only had one arm.

It seems that he gave up all hopes of becoming a vet when he realised that the exams meant maths. But an aunt died, leaving him a little money – she was a member of an obscure religious sect; he assured me that she had returned to earth and still lived with him in the form of a stuffed airedale – and he had decided to spend the rest of his life in tending animals in an amateur way. For that purpose he went for little walks, always carrying with him a thermometer and a used lolly-stick so that when he encountered an animal he could make it say "Aaah!" and take its temperature. It was work he loved.

But, he confessed with a sudden flush, he had not as yet managed to examine an animal. No sooner had he pressed his used lolly-stick on the little, or large, or forked tongue than the creature sank its teeth into the nearest available piece of Oliver and was away. Not one "Aaah!" had he achieved.

And worse than that, a blow from a robin's wing had lost him his arm. Oliver was up a ladder at the time, trying to take the temperature of this robin who was on a branch of an apple tree. Apparently Oliver thought the robin looked rather flushed so approached it with his lolly-stick and said "say 'Aaah!'" whereupon the robin flapped a wing which dislodged an apple which fell upon Oliver's fingers and he let go of the ladder.

Less obvious but just as regrettable was the loss of his left big toe when the tortoise he was trying to examine fell from his hands, and the loss of two medium toes on his right foot due to circumstances which I did not quite grasp but which entailed a rabbit and Oliver wearing green socks.

That was the last time I saw what was left of Oliver alive. I read an account of his passing-over in a local paper I was folding up the other day (I had a hole in my shoe and it was coming on to rain). The newspaper report said that Oliver Sinclair Yarrop had bent down with a lolly-stick to a young lamb and was trying to persuade it to say "Aaah!". What Oliver had not noticed was that there was a large goat just behind him. But the goat had noticed Oliver. And the temptation was too great. It had charged.

As the coroner said, it was not the butt which hurt Oliver so much as the landing, which took an appreciable time to occur during which time Oliver was accelerating at the rate of thirty-two feet per sec. But what did the deceased think he was doing, fooling about with a lamb on the edge of Beachy Head?

So the Forgettable Oliver died, and is almost forgotten. But if there is a hereafter, and I think there is, he will be happy at last. There will be green fields there. And hundreds and hundreds of little woolly lambs.

And more than that:

The lambs are going "Aaah!" to Oliver Yarrop.

Oh the little more, and how much it is

Robert Browning
'*By the Fireside*'

SOME time ago Frank Muir and I wrote a television series which turned out so dire that one newspaper considered reviewing it in the obituary column. The comment which caused Frank most distress, however, appeared in a Sunday rag. "It is now obvious that Muir and Norden have exhibited themselves so frequently as performers, they no longer possess any ability to write. They are now to be regarded merely as talkers."

I cannot recall ever seeing my colleague more choked. "Do you realise," he said, "do you realise the implications if what that paper says is true? Bang go my chances for Posterity. And you know how I feel about Posterity."

I do. He's very keen on it. "When I go," he said, "I want to be remembered."

"Well, I'll remember you," I said. "I bet I will. Burly chap with a bow-tie. Swiped my felt-nib pen."

"Nobody'd call you Posterity, would they? I'm talking about real *afterwards* Posterity. 'Merely talkers!' What a shameful rotten thing for a paper to write. Name me one 'talker' who's been remembered by Posterity. Eh? Name me one! Yes, all right, Dr Johnson. But he had Boswell, didn't he. All I've got is you."

Frank is inclined to do that. Ask you a question, answer it himself, then tell you you were wrong. This time, however, something different happened. He suddenly sat up and stared at me. Then – "Sir," he said. "Sir, it may be that you will suffice."

He had never called me 'Sir' before. Within the tundra of my heart, something thawed and started trickling. "Dear old Frank," I said. "What are you chuntering on about?"

"Boswell and Johnson," he said. "Boswell just followed Johnson around everywhere and jotted down every observation Johnson uttered into a notebook. Then he transferred all the notebook stuff into five volumes and came up with *Boswell's Life Of Dr Johnson*. One of the all-time Posterity chart-toppers! Well, why can't you do the same thing?"

"Because," I said, "I think he's dead. We could check with the British Medical Council, but they must have so many Dr Johnsons on their –"

"Sir," Frank said. "Follow me more closely. *Norden's Life of Mr Muir!* Using exactly the same technique. By cracky, the more I think about it, the more I like it. Can you give me a good reason why we can't start right away?"

"I think so," I said. "I haven't got a notebook."

"Sir," Frank said, and one could tell he was already living the part. "Sir, you will need more than one notebook. Five volumes at, say, three hundred pages per each, let's see." He stabbed expertly at his pocket-calculator. Then he took it out of his pocket and stabbed again. When we'd checked the answer with my Ready Reckoner, we set off for that Office Stationery shop in Maddox Street. The manager, I thought, seemed a little anxious when we explained ourselves.

"Sir," Frank said, not only living it now but loving it. "Sir, I am Mr Muir and this is my biographer. Do you stock those 3p notebooks with a spiral wire going up and down the spine?" We had agreed that those would be the best form of notebook for me to carry, as they wouldn't spoil the shape of my good suit when accompanying Frank to coffee-houses or journeys to the Highlands.

"I think I can find you one," the manager said.

"Sir," Frank said, "eight hundred and seventy."

One thing about that manager, he did help stack the eight hundred and seventy notebooks inside a wooden crate, in order to make them easier for me to carry. I say 'me' because, as Frank pointed out, if he were to give a hand in the humping about of a dirty great wooden crate, how would he have the puff to utter any observations for me to copy down.

As we tauntered back along Regent Street – 'taunter' is a labour-saving word I'm using to describe the appearance of one person sauntering, the other tottering – so clement and agreeable was the autumnal sunshine that Frank was moved to utter Observation One.

"Sir," he observed, "could the fact that new cars are invariably introduced in the autumn be the reason why they are sometimes known as autumnobiles?"

Unfortunately, the blood was now pounding so hard in my ears, I didn't hear what he said. "Do what?" I asked.

"I just did an observation," Frank said.

"Sorry. Hang about." I lowered the wooden crate to the pavement and took out the top notebook. "Sir," Frank said, "could the fact that new cars are invariably introduced in the why aren't you writing any of this down?"

"You've still got my felt-nib pen."

He threw it at me. "Get it down while it's fresh."

I wrote feverishly then stopped. "I didn't really hear what you said." A few people had now gathered round us. "Please," I said to Frank, "just one more time."

As he reiterated it, very slowly this time and quite loudly, I wrote it carefully into the notebook. While I was doing so, a small elderly lady plucked at my sleeve. "Excuse me, officer," she said. "What are you charging him with?"

Now it must have happened during the time that I was explaining to that lady that I was not a plain-clothes policeman, I was a biographer just starting on the first page of the first notebook of a five-volume biography, it must have been while I was busy doing that that some alert mafioso swiped the wooden crate.

That is the reason why the publication of the not-much-heralded *Norden's Life Of Mr Muir* has been unavoidably delayed. The fact is, all I have of it to date is one measly observation and a bill for eight hundred and seventy spiral wire notebooks at 3p each which comes to a sum of no less than would you believe £26.10. As Browning damn near got round to commenting:

"Oh, the little Muir, and how much it is!"

I was desolate and sick of an old passion

Ernest Dowson
'Non Sum Qualis Eram'

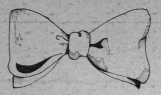

I have rather gone off Denis Norden. One does go off people from time to time. Other people I have been off (off whom I have been?) include Crippen, Hitler, Mrs Mary Whitehouse, Pontius Pilate, Patrick Campbell, Professor A. L. Rowse and Charlie Chaplin, so Denis is in good company. It's just that he was a bit infuriating this afternoon.

We had arranged to meet at his office at 3 p.m. on a matter of business – he was trying to sell me a camera which he had dropped – and when I arrived at seven minutes past the hour he said to me, with a trace of irritability in his normally suave voice, "You're late."

Well, I mean to say. He was the cause of it. Just as I was leaving home I received this garbled message from his secretary, Hedda Garbler, saying that Denis had been having lunch at a Chinese restaurant and had left something there which belonged to his aunt and would I pick it up on my way in and thank you.

Ever the one to oblige an old friend I dropped in to the restaurant and collected the thing, of which the management was visibly glad to be relieved, which appeared to be a rolled-up, dark grey, very tatty sheepskin rug – and rather smelly with it.

I proceeded blithely along Kensington High Street in an easterly direction, playing with the thing the way one does when carrying a thing – tossing it in the air and catching it, punting it along the pavement for a bit, shoving it under the arm and carrying it like a rugger ball – when I realised that it was giving off warmth. This was a little alarming so I stopped and began to unwrap the bundle. Or rather, I tried to unwrap the bundle. It was not a bundle. Or a rolled-up rug. It was a very, very old, mangy Persian cat.

Now I am not a cat man. I am unable to exchange minds with a cat. Sigmund Freud spent thirty years researching into the feminine soul before confessing that he could find no answer to the question: what does a woman *want*? I feel the same sense of inadequacy with a cat.

I looked at the cat and the cat returned the favour with a steady look of cold, implacable malevolence.

I decided upon a show of strength.

"All right, Moggy," I said firmly, "let's go."

She gave a sort of sweep with one arm and my hair had four partings in it.

Cats have these scimitars built into their paws for just this sort of aggro and my old lady had hers locked in the 'attack' position. A sharp pain in my side told me that she was putting in some serious work on my jacket – obviously trying to get at my liver.

In a flash I grabbed her by the neck and stuffed her into my jacket pocket. I left her head sticking out so that she could breathe but by clamping my hand against the pocket I had her tightly pinioned.

"Get out of that!" I chortled.

I felt her go rigid. I realised later that she went rigid when she was thinking things out; planning her next move.

It came just as I was about level with the Albert Hall. My right thigh began to grow hot. Then it grew cold. And my right ankle felt distinctly damp.

She had gained the initiative once again.

Hoisting her out of my pocket by the neck and holding her at arm's length I nipped into that little ironmonger's shop near Albert Hall Mansions, bought a ball of shiny string, tied one end round her neck and paid out the string until I had her on a ten-yard-long lead. My thinking was that by the time she had run that ten yards, scimitars bared, I would have had a chance to take evasive action.

She was furious. She immediately went rigid, pondering, and I was able to make quite a bit of distance, dragging her along on the end of the string.

She got my measure just as we came up to Hyde Park Corner. There was a quick flurry of fur and she emerged out of her trance like a streak of lightning, tearing round and round me in a clockwise direction. I couldn't think what she was up to at first but I soon found out. In a moment she had me trussed up in string like a mummy. I teetered for a second, trying to keep my balance, but, very gently, she gave a little pull on the string and I crashed to the ground.

I extricated myself from the string and then it was I who went rigid. After some thought it seemed to me that I should not attempt the impossible, i.e. to outwit the cat or overcome it by strength, but concentrate on solving the immediate problem: how to prevent myself from being wound up in the string and brought crashing to the pavement every few yards. As the cat acted – I would have to react.

And so that is how we proceeded along the length of Piccadilly and into Denis's office, in a kind of screw movement; the cat sprinting round me in a clockwise direction while I sprinted round the cat in an anti-clockwise direction.

I arrived at seven minutes past the hour and he said "You're late." Can you wonder that I have gone off him?

Indeed I was late. But I was a little more than late.

I was dizzy, late and sick of an old Persian.

Hope springs eternal in the human breast

Alexander Pope
'*Essay on Criticism*'

IF you saw, some months ago, a rather tangled version of this quotation headlining *The Times* music critic's column, I'm afraid that was my fault. It was the outcome of an incident where I saved a young Dutch girl from being mowed down by a runaway hors d'œuvre trolley.

What happened was, I was having lunch with an American producer who'd had the idea of making a film called *Marty*, to be based on the life of Luther. And while he was going on about it, I saw an hors d'œuvre trolley start to move forward.

Now as you know, in elegant London hotels the hors d'œuvre trolleys are always about the size of small trams. As, at this place, the dining-room floor also had a slight incline, once the trolley got rolling, it gathered speed at an enormous lick and, in no time, was hurtling down the room, rocking and swaying and spilling out Russian salad and sardines.

Then I noticed something else. Directly in its path was this girl. To make matters worse, she happened to be bending forward – not consciously, I don't think, she just had rather heavy ear-rings on. Anyway, without even thinking, I dived forward and swept her aside. The great trolley hurtled past and splattered itself harmlessly against an elderly waiter. (A team of surgeons, I've been told, were still picking black olives out of him six hours later.)

The girl's husband, a prosperous Dutchman, was quite embarrassingly grateful. Apparently, they'd only been married three days and were having a week's honeymoon in London. So if that trolley had claimed her, it would have been a really rotten waste of a double room.

"Mijnheer," he said to me, with more emotion than I had thought the Dutch capable of, "for what you have done, I will send to you the largest token of my gratitude that my craftsmen can manufacture."

All right, what would you have reckoned he had in mind? So did I. Cupidity glands started extruding like icing-bags. Seven complete days passed before it was borne upon me that diamond-cutting is not the only craft for which the Dutch are renowned.

The reminder came from the man from British Rail Services. When I opened the door of my flat to him, he said, "It won't go in the lift and I'm not humping it up them stairs."

I accompanied him down to the entrance hall and there it was. A cheese. A Dutch cheese, the size of – look, do you remember that cartwheel Bernard Miles used to lean on? Well, imagine something the same diameter, but about two feet thick and bright red.

I stood gazing at it for quite some time. As it happens, I am allergic to cheese. It dates back to an incident in my boyhood when I pulled on a pair of swimming trunks, inside which someone had left a loaded mouse-trap.

So I said to the van man, "Can't you possibly take it away again? Share it out among the lads?"

He turned out to be one of those people who talk in A's and B's. "A," he said, "I'm not ruining myself trying to lift that thing up again, B, how would anyone cut it?"

It was then I had a brainwave. In Flat 14, there was this young musician, a student at the Royal Academy of Music. And what was he studying? The harp.

Do I need to spell out the rest of it? After all, in existential terms, what is a harp but an oversized cheese-slicer with cultural pretensions?

In the event, it worked a treat. The van man had no trouble carrying the Dutch treasure away in lightweight slices and, no doubt, his depot is still acclaimed for the lavishness of its wine-and-cheese parties.

And that should have been the end of the story. But unfortunately – and I honestly do feel badly about this – that very night the young music student had arranged to give his first recital. A test piece by Schumann, at the Rudolf Steiner Hall.

I blame no one but myself. Even today, I still don't know whether it was the after-effect of the van man and me sitting so heavily on the frame of the harp to force the strings through the cheese; or whether it was just that cheese itself exerts some kind of emancipating effect upon harp-strings.

All that anyone knows for certain is, on the eighth bar of the

Schumann piece, when the young man from No. 14 grabbed a handful of strings and then, as is the way in harp-plucking, released them, they all flew out of the harp and struck a gentleman in the fourth row, a retired colonel who'd wandered in under the impression it was going to be that lecture on 'How To Cure Stammering'.

It's not a sequence of circumstances of which I'm in any way proud. But if relating it has done nothing else, it may have helped clear matters up for those of you who still puzzle over the headline which appeared the following morning above *The Times* music critic's review of the performance:

"Harp Strings Hit Colonel In The Schumann Test."

> 'Old Soldiers Never Die'
>
> *Song. 1914–1918*

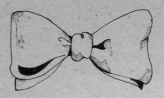

THE other morning I was sitting over my breakfast egg – I hadn't finished my toast and marmalade and I didn't want my egg to get cold – when my wife suddenly said, "Do you know what I was doing exactly ten years ago this morning?"

I raced back down Memory Lane. It was empty.

"No, what?"

"I was sitting in the top room of a Genoese watch-tower in Corsica, writing postcards under an umbrella."

She was right. As I retrieved the egg from beneath me and started digging into it, memory flooded back. Of course – the priest and the eggs!

Ten years ago we bought a sort of mediaeval potting-shed in the hill village of Monticello, which sits six hundred feet above the small port of Ile-Rousse. We went out and moved in exactly ten years ago, on Easter Monday.

In no time we had the place shipshape; fresh newspaper on the table; packing-case lined with straw for the children to sleep in; and our own bed made up in the little room across the bridge, which was the top part of an ancient watch-tower. Pleasantly fatigued after all that, we strolled across the square to the bar for a quick Casanis, a Corsican aperitif based upon, I think, torpedo fluid and marine varnish. The first sip had hardly started corroding the fillings before the bad news was broken to us.

It seems that you must never sleep in a house in Corsica before it has been blessed by a priest.

And, more than that, there must be coloured eggs in every room to be blessed.

And so the awful chain of events began. There was not an egg to be had in the village, brown, white or variegated, and the shops were shut for the holiday.

Things were getting a little desperate and I couldn't think what to do next, apart from shout at the children, when I noticed some vaguely egg-shaped pots lying about. They were about a foot high and made of dirty-white earthenware. Apparently the villagers filled them with soil and grew things in them, like geraniums and carrots. We bore six of these off to our place and set about getting some colour into them. We boiled up my wife's new blue dress in a bucket, steeped the pots in that and they came out quite a pleasant pale blue. We steeped the other three in hot beetroot juice and they took on a fine mauve tinge. We had our coloured eggs. Now for the priest.

The nearest priest lived in Ile-Rousse, which was down three miles of hairpin bends. I borrowed a car from the man next door and set off. It was one of those tiny Citroens which the French are so fond of; they are made of corrugated iron and cock a leg going round corners. As the layout inside the car was totally alien I decided not to risk using the engine and just gave the thing a shove, jumped in and coasted all the way down to the port.

By the time I had located the priest and persuaded the priest to come up to Monticello – a triumph of diplomacy; he was ninety-two and had earache – it was dark. And it began to rain. Now Mediterranean rain differs from British rain. You don't get it so regularly but when you do it is bigger, faster, wetter, and it bounces higher.

It was when we were in the car, with the stuff pounding down on the roof, that I realised that I had no idea how to put the car into motion. Starting the engine was simple enough, merely a matter of turning the key. But the gears . . .

Citroen 2CVs don't go in for a gear-lever, as one understands a gear-lever. Instead, there is a white toffee-apple sticking out of the dashboard. And there is no indication anywhere as to which way the thing has to be turned, bent, lifted, pulled, inclined or thrust in order to locate first gear.

I wrestled with the toffee-apple for quite a long while, with the priest sitting quietly beside me mumbling to himself in Latin, when suddenly we lurched backwards. I had found reverse.

I resolved not to push my luck any farther, and backed gently towards Monticello.

All went well within the street lights of Ile-Rousse but once we had started reversing up the steep, twisted road to Monticello two things became apparent: a car's headlamps point forwards not backwards, and although windscreen wipers keep a driver's vision clear in the heaviest of rain there are no windscreen wipers on the rear window.

There was nothing for it but to ask the priest to get out and walk ahead of the car to guide me.

It took us nearly an hour to climb the hill and I must say that it was a very tired, sodden and cross priest indeed who allowed me to propel him into our residence.

"There you are, Father," I said, with a sweep of the hand. "Coloured eggs as per instructions. Bless this house."

But something had gone wrong. The 'eggs' were no longer coloured. In the two hours I had been absent the colour had completely faded from them and they were clearly just six earthenware pots, albeit egg-shaped.

"Ostrich eggs, Father," I mumbled, without hope. "Colouring very pale . . ."

He broke into words. "These are not coloured eggs. These are jars which the villagers fill with soil to grow things like bougainvillea and turnips."

"Now you come to mention it, Father," I cried, fighting to the last, "they DO look like jars used for growing things in. A fantastic resemblance . . ."

It was no use, of course. He wasn't fooled for a second by our anæmic pottery. The last we saw of him was his frail figure making for the bar.

So our house was not blessed.

And during the night a wind rose up and stripped half the tiles from the tower roof. And the rain continued to rain.

And next morning, when my wife wrote her postcards home, she had to do so sitting in the tower under an umbrella.

The irony is that I would never have made such a pathetic attempt to deceive the old priest if I had known then, as I know now, an ancient Corsican proverb:

"Old soil-jars never dye."

'Forever Amber'

Title of Novel
Kathleen Winsor

ONCE in a lifetime, every scriptwriter gets an idea that really fires him. In my case, from every film-studio that I've approached with it. But this idea, I pledge you, this is a blockbuster, it's the big one. What makes me so sure is – and isn't this always the real test? – I can outline the whole idea in just five words. Three, if hyphens count. A peace-time war-film!

What do you mean impossible? Will you just *listen*!

When you get right down to it, what is a war-film? Isn't the story always the same one? Some kind of mixed group – a fighter squadron, say, a commando platoon, a squad of marines, doesn't matter – an assemblage of individuals from all walks of life who finally, under the stress of combat and danger, learn how to work together as one unit? Right. So here's what we do. We take a peace-time equivalent of that kind of group and – now follow me here – we tell their story in exactly the same kind of terms.

I know what's going through your mind. What kind of peace-time group in any way resembles a group of war-time commandos, marines, fighter pilots? Okay, try this on for size. A Formation Dancing Team?

Suddenly gone quiet, haven't you? So let me fill the story in, just broad brush-strokes.

We open, like all those war-films do, at the place where 'it all happened'. But – as the place looks *now*, present day. Abandoned, empty, deserted. In our case, it's a ballroom. An abandoned, empty, deserted ballroom.

Into it wanders our hero. No longer a young man. Touches of grey here and there. But still looking good, of course. Sexy. Slowly he walks across the empty ballroom – we do the echo-thing with his footsteps – then he pauses. Looking down at the maple dance-floor, he rubs his shoe on its dust. As the camera moves in on his face, into his eyes comes that look that tells us he's going to have a flashback. Far-off sounds creep in! Shuffle of patent-leather shoes, rustle of taffeta dresses, chickychickybomchick of a samba. As they get louder, louder, the whole screen goes sort of ripple-y – and when it clears up again, boom, we're in.

It's ten years ago – and there they are. The Mrs Eva Swaythling Formation Dancing Team. Six men, six women. The Clean Dozen. Heading them up – the Skipper. Mrs Eva Swaythling herself! Hard-bitten, loud-mouthed, ruthless. Joan Crawford if we can get her, if not we go for Charles Bronson.

She's barking out orders. "I'm going to make dancers out of you if it means you rhumba on the stumps of your ankles!" Tough as they come, see? But, underneath it all, deep down – golden syrup.

Cut to cameos of each of the team. John Mills, the spoilt rich kid who finally learns humility. Richard Attenborough, the lovable cockney. ("Time for a brew-up, Skipper?") Sarah Miles, whose puppy is dying and medical science is baffled. The coloured boy, you can do this now, the coloured boy who turns out braver than anybody. Susan George, who gets raped by a second-trumpet player, but off-screen so we keep the U Certificate.

The Mrs Eva Swaythling Formation Dancers. . . . We do a mon-tage of their training. Mile after mile in quickstep tempo, carrying 250 lb of sequins on their backs. The pitiful shortage of equipment. "How are we gonna get the material for the girls' dresses, Skip . . .?" "Give us the tulle and we'll finish the job."

Their first night-op. The Hammersmith Palais during a power-cut. We show their triumphs, we show their reverses. And not only their reverses, their chassis-turns, their scissors-steps. And always, right out there in front, Mrs Eva Swaythling. Threatening, cajoling, exhorting, "There are no atheists in a foxtrot."

Finally comes the this-is-the-moment-that-all-your-training's-been-the-preparation-for moment. They're going in against Jerry. It's the Eurovision Area Championships.

They're in the dressing-room of the Streatham Locarno. Waiting. "It's quiet out there. . . ." "Too damned quiet. I don't like it. . . ." "Time for a brew-up, Skipper?"

Crash of sound – and they're plunged into the maelstrom! Into the shrieking, pounding bombardment that is the Ken Mackintosh Orchestra. Thrills! Spills! Chills! In the fourth sequence of the

Military Two-Step, the Number Three man suddenly staggers. His shoe lace has snapped! But, like a well-oiled machine, the two girls either side of him move in and, without breaking step, support him between their puff-sleeves. He finishes the flower-pattern on one shoe!

It looks like nothing can stop them. But then, just as the Latin American heat starts – tragedy! Mrs Eva Swaythling winces, claps her hands to that iron bosom. Her face contorts. The Souvenir Brochure slips from her nerveless fingers. . . .

Around the ballroom the word flashes. "Mrs Eva Swaythling's bought it!" In that great dance hall in the sky, there'll be a new pair of silver shoes tonight.

Momentarily the Team falter, become ragged. But it is the coloured boy who rallies them. "Okay, gang. Let's get this one for the Skipper!"

The ballroom will never see Formation Dancing like that again. And, as the samba chickychickyboms to its climax, the Mrs Eva Swaythling Team realise they've done it. They've brought the Common Market Latin American Area Trophy back to Britain. . . .

Must be a milestone in screen history. Eh? Must be. There's only one thing that's still holding me up on it, apart from the fact that everyone thinks it's rotten. Finding the right title for it. *In Which We Swerve? . . . Last Military Two-Step In Streatham? . . .* Nuh.

No, I think there's only one title that captures the sweep and majesty of the story – that broken rallying-cry which snatched victory from the jaws of Latin American defeat. How does this grab you? . . .

"For Eva – Samba!"

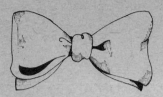

THE pure unalloyed joy, the flight of the heart on wings of song, the flowering of the spirit like the opening of a jacaranda-tree blossom at the prospect of my wife returning tomorrow after a week away is tempered by the thought of the squalid state the kitchen is in.

In order to preserve the balance of nature it is vital that I maintain the fiction that I am capable, at a pinch, of looking after myself and can be left for a few hours without change and decay taking over the household.

So, in the few hours left me, I have an alarming number of important things to do, most of which have been brought about by my firm conviction that women run things on old-fashioned, traditional lines which would benefit from the application of a cold, rational, male intelligence; i.e. mine.

First of all I must replenish the stock of tinned soup in the store cupboard. Round about Day Two I realised that man could live on tinned soup alone. It heats up in a jiffy and, more than that, the tin can be used as a throwaway saucepan. With the help of a pair of pliers to hold the thing, the empty tin can be used to boil eggs or anything else and then thrown away; the soul-numbing process of washing-up is thereby minimised. The trouble is that a keen female eye, viewing the stock cupboard, will spot at a glance that a suspicious quantity of tinned soup has been consumed. So it must be replaced.

On Day One I had realised that, as master of all I surveyed, I did not have to eat vegetables. I have no religious or moral objections to vegetables but they are, as it were, dull. They are the also-rans of the plate. One takes an egg, or a piece of meat, or fish, with pleasure but then one has, as a kind of penance, to dilute one's pleasure with a damp lump of boskage. However, this puritan attitude that no meal is worthy without veg. is strongly held in this house so I must somehow give the impression that vegetables have been consumed in quantity. What I must do is to buy a cauliflower and shake it about a bit in the kitchen. Fragments will then be found under the table and in corners, giving the impression that vegetables have been in the forefront of my diet.

And then there is the refrigerator. This seemed to me a most inefficient instrument, yielding up stiff butter when I wanted it to spread, ice-cold milk when I wanted milk to warm up for the coffee, and when I needed some ice cubes the ice container was apparently welded to the shelf with cold. So I instituted a system whereby I switched off the fridge at breakfast, thereby making the contents malleable when I needed them, and switched it on again at night. This has worked quite well except that the contents of the fridge are now a cluster of variously-sized rectangular snowballs. I must remember to take a hammer and chisel to them before tomorrow.

And I need a stout elastic band because I have done in the vacuum cleaner. I used one of my gumboots for kitchen refuse to save messing about with a bin but liquids seeped through a hole in the toe. The obvious solution to a hole in a gumboot toe is to bung it up with a mixture of sawdust and the remains of that tin of car undersealing compound which one has in one's garage. I poured the underseal and the sawdust into a thing called a Liquidiser, which is a kind of electric food-mixer, but what I failed to note was that one is supposed to put the lid on before operating it. And when I began to vacuum clean the mixture of tar and sawdust off the kitchen ceiling it seemed to jam up the works. The motor went on running but there was a smell of burning rubber and now I must, before tomorrow, provide the vacuum cleaner with a new rubber band.

And eggs. We have an ark in the orchard containing nine hens, which provide us with a regular intake of beige eggs. I went out to feed them on Evening One and I think that they missed my wife. They greeted me, I felt, reproachfully, making sounds not unlike those made by Mr Frankie Howerd. "Ooh!" they went, "Ooooh, OooooOOOh." So I undid the door of the ark and led them on an educational tour of the garden, pointing out where the new drainage is to be laid, the place on the lawn where I had lost my lighter, the vulgar shape which one of the poplar trees had grown into. And then the dogs joined us and helped to take the chickens out of themselves by chasing them, and soon the air was filled with feathers and joyous squawks. I finally got the chickens back into the ark by midnight but, oddly, they haven't laid an egg between them the whole week. Since my wife will be expecting to be greeted by about three dozen beige eggs, I must do something about this before she returns.

I also had a spot of bother with a packet of frozen peas. I thought I would vary my diet by making myself a Spanish omelet, i.e. as I understood it, an omelet with a pea or two in it. Now the packet stated clearly that if less than four servings was required the necessary amount could be obtained by giving the frozen pack a sharp buffet with an instrument. I had my soup tin on the gas-stove, with a knob of butter in it, and I obeyed the instructions; that is to say, I held the frozen lump in my left hand and aimed a blow at it with a convenient instrument – my dog's drinking bowl. It worked up to a point. One frozen pea detached itself, bounced off my knee, and disappeared. Where had it gone? My Afghan hound was right next to me at the time, watching keenly what I was doing with her bowl, and I had a sudden horrible suspicion that the pea had gone into her ear. I called to her. She evinced no interest. I went round the other side and called again. She looked up. I made a mental note to take the dog to the vet for a swift peaectomy operation before tomorrow.

Lastly there is the problem of my breath. Last night I made myself a casserole of sausages – or rather, a soup-tin-role of sausages – but I seemed to have lost the salt. After a deal of searching I found an alien-looking container marked 'Sel' and applied it liberally. It seems that it was garlic salt. I did not realise what it had done to my breath – one doesn't with garlic – until this afternoon when I stood waiting for somebody to open a door to me and suddenly noticed that the varnish on the door was bubbling.

So I have a number of things to remember to do before tomorrow, such as tinned soup, a cauliflower, de-frosting the refrigerator, buying an elastic band for the vacuum cleaner, getting in three dozen beige eggs, seeing the vet about the pea in the dog's ear and taking something for the garlic on my breath.

How, you are perhaps asking yourself, will he possibly remember all these things?

Well, hopefully I have put them all together into a kind of chant, or song. It goes:

"Soup . . . a cauli . . . fridge . . . elastic . . . eggs . . . pea . . . halitosis."

'Great Expectations'

Title of Novel
Charles Dickens

IF it's true that we laugh loudest at that which we hate most, then my favourite joke is the one that Ronnie Scott tells about the fellow who says to a girl "Do you like Dickens?" and she says "I don't know, I've never been to one." Because I just can't be doing with Dickens. It's some kind of blind spot, I'm sorry, he holds out nothing whatever for me. That's why, if it hadn't been for a story in this morning's newspaper, the above quotation would have put me in a right hiatus.

It was a story about smuggling immigrants into Britain. As you must know by now, there is, in this ancient seat of freedom, a growing body of organised apoplexy which refuses to believe that immigration is the sincerest form of flattery. Consequently, a minor but lucrative hustle has grown up, based on smuggling persons of foreign origin across our frontiers at a hundred and fifty pounds a nob.

Well, according to the newspaper story, one clever youngster hit on a bright variation. He loaded sixteen Asian nationals inside a large wooden crate, drilled the necessary air-holes, then had the crate flown Air Freight to Heathrow. The intention was that once a lorry had off-loaded it into the Freight Shed, he would then, prior to Customs inspection, prise open the crate and assist its occupants to effect a stealthy exit through the Spectators' Car Park.

And had it not been for the uncertain state of industrial relations at London Airport, it would have made an exemplary essay in Creative Smuggling. The crate was off-loaded from the plane, all right. But just as the lorry was about to take it to the Freight Shed, a twenty-four-hour strike was called.

The driver slammed on his brakes, switched off the ignition, climbed out of his cab and scampered off to join his colleagues harmonising "We Shall Not Be Moved" hard by the Departure Lounge. In consequence, the crate of sixteen Asians was left at the far end of the runway until such time as the twenty-four-hour strike finished.

Well, another fact of life that will not have escaped you is that, in this country, the twenty-four-hour strike is like the twenty-four-hour 'flu. You have to reckon on it lasting at least five days.

This proved about three days too many for the crated Asians. On the second day, they held a whispered consultation. That, in itself, is no easy task when you're packed in layers of four. By a show of hands – again, not easy – they agreed that further confinement might prove too irksome to endure. So, using a system of co-ordinated inhaling and exhaling, they burst open the sides of the crate.

Too bad, really. They were immediately apprehended by the Chairman of BOAC. It just so happened he was taking a stroll out to the far end of the runway to try to get away from the sound of Clive Jenkins' voice.

Sad, isn't it, typical of the times in which we live, all goes to show, etc., etc.

Far as I'm concerned, though, if it hadn't been for the Heathrow Sixteen's resentment of their prolonged incarceration, I'd never have found that newspaper sub-head which circumvented my Dickensian block:

"Crate Irks Packed Asians."

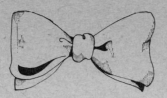

I propose to tell you pretty well all there is to know about an animal which is very popular among dog-lovers though less so among dog-haters. I refer to the dog. Dogs, like horses, are quadrupeds. That is to say, they have four rupeds, one at each corner, on which they walk. In many other ways dogs are like horses – for example, they both like eating biscuits and being photographed and being tickled behind the ear – but they are not all THAT much like horses because they are smaller. Except, of course, if you match a very huge dog indeed up against a tiny, tiny horse who hasn't been well, when it is quite difficult to tell the difference between them.

If you find yourself in the predicament of facing a very large dog and a tiny horse, not knowing which is which, the wisest thing to do is to wait until they are both moving towards you then shout "whoa!" The one that doesn't stop is the dog. This is a reasonably safe test unless the name of the horse is Woe, in which case they will both approach. Or the horse is deaf.

Dogs are very historical, some of the earliest being found by Marco Polo up Chinese mandarins' sleeves.

The Romans had dogs and named the Canary Islands after them, although this was by way of being a bit of a mistake: the Romans had very, very large and hairy canaries and very, very small yellow dogs and they got the two mixed up.

Much mention is made of dogs in English literature. The popular dog's name, Prince, comes from Shakespeare's *Hamlet*, where Prince was a Great Dane. From the same play comes a popular doggy expression "Down, Prince!" uttered by Ophelia.

Another reference occurs in *Macbeth*. A dog misbehaves himself in the castle and Lady Macbeth, very cross, cries "Out, damned Spot!"

Keats mentions a dog in one of his longer poems but I can't remember which one.

Elizabeth Barrett Browning had a King Charles spaniel which sat on the end of the sofa with her and helped her pine for Robert Browning but it did not have a memorable name.

Bill somebody-or-other in a novel by Charles Dickens had some sort of dog – I think it was a black-and-white one – but I've forgotten its name.

That is all I remember about dogs in English literature.

There is a large selection of various sorts of dogs for those interested in acquiring one. Poodles are very popular because they do not moult, or run amok and get their names in the paper, and they would much rather be people than dogs so – except twice a year – they do not bother much with each other. Poodles usually come in three shades, black, white and brown, though not all at once. Black ones are nice in that they don't show the dirt but when they sit down in the shadows they are invisible and you tend to tread on one by accident causing you to pitch forward, graze your knee on the radiator and end up with your elbow in the potatoes.

The Chow is a large, hairy dog with eyes rather like raisins and a mauve tongue which is the same mauve as that wine-gum which when you come to it you cover with your thumb and stop handing them round. They are very popular in Italy where a song was written to a Chow puppy: 'Chow, Chow, Bambino'.

Another large dog is the Afghan Hound, which looks like a greyhound in a fun-fur. Afghans are very beautiful. They eat meat, biscuits, fish, books, chairs, bicycle tyres, mattresses, carpets, tables, raincoats, trees, car upholstery and milkmen.

Greyhounds were once much more popular than they are nowadays, perhaps because they need so much exercising. Very few men are willing, after a hard day at the factory bench or in the boardroom, to arrive home and then take the greyhound out for its run, and many middle-aged men find it increasingly difficult to squeeze themselves into the trap.

Flat-dwellers in the modern world are turning increasingly towards smaller dogs and small dogs are becoming extremely popular. The smallest of all is the Chihuahua, a naked Mexican animal the size of a pound of stewing steak.

Not surprisingly, the Chihuahua is supplanting the bigger dogs in the affections of pet-owners. It is very difficult indeed to mistake a

Chihuahua for a horse. It requires very little exercise – a swift daily trot round the back-door mat suffices – and it could live happily in a telephone-box let alone a small flat. So no wonder the latest copy of the trade journal, *The Doggy Times*, carried a banner headline:

"Chihuahua Boom Today."

Now is the time for all good men to
come to the aid of the party

Edwin Meade Robinson
'The Typewriter's Song'

FOR the thinking man, there is much to be learned
from that piece of advice printed on most bottles of patent medicine:
"Keep Away from Small Children". Personally, I've always avoided
them as much as possible. However, when the child is your own and
it's her fifth birthday party. . . .

It was an illuminating experience, if repulsive. One moment a tiny
shy thing, in her party dress, had her hand in mine, waiting for the
first of her little friends to arrive. A ring at the front door – then this
bulldozer hurled past me, wrenched the door open and with a
"Where's my present, where's my present?" shoved the small guest up
against a wall and frisked him from head to foot. It is something of a
jarring moment when you realise you have brought another Customs
Officer into the world.

"She's over-excited," I muttered to the boy's mother. But that lady's
gaze had already swept past what was going on in the hall and was
busy in the kitchen, pricing our units.

Ten minutes later there were twenty-three guests present. I spent
quite a while watching the little boys at play. What I found interesting was not so much that early defining of sexual roles about
which there's so much chat-show chatter these days, more how the
actual playing of the role has altered since my time. When I was that
age, small boys used to point pistols and say, "Bang, bang, you're
dead." Now they point pieces of plastic and say, "Zap, zap, you're
sterile."

While I was having a ponder on that, I felt a tug at my trousers. It
was one of the little girls. "I'm Caroline."

"I know, dear. So's practically everybody."

We had eight Carolines present. Eight Carolines, five Rebeccas,
four Jakes and about half a dozen Jamies. Where have all the Harolds

and Muriels gone? Who was the last child to be christened Sadie? Caroline said, "Do you like my new dress?"

"It's lovely, dear."

"I'm wearing a bra."

True as I'm sitting here. Didn't come up as far as my knee-cap. Don't you find something chilling about someone wearing uplift before they've got any up to lift? I had the greatest difficulty, the rest of the afternoon, restraining her from showing it to me.

Her persistence was only diverted by the announcement that tea was to be served. The tea also proved to be what Jimmy Durante used to call a revolting development. Talk about eat, drink and be messy. Has science ever explained why, at that age, the only time they sneeze is when they've just taken a mouthful of sponge cake?

But it was after the meal that the really interesting problem arose. There is one lesson to be drawn from it that I can pass on to you immediately. When giving children's parties, never serve eight jugs of orangeade in a house which has only one bathroom. What you are immediately brought up against is the myth that the British are united by a common language. It was one of the Simons who came up to me first. "Mister," he said, "I want to go soo-soo."

I narrowed my eyes at him. "You want to what?" But the fattest of the Rebeccas was now pulling my sleeve. "Yes, dear?"

"Where do I tinkle?" she said. As I stared at her blankly, a rather red-faced Jake came dashing in. Very fast. "Make whistle-whistle," he announced. Urgently.

"Look, children," I began – but, at that moment, the most soignée of the Carolines entered the room. "I want to go to the loo," she said.

The penny dropped. I turned back to the original Simon, the one who'd uttered the first request. "Hear that, lad?" I asked him. "That's what you should have said. 'I want to go to the loo.'"

"Not any more," he said.

What has the education explosion really achieved, I wondered to myself later that evening as I was rubbing away at the carpet. What kind of society is it where parents have narrowed the range of names which their children can be christened down to little more than half a dozen, while at the same time creating an infinity of names for the potty?

What's needed, I decided, is a standardisation of appellation in the second area. And it's needed right away, before we all disappear down the generation gap. What I suggest is a Royal Commission – headed, preferably, by someone of the stature of Lord Goodman – to decide on one official phrase to which everybody's children will then conform.

If you're with me on this, please send S.A.E. You will receive by return a sticker for the rear window of your car:

"Now Is The Time For Lord Goodman To Come To The Aid Of The Potty."

They bore him barefac'd on the bier

Shakespeare
Hamlet, Act IV, Sc. 5

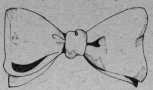

I wonder whether you share my delight in Fanny Hill? I find it really pretty there in the Spring, so easy to get to from Godalming by bicycle and there is a lovely view from the top if you stand on your saddle. I was doing just that some five years ago when I detected that something was amiss. "Hello, Frank," I distinctly remember saying to myself as I balanced precariously with one foot on the saddle, "all is not A.1 at Lloyd's."

The reason for my perturbation was that I seemed not to be seeing quite as much of the lovely countryside as I was accustomed to see: the lady who took her Sunday afternoon bath at exactly four o'clock in the small cottage two hundred yards beyond the hedge was still visible. But only from the neck up.

I pondered. Either the thicket hedge had grown sharply since the previous Sunday thus cutting off the view, or I had sunk slightly.

I checked. Bicycle against the same telegraph pole. Same shoes. Socks no thinner; the same hand-knitted heather mixture. Then I saw. My rear tyre was quite flat. I had a puncture.

No problem, of course, to a practical man. I levered the tyre off with the tablespoon I always carry with me for my hourly spoonful of Queen Bee honey, licked round the inner-tube until I detected the bubble and started to apply the tube of sticky stuff. Then happened what frequently happens when, for instance, one is faced with a particularly intricate crossword puzzle clue – the solution did not immediately present itself. I squeezed the tube, jumped on it and bit it but it was hopeless; the stuff inside had perished. I resolved to seek help. Lying some way back from the road was a house I had often noticed when I was idly waiting for four o'clock to arrive; an odd Victorian gothic residence set about with fruit trees and a croquet lawn.

The door was opened by a prim, middle-aged maid, clad in the uniform of her kind. She dropped a little, old-fashioned curtsey and murmured that she would inform the master. As I waited in the hall, contemplating the mezzo-tints of past-Presidents of the Royal Philanthropic Society, my mind was troubled. There was something about the maid that was curious, unusual. But what? "Come along, Frank," I remember saying to myself, "there's something about her that's not all tickety-boo." Then I realised what it was. She had a vast spade beard.

At that moment another woman, visibly the housekeeper, came in to say that Mr Pennithorne Phipps would see me. She was middle-aged, dressed in black, and her beard, though luxuriant, was a faintly fictional shade of auburn. Perhaps – who knows a woman's wiles – aided by a dab from a bottle?

Mr Pennithorne Phipps, a kindly, elderly man, received me affably, gave me a tube of rubber solution and a glass of cloudy sherry and insisted on telling me his story.

As a comparatively young man he had inherited a large sum of money which he resolved to put to some good purpose. A close friend, after trying unsuccessfully to sell him a gold-mine in Basingstoke, reluctantly accepted this philanthropic intent and advised him to do what he could to alleviate the plight of circus folk, who were being put out of work in their thousands due to people being more interested in the wireless and the cinema than in going to the circus.

Young Pennithorne Phipps set to with a will, which had been through Probate and had made him a very rich man indeed. He persuaded motor-car manufacturers to hire the India-Rubber Men to demonstrate how simple it was to get in and out of their smaller cars. He talked restaurateurs into engaging the Lilliputian Midgets to sit in their restaurants and so make the servings look bigger. He hired the Human Cannonballs to seaside landladies – after the flight was timed the landlady could legally advertise "Only one minute from the sea".

But he could find no work for four bearded ladies. They were shy of other people. It was obviously too dangerous for them to go into industry and have to bend over lathes or sewing-machines. Their chances of a modelling career were slim. So he decided to take them into his house to look after him. And this they did most delightfully, one gardening, one cooking, one housekeeping, and one maiding. And in the long winter evenings, when the shadows drew in, they would plait each other's beards with pale ribbons on the ends of which were little wooden balls. Then the four of them would bend over their dulcimers and, with little twitches and nods of their heads, play for him the airs he never tired of hearing, like Corelli's Concerto Grosso in G Minor, and 'Put A Bit Of Powder On It, Father'. And when he was down in the dumps and *triste* they would amuse him by playing Beard Football, which was like Blow Football but instead of blowing down tubes to urge the ball into the goal the ladies tried to sweep it in with their beards.

That was five years ago. I never returned to the house, nor to the hill, because of a serious accident which befell me a few minutes after leaving the house. I mended my puncture and took up my usual position on tiptoe on the saddle, observing the scenery. All was as usual. The lady enjoyed her bath, as did I, until, quite unexpectedly, the lady did something most imaginative with her loofah and I fell off the bike.

The hospital did what they could but it was a complicated fracture. "Give it to me straight, Doctor," I said. She paused for a moment, then said, "I live in a cottage about two hundred yards from a hill – you won't have heard of it – Fanny Hill. It's only a weekend cottage – I go there for a rest, and a bath, on Sundays – but I love that little hill. I'm sorry . . . but you will never be able to cycle up any sort of hill again."

Nor have I. But last week a friend lent me his light van for the week-end and I had a sudden urge to recapture the pleasures of those Sundays five years ago. I drove to Fanny Hill. As I had ten minutes in hand before four o'clock I, on an impulse, called at the old Victorian gothic cottage.

What a change I found. The door was opened by the same maid – but she was clean shaven, and she smelt very strongly of brown ale.

"Dunno where he is," she said, and left me.

I glanced behind me. The lawns were lumpy and the croquet hoops were mottled with rust.

A noise made me turn back. It was the housekeeper descending the stairs; the last two on her behind.

"Hang on, cock," she said, "I'll fetch the old fool."

She, too, was clean shaven.

It was a sad Pennithorne Phipps indeed who faced me. It seems that he grew troubled about his four bearded ladies shortly after I had last seen them. Although they were entirely content he felt that perhaps he was being selfish in keeping them within the confines of the house. So he brought a specialist man down from London and paid for him to remove their beards by electrolysis. They were now normal women, able to take their place in society.

"It's been frightful," he said. "They troop down to the village every evening; they spend most of the time in the pub downing gallons of brown ale . . . there's no dulcimer playing . . . they can't now . . . nor Beard Football . . . instead of being happy, perfectly adjusted people they have become quarrelsome, competitive and, well, just plain dreary. They are now very dull people indeed."

A few minutes later, as I took my aluminium ladder from the back of the van, adjusted it against the telegraph pole, got myself comfortably into position, binoculars at the ready, I thought over the sad story of Pennithorne Phipps and it seemed to contain a moral: Kindness is a lovely thing, but too much kindness can, in a funny way, corrupt.

Poor Pennithorne Phipps's ladies. Bearded and out of the ordinary, they were delightful people. But now . . .

They bore him – bare-faced, on the beer.

The least said, soonest mended

Charles Dickens
'*The Pickwick Papers*'

THIS is the phrase on which the Glastonberrys have based their lawsuit against the ground-landlord. Tell you about the Glastonberrys. They're our local monied couple. Rich, rich, rich. Mr Glastonberry has some sort of corner in flagpole manufacturing, a small-boned man whose life seems dedicated to the proposition that Neatness Counts. He always looks so exceptionally dapper, the local theory is that she keeps a plastic cover over him when not in use. Mrs Glastonberry is all Wedgwood hair and lipstick on the teeth, the sort of woman who asks for the wine-list in a Wimpy Bar.

Their passion is houses. They buy and discard houses as though on a winning streak in Monopoly. Over the past ten years, they must have lived in eight different houses, each one featuring some conspicuously exotic adjunct of gracious living. One house had a conversation-pit, another a barbecue-terrace. I can remember an indoor ski-slope, a set of pornographic stained-glass windows, a pelota court. . . .

But it was the novelty-item in her latest home that brought on the lawsuit. "Do come and see our new pad," she called to me in the Washeteria soon after they moved in. "We got it because of the sauna."

That statement was true, as has since been revealed, in a very exact sense. It was only by reason of the sauna that the house had come on the market at all. The previous owner had perished in it.

Poor old soul, it was one of those chance-in-a-million situations. He'd entered it – if you've never seen a sauna, it's like a sort of sweating-hot garden-shed – he'd turned the temperature up to about 120 degrees, lolled about till he was the colour of shrimp-cocktail, then gone to open the door to go out for a cooling shower. The handle of the door had jammed. . . .

I must say, when Mrs Glastonberry recounted this to me that

evening, my keenness to enter the sauna waned. "Oh, it's in perfect working order now," she assured me. "The landlord's had it repaired. We made that a condition of the lease. But, anyway, Walter insists that he should be the first one to try it."

Walter is the son. A somewhat unhealthily complexioned fifteen-year-old, who always puts me in mind of one of Krafft-Ebing's footnotes. What my Mother calls 'sly'.

He came bustling up with a towel round his middle. "Mother," he said, "if we want to do this right, we've got to do it the Scandinavian way."

"What's the Scandinavian way, dear?"

"Mixed."

They have this au-pair girl called Gia. A rather striking-looking Italian, who walks as though she never exhales. Mrs Glastonberry looked disconcerted.

"Oh, Mum, don't be a wet. It's only ten minutes. For heaven's sake, if a thing's worth doing –"

Enter Gia wearing a towel that started late and finished early. Walter took her hand, and they entered the sauna. It's a converted cupboard under the stairs, really, which the poor old previous owner had lined with lead and had a special kind of stove put in.

We waited outside it, sipping drinks and munching squares of toast which had been smeared with foodstuffs of such unidentifiable blandness, they were a kind of gastronomic Muzak.

After about half an hour, uneasiness was noticeably prevalent. "Are you all right in there, Walter?" Mrs Glastonberry called, tapping on the door with her solitaire.

"Mum, the handle's jammed again."

Consternation. "Harold," said Mrs Glastonberry to her husband, "your fifteen-year-old son is locked in there with a nude Italian!"

After some consideration, Harold said, "And think of the heat."

We tried opening the door from the outside. It rattled a bit but didn't budge. Five of us got our shoulders together and charged the door. Not a hope. Lead-lined, you see, for the insulation.

"Mum," came Walter's voice, "Gia's fainted."

"Move to the far side of the sauna immediately," said Mrs Glastonberry.

"Don't worry, Mum," Walter said a moment later, "I'm giving her the kiss of life."

He continued giving it to her, according to my Timex, for the next hour and a half. At midnight, someone suggested we fetch the vicar and try to persuade him to marry them through the keyhole.

Five minutes after that, the door opened and Walter and Gia emerged. They looked, as newspapers say, little the worse for their ordeal. Looked, in fact, all things considered, extraordinarily cheerful. Another note I made, but nobody else seemed to, was that on emerging Walter extracted a key from the inside of the door and slipped it under his towel.

It was when the Sicilian relatives started coming over for the wedding that the Glastonberrys instituted their lawsuit against the landlord for failing to carry out stipulated repairs. Personally, I think they've got a good case. After all, as Mrs Glastonberry keeps trying to translate into Italian:

"The lease said sauna's mended."

Ring down the curtain, the farce is over

Rabelais's last words (attributed)

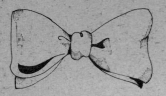

I was in the morning room. I shouldn't have been in the morning room because it was half-past two in the afternoon, but I couldn't go into the sitting room because I wanted to stand. Or, to be more accurate, I wanted to walk. And the sitting room is hardly the place in which to walk, let alone stand.

It was my desire to walk backwards and forwards. I much prefer walking backwards and forwards because it saves turning. I walk forward as far as I can go – usually until the tip of my nose comes to rest against the wallpaper – and then I walk backwards as far as I can go – usually indicated by the back of my head gently bumping against the wall. I then proceed forward again and repeat the process until I have walked enough.

If, on the other hand, I turned when I reached the wall rather than reversing, then this would mean that the sole of my right shoe would wear out more quickly than that of the left – I find that I usually turn on my right foot – which would lead to difficulties when the right shoe became due for repair at a time when the left shoe was still serviceable.

The need to reverse rather than turn was further strengthened by the fact that I was carrying an anvil in my right hand. The weight of this would have considerably accelerated the wear on the sole of the right shoe.

I had passed a length of stout rope round the anvil, leaving a loop by which to carry the thing. It was this loop that I was holding by the right hand as I walked up and down the morning room that afternoon. I was carrying the anvil because I wished to make my right arm half an inch longer – I had bought an inexpensive tweed sports jacket the right arm of which was half an inch longer than the left.

After perhaps an hour of walking a friend of mine, a retired tee-planter – he used to be a golfer's caddy – came in to see me. They say that the definition of a friend is someone to whom you don't feel obliged to speak. My friend sat watching me for an hour in silence, and then left.

Shortly after that I heard my wife calling. I put down the anvil and made my way into the drawing room where I found my wife quietly drawing. She is quite artistic and has made a fine collection of English kitsch which she has on display in the kitchen.

"Yes, my love?" I began, when I suddenly noticed with mounting horror that neither of her feet was touching the ground.

I started forward, but a closer examination revealed that she was lying on the sofa.

"Why is there a hole through the drawing-room wall just by your chair?" she asked. "Did you make it?"

"Indeed I did!" I said warmly. "With a hammer and a cold chisel only this very morning."

"Why did you knock a hole through our drawing-room wall?"

"Quite simply, my love, to enable me to play the bass flute should I ever wish to take it up. You will notice that my chair is hard up against the wall and that the wall is on the right of the chair. If the urge ever came upon me to learn to play the bass flute I now have enough room to the right of me – an essential prerequisite of bass flute-playing just as enough room in front is necessary to a trombonist."

"Yes, but the wind blows straight through the hole and the rain comes in. Surely there is something you can put over the hole until you decide whether or not to take up the bass flute?"

"Good thinking, my dear," I said. "You know what would answer the purpose if we could lay our hands on one – a framed aquatint of Lowestoft Harbour showing the Old Groin."

It took us days to find one.

Then in came this auction catalogue of the village roadsweeper's effects. He had won the pools and bought the Uffizi Palace in Florence so was selling off his former possessions in five lots, namely, lot one – a gas ring, circa 1952, with a faulty tube; lot two – a pile of down useful for stuffing pillows; lot three – a double-damask curtain of great age which did him in lieu of a front door; lot four – his sole article of furniture, a rickety Victorian sofa covered with carved squiggles and ornaments; and lot five – a framed aquatint of Lowestoft Harbour showing the Old Groin.

I hurried round to the auction-room with a feeling that destiny was on my side. The man there said that lot five would come up at about a quarter to four, so I was in plenty of time.

Bidding started briskly for the gas ring. It had reached 5p when I thought I had better check the time. Now I wear my watch on my right wrist to confuse thieves and I was wearing my new, inexpensive sports jacket with the overlong sleeve. I put my arm up and wriggled it so that I could read the time on my watch and found that I had bought the gas ring.

This was most vexing. But even more vexing was that exactly the same thing happened with the pile of down, the double-damask curtain and the fussy Victorian settee. And when the auctioneer did get to lot five – the aquatint – I had no money left to buy it.

I trailed miserably home and found my wife busy doing some sums in the summerhouse.

"Well?" she said, eagerly. "Did you bid?"

"I did," I replied.

"And did you buy it?"

"I bought," I said, picking my words carefully. "But not it."

"Now look here, Rover," said my wife, using the pet name she always applies in moments of anger, "just what have you bought?"

In a very small voice I whispered:

"Ring . . . down . . . the curtain . . . the fussy sofa."

His word is as good as his bond

Proverb
Seventeenth century

FULL-FRONTAL nudity – and there's as catch-penny an opening as you'll ever see – has now become accepted by every branch of the theatrical profession with the possible exception of lady accordion-players. There is, however, one group of performers whom it threatens to relegate to the status of an endangered species. Conjurors.

It takes but a moment's reflection to realise why. Think of all those live doves, lighted cigarettes, steel rings. Where, with no clothes to secrete them *in*, is a conjuror to produce them *from*? A naked conjuror is at as much of a disadvantage as a vegetarian vampire or a cautious lemming.

That's why my heart went out to Nigel Gascoyne, Society Illusionist. Particularly as he was already under a bit of a cloud, following an unfortunate lapse of concentration during his 'Sawing A Woman In Half' illusion. "Oh, it's a swine of a trick, that is," he confided to me afterwards, "if you allow your mind to wander for even a *second* . . ." Fortunately, the mishap didn't prove fatal and the lady concerned is now living contentedly in Scarborough. And Devon.

But the ensuing publicity, coupled with the growing public hunger for more and more nudity in entertainment, meant hard times for Nigel. From the elegant purlieus of London's glittering West End, he was reduced to performing in cheap Holiday camps, convalescent homes for the more obscure diseases, TUC Conferences . . .

"You just got to find a way of sexing-up the act, Nige," his agent kept saying. "It's flesh they want these days."

"From a *conjuror*?" Nigel said bleakly.

But remonstrance was futile. The downward drift continued. Gradually he found himself performing to smaller and smaller audiences – The Clarence Hatry Dividend Club, the Vladivostok Young Conservatives, the ITA Opera Appreciation Society.... Piece by piece, he was reduced to selling-off his equipment, the very tools of his trade. The interlocking steel rings went to a scrap-metal merchant, the doves to a pacifist rally, the fifteen tied-together multi-coloured silk handkerchiefs to a Property Developer with hay-fever.

By Christmas Eve, all that remained of that rich diversity of exotica which Nigel had been wont to produce from about his person was one egg – a pathetic relic of his 'disappearing an egg from inside a black velvet bag' illusion. Oh, it had been a sensation in cabaret, that illusion. The awed murmurs that the egg's disappearance used to evoke from highly-placed executives at Management-By-Objective banquets! ("Surely he must be a devotee of witchcraft, a follower of the left-hand path?")

But life is not always a cabaret, old chum. Today that egg was all that stood between Nigel and starvation. Alone in his squalid bed-sit, he gazed at it, wishing there were only some way he could cook it. Oh, there was a gas ring by the grimy wall – but he no longer had the wherewithal to replenish its greedy slot. "That's show-business, all right," he reflected bitterly. "When a 10p piece for the meter is beyond the means of someone whose very name is Gascoyne."

Perhaps he could kindle a fire in the grate with his faded pressnotices? But would they burn strongly enough to boil an egg? Probably not. Something more solid in the way of fuel was needed. A piece of wood of some kind? A piece of wood. . . .

Can there be a more tragic symbol of surrender than a conjuror burning his wand? The wand, after all, is at the very heart of the conjuring experience. A wandless conjuror becomes, almost by definition, as incapable of function as a deaf lumberjack (can't hear TIMBER!) or a bow-legged wine-waiter (can't hold the bottle between knees for pulling cork out).

Or so one would have said. However, in a nearby room of that dingy lodging-house, crouched another practitioner of the performing arts: a former strip-tease artist named Alice B. Topless. She also had become a casualty to the sociological malaise which Veblen has called 'conspicuous display', but she preferred to describe as 'too much bleeding amateur competition'.

Now – alone, penniless, starving – she was contemplating putting an end to it all by impaling herself on a portable TV aerial. But as she moved towards it, she suddenly paused – sniffed. So sharpened by hunger had her senses become, her delicate nostrils had detected, drifting across that sordid hallway, the aroma of boiling egg! Timidly, she went out into the hall and tapped on Nigel's door ...

Today 'Nigel Gascoyne & Alice – The Daring Deceivers' are a show-business legend. Did I say a conjuror without a wand is incapable of functioning? That must now be qualified. What we failed to consider was the *purpose* of a wand. Why does a conjuror make such play with the wand when tapping it sharply against the rim of a black velvet bag? For only one reason: to draw your eyes away from what his other hand is groping for inside the recesses of his tail-coat. In other words, the wand is only there to 'misdirect', to distract the audience's attention.

Bearing that in mind, suppose now that, instead of a wand, your conjuror has an extremely beautiful bird standing at his side. And, at the point in the illusion when he wants all eyes diverted away from him – at that exact moment, every stitch of that bird's clothing *falls to the ground*!

All requirements are satisfied, aren't they? The moral seems to be that, these days, a nude lady-assistant can serve a conjuror's purposes every bit as effectively as his little bit of wood used to. Or, as Alice herself puts it:

"His bird is as good as his wand."

The Law is not concerned with trifles

Old legal maxim

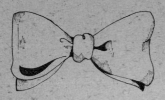

To His Honour, The Chief Judge,
The Centre Court,
Old Bailey,
London.

Dear Honour,
 No doubt you wondered why I did not present myself, as the policeman told me to, at your court last Wednesday at 10.30 inst. to answer the charge which had been levelled at me, viz. and to wit as under. Namely, that I did heave, with malice aforethought, a quantity of hot food over the personages of Lord Ickenham, Lady Ickenham, the Hon. Ickenham and their three guests, causing them to sustain distress, a bill for dry-cleaning and, in the case of Lady Ickenham, half a pint of hot gravy down the cleavage.
 The reason I did not turn up for my trial, Your Worship, lies in the circumstances as follows.
 Until the day before the occurrence occurred I had been, by profession, unemployed. Then I saw this advertisement that a waiter was required for the restaurant up the Post Office Tower. Your Grace probably does not eat out much of an evening what with having to wear that wig and the funny clothes and being laughed at by other diners so I will fill you in a bit about the restaurant. It resides, as I said, five hundred and ninety feet up the Post Office Tower. It gives a pretty view over London and the menu is about four foot square.
 I arrived for my appointment with the manager an hour and a half late and had to have a lie-down before he could ask me any questions (I have since learnt that it is possible to get to the top by lift), but he

decided that as he was so short-handed he would give me a try-out and I was to start immediately.

What he forgot to tell me, what with me being late and lunch having started and the tables full of rich people looking out of the windows and saying "That must be Highgate", was that the restaurant revolves.

This is a most important part of my case, Lord. I should have been told that the restaurant revolves. It is not – I maintain – a normal thing for a restaurant to do and unless one is given the nod beforehand one's natural expectancy is that the place will stay put.

How it works is like this. The whole thing is circular, that is to say, round. The kitchen and the Ladies and Gents and the wine cellar and so on are in the middle. In a sort of circular core. Round this is a perimeter, about twelve feet wide, on which are the tables. It is this outer ring, with the people on it, which revolves. It does not whizz round at a great lick, My Honour, or the eaters would be flung out of the windows and scattered all over Soho. It revolves very slowly so as you hardly notice. And I should have been told.

I emerged from the kitchen and at the first table in front of me was Lord Ickenham's party. I adjusted the carbon in my pad, briskly noted their first order, which was for soup, about-turned and walked straight into the Ladies. I covered up as best I could by mumbling "Sorry gentlemen" and found my way back to the kitchen next door, but it was an unnerving experience; the two rooms seem to have changed places behind my back.

I put six bowls of soup on a tray and headed out again. But Lord Ickenham and party had apparently got fed up with waiting and left. At their table was a party of Japanese tourists. They did not want soup so I turned to go back to the kitchen and found myself in the manager's office. By now I was beginning to feel ill. I returned to the Japanese to find that they too had left and the table was now occupied by a jolly party from Uttoxeter who gave me a huge order for spaghetti and asparagus with butter sauce and roast beef and fish.

By this time I had realised that all was not what it seemed to be, so I walked very carefully through the door which I *knew* was the kitchen. It was the wine cellar. The kitchen proved to be right round the other side of the curved wall of doors. I loaded up my tray with the mass of food ordered by the Uttoxeter party and emerged cautiously from the kitchen. . . .

Imagine my surprise, and delight, to find sitting seated at the table in front of me my original party, consisting and comprising of Lord Ickenham, Lady Ickenham, the Hon. Ickenham and their three guests.

I was so pleased at things returning, as it were, to normal that I rushed forward to greet them, bearing the loaded tray above my head.

This, I now realise, was a mistake. For one thing it is never a good policy to rush forward bearing loaded trays. For another thing, there is a join where the bit which revolves meets the bit which stays put. Not a huge join, but just big enough a join for one's toe to catch in.

Suffice it to say, Your Lord, that I tripped and my whole trayful of hot nosh deluged Lord Ickenham and party – particularly Lady Ickenham.

Quite naturally I fled the scene. I rushed for the manager's office to offer him my personal resignation. But it was not the manager's office which I entered. Once again something had happened to the geography and what I entered was, in point of fact, the service lift. Or more precisely the service lift-shaft, the lift itself being at ground level at the time.

And that is why I was unable to be with you at the trial last Wednesday, and why I am writing this from my hospital bed. The surgeon said I was very lucky in that I fell on my head and I should be out and about again in a month or so. I will certainly pop in and see My Lordship when I am my old self again.

But in the interim I would like to point out, Worship, that I do not think that Lord Ickenham has a case. I am sure that I do not need to remind Thee of the rules which govern English Courts of Justice, and have done from time immoral. And I would bring to the court's notice that great maxim which is the cornerstone of British justice and jury's prudence:

The Law is not Concerned with Trayfulls.

Frank Muir

Where there's a will, there's a way

G. Herbert (1640)
'Outlandish Proverbs'

WHEN it finally became apparent that the entertainment business was the only career for which I was suited – and that's quoting my Latin Master more or less exactly – I went to a large cinema in Leicester Square and pleaded with them to take me on, in any capacity, however menial. The Manager said, "The only vacancy I've got is for an Ice Cream Girl."

"Try me," I said.

I can't say I enjoyed the experience. The shoulder-straps of those trays are calibrated for feminine sizes, which meant I had to wear the tray itself so high on my chest, I kept getting the orange-drink straws up my nostril. So I was fairly relieved when the Manager told me I was to be moved to another post.

"You wanted to start at the very bottom rung of the ladder?" he asked. I nodded. He pointed towards something propped up against the cinema canopy. "There's the ladder."

The new job was rather grandly titled 'Head of Display'. All it really entailed was climbing up the ladder and affixing, high on the front wall of the cinema, those four-foot-tall metal letters which spell out the name of the film on that week.

I can't say it was a glamorous task. In a high wind, it was often dicey and – artistically – it was something less than fulfilling. Unlike a painter or a sculptor, I was in no position to step back and survey my finished work. This led, in the first few weeks, to certain errors of judgment, among which I can remember WEST SIDE SORTY, THE SNOUD OF MUSIC and SANE CONNERY IN GLODFINGER.

Nevertheless, the work did make me feel that little bit nearer to the great throbbing heart of show-business. If it were not for me, I used to think, as I surveyed the entertainment-hungry crowds milling around

Leicester Square, those people would have to make guesses at what we're showing tonight.

But it is only the moment of emergency which really transforms us into troupers. My moment came when the telephone rang at three o'clock one morning. It was the Manager. "I just passed the cinema on my way home from a Ban The Pill meeting," he said. "Your Y has dropped off."

Fuddled with sleep as I was, I immediately comprehended the urgency of his concern. The film we were showing that week was *My Fair Lady*. Although the new liberalisation of attitudes had begun to emerge and Gay Power was already nascent, it was still not yet on for a Leicester Square first-run house to appear to be exhibiting a film called MY FAIR LAD.

When my hastily-summoned taxi reached the cinema, I found the letter Y lying, twisted and splintered, on the pavement. Obviously, it was ruined beyond repair. I hastened to the store-room where the spare letters were kept. There was no spare Y!

Perhaps I can construct one, I thought. Attention was already beginning to be paid to John Schlesinger, Ken Russell and Sam Peckinpah, so we had no shortage of Xs in stock. Perhaps I could take an X and change it into a Y by just sawing off the, as it were, south-east leg?

No luck. I did it all right, but it wouldn't stay up on the wall. What to do? Where, in London, at four o'clock in the morning, can one lay hands on a four-foot-tall letter Y?

Well, if necessity is the mother of invention, there are times when it is also the mother-in-law. In other words, it can occasionally spur one to the kind of expedient which one would rather not think one-self capable of.

In my case, theft. From the cinema on the opposite side of Leicester Square, which was showing a film whose title contained the letter I wanted. As, at that time of the morning, people get up to all sorts of strange things in the West End, nobody even paused to stare when I shinned up the facia of that cinema and removed its enormous Y.

The only nasty moment came when I was carrying it across Coventry Street. A policeman stopped me – "Excuse me, sir. What might you be doing walking along at 4.30 a.m. carrying a four-foot letter Y?"

Fortunately, I kept my presence of mind, or cool, as it was only just beginning to be called. "This is not a letter Y, officer," I said. "I am an itinerant water-diviner. My preference happens to be for the larger-sized twig."

He even touched his helmet to me as he went on his way. By 5 a.m., the fair name of *My Fair Lady* was restored. True, the cinema opposite, which had been packing them in with a magnificent John Huston classic starring Gregory Peck and Orson Welles, now appeared to be showing a film called MOB DICK. But that's, as I felt myself entitled to say for the very first time, show-business.

I've had warm feelings towards the screen version of Herman Melville's great allegorical novel ever since. Indeed, I recommend that any other aspiring Head of Display who ever finds himself in a similar predicament to mine seek around for a cinema showing it. You'll find what I found:

Where there's a whale, there's a Y.

My love is like a red, red rose

Robert Burns

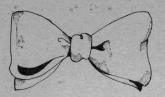

ARE you there, Jimmy Young? You of the cheerful chatter and the gramophone records and the recipe of the day? I have been a staunch listener this many a year, Jimmy Young, and I have just tried out one of your recipes so I thought perhaps you might like to know how it turned out.

I did everything exactly as you said, picking up pad and pencil exactly when you told me to – I had to steer with my teeth – and I obeyed the recipe to the letter.

You do an awful lot of recipes, usually for strange delights like Savoury Baked-bean Meringues or Pilchard Tartlets, so you probably don't remember mine offhand – but it was for a Farmyard Cottage Loaf. Good, old-fashioned home-made bread.

You began by asking me to grab hold of two pounds of 'plain' flour. You kept repeating that it must be 'plain' flour but you didn't spell the word 'plain'. Well, Jim, I live quite near the airport so I dropped in on the way home. Do you know something? They don't bake on planes. Those ice-cold sandwiches they hand round are not made on board; the bread is baked on the ground. So I bought some flour which the grocer said was 'Self-raising'; it seemed the next best thing.

Then you said "take a pint of water". Bit of a problem there because the bathroom scales only work in stones and pounds. But I found a quart bottle, took this round to the pub and asked the barman to put a pint of draught in it. Once home I got a milk bottle of water and measured how much water I had to add to the beer to fill the bottle. I then emptied the bottle and poured in this same, measured, amount of water. The empty space in the bottle now represented exactly one pint. All I had to do then was fill the bottle and measure how much water it took and I had my pint. As a point of interest, Jim, a pint is roughly the amount contained in a small milk bottle.

Next you said salt – a pinch. No problem; the kitchen window next door was open.

Then came yeast – a lump the size of a walnut – which you said could be obtained from any Baker. I tooled straight round to my nearest Baker, Ernie Baker who mends bicycles, but he'd never heard of the stuff. Luckily I managed to pick up a knob from the cakeshop. It's a sort of yellow dough, Jim, and it stinks.

You then told me to put the flour, yeast, salt and water into a bowl, which I did. You then said that for twenty minutes it had to be kneaded. That was a tricky business, Jim, and I have a couple of hints which you might give your listeners if you repeat this recipe some time in the future. When kneading it is advisable to roll the trousers up first. If you forget to do this and you can't get the dough off with hot water or petrol quite a good tip is to burn the trousers. I found the most practical way of kneading was to divide the dough into two large bowls, put these on the floor and use one knee to each bowl, hanging on to the edge of the kitchen table for balance. Another advantage to this method is that if, as happened to me, the vicar calls in the middle of the process, you can make your way slowly to the front door, Toulouse-Lautrec style, without interrupting the process.

Your next instruction, Jim, was to find a warm place, about 80 degrees Fahrenheit, and put the bowl in to prove it. I found a nice warm spot under the dog and put the bowl in but it didn't prove anything to me. Could have been 20 degrees or 100 degrees, Jim. So I took the bowl out again.

Next I had to grease my baking tin. Now that was something I did know a little about. Out to the garage for the grease-gun. Pump-pump. Done.

Finally you told me to put the dough into the greased tin, press it down well, and bake it in a low oven for four hours. Oh, Jim, that was a tricky one to be faced with right at the end of the recipe. You see, our stove is a pretty old one and it is up on cast-iron legs; the oven is at least eight inches off the ground. But – you wanted a low oven so a low oven you had to have. It took me about twenty minutes to hacksaw off each leg, but I managed it, and in went my bread.

I will be frank with you, Jim, and confess that when I took my loaf out four hours later I was disappointed. It did not even look like a loaf. It was sort of black and blistery and it sat very low in the tin. Nor did it smell like a loaf. It smelt like an Italian garage on a hot day. And I couldn't get it out of the tin. I remember you saying to pass a knife round the edge and shake it out but the knife wouldn't go in. Eventually I drilled a hole in the crust of the loaf, inserted the end of a crowbar and, using the edge of the tin as a fulcrum, threw all my weight on the other end with the object of prising the loaf out. It sort of worked. There was a splintering noise, the crust gave way and I was flat on my back. There was no sign of the interior of the loaf.

I found the interior of the loaf the following morning. On the ceiling. A great lump of semi-cooked, rancid dough had hit the ceiling, started to droop, and then congealed into a cross between a gargoyle and one of those conical plaster ceiling-fittings which electric lights used to hang from.

Far be it from me to criticise, Jim, but are you sure that your recipes aren't a wee bit complicated? I happen to be a handy, practical sort of chap, but many of your listeners are women, Jim, and how some of them would have coped . . .

Well, you said at the end of the recipe that you would like to hear how our bread has turned out so I am only too happy to oblige:

My loaf is like a weird, weird rose.

Prevention is better than cure

Thomas Fuller
'The Histories of the Worthies of England'

UNTIL recently, my knowledge of Herbert Tozer, last of the literalists, was confined to a couple of indignant messages from him. "Kindly refrain from saying 'best foot forward'," he wrote after I had used the phrase in a broadcast. "No one has more than two feet. In future, please amend to 'better foot forward'." Similarly, after I'd uttered publicly the proverb "Still waters run deep", I received a telegram from him – "If waters are still how can they run at all question-mark."

Impressed, I showed these admonitions to Sir Jack Longland, our Chairman on that last infirmity of noble minds, the 'My Word!' quiz programme. To my surprise, Jack coloured up like a girl. Then, after some hesitation, he admitted acquaintanceship with Tozer. "It was exactly that trick of literalism," he said, "which helped Herbert work his ticket out of the Army."

It was an odd story. Tozer, a National Service conscript, had only been in Catterick Camp two days when he came to the conclusion that the Army was no kind of life for his kind of man. But how to persuade them to sever the connection? He fell back upon literalism.

When, the following morning on the parade-ground, the Sergeant Major instructed his squad to stand at ease, Herbert left the parade-ground and went absent without leave. They picked him up a week later in a South of England town. On being brought before his C.O., Herbert claimed firmly that he had only been obeying orders. "I was told, sir, that a good soldier always obeys the last order given."

"Your last order, Tozer," the C.O. said coldly, "was to stand at ease."

"With respect, sir, that was not what the Sergeant Major said If, sir, you would request the Sergeant Major to repeat the order exactly as he uttered it, sir?"

The C.O., a just man, nodded at the Sergeant Major. The S.M.

cleared his throat obediently. Then, in traditional manner, he bellowed – "Squa-hod . . . Squad, stand at . . . *hayes!*"

"Exactly, sir. And Hayes is a small town in Middlesex, not far from London Airport. That was where I proceeded to go and stand, sir. As I received no orders rescinding that instruction, sir, I have been standing there these past seven days."

They had no alternative but to acquit and release him. The Army is possibly the last bastion of literalism, particularly with respect to what it calls 'words of command'.

It was this sensitivity that Herbert continued to exploit. Ordered, a couple of days later, to "Quick March!", he again left the parade-ground. This time he secreted himself within a large ammunition box, inside which he had taken the precaution of boring air-holes and storing ample provisions.

It was five days before they found him. Brought before the C.O., he again requested that the N.C.O. responsible for the quick-march order repeat the word of command. Grimly the C.O. motioned the N.C.O. so to do. "Squa-hod," bellowed the Drill Sergeant, "Squad, quick . . . *hutch!*"

"The verb 'hutch', is a sixteenth-century word," explained Herbert. "It means 'to lay up in a hutch or chest'. And the word 'chest' is defined as 'a large box of strong construction' – an adequate description, I would venture to say, sir, of the container to which I proceeded. And, *en passant*, sir, may I make a suggestion regarding the use of the word 'quick'. It is an adjective, sir. The more correct qualifier would be 'quickly' . . . 'Quickly hutch!' "

The C.O. had little bits of spit showing at the corners of his mouth but, stickler that he was for the niceties, he motioned to Prisoners' Escort to march Herbert away. It was when Herbert appeared before him the very next day, this time following an unconventional response to the command "Eyes Right!", that a despatch-rider was sent to purchase a copy of *The Shorter Oxford English Dictionary*. The command to eyes-right had, as is the Army way, been vouchsafed in the form of "Eyes . . . *hight!*" – whereupon Herbert had smartly proceeded to pull a box of mascara from his battle-dress and daub it profusely upon his eyelashes and eyelids. To the C.O.'s chagrin, the *Shorter Oxford* unequivocally confirmed that 'hight' means 'to embellish or ornament'. (Early M.E., huihten, of doubtful origin, 1633.)

The decisive battle was fought, appropriately, at Herbert Tozer's Passing Out parade. On the very first word of command – the order to come to attention – Herbert marched himself away. This time, however, he was immediately intercepted by the waiting Military Police who had been set to observe his every movement.

On the C.O.'s desk, next to his latest amended copy of Q.R.s – Queen's Regulations, for the non-military – lay the by now well-thumbed *Shorter Oxford*. "All that happened," snarled the C.O., "was that the parade was called to attention. Those were the only words of command given."

"But may I remind you of the manner of their utterance, sir?" Herbert said. "We were told 'Parade . . . *shun!*' The verb 'shun', sir – and do, by all means, look it up – the verb 'shun' means 'avoid, eschew or seek safety by concealment from'. Which I did, sir."

"And over-reached yourself, Tozer," the C.O. said. "Look, lad." The dictionary flipped open immediately to the correct page, for a bookmark had already been inserted there. "The verb 'shun' can only be used *transitively*. In other words, for it to have the meaning you gave it, there has to be an *object* after it; as in 'shun drink', or 'shun intellectuals'. Without that 'object', its only possible definition is 'Diminutive of stand to attention'. Which you didn't do, cockychops." The C.O. turned to the Adjutant. "Well done, Simon. Think we've got grounds for a court-martial?"

"If you want my opinion, sir," the Adjutant said, "We've got grounds for a firing-squad. Just to make sure, though, I'll send the papers off to the Education Officer, together with a copy of the appropriate Q.R. regarding punishments for desertion."

"In that case, sir," Herbert said, "may I submit a defence-brief to him? Quoting some further references anent the disputed definition?"

"Submit all the anent you wish," said the C.O., who was not without style.

You can't help feeling sorry for the man. What he had forgotten was that no literalist relies on the *Shorter Oxford*. Herbert's brief was based firmly on the thirteen-volume *Oxford*. There, with massive authority, is printed an alternative use of 'shun' – as an *intransitive* verb. Its meaning is 'Move away, go aside, fly'.

Herbert was honourably discharged from the Army within two weeks. The other factor which the C.O. had forgotten was that the Div. Educational Officer was Brigadier J. Longland. Jack's judgment on the relative merits of Herbert's argument as against the Army's was characteristically cogent:

"Brief on 'shun' is better than Q.R."

If winter comes, can spring be far behind?

Percy Bysshe Shelley
'Ode to the West Wind'

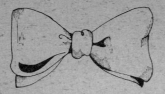

A year or so ago I had occasion to go to Moscow (a cool sentence which tells nothing of the panic, soul-searching, worry and frantic organising which actually took place prior to embarkation). It fell to me, a thrusting, youngish television executive, to see a Russian about a play.

The time of the year was February, and Moscow in February, according to a vodka-pickled ex-foreign correspondent I happened to meet on a 14A bus, is cold enough to freeze the wheels off a brass cannon. So off I went to Moss Bros. and hired myself a fur hat with flaps, galoshes, ski gloves, and an enormous fur-lined overcoat. I held a dress parade when I reached home and my wife said that I looked like a cross between a used flue-brush and a pregnant yeti. Happily my wife was coming with me and I was able to point out that, dressed for the Steppes, she looked like a fur-bearing pear. But at least we reckoned that we would be warm; poor trusting innocents that we were.

I never did like flying and when we arrived at London Airport I had the familiar sensation of disquiet; as though a cold potato had lodged half-way down my gullet.

We arrived in comfortable time, as is our custom; that is to say, two hours before we needed to. Our nerves were not helped by the broadcast announcements. Moscow is a peculiarly upsetting place to be bound for because almost all the half-heard announcements seemed to refer to it: "Last call for flight 724. All passengers mus' go to . . ." "All passengers for BOAC mus' go . . ."

A further disagreeable factor was the temperature in the Departure Lounge. Reading outwards from my long woollen combs, I was wearing about eight inches of heavy insulation. After five minutes I was sweating like a carthorse.

But we arrived in Moscow safely and perhaps I can pass on a few tips and wrinkles to others preparing a similar expedition.

If you are approached on the tarmac by a photographer who asks you to stand at the top of the aircraft ladder, wave happily, and then step backwards into the aircraft, do benefit from my experience and first make sure that there is an aircraft backed onto the ladder.

Do not have a comeover when you land and find that you are at a place called 'Mockba' and scream that you've been hijacked and try to shut yourself in the loo and have to be given brandy by your wife; 'Mockba' is the way the Russians spell Moscow.

Don't expect too much from Russian plumbing. All Russian lavatory cisterns are made by the same firm and none of them works. Or rather, they overwork. Instead of the water gushing forth on demand, building up again, and then stopping, due to a small design deficiency there is no build-up and no gush on demand, just a steady, noisy trickle of water through the works night and day. So what you do is this. You take the porcelain lid off with your right hand and feel down in the water with you left hand. Somewhere at the bottom there is a rubber seating-valve thing. Press this firmly down and the trickle ceases.

Note to the above: A little way up Gorki Prospect, on the left, is a small jeweller's shop which specialises in drying out wrist-watches.

The steward on the aircraft told me always to wear my fur hat and always to wear it with the flaps down and the strings tied firmly under my chin, and I think this was very good advice. The only thing is that fur hats are very bulky things and at first I kept rolling out of bed. This can be avoided by stacking a couple of bricks on the pillow either side of the head.

I have left the Golden Tip until last, because it is very important and I had to find it out for myself.

There is a fallacy in the system of clothing you are advised to wear to combat the Russian winter. When you are standing erect the clothing is warm enough; but when you are walking, or bending down . . .

All fur-lined overcoats have a slit up the back. All jackets have a slit up the back. All winter long-johns have a slit at the back. When you bend down in Red Square there is nothing between your vitals and the east wind of Siberia but the seam in your trousers – virtually a dotted line. Your rear portion is almost totally unprotected; a sitting target for frostbite.

I gave the problem considerable thought and came up with a practical answer. You take *two* fur hats with you to Moscow. Each morning, before dressing, in the privacy of your own bedroom, you arrange two basins on two chairs. In basin A you stir a mixture of flour and water until it reaches the consistency of cream. You then take a pair of scissors and your second fur hat and snip off enough fur to fill basin B. Lowering your pyjama trousers (or raising your nightdress, as appropriate) you sit in basin A. You then walk about a bit until tacky and sit in basin B. A further turn round the room to dry off and you are fully protected for twenty-four hours against the iciest wind blowing round the Urals.

But, you are probably saying, the flaps on my long winter underwear always stays shut; and anyway, I won't be bending down.

I say, don't take chances. They can spring open with the ordinary movements of walking. So:

If winter combs can spring – befur behind.

A crown is no cure for the headache

Benjamin Franklin
'*Poor Richard's Almanack*'

MY grandmother was a great one for axioms. Her favourite was, "The unexpected doesn't always happen but when it does it generally happens when you're least expecting it." As with everything else about my little smiling Granny, that axiom is sagacious, perceptive and, when you get right to the core of the situation, absolutely no help at all.

If you require some elaboration of that touch of bitterness, stay with me. We'll go back to the time when I was seventeen years old.

When I was seventeen, it was a very good year for small-town girls. Mainly because not one of them would have anything to do with me. This was due to the appearance I presented. At that age I was all wrists and ankles. Six foot three, a neck like Nat Jackley's, so gangling and painfully skinny that, in repose, I looked like a pair of discarded braces.

Such a configuration made me achingly shy of girls. In fact, at the time of which I speak, I still hadn't kissed any female who was not either a blood-relation or four-legged.

Then one day, a Tuesday afternoon, while Jan Berenska belted out his concert arrangement of 'Little Curly Head Upon A High Chair' direct from the Pump Room, Leamington Spa, my Mum came into my bedroom. "Mrs Forbush is coming to tea," she said. "And she's bringing her daughter with her. You two can play together while we talk."

The news did not stir me. Although I'd never seen the daughter, I had seen Mrs Forbush. About as sexy as the General Council of the TUC. So I just grunted and continued cutting out the advertisements for half-slips in *The Draper's Record*. An hour later, the door opened again and my mother pushed Lila in.

Lila. Thinking back on her, even across this arch of decades, my marrow-bone still melts. A raven-eyed, black-haired shimmer of wet-lipped ripeness. Just turned sixteen, and wearing those shiny artificial-silk stockings with the overstated seam.

"Well," my Mum said as she left us, "play nicely." I remained inert, just staring at Lila. Never, in the whole of my life-span, had I ever gazed on anything so utterly – *tangible*.

She scanned me the way a decorator does a house when you've asked for an estimate to do the outside. I said, "Would you like to look through my Meccano catalogues?"

She shook her head. The movement rippled right the way down! I could hear my own breathing. "Tell you what," she said, in a light, clear voice, "let's kiss."

It was just the one kiss. What must be said about it, though, is that it lasted twenty-three minutes. Moreover, the embouchure which Lila employed can most nearly be conveyed by the phrase 'as though eating an over-ripe pear'. My Chilprufe vest ran up my back like a window-blind.

Immediately after it, we were called downstairs for tea and Lyons Snow Cake, so that's all there ever was between Lila Forbush and me. She showed no inclination to go upstairs again after tea, spent the rest of the afternoon chatting to my Mum and Mrs Forbush, without even glancing in my direction. I sensed that she'd found me to be what educational circles now describe as an under-achiever.

Episode closed. But where does an experience like that, with a Lila like that, leave a man for the rest of his life? I am in a position to tell you. Ever afterwards, she becomes the measure against which every other woman fails. Then, as he moves towards middle-age – "If only," he keeps finding himself thinking. "If only we could play it again, Sam. With me as I am now – but Lila as she was then!"

Impossible? Well, hold your horses. Cut to thirty years later. This month, in fact. Two weeks ago, if you want it to the day, at a friend's cocktail-party in the King's Road. He'd just taken over a disused telephone-box and opened it as a boutique. There I was, milling with the fashionable throng, when – suddenly, right in front of me, across a crowded room – ! Unmistakable. Those raven-eyes, the black hair, those pouting wet lips! It had happened! Life had managed to work me its jackpot – a second chance!

I bounded across that room like an antelope. Trying to control my voice, "My dear," I said. "Please don't be startled, I'm not accosting you. It's just that, are you – oh, you must be, I can see it in every feature – are you Lila Forbush's daughter?"

The light, clear tones which answered me erased three decades as though they had never been. "Up your kilt, squire."

"No, please," I said. "Don't turn away, I mean no offence."

"Well, you're giving it, aren't you."

"Why?"

"I'm Lila Forbush's son."

I refer you back to my grandmother's axiom. Also, and more importantly, to that assertion that axioms offer the thinking man everything except consolation.

Or, as Ben Franklyn used to walk around America snarling:

"A Gran is no cure for the heartache."

A rose-red city – 'half as old as time'

Rev. John William Burgon
'Petra'

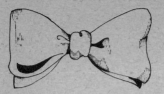

I have been near tears many times in my crowded life but I can only recall having actually wept but twice – once when I rounded a bend of the road in Corsica and the unbelievable beauty of the rock formations known as Les Calanches were bathed in the warm, rosy glow of the late afternoon sunshine, and once when a horse trod on my foot.

But I was near tears today, when the post brought me a birthday card from a dear old lady in the village. She was in hospital – she had twisted her ankle water-skiing in Hendon – and had taken the trouble to make me a birthday card with her own hands. Just a folded piece of simple paper, with a pressed flower pasted on the front, and a simple legend within: "Happy Birthday. With all the money you're making, how about sending an old lady a gallon of gin. Mrs Tobler."

Oh, it wasn't the words, simple and sincere though they were. It was something about the faded flower pasted on the front. And the name Mrs Tobler. Where had I seen that flower before?

Later on that morning, as I was cleaning my spectacles, everything became clear.

It was twelve years ago, give or take a day. And it was to do with my children. Jamie was then six feet tall, with an engaging smile and a lot of blonde hair. He was eight. A quiet lad, for the past few months he had been spending most of his spare time industriously loosening and removing his teeth in order to save up the sixpences thereby obtained to buy a chemistry set to make ice cream. My daughter Sally was six; gentle, beautiful and practically toothless because Jamie was helping to loosen her teeth in return for half her sixpences.

The children had a part of the garden for their very own, to make of it what they would. Jamie had made a mine of his. He was down about eight feet, prospecting for old clay pipes, coal, Roman coins, mud; anything on which he could make an honest buck.

Sal's patch was quite different. She loved colour, and simple things, and beauty. Her little square was neatly raked and levelled and she had put little labels where she had planted things. She had planted a number of things. There was a sandal. It showed no signs of growing but nor did it seem to deteriorate; it stuck out of the ground and sort of retained its status quo. There was one asparagus which had roared up to a height of four feet and waved in the breeze like a ghostly, emaciated Christmas tree. A packet of frozen peas. In their packet. And a rose bush. Sal was very, very attached indeed to her rose bush. She had cut a clipping on a country walk and planted it and it made a brave patch of colour – mostly brown and green – but there was one small, red flower. Sal called it *Red Setter*. Because it was a dog-rose.

Now we had an actor staying with us at the time named Arthur Howard. A very nice actor indeed. The sort of actor who when you say to somebody "We've got Arthur Howard staying with us" they say "Oh, ARTHUR! How IS he?" But Arthur was not a gardener. Actor, yes. Gardener, no. *The Tempest* – fine. The compost – not a clue.

That afternoon we had to go out on a charity walk – well a sort of charity walk; my wife was breaking in a new pair of boots for the parish priest – and Arthur could not come with us because he had caught his ear in the egg whisk. It was one of those hand-held ones like a bow-legged ballet dancer doing an entrechat and, thinking two of the tines were touching, he whirred it round and put his ear to it . . .

So we left Arthur to look after the estate.

When we arrived back it seems that a woman – a Mrs Tizer, or Tusser, Arthur couldn't be sure – had arrived at the back door and asked whether she could buy some of my wife's herbs. My wife had her little herb garden right next to the children's patch.

Ever eager to oblige, Arthur had pulled up handfuls of this and that and sold them to the woman for a shilling.

"What did you give her?" asked my wife, a little puzzled.

"Well," said Arthur, "there was rosemary, chives, tarragon, and – oh yes – thyme!"

"Are you sure?" asked my wife. "I don't remember planting thyme."

The next thing there was a tremendous cry and Sally hurtled into the scene, tears streaming down her face. "My rose has gone!" She sobbed. "Somebody has stolen my lovely rose!"

And gone it had. Her single little dog-rose had vanished from the face of the earth, it seemed for ever.

But this morning it returned. Dried, pressed, and stuck to my birthday card from the old lady; twelve years later.

So a few minutes ago, when Sally looked at the card in my hand in a rather puzzled way and said "What is that flower? It seems – sort of – familiar," who can begrudge me a vagrant tear as I answered, "It is a rose, dearest . . .

"A rose, *Red Setter*, Arthur sold as thyme."

More matter with less art

Shakespeare
Hamlet Act II, sc. 2

EVER see a Burt Lancaster war-film called *The Train*? A dull title, but an interesting premise – a group of French civilians who risk their lives smuggling certain masterpieces of French art out of the occupied zone, so that the noble culture of La Belle France can continue to enrich the spirit of the Free World. The question the film posed was this: is the preservation of any work of art, however great, worth the sacrifice of any human life, however humble?

I found myself facing the same philosophical dilemma when my small nephew got his head jammed in the hole of a Henry Moore statue. It was during a class outing to the Tate Gallery and young Arthur had paused in front of Moore's *The Mother*. What the teacher should have remembered was that, the previous week, the same class had been on a day-trip to Brighton. There, on the Palace Pier, Arthur had posed for a comic photograph in one of those 'fat lady' cut-outs with a hole at the neck for you to stick your own face through.

To the mind of a twelve-year-old, the association of ideas must have been irresistible. Even the Gallery authorities admitted that it was a justifiable impulse, not to say endearing. It only began to take on dimensions when they found Arthur couldn't get his head out of the statue again.

"We've tried everything," the Curator said when he visited me that evening. "Cutting his hair, greasing his ears . . ." He gestured helplessly.

My own knowledge of modern sculpture can be evaluated from the fact that I once put down £75 deposit on a Giacometti under the impression it was an Italian sports car. So I cannot say I really appreciated the Curator's agitation. Not even when he said, "It looks as though the only way we'll ever extricate your nephew is by smashing that statue to pieces."

"Fair enough," I said. "Want the lend of a big hammer?"

He twitched. "Henry Moore's *The Mother*," he said, "is one of this country's finest cultural treasures."

"I see," I said. "Well, that's more than anyone could say about Arthur. Judging from his school reports, that hole is about the only 'O' he'll ever get through."

The Curator drew a shaky breath. "Look here. Are we to demolish a masterwork just because of one idiot schoolboy?"

I stared at him. There was a cold glitter in his eye. "I want you, as his uncle, to persuade his parents to let him . . . stay there."

"Stone me," I said.

"We'll do everything that can be done to ensure that he leads as normal a life as is possible under the circumstances. The Arts Council has already promised a special grant."

"It's still not much of a future for the lad, is it," I said. "Oh, maybe all right for the time being, but what about when he's a bit older? Girls? Marriage? You'd have your work cut out then, wouldn't you? Oh, I suppose he could manage some kind of married life, not the easiest, but what about if he has children? I mean, think of things like Speech Day? Couldn't very well turn up with a statue round his neck, could he, you know how kids are about their parents looking conspicuous."

"It's the boy," said the Curator, "or the statue."

Well, it was one of your real metaphysical posers. 'Art versus Life'. Oh, I know your Jonathan Millers and your Dr Bronowskis can bat a topic like that up and down for hours, but it was outside my range. Deepest I've ever been on a chat-show is Are Blood Sports Cruel. So I said "Mind if I go and have a look at Arthur?"

The Tate Gallery at midnight can never be what a person would call groovy. That night, however, the sight of that enormous statue with a schoolboy's head in the middle . . . macabre. I said to the Curator, "You could at least have altered the label. Called it *Mother And Child*."

Young Art, I must say, was in excellent spirits, considering. "Hallo, uncle," he said. "Got me head stuck."

There was something in his tone I recognised. "Arthur," I said, "you're enjoying this."

He smiled. "Got 'em all at it, haven't I."

I realised what was needed. "Arthur," I said, "when your parents had the wall removed between your lounge and your dining room, do you remember what they called that?"

"Yes," he said. "Knocking-through."

I brought the big hammer out of my pocket. "That's the phrase I was looking for."

In ten seconds he was standing at my side. "Can we stop for a kebab on the way home?"

It was, I think, the magazine called *Studio International* which made use of the *Hamlet* quotation. They displayed two photographs – one showing the scene before Arthur was extricated, the other showing the scene afterwards. The 'before' one was captioned, "Henry Moore's *The Mother* With Arthur Inside". On the photo of the empty statue, the caption read:

"Moore *Mater* With Less Art"

Stand a little less between me and the sun

Diogenes to Alexander, when the latter asked
if there was anything he could do for him.

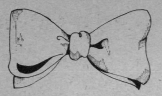

I was very interested to read in *The Times* the other day that Claude Monet's painting, *Girl walking by the river near St Cloud*, had been sold at Sotheby's for £1,000,000,000. The buyer was an American from Texas who wanted it very much to make into a drinks tray. I wasn't able to read the buyer's name because it was just below the chips and the paper had gone transparent.

I suppose it went for what these days is a largish sum because it is such an important painting; the first painting in which the great Impressionist had included a human figure. Just what induced him to break the habit of a lifetime and shove in a girl I am now able to divulge.

Monet started to paint his picture – the one he put the figure in – on the morning before the first Impressionist exhibition. This took place in Paris, in 1874, in the studio of the photographer Nadar – 35 Boulevard des Capucines, first door on the left, over the chemist's shop.

That morning all the young painters met in a café – the Café Guerbois, second on the right past the horsemeat shop – and a very excited batch of poor young painters they were, to be sure, laughing and shouting and ordering drinks.

There was Toulouse-Lautrec; he was on shorts. There was the nervous, brooding young Vincent Van Gogh, who tossed back his drink and strode off ("Young Vincent is so restless," murmured Monet, "ear today – gone tomorrow"). There was Sisley, Fantin-Latour, all drinking down litres of cheap beer. Only Cézanne was conspicuous by his absinthe.

But the figure of Claude Monet sat apart from the others, moodily stirring his coffee with a used tube of Chrome Yellow, and not joining in the general fun of pouring beer over each other and throwing bread at the waiter.

"What's up, Claude, *mon vieux*?" cried Alfred Sisley, flinging himself bestride the chair next to Monet and wincing a moment with agony.

"Well, you've done it all wrong, lads," replied Monet. "All you've painted is women. Dozens and dozens of plump birds. The public doesn't want plump birds – they're a drug on the market. I doubt if you can flog another painting of a plump bird even if you give trading stamps."

"But," stuttered Sisley, adjusting his chair, "have you seen Renoir's study of the girl bathing by the river? Beautiful . . . meaningful . . ."

"Like a mauve sea-cow sitting on wet grass, old son. He'll be trundling that home on the old pram tonight, mark my words."

"But . . . have you seen Degas' pastel of the naked woman bending over a bowl of water?"

"A flash in the pan, squire. He'll get ten francs for it, top weight, frame thrown in. No, laddie, it's the old pastoral scene they want these days; the old sun through the trees and glinting off the old water and not a body in sight. So good luck with the exhibish – I'm off to dash off a quickie along the banks of the Seine; there's a nice bend near St Cloud where the water's a dark brown colour; I've got rather a lot of brown left over from that thing I did of Rouen Cathedral . . . *allez-au'voir!*" And he was gone.

And so, on the evening of 15 April, 1874, the young Impressionists startled Paris with their first exhibition. In no time at all the little salon was filled to bursting point with the cream of Paris.

Emile Zola was there with his lovely wife, Gorgon. The poet Baudelaire rushed about all over the place, uttering little cries and simply reeking of 'Fleurs du Mal'.

The British Ambassador, Lord Macbeth, was there with his lady wife. Lady Macbeth was visibly startled at the painting of the woman bending over the bowl and cried "Is that a Degas I see before me?"

George Sand, the eminent lady novelist, swept in like a ship in full sail with her usual two admirers in attendance; a Chopin to starboard and a Liszt to port.

Probably the most excited person present was the Spanish consul, who stood in front of Renoir's picture of the large nude lady sitting on the turf crooning "*Gracias!* Oh, *gracias!*"

In one hour and ten minutes every picture had been sold. Not for thirty for forty francs, as the poor young artists had hoped, but for a hundred francs and more.

The Spanish consul paid two hundred francs for Renoir's nude and insisted on taking it with him. He cried, "I just cannot leave her behind alone!"

As the evening light began to fade, Renoir took a cab to St Cloud to find his old friend Claude and tell him the good news. He soon found him, on a corner of the Seine, dabbing away at the brown bits of his picture.

"Claude!" he shouted, "Claude, you must paint women! Put one in your picture now. This instant! We have all sold every one of our figure pictures!"

"And how much did you get for your purple sea-cow, matey, eh? Five francs? Ten?"

In answer, Renoir counted out his two hundred francs.

"Good grief!" said Claude, "Deux song frong for embongpong?"

He looked down at his painting of the river and the empty riverbank.

"Would you do something for me?" he asked, a strange look coming into his eyes.

"Of course," replied Renoir. "What do you want me to do?"

Claude Monet took up a great brushful of pink paint:

"Stand a little lass between me and the Seine."

Dressed in a little brief authority

Shakespeare
Measure for Measure, Act II, sc. 2

THE outpost of Arcadia in which I live is called Golders Green. It features a Mrs Thora Tidmarsh who gives the kind of parties that could count as qualifying heats for the Olympic Yawning Team. At one of them, a piece of paper was pinned on your lapel as you came through the front door. On this paper was written an anagram and you had to promise faithfully you wouldn't help yourself to a drink until you'd worked out what word the anagram was supposed to be. My anagram was CXLNOIE.

That was eighteen months ago. Last week I met Thora Tidmarsh in the Chinese takeaway and she said, "I'm having another party next Saturday, you must come. Everyone's got to dress up as a famous quotation."

"Mrs Tidmarsh," I said, "Oh, Mrs Tidmarsh."

'Lexicon.' That's the word. 'Lexicon!' CXLNOIE. Look, you won't mind if I rush this a bit from now on, will you, but it's been eighteen months since I tasted alcohol.

When I got home, my wife said, "I'm going as, you'll never guess the quotation, it came to me like Flash, I'm going as, no I won't tell you."

'I said, "What are you going as?"

She said, "I'm going to carry a flask of wine and a loaf of bread and a big card with the word OHTU."

I said, "I've got it. I bet I've got it. It's 'OHTU be in England now that –'."

"It's not," she said. "It's 'A flask of wine, a loaf of bread and thou'. OHTU is the anagram."

I said, "But anagrams were only for the last party, this party it's – oh, you get on with it then."

But every day from then on, she kept exclaiming things like, "You'll

89

never guess what Mrs Thing from 74's going as. She's going to hang a convector heater on her bottom and be 'O that this too, too solid flesh would melt'." Or, "You know the lady who lives at 'Done Rome In'?" (The husband claims to be a descendant of the Visigoths.) "Well, she's embroidering the minicab company's price-rises on her blouse, so as to be 'Earth has not anything to show more fare'."

People can be so creative sometimes, can't they. Me, I just gloomed about for the whole week, brain-racking. Friday night, I still hadn't an idea in my head, so I said, "Listen, why don't I just pitch up at the back door and instead of going in, I'll hang about outside and be 'Come into the garden, Maud'?"

She said, "Where does the Maud bit fit in?"

I said, "You're getting more like your mother every day."

Comes Saturday night, I'm no further on. Away she went with her flask of wine and her Hovis and I said I'd join her a bit later because my mind works better under deadline conditions. After about an hour of sitting with my eyes closed, the hunger pangs struck, so I wandered into the larder ("When did you last see your larder?"?). All I could find were a couple of rather pallid soft roes ("Go, lovely Roes"?), a box of Matzos ("You Matzo been a beautiful baby"?), and a – ah now! Wait a minute.

On the bottom shelf there was this bit of cheese. A large slice of Brie that we used for the mousetrap, the mice round N.W.11 being a bit sophisticated.

I took off all my clothes, stripped right down to the skin, smeared myself from head to foot with the Brie cheese, which luckily was fairly ripe, or 'Muir' as the French call it, slipped on my raincoat, then off I trotted to the party.

I was, though I say it myself, a sensation. Mainly, I think, because I went to the wrong house. There were about eight people round the table when I was ushered in, all of them in evening dress like one of those after-dinner mint adverts, and they evinced some consternation.

"Sorry," I said. "Mistake. Thought this was Thora Tidmarsh's place. She's giving a party and I'm a quotation."

"Oh, quite understandable," they said. "Not to worry. Think nothing of it. My hacienda is yours, señor. But," they said, "why are you smothered all over in runny cheese?"

"Ah, that," I said. "Well, it's *Shakespeare*, isn't it?

" 'Dressed in a little Brie for Thora T'."

Upon
My Word!

'The Light That Failed'

Rudyard Kipling
Title of Story

Iᴛ'ꜱ fair to say that, even at my most unbuttoned, I am
to the Fun People what Marcel Marceau is to radio. For that reason, it
was perhaps unwise even to have considered accepting that invitation
to Bernice's Housecooling Party. Bernice, by common agreement of
every After Eight consumer in the Garden Suburb, is more or less a
registered Fun Person. So for me to receive an invite to one of her
celebrations was very akin to breaking through the Roundhead
lines.

For the benefit of those of you who don't live at that pace either, I
should explain that a Housecooling party is one thrown to mark the
departure from a house. In Bernice's case, this was occasioned by the fact
that she and Lionel had finally split up. I say 'finally' because although
divorce had been on the cards for ages, they'd been trying to make a go
of it for the sake of the home movies.

Now, however, the split was official and Bernice was launching her
new status with champagne and the chums round and I felt no end
chuffed at being included among those cavorting. The only snag was,
what should I take along as a present? What sort of gift is *appropriate*
to a Fun Person? Yes, obviously a Fun *Thing* – but then again, what's
that? I did a tentative wander round our local Gift Boutique, but that's
not really an Aladdin's Cave even at the best of times and especially
not since it branched out into Suede Cleaning and Sheepskin Renewal.

Contact sunglasses? An electric kettle with a stereo whistle? A
musical toilet-roll holder that plays 'Dream The Impossible Dream'?
Everything I considered seemed far too *stolid* for a fun-gift. Then, the
following Sunday, my eye lighted on an item in the newspaper: a
trendy foundry in the Midlands was offering reproduction

chastity-belts! Perfect replicas, in cast iron, of the famed mediaeval securi-corps. complete with padlock and key.

When I presented one to Bernice, I must say its reception proved all I could have hoped for. "Oh, what a Fun Thing!" she ejaculated. "Do look everybody, oh do look!" She's a large lady, Bernice, and as she never wears undergarments, when she walks everything seems to move more than her feet do. Right now, her motion was that of a blancmange in a railway dining-car. "Isn't it a hoot!" she shouted. "Oh, Giorgio, do come and look."

Giorgio turned out to be an Italian water-skiing instructor she'd recently imported from Portofino. About seven foot tall, sun-tanned, muscles even unto the eyebrows, and didn't speak one word of English. "Isn't it absolutely darling?," she yelled, waving the belt in front of him, "Chastitia Belta!" He nodded uncomprehendingly and grinned, exposing teeth you could read small print by.

"Bags you try it on," shouted the man who manages the Driving School, an ex-major with gin leaking out of his ears. "Go on, Bernice, put it on!"

"Oh I must, I must! Give me just five mins."

While she was upstairs, I was man of the moment. Everybody crowded round me and said what a brilliant idea, what really fun-thinking, how absolutely knockout, and you really must come round to our pad for fondue. And when Bernice came down again, "It fits as if it was made for me," she squealed. "Absolutely superb, darling."

Then, while everybody was uttering cheers and upping their glasses to me, she waved her hands in the air. "A moment's quiet now," she said. "Best of order, please. It's time for Bernice to make the big announcement."

She moved over to Giorgio and leaned back against the brown wall of his chest. "This morning at eleven o'clock, Giorgio and I were married in Hampstead Registry Office. Tonight we're off to Portofino for the honeymoon bit."

A moment's gaping – then whoops and yoicks. Hugging, back-slapping, cries of congratulations from all the males, envy from the females. They poured champagne the way Wimpeys pour concrete and, after someone had put the Marriage Theme from *The Godfather* on the record-player, dancing took place.

So when, an hour or so later, Bernice came quivering up at my side, I was feeling no angst at all. "Just off to change into the going-away gear, darling," she smiled. "Can I have the padlock key?"

"By jove, yes," I chuckled. "Jolly well better have that, I should think, what?" I don't know why I seem to fall into that playing-against-type sort of dialogue in Fun People environments, nerves I suppose, but anyway I reached jovially into my pocket for the small cast-iron key.

It was the first time I ever really comprehended the meaning of that expression 'suddenly taken sober'. As I groped from pocket to pocket, I could *feel* the room cooling. Slowly all conversation died, the record-player was switched-off, more and more eyes turned to me as I patted myself, poked, dug, scrabbled, tore. By the time I had every single one of my pocket-linings hanging out, the place was in complete silence. The only sound to be heard came from the TV set next door. It was a commercial; the one about 'all that locked-in goodness'.

"Surely," said somebody finally, "surely they come with a *spare* key."

"Well, no. Not if you think about it," I said. "I mean not for a chastity-belt. A spare key, I mean, it'd sort of defeat the whole . . . " It was a trailing-off kind of statement, because nobody seemed all that interested in pursuing its logic. From upstairs we heard Giorgio burst into sudden song. Having gone up to change into his other T-shirt, he was cheerfully belting out the Italian version of 'Tonight, tonight, Won't be just any night.'

"Send for the Fire Brigade," said Bernice, her eyes never leaving mine and all that mighty mass at rest.

The first thing the Head Fireman said when he came through the door was "Will I need the extension ladder?" I took him out on to the patio and gave him a complete, if muttered, explanation of the circumstances. He stared at me. "I've got two engines and an appliance out there," he said. "We've halted the traffic up as far as Swiss Cottage."

"An appliance," I said. "That's exactly what's needed. Some kind of appliance."

He shouldered the hose and spoke a few dismissive words into a walkie-talkie. As the mighty engines roared into life and started moving away, he said, "Don't you know it's an offence to make unnecessary 999 calls? I'll lend you a six-inch cold file and consider yourself lucky."

Clutching the ugly metal implement he'd pushed into my hand, I said to Bernice, "Let's go up in the bathroom then." When I felt the little stir of air caused by a whole roomful of eyebrows lifting, I quickly added, "I'll wear some kind of blindfold, of course. Whole thing won't take more than a few minutes."

Nor would it have done. Except that Giorgio, sensing his new bride's presence in the bathroom, took it into his head to burst joyously in upon her.

I've tried many times to interpret the scene as it must have presented itself to his eyes. Bearing in mind that he hadn't grasped the function of my gift in the first place, all he registered was this stranger wearing a rubber shower-cap pulled down over his eyes, kneeling in front of Bernice – and creating this *rasping* noise. . . .

Well, it's all water under the bridge now and I'm not really complaining. As soon as I was considered well enough to eat solids again, Giorgio even had the generosity to send me a box of fruit jellies. But what's beyond all doubt is this: as far as moving in on the Fun People is concerned, I've blown all chances.

In fact, I doubt if my name is even acknowledged by any of them any more. If I'm ever mentioned at all, it's only by the fun-soubriquet Giorgio used in addressing his jellies – 'Lo zotico que limó'.

Don't bother getting out the Italian dictionary. The translation is etched upon my cortex:

'The Lout That Filed.'

Let us now praise famous men, and the fathers that begat us

Ecclesiasticus xliv. 1

I answered the front door one evening and there stood a thinnish, faintly familiar figure.

"Yes?" I said.

"It's me!" said the figure. "Nicholas. Nicholas Menon. Husband of Carol. Your vicar."

I peered. "So it is! Come in, old friend!"

I persuaded him to accept a glass of herbal mixture – the juice of juniper berries, distilled, with ice and lemon and not too much tonic – and brought the conversation round to the change in his appearance.

"You used to be thick, Nick," I said, groping for tactful words. "But you've lost a lot of weight. You're now, how can I put it, a slicker vicar. What pared away the pounds? A diet? Dietary biscuits? A cellular wafer?"

"A glandular fever. But herein lies my problem. My clothes are now four sizes too large and I am to officiate at a wedding tomorrow."

"As indeed I know," I answered warmly. "The *Staines and Egham News* is my bible. Sunninghill Parish Church. Morning-suits, marquee among the rhododendrons and the cream of the *Tatler's* photographic staff."

"Even so," he said. "Now, I have found one suit that fits me, a clerical grey number from my student days which was lagging the church boiler, and I have taken it to the cleaners in Virginia Water. They assure me that it will be ready for collection just before I have to set out for the wedding tomorrow."

"Well, that should do the trick, Nick." I replied. "Wherein lies your problem?"

"The manager of the cleaners has just telephoned to say that his

97

pressing machine has expired in a cloud of steam. My suit will be cleaned, spun in a drum until dry, but, alas, not pressed."

"Ah!" I said. "So you either officiate tomorrow looking like Stan Laurel wearing Oliver Hardy's suit, or wearing a suit straight out of the spin-dryer, wrinkled like a walnut."

"There seems no other choice."

I mixed us another half-litre of herbal comfort.

"Timings?" I asked.

"Collect suit, 2.30. Drive back to Thorpe Vicarage and change at great speed. Arrive at the church at 2.50. I can just do the journey in 16 minutes – Carol timed me yesterday with the kitchen plinger."

I am a firm believer in Lateral Thinking in problems like these. So I assumed a Lateral position on the carpet and gave myself up to Thought. After, I suppose, some nine minutes I sat up.

"We will be waiting for you at the cleaners tomorrow with a vehicle," I said, emphasising each word. "You will enter the vehicle, with your suit, and be driven to the church. On the way your suit will be neatly pressed – WHILE IT IS ON YOU!"

His face was a study.

There were all too few hours left for preparation, for racing round to the builder's merchants, the camping equipment shop, the iron-mongers, to say nothing of persuading Mr Marshall to lend us his Mobile Greengrocery van.

2.30 the next day saw my wife, son and I, in Mr Marshall's van, waiting outside the cleaners in Virginia Water. My wife had lit the two camping stoves and fixed the rubber tubing to the spouts of the two kettles. Jamie was keeping the engine running for a smooth getaway.

Nicholas emerged, clutching his clean but crumpled suit, and looking, I thought, a shade apprehensive.

Once Nick was in the van, Jamie let in the clutch and proceeded towards Sunninghill. Nick changed into his suit in a secluded corner by the cabbages and on my word of command assumed a prone position on the floor.

Rolling forward the two three-foot lengths of six-inch diameter, salt glaze pottery drainage pipes I deftly slipped them up Nick's legs. There was an awkward moment when his right shoe jammed in the pipe but a blow or two with the starting handle freed the foot and no time was lost. Polly's kettles were then on the boil and, on the word of command, she inserted the rubber tubes up the pipes.

We allowed the steam to play through the pipes for six minutes. I then slid the pipes away from the legs and Nick stood up for the next stage, which consisted of applying bulldog clips so as to form creases in the damp, hot fabric. Eighty of these were clipped on, twenty to each crease, back and front, both legs. As Nick sat on the tailboard of the van, dangling his legs in the airstream to dry off his trousers, we began on the jacket.

First we removed the jacket, replacing it with a heatproof waistcoat made by my wife from eighteen oven gloves sewn together. Next we dampened the jacket with water from the watering-can Mr Marshall used to freshen up his lettuces. We then replaced the jacket on Nick, and covered the entire surface of the jacket, sleeves as well, in oven-proof aluminium foil. After checking that Nick was completely foiled, I lit my little calor-gas blow torch and began playing it carefully over the foil, keeping it moving, watching for tell-tale puffs of steam which told me that the scheme was working.

At one point Nick seemed to slump.

"Are you all right?" I enquired, anxiously. "Not the old ticker, vicar?"

But it was only some large potatoes which had fallen off a high rack, when Jamie had taken a right-hand bend at speed, and hit Nicholas on the head.

We stripped off the hot foil, held the jacket out of the window to cool it off, and the job was done.

At 2.49 precisely my son pulled up with a jerk outside the gates of Sunninghill church, a rain of assorted choice veg. descended upon us, and Nick got out of the van and made his way towards the vestry door, looking smart and neat in his well-pressed suit.

He was still steaming a little here and there but we reckoned that anybody noticing it in church would assume it to be a kind of nimbus.

"Well," said my wife, plucking a Brussels sprout from her hair. "Thank goodness that's over."

"Over?" I said, incredulity in my voice. "Over? It hasn't really started yet. We are on our way to our first million with the Muir On-Site Valet Van!"

"You don't really suppose you can make money with this . . . this . . ."

"Consider," I said, my voice rising with boyish enthusiasm. "It'll be the Fourth of June soon. Founder's Day at Eton. Statesmen, judges and millionaires trudging along Eton High Street, suits crumpled after sitting all day in deckchairs watching cricket. I step out of the van, parked by the kerb. 'Touch up, my lord? Just step inside!' And then there's Henley Regatta. Hundreds of old chaps in little pink caps – Leanderthal Man – watching their sons skulling up and down and wondering how they are going to make the old blazer last through the week. 'Care for a spruce-up before your son wins the race, sir? Polly – put the kettles on!' Thank goodness that Nick started us going.''

"What are you trying to say?"

"Let us now press famous men, and the fathers at regattas!''

Discretion is the better part of valour

Proverb

I was watching a blue movie the other night – it wasn't meant to be that colour, but my TV set hasn't been the same since I turned it over on its side to watch more comfortably while lying in bed – and it was one of those wartime flying stories.

My mind immediately snapped back to that summer of 1941 when I was a Lab. Technician in the Photographic Unit of an RAF Training Station up in Northern Scotland. Our task was to teach budding Intelligence Officers how to 'read' Aerial Reconnaissance photographs. (Oh, you remember what they were – those photos of enemy terrain which were taken from a great height by our reconnaissance planes.)

My part in this training operation was boring but simple. Whenever we received an A.R. photo ('Aerial Reconnaissance'; come on now, don't make me have to explain *everything*), I would inspect it, select an appropriate square of it, blow that square up into a ten-by-eight glossy, then pass out several copies of this enlargement among the I.O.s. They would study their ten-by-eights through magnifying glasses, then each would take his turn interpreting the significant topographical features suggested by the photo: reservoirs, high ground, railway lines, wooded areas, etc.

Got the hang of it now? I hope so, because I now have to explain some of the handicaps under which I worked.

The principal one was that I never *received* any Aerial Reconnaissance photographs. Oh, Reconnaissance Command posted them to me all right, but as they were somewhere down in the Home Counties and the part of Northern Scotland we were in was really excessively Northern, the mail never reached us. Consequently I was obliged to obtain my supply of A.R. photos from whatever alternative sources I could find.

Well, at that time and in that place, there was only one alternative source – elderly back-numbers of the *National Geographic Magazine*, which the Dental Officer kept in his ante-room, presumably because anaesthetics were also in short supply. Several of these contained Aerial Photographs which were quite adequate for my purposes. As they were usually of places like The Great Barrier Reef or Popacatapetl, I must admit the trainees didn't get that many marshalling-yards or heavy-water factories to recognise. Still, in wartime, improvisation itself becomes a virtue.

The other handicap I had to surmount was that as, in this remote corner, there was little else but scenery available in the way of off-duty pleasures, the Station had a thriving Camera Club. This meant that every moment of my spare time was taken up in developing and printing snaps for an entire squadron of keen amateur photographers.

It was this keenness which precipitated the awkward incident. For some time, the Flight Sergeant in charge of our Cookhouse had been paying court to a crofter's daughter named Ella McGivern. The only female in twenty-five square miles, she was an unprepossessing girl with a skin like a water-biscuit and legs like two vacuum-cleaner bags. Nevertheless, because of the sheer lack of competition, she functioned as our neighbourhood sex object.

For that reason, excitement ran high when it was announced in DRO's that, on the following Friday evening, Ella had agreed to act as a live female model for the Camera Club. Fever pitch was reached when it became known, through less official channels, that the Flight Sergeant had persuaded her to pose in the nude.

In those days, of course, the word 'nude' was hardly the absolute term that it is today and Ella was insisting on retaining a pair of P.T. shorts below and a square of transparent net-curtaining up top. But when you've been the best part of eight months in a remote corner of Northern Scotland, even that is a fairly heady prospect.

Accordingly, come Friday, not only was the entire Camera Club to be seen clicking away at her but also a neighbouring platoon of Pioneer Corps, the complete intake of Intelligence Officers, all the sentries and two German parachutists.

For me, however, it meant only a virtually insuperable workload. For in addition to the task of developing single-handed all the figure studies of Ella that were snapped that evening, I also had to make ready an adequate supply of ten-by-eights for the official Aerial Photograph Interpretation Test which the C.O. had laid on for the Intelligence Officers the following morning.

The aerial photograph which I'd selected as the subject of the Test was of an area that, again, could hardly be described as a raging battleground. As time was short and the copies of the *National Geographic Magazine* were dwindling, I'd chosen a picture of a place called Karakorum, which is a mountain range in Tibet. As was my practice, I squared it off, selected an appropriate square and placed it under the enlarger.

At least, I think that's what I enlarged. To this day I can't be really sure. Bearing in mind that I also had in my Lab at the time three hundred or so Art Poses of Miss McGivern, the possibilities of error were considerable.

Mind you, the thought that I might have erred did not strike me until the following morning when the Test was already under way. I wandered in and watched the Intelligence Officers scanning their ten-by-eights of what they'd been told was 'mountain terrain'. Only then did it occur to me that what they were all studying through their magnifying glasses might, conceivably, through sheer pressure of work and lack of sleep, be a monstrous enlargement of some section of Ella McGivern.

"Excuse me, sir." I tugged at the C.O.'s sleeve. "There is a possibility I may have made a boob."

The C.O. was a man who could have given irritability lessons to Captain Bligh. "Belt up, Corporal," he said. Then, to one of the Intelligence Officers – "Come on then, Pilot Officer Lacey. Make anything of it?"

Pilot Officer Lacey nodded confidently. "It's at least five thousand feet high," he said. "And there's cart tracks leading up the lower slopes."

"There's also traces of volcanic activity," volunteered a fellow Intelligence Officer. "And is that a small hut at the top?"

I could not, in all conscience, allow this to go on. I leant towards the C.O's ear and quietly confessed the possibility that I had submitted an error. Equally quietly he reduced me to AC2 and confined me to camp until 1957.

Then he turned to the officers. "I'm afraid the Test must be aborted, gentlemen," he said. "A certain measure of uncertainty has arisen regarding its subject matter."

With some distaste, he picked up a ten-by-eight. Surveying it, he said:

"This creation is Tibet, or part of Ella."

There's many a slip 'twixt the cup and the lip

Proverb

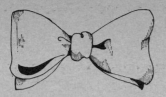

Paris was baking hot that May in 1863. The sun shone down, the temperature went up, tempers frayed, farmers prayed, the level of the Seine dropped, a revival of Gluck's opera *Iphigenia in Aulis* flopped, Sarah Bernhardt made her debut, people walking past drains went "Pheew!", and the pavements were hot enough to *flamber* a crêpe-suzette on.

Idlers of the town strolling past Maxim's restaurant, picking their way carefully over the kneeling chefs and the suzettes, could only envy the rich courtesans who clip-clopped past in their open carriages, the moving air cooling their brows and disturbing such traces of lovely hair as escaped from beneath their characteristic, egg-shaped hats (*oeufs en cocottes*).

At a table in the Café de Bade, Émile Zola tried to stop the sweat dropping off his chin onto his manuscript as he put the finishing touches to his searing exposé of slavery in the banana plantations, *Nana*.

In a cheap bistro, a gaunt unhappy-looking English painter of draperies, by the name of Jack Hughes, put a paper doily on his head, balanced a silver sugar-sifter on top, puffed out his cheeks and said "Look everybody – Queen Victoria!" Few of his laughing fellow-artists guessed that his ambition was to become a leading Impressionist.

Perhaps the coolest spot in all Paris was beneath the great trees of the Bois de Boulogne. And it was there, in the very heart of the Bois, that the painter Édouard Manet was making his final attempt to win recognition. As he told his friends, "If the public does not like this last picture of mine, I shall do myself, as the English say, in."

It was a beautiful setting for a painting. Manet had erected his easel in the shadow of a huge pile of granite boulders known to Parisians as

Lover's Leap. There was grass, and trees, and in the background a pond full of carp which blew bubbles and swam about and did whatever mysterious things carp do to while away the time.

The picture was to be called *Déjeuner sur l'herbe* (Lunch is on Herbie), and was to depict Herbie giving a picnic lunch to a friend and a couple of girls. All of them nude. The nudity was partly to give the picture a neo-classical appeal but mostly because Manet was hopeless at painting dresses and pairs of trousers.

And so Manet painted furiously, while his mistress, Suzanne, and three friends sat with nothing on and tried to keep still.

"Herbie!" cried Manet, suddenly. "You're the host. You're supposed to be lolling at ease, chatting Suzanne. Why have you turned on to your left side?"

"Boil on me bum."

Manet muttered a Gallic imprecation.

More painting. Then:

"Ow!" from Suzanne. "Ow! Cor! Ow!"

"Now what?" from Manet.

"Ants! In the pants. Or where the pants would be if I was wearing any. Which thanks to you I'm not." She jumped up and danced about.

Manet gritted his teeth in exasperation. "I don't know why I keep you on as a model" he muttered.

"I do," she muttered back, "judging from last night."

"What was that?"

"Nothing. Nothing."

More painting. Then Manet flung his brush down in exasperation.

"You, girl, whatever your name is!" he bellowed. "You're supposed to be reclining on one elbow on the grass. What are you doing back there in the pond?"

"Paddling!" she bellowed back. "Got a bunion. It's hard on a girl's feet in my profession."

Somehow, just one day before the picture had to be entered for the Salon, it was finished. Manet sent for his friend, Émile Zola, and waited, trembling, for his verdict.

"Sorry, Éd," said Zola, shaking his head sadly. "You have here a stinkeroo. A floperoo *formidable* (formidable). It's the nudes, old lad. Everybody's painted them this year. Nudes bathing, nudes up trees, nudes chasing each other round urns. Another nude painting doesn't stand a snowflake in hell's chance. Disappointing, I know, but I'm sure you want me, your old friend Zola, to be realistic."

Manet went white, including his ginger beard. "But there is no time to paint another!" he whispered. "And I can't paint clothes on to the figures – I can't DO clothes! This is *rideaux* (curtains) for me. Be so kind as to hand me that poison-bottle marked 'Poison' . . ."

"Wait!" cried Zola. "There must be a way . . . ." He strode up and down for a while. Then he lifted a clenched fist to the ceiling and cried in a great voice, "*J'accuse! J'accuse!*" (Jack Hughes! Jack Hughes!)

"It is a name I have heard . . ."

"He is a gaunt, unhappy English painter who gives impersonations of Queen Victoria. But he is, my friend, a Drapery Man! You know, do you not, how those execrable English society portrait painters work? They paint in only the hands and the face and then engage a Drapery Man to paint in the clothes. Some hack like – Jack Hughes!"

The colour began to suffuse back into Manet's beard. "Suzanne!" He commanded. "Put some clothes on and fetch Jack Hughes!"

It was arranged within the hour. For the sum of ten francs, cash in advance, Hughes agreed to clothe the four figures in the painting.

"A nice pink dress for the girl paddling in the pond, if I might make a suggestion, sir," he said. "And a modish green muslin for the foremost bird. For the two gents I would suggest dark jackets and light trousers. With a smoking hat complete with tassel for the lad in the foreground." And he left.

Alas, how often in the history of Hope has the goblet been dashed from the lips before a drop of liquor had graced tonsil?

Hughes bought a bottle of absinthe with the ten francs and in three hours was as stewed as an eel. He managed to paint clothes on to the two men, but the paddling girl was left in what looked like a white underslip, and Suzanne was, as she usually was, stark naked. His landlady delivered the picture to the Salon.

Manet slipped into the Exhibition Hall the following night, but he only got as far as the door. The howls of rage and anger from the critics jostling round his picture were enough. He went very white. Whiter than white. And slipped away into the Paris night.

It's a pity he did not stay, really. An hour later a remarkable change had come over the gallery. Word had spread round the city that there was a beastly, degrading picture in the Salon and a hundred thousand excited art lovers were trying to batter their way in. And the artists of Paris had decided that Manet was an important pioneer in modern art, daring to combine classical nudes with fully-clothed figures in a contemporary setting.

Zola went round to Manet's studio to congratulate him, only to be met by a sobbing Suzanne. He put his arms round her to comfort her, and patted her.

"There, there, my dear," he said, "And, if you will permit an old friend, perhaps there?"

"Édouard has gone!" she sobbed, nodding. "He came in, asked for his poison-bottle marked 'Poison' and rushed out again!"

Together they searched Paris. But nowhere did they find any trace of a pale-faced painter with a ginger beard carrying a poison-bottle.

"There is one tiny hope left," wheezed Zola as they climbed back up to Montmartre. "Put some clothes on, then we'll try the Bois de Boulogne. There's just a chance that he returned to the spot where he painted his picture."

And so they crept through the dark wood towards the little patch of grass between the granite bluff and the pond. Suzanne made Zola go on ahead, because of what he might find there.

What he found was a familiar figure, supine on the turf, motionless, clutching a small bottle. But not a poison-bottle marked 'Poison'. It was a quarter-bottle marked 'vin ordinaire'. And the figure was gently snoring.

Zola retraced his steps back to where Suzanne was anxiously waiting. "He grabbed the wrong bottle", he said.

"Then –" she cried, "he has not done himself, as he has so frequently threatened to, in?"

"Indeed no," said Zola, pivoting her until she was facing the horizontal genius –

"There's Manet. Asleep. 'Twixt the carp and the Leap."

A stitch in time saves nine

Proverb

LOOKING back on my literary career, I think the most fulfilling period was when I was writing the Society Column for the *Barbers' and Hairdressers' Quarterly*. Although the work brought me into contact with most of the leading people in the trade, the one who has lingered longest in my memory is old Dino Goldoni.

A small, balding man, with a face like a melancholy knee-cap, he ran The Short Sharp Shave Shop, a two-chair lock-up off Camden Town High Street. His establishment owed its name to the fact that Dino, a three-time winner of the Masters Shaving Competition sponsored annually by my publication, had retired as undisputed champion of the art.

Now, however, he had received a challenge. A new man, a Greek called Andreas, whose saloon in Kensal Rise was the first to feature a basin into which you leaned *backwards* for a shampoo, had challenged Dino to a Shave Off.

For those of you unfamiliar with the rules of this contest, a Shave Off is a sudden-death competition in which two barbers vie with each other to see which can shave the most people over a given ten-minute period, any severed eyebrow or ear counting as two faults.

Old Dino, as the holder of three Golds, was fairly indulgent about the event at first. In the preceding week, he did put in a little practice on his backscrape, using as target his customary assistant, an Irishman called No Nose McGinty, but such was his confidence he spent little more than an hour a day at wrist-flexing and lather-rubbing. I must admit that I too regarded the occasion as no more than a work-out for Dino, even wondering a little at Andreas' temerity.

On the day of the Shave Off, however, my eyes were opened. As

usual a guest-manicurist had been brought in to act as Official Starter –
in this case, a very popular girl called Florence, known throughout the
trade as Cash Flo. My Editor and a man from the board of Silvikrin
were along as judges. But just as Flo was about to drop the hot towel –
the time-honoured signal for the start – Dino let out a startled yell.
"Where's-a my brush? Who's-a swipe my brush?"

To the layman, the most important item of equipment in this kind
of event would appear to be the razor. Not so. In competition shaving,
the brush is all. Over years of use a barber will have moulded it to his
individual hand, rendered it smooth and swift, learned just how much
pressure to apply going round corners and across the cheekbone.

Now, at the crucial moment, Dino's brush had disappeared. When
Andreas stepped forward smirking, I realised how dangerously we had
underestimated him. Noting that he was clad, not in the grey overall
of the old school, but in one of the new-fangled white nylon smocks, I
reminded myself of the old adage: beware of Greeks wearing shifts.

"I claim a walkover", Andreas said with a white nylon smile. My
Editor cocked an enquiring eye at Dino. He spread his hands miserably,
acknowledging defeat.

"One moment, please," I said. "May I respectfully remind you of
the BBC rules?" My Editor frowned but I held my ground. According
to the official body which has established the conventions for these
events, the British Barbers' Committee, if a competitor loses an item
of equipment, he is allowed fifteen minutes to replace it before being
disqualified.

"Very well," said the Editor. "You have a quarter-of-an-hour." He
started his stopwatch.

Dino shook his head hopelessly. "What's-a good?" he said (or
possibly "What's a-good?"). "How'm I gonna find a good brush
round these-a parts in fifteen minutes?"

"Listen," I said. "These-a parts are Camden Town. Right on the
door-step of the London Zoo. Do you shave any of the keepers there?"

"My best customers," Dino said with a flash of the old pride. "They
all-a come to Dino."

"Right," I replied. "Then we get on to the Head Keeper."

"What for do I need a Head Keeper?"

"Because it's a question of keeping your head. Seeing that there's no
time to skin a badger, what's the next best animal for making a soft
pliable shaving-brush?" When Dino shrugged in bewilderment, I
pressed on urgently. "Ostrich feathers! The tail-feathers of an ostrich."

"He's-a not gonna pull all-a the feathers off his best ostrich just-a because Dino – "

"We're not asking him to," I interrupted. "Tell him to bring the ostrich itself along. Preferably a docile one."

Dino sighed and moved to the phone. It did take a certain amount of explaining on his part and roughly the same amount of expostulating on mine but, praise be, no more than twelve minutes had elapsed when the door opened and a tall sun-tanned man entered, leading an amiably-visaged ostrich.

I had a piece of twine ready waiting. It was the work of a moment to tie it round the ostrich's tail-feathers, pulling them tight so that they formed one uniform, manageable plume. As my Editor's fingers moved to his stop-watch knob to signal the end of our quarter-of-an-hour's grace, the plume was completed.

Down went Flo's hot-towel, and the contest was on. Into the shaving-mug went the plume, on to the customer's face went the lather – Dino was off and away.

Today, wherever men with cut-throats foregather, they still talk about Dino's performance that afternoon. Up till then, the world record for the ten-minute Shave Off had been seven customers. Dino did not simply break that record, he shattered it. The new figure he established still stands.

As I mentioned earlier, in terms of emotional experience it was one of the most fulfilling episodes of my life. Whenever the bad times come now, or the old fire flickers, I still summon up remembrance of the phrase I headlined my story with:

"Ostrich And Twine Shaves Nine."

A jug of wine, a loaf of bread – and thou

Omar Khayyám
'Rubaiyat'

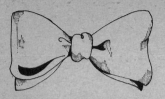

WELL, Jeremy, I understand from your aunty
that you are going to be married to that nice girl in the gas showroom.
No, I wouldn't agree that she is all that enormous. A little bulky,
perhaps, particularly when she is demonstrating an oven, but no doubt
once safely married she will moderate her present enthusiasm for
eating things like chocolate fudge and cold roast potatoes.

How wise you are to get your ferrets used to new sleeping quarters;
I think you should consider moving them right out of your bedroom
now that they have got used to not sleeping in your bed.

Faintly on the same theme, I have a word of warning to you. It has
been said that a bride's attitude towards her betrothed can be summed
up in three words: Aisle. Altar. Hymn. You must prepare to resist
alteration in those areas where a change is not an improvement.

It may come as a shock to you when you are married so perhaps now
is the time to prepare yourself mentally to face a generally acknowledged
fact; most women have an eccentric attitude towards personal hygiene.

For instance, women tend to underestimate, some of them by weeks,
how long a pair of socks can be worn before they need to be changed.

Brides also fail to appreciate that when a man's hands become soiled,
say through dismantling a carburettor or shifting a heap of coal, Dame
Nature has provided absorbent matter for him to wipe his hands on in
the shape of drying-up cloths, bathroom towels, and the edges of
table-cloths. You will find that this natural practice will be frowned
upon.

But much more important, and in some cases downright dangerous,
is the feminine insistence that the male should wallow in a hot bath at
least once a week.

The bath is not a British thing, Jeremy. Like a lot of other things, such as polo, cats, markets and carpets, it was imported from ancient Persia. However, the Persian version had an additional attraction; it was mixed bathing.

The bath next cropped up in ancient Greece. Mrs Archimedes used to fill her husband's bath right up to the brim. Archimedes found that the water slopped over the sides when he jumped in, and by weighing the amount of water spilt, and weighing himself, he discovered a formidable argument against baths, or at least full ones, in that a floating body displaces its own weight of water. He also discovered that the displaced water wet the bath-towel and made it so heavy that when he hung it on the towel-rail it pulled out the nails and the rail fell off the wall. So he invented the screw.

The idea of washing one's person seems to have been introduced into England during the reign of Henry II by a cleric of advanced views who used to give himself an all-over wash in a pail. He became known as Thomas O'Bucket.

The full obsession with immersing the body in the alien element came into fruition in Victorian times. They had a motto then, 'Cleanliness is Next to Godliness' – a sentiment about as logical as 'Lawn-mowing is Next to Madrigal-Singing'.

Consider the matter from a scientific point of view. Your skin is like a Fair Isle sweater (yours more than most people's, Jeremy, but I am sure the blotches are mostly due to nerves). Think of yourself as entirely covered in a kind of knitted garment which keeps your bones in place. It has neat edging round the lips to stop your mouth from fraying, and has some loose embroidery on top which we call hair. And like a Fair Isle sweater, it is a living, breathing thing, full of natural oils. Now if you soak this continually in hot water, and rub it all over with a cake of chemical substance made from rancid grease boiled up with caustic soda, then the natural protective oils will be washed away and all sorts of things will happen, beginning with colds and chills and ending with the skin shrinking, moisture getting in and, eventually, rusty ribs.

My own plan for personal cleanliness is simplicity itself and entirely in concord with nature.

Once a week – or so – stand naked in the bath and dab yourself lightly all over with a bit of cotton wool moistened in rainwater. Don't use tapwater, which has chemicals and impurities in it to make it taste nice. Keep an old jug handy and stick it under a drain pipe, or the down pipe of a gutter, so that you have a supply of rainwater always to hand.

Areas of mud, axle-grease, dried paint, and tar should be given individual treatment with a loofah. Not a wet loofah, which is flabby and useless, but a dry loofah. Scrub away hard until the offending matter is dislodged, pausing only if you find that you are about to draw blood.

For a final toning up, rub yourself down with a slice of stale bread, using a circular motion and no butter. Bread has the property of absorbing water and grease, and erasing any pencil marks you might have overlooked.

Dash about a bit on the bathroom lino to dry off and the job is done, using pure, natural means.

So, Jeremy, take a firm stand on the question of frequent hot baths, which are foreign, pagan, and dangerous. All your bride needs for a clean and decent husband is four things:

A jug of rain, a loofah, bread – and thou.

He who hesitates is lost

Proverb

THOSE Kung Fu entertainments are an intriguing blend of bone-fracture and sententiousness. I was watching one the other night where the hero – a right prosy beggar, but the owner of a lethal left leg – observed to the baddie, "The man who loves unhappily will never finish first in the obstacle-race of Life." Then he kicked him in the groin and rode off into the commercial.

His remark, however, stayed with me. "Could that possibly account for it?" I mused. "Could that explain my own failure to break Life's tape ahead of the field?" For when I catalogue the various romantic attachments which have decorated my days – nights were generally out of the question, they had to wash their hair – the list does emerge as a pretty miserable series of encounters.

It's possibly because I started off on the wrong foot, if that's the correct anatomical referent in these matters. My adolescence, you see, was too early for what's become known as the sexual revolution. In fact, when I was seventeen, there appeared to be a sexual cease-fire. True, a roped-off section of the lending library called 'Modern' Novels offered the odd inflammatory chapter-ending, but you had to be twenty-five before you could borrow one and even then it was two old-pence per day. And when I did once manage to nail a book called *Learn to Love*, it turned out to be the sixth volume of a set of encyclo-paedias, the next volume being *Luana to Membrane*.

So, with no Dr Reuben or Martin Cole around to direct our urges, what the panting young oicks of my era adopted as behaviour-models were the sentimental Hollywood films of that period. I grew to man-hood fully believing that all girls shut their eyes when kissed on the lips, most of them standing on tiptoe with one leg bent upwards. And, at my most impressionable period, a scene in one of those films – a Charles Boyer/Jean Arthur romance – left an absolutely indelible imprint.

I can see that scene now. They were dining in a fashionable restaurant and, coffee having arrived, Boyer beckoned. A strolling violinist entered the scene and, leaning over Jean Arthur, he softly played their particular our-tune into her left ear. And as she listened, her hand involuntarily stole across the table and her little finger linked into his. (Into Charles Boyer's I mean. Had it been the violinist's, it would, of course, have cocked-up the melody-line utterly.)

Well, I can't tell you to what heights of dewy-eyed soppiness that moment sent me. To the sort of male I was then – and, if truth be told, have been ever since as well – all of romance was in that scene. "If only," I thought, "if only I could arrange an identical set-up for myself, Life need strew no other rose in my path."

For more than one reason it wasn't easy. Snag A was that no restaurant in my postal district featured a strolling musician; Snag B, there was no girl I fancied anywhere near strongly enough to buy a whole meal for. However, within a month both A and B were taken care of.

First, right next door, a new family moved in containing an eminently molestable daughter called Lily. For the statistically-minded, her measurements were 36, 24, 36, 27; the last figure being her I.Q. But so besotted was I by the other three numerals I cared not. The other happy circumstance was that the haberdashers in the High Street closed down and reopened – after some initial difficulties with the spelling of the neon sign – as 'The Hendon Brasserie'. More important, it was owned and personally managed by an ex-member of Bram Martin's Orchestra. Anticipating the imminent demise of the Big Bands, he had decided to invest his savings in something less transitory.

So I had it all going for me – the place, the girl, the strolling violinist. Getting Lily to agree to 'date' me, as the operation was then called, proved easier than I had anticipated and when she met me at the Brasserie she looked a knock-out. Admittedly she appeared to be about two foot taller than when I'd last seen her but that was because of the hairdo that girls of that day adopted for formal occasions – a sort of black-gloss beehive. She proved to have a healthy appreciation of food so there was little conversation through the three-course table d'hôte, Lily being occupied in stuffing herself like an out-of-work taxidermist. But when coffee was finally served, she pushed away from the table and looked at me for the first time. Taking it to be a good augury that she was still breathing quite heavily, I moved in closer. "What's your favourite tune?" I asked, giving her the Franchot Tone turned-down-on-one-side smile.

As I mentioned earlier, she was a bit hard of thinking so there was quite a pause before the answer. "I beg yours?" she said.

"Your favourite tune."

"Oh, I'm not all that musical really." She pondered. "What's the one that goes –" and she hummed a few bars.

"That's the National Anthem," I said. "Tell you what, I'll pick one." And beckoning the manager-violinist over, I said "Listen, my good fellow. Can you play 'Time After Time I Tell Myself That I'm'?"

He nodded and winked. Then, leaning forward to Lily's ear, he began – on that low, sexy string they hardly ever seem to use any more. I locked my eyes into Lily's and awaited developments. She was still blowing a bit but, sure enough, after no more than a half-chorus, her hand came creeping across the table.

As I found out afterwards, it was only groping for a toothpick, but no matter. I seized her little finger, curled my own little finger into it, gripped tight, and closed my eyes in bliss. Pure and unalloyed bliss.

In fact, so utter was the bliss that when the music ceased playing, I didn't even notice it at first. It was only when I heard a strange kind of *sawing* noise. . . .

He'd somehow got his violin-bow stuck right through her beehive! Remember how peculiarly unyielding the lacquer was that girls used in those days? If you ever ran your fingers through their hair you stood a fair chance of breaking your nails. Well, this clown, this poop, he'd managed to push his bow right into the interior. And now the resin had somehow *bonded* itself to . . . oh, it was just so dispiriting, so awful, I can't even bear recalling any more of it.

Anyway, when that's the kind of foot a fellow gets started off on in the romance line, you do see how miserably his later liaisons are going to turn out. And so it proved. That's why that line of Kung Fusion set me brooding so much. "The man who loves unhappily will never finish first in the obstacle-race of Life."

Or, if you prefer the Western version:

"He who has sad dates is last."

None was for a party; all were for the state

Lord Macaulay
Lays of Ancient Rome: 'Horatius'

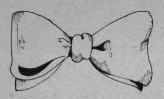

THE only bit of Spanish I remember after wrestling with it for a term at school is an ancient proverb which went: 'Whoever Spitteth at Heaven Shall Have it Fall Back in his Eye.' A good thought; cautionary, ballistically sound. And it seems to me that we should have a similar proverb in English to warn the impulsive of the dangers of doing the opposite; not spitting at Heaven but trying to get a bit nearer to it. I propose the following: 'Whoever Foolishly Attempteth to Bring About a Social Reform Very Likely will Find that it Falleth Upon Cloth Ears and Lo the Ground Will be Stony and Before He Knoweth Where He is He Will be Back Where He Started having Achieved Sweet Fanny Adams and Made to Feel an Utter Nana.'

That's only a first draft, of course. It will need honing before it goes into *The Oxford Dict. of Eng. Proverbs.*

The need for such a proverb was brought home to me recently when I attempted to set on its way a small but, it seemed to me, vital social reform.

The Classless Society is the dearest wish of all of us but spreading the word that beans-on-toast are chic and Rolls-Royces are heavy on brake-linings is only nibbling at the problem. There is one real bastion of class-consciousness which must be removed.

Until recently the main Class giveaways were speech and dress. If somebody spoke a little too loudly, with a pre-war BBC announcer's accent, keeping the vowels well open, then he or she was an Upper. If all this was attempted and it just failed, then he or she was a Middle. Mumbling mangled vowels, and local colour in the accent indicated Lower. But nowadays, thanks to telly, pop-music, and the media generally, our youth and our trendier middle-aged now talk what might be termed Standard Received Disc-Jockey. If you meet a lad in Windsor High Street it is now no longer possible to tell from his speech whether he is Eton or Slough Comprehensive.

Clothes have also ceased to be reliable indicators of Class. If you spot a little riot of colour ambling along the King's Road it could well be the rhythm guitarist of The Who. It could also be The Right Hon. Leo Abse M.P. on his way to the opening of Parliament.

But there is still one infallible way of separating the sheep from the lambs, the ewes from the non-ewes, and that is what we call the place where we all, from time to time, are compelled to go. Roughly speaking, Uppers go to the Lavatory, Middles to the Loo and Lowers go to the Toilet.

This is oversimplifying the picture to an enormous extent; in fact, the situation is in a state of flux. Loo is holding its own fairly well but there is a strong, perhaps 14%, swing to Toilet and most of these gains are at the expense of Lavatory.

These terms are totally non-interchangeable in society. Uppers and Middles recoil from the vulgarity of the word 'Toilet'. Uppers and Lowers both regard 'Loo' as being a hopelessly twee euphemism. And Lowers and Middles join in finding the aristocratic use of the word 'Lavatory' utterly disgusting.

Now it wouldn't be too bad if we had just those three words – the U.S.A. manages happily with two, the John and the Can – but unfortunately we have a great many more words for the Unmentionable Thing. Consequently when strangers meet in an English house, and nature calls, our society breaks into a *mille-feuille* of social strata, the guest trying frantically to sort out in his mind which euphemism his host is most likely to embrace and the host similarly trying to fit euphemism to guest.

Many older hosts and hostesses, who grew up in a protected, non-permissive society, can't bear to apply any word at all to It. They say, "Would you like to . . . (faint upward wave of right hand). . . ?" Or simply, "Are you . . . all right?"

Schoolchildren are brought up to avoid a confrontation by being taught to use such evasions as "Please, Miss, may I be excused?" "Please, Sir, may I leave the room?" The confusion which this produces in the delicate, growing mind is illustrated by the small boy who suddenly put his hand up and said "Please, Miss, Johnny's left the room on the floor".

Keen euphemismaticians often study a stranger's house for clues before taking the plunge. Framed prints of vintage cars on the walls, pewter tankards, and 'Match of the Day' on the telly indicate an approach along the lines of:

"Where's the geography, old son?" Or:

"Excuse me, but I must go and see whether my horse has kicked off its blanket".

(*Note:* These phrases are rarely necessary as this host invariably greets his guests with a cheerful, "By the way, the bog's on the landing.")

Colour Supplements lying about, Hi-Fi, and Spanish Claret indicate a slightly more roguish approach from the host:

"Ah – if anyone needs the House of Lords it's at the end past the au-pair's room." Or:

"Comforts anyone?"

And in between these phrases there are a hundred others, each one clung to by a section of the population as being the one socially acceptable phrase which will protect them from hideous embarrassment.

Obviously something must be done to straighten this situation out, and the answer to the problem is to find a word for the Thing which is acceptable to all ranks. But which word? 'Lavatory' is useless; it is the word plumbers use for a washbasin. 'Toilet' is a horrid euphemism, imported from the U.S.A., which really means a lady's dressing-table. 'Loo' doesn't mean anything at all, being a hangover from eighteenth-century Edinburgh when folks were wont to empty their chamber pots out of the top stories of tenement buildings with a cheerful warning cry of, "Guardy-loo!"

The problem was solved for me one evening when a small, round, innocent face looked up into mine and said, simply, "I want potty". It wasn't a child who spoke, in fact, it was a shortish Rural Dean who had come round about a subscription and had stayed to bash the sherry. But the simple, child's word 'Potty' was the word I had been searching for. An old, honourable, easily remembered word, and the only word of the whole bunch which described the Thing itself.

My mind went immediately into overdrive (unhappily, I recall, forgetting the Rural Dean and his pressing problem) and it seemed to me that I should form a society to promote the use of the word 'Pot'. Perhaps calling the society Pioneers of Truth (thus making clever use of the initial letters), with myself as (paid) President. Perhaps I would write the society a brief, expensive manifesto. . . .

I saw the Rural Dean out of the front door and into the bushes and immediately sat down and wrote out a questionnaire, to send to a hundred people to test whether I had judged the people's mood correctly. I asked them to state clearly whether they would be in favour of everybody settling to call the Thing something like 'Potty' rather than messing about pretending that they were nipping outside to check whether the trusty steed had kicked off its saddle.

It was when the results of my referendum were all in that I realised a sad truth. A truth encapsulated in the proverb 'Whoever Foolishly Attempteth to Bring About a Social Reform Very Likely Will Find that it Falleth Upon Cloth Ears . . . (etc.)' The figures were conclusive:

None was for a Potty; all were for The Steed.

The rank is but the guinea's stamp

Robert Burns
'For a' that and a' that'

Yes, I've had some odd experiences in Gents'
Loos – I still chuckle at what happened when I used the one in the
Leaning Tower of Pisa – but the oddest, I think, occurred behind the
door marked 'Maharajahs' at a certain well-known Indian restaurant
in Mayfair.

Immediately upon entering its marble vastness, my attention was
caught by the behaviour of a tall, red-headed gentleman. Standing in
front of a mirror, he was inspecting himself keenly, all the while
nodding his head rapidly up and down, then shaking it equally
forcefully to and fro. After watching his vigorous nodding-and-
shaking for some several minutes, I could no longer restrain my
curiosity. "Excuse me, sir," I said. "Are you in the throes of some deep
internal conflict?"

"I fear my dilemma is of a more external nature," he replied. "I am
endeavouring to ascertain just how far – look, sir, perhaps you can
enlighten me." Performing some further agitations of his head, he
asked, "When I go like this, do you chance to notice any marked
alteration of my visage?"

I gazed at him intently. Finally, "Yes." I replied. "Your forehead
appears to – diminish."

He sighed heavily. "As I feared," he said. Then seating himself upon
the chinchilla top of the used paper towel basket, he told me his story.

At a very early age he had had the misfortune to lose his hair. Not
all of it, but enough to impart to his scalp in adult life a kind of see-
through look. It had rendered him acutely, and perhaps unduly,
sensitive about his appearance; to such an extent that he had, as far as
was possible, shunned all contact with the opposite sex.

As he was a gynaecologist by trade, such a withdrawal had proved as damaging professionally as it was socially. However, quite recently a patient's husband had drawn his attention to a startling advance in masculine embellishment: the false hairpiece, or toupée. On impulse he had purchased one – a red one – and after trying it on, he adjudged his appearance so enhanced that he took courage in both hands and joined a mixed pot-holing group.

There, while descending a narrow chimney, he had found himself sitting on the nose of an extremely pleasing younger lady. Their acquaintanceship had ripened and now, after some months of courtship, he had invited her here to this caravanserai of curry with the express purpose of asking her to become his wife.

"And does she know about your false roof?" I broke in at this point. "Have you told her that you are, as it were, carrying on business under an assumed mane?"

He shook his head mournfully – causing another slight subsidence of the thatch. "I have not yet summoned up courage," he said. "That is why what happened during the dessert course was so dismaying. I had chosen the Gooseberry Compôte and when she asked me whether she could have my glacé cherry, I nodded my head. As I did so, suddenly I felt this unaccustomed current of air upon my cranium."

"It fell off?" Involuntarily my voice rose, for there can be few mental images more chilling than that of an upside-down red toupée in a plate of stewed gooseberries.

"Fortunately no. But it did make a significant skid forward. Happily she didn't notice, being fully occupied with her Rum Baba. So, making a trumped-up excuse, I hastened here. And now – well, now every movement seems to loosen it further. See?" He made a nodding movement again, causing another manifestation of what astronomers call, I believe, the Red Shift. "What's happened, you see, is something for which I have only myself to blame. You must understand that these things are held firm to the head by means of a strip of sticking-plaster which one is supposed to renew daily. Tonight though, such was my excitement, I neglected to effect the renewal. In consequence, unless I can now find some other means of adhesion, it's – farewell, Rozella!"

"Is that what you call it?" I asked.

"That's the young lady's name. Sir, can you perhaps suggest something by which I may anchor it?"

"Well, if all you need is a sticking-plaster, surely that First Aid

Cabinet on the wall, the one with the minarets? Something in there –?"

"I have already searched it. It has everything but sticking-plaster. Bandages, lint, iodine – even splints."

"Bandages!" I said. "What about going back with your head covered in bandages? Say that on your way here, some indigent immigrant mugged you for your lighter fuel."

"One can hardly propose in a turban. Especially not in an Indian restaurant. Have you not, perhaps, something about your person?"

I explored my pockets. "Nothing I'm afraid. Tell you what, though. In my brief-case I've got some drawing-pins. Couldn't we try to . . . no, perhaps not. What's really needed is some kind of adhesive substance, isn't it. Look, I say, here's a thought. Suppose you go back to the table and tell the waiter you've gone off the idea of stewed gooseberries, you really fancy a baked apple. Then when he brings it, you fetch it in here. Baked apple, you see, always has that toffee-bit on top. Sometimes that's of quite startling stickiness."

"But won't Rozella question my reason for taking a baked apple into the Gentlemen's Toilet?"

"Let her. In any relationship there have to be certain areas of privacy. Mind you –"

"What?"

"I don't think Indian restaurants serve baked apple."

His face, which had brightened, fell again. "Don't despair," I said. "Not yet." I hardened my eyes and gazed upwards, a habit I have when concentrating. "No use staring at the ceiling, boy," my old Maths Master used to say. "You won't find the answer up there." It never crossed his mind that I'd sneaked in the night before and scribbled out the Trig. tables all round the light fitting.

The ceiling! Wait a minute, when was it? Last Christmas? Yes! The pennies! Ten pound in pennies!

"Just wait here," I said to my toupéed friend and hurried out. Within three minutes I was back. "Ever been in a pub that's collecting for a favourite charity?" I panted. "They stick the pennies you contribute up on the ceiling. Know how? With *this*!" And I held up the bottle of stout I'd purchased from the off-licence down the street. "So if we just pour out a little, then moderately dampen the inside of your wig with it. . . ."

Two months later a small box came through my letter-box. Inside was a rather stingy piece of wedding cake.

Since that evening, I never see an advert for those hirsute artifices without recalling my friend's last-minute repair job and I wonder whether other users of hairpieces ever find themselves relying upon a similar emergency fixative. I hope not. For how precariously perched must such crowning glories be, when – in Burns' phrase –

"Their anchor's but the Guinness damp."

O, for the wings, for the wings of a dove

Mendelssohn
'Hear My Prayer'

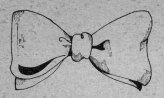

THERE has been a lot of loose talk going on in places where thinking men congregate, like the fruit-machine salon at the Athenaeum Club and the House of Commons Sauna and Massage Parlour, as to why Britain has declined to the status of a second-class power.

Ignoring for a moment the fact that many of us see nothing disastrous in this – dropping from being Top Dog, with all the duties and responsibilities which go with it, to being Number Two can be a merciful release, as many a husband knows – the reason for this supposed decline in Britain's might seems to be in doubt. Various reasons have been advanced.

On the global level my researches have revealed the following: America thinks we are bankrupt. Scotland thinks we have too much money. Japan thinks we are too tall. Mr Enoch Powell thinks we are too tinted. Germany thinks our working-class doesn't work. Russia thinks our working-class is crushed by the rich. Switzerland thinks that according to her standards we haven't got any rich. The Confederation of British Industries thinks we are trapped between the Devil and the TUC.

On the more local level I have had meaningful dialogue with a retail-outlet contact; a piece of trendy jargon meaning that I spent an hour trotting behind Mercer the milkman as, whiff ablaze, he strode round the village bestowing pintas on doorsteps. According to Mercer, who has a fine ear for this sort of thing, local opinion holds that the sad state of the nation is attributable to one or more of the following reasons: they are putting fluoride in the water at Staines reservoir; the new motorway workings have fractured the pipes leading to Lyne Lane sewage farm and the stuff is leaking into the soil; there was a shortage of bees last summer; it's the rubbish on the telly.

All these might be contributory factors but the whole lot together would only add up to a temporary *cafard*, not a national decline. No, the real reason is more fundamental. In my opinion the decline of the British nation as a great power is directly connected with the decline in our consumption of boiled pudding.

It is an undeniable fact that our nation began to lose its pre-eminence at the same time as the good, old-fashioned steamed suet pudding fell into desuetude.

I am prepared to support my theory with facts. In medieval times the Englishman, be he noble or lewd, stood about five feet in height and, because vegetables were not invented until the eighteenth century, went to an early grave riddled with scurvy. So where did he get the energy to win at Agincourt? From boiled puddings. For centuries the ability of the English to consume boiled puddings was a matter of wonder to continentals. What hope had French or Spanish troops, fed on hot water with stringy bits of meat floating about in it, against our English bowmen, belts bursting with good pudding; suet to keep out the cold and damp, flour for bulk, and meat for energy?

Almost everything was shoved into the puddings to begin with; veal, pork, mutton, various interior organs of the deer, but latterly, from the eighteenth century, puddings came to be eaten more and more as puddings and were stuffed with plums or coated with jam.

At the height of the British Empire our public schools supplied a stream of splendid chaps to be administrators in those far-flung countries coloured red on the map. Straight from boarding school they went, honking with adenoids, and after five years of digesting roly-poly puddings and figgy duffs, constipated to the eyebrows and thus impervious to dysentery.

All gone now, of course; both the red bits on the map and puddings. Since the last war puddings have been called 'sweets' and usually consist of either a mess of artificially tinted and flavoured froth, or a baleful mixture of semi-edible substances called something like Baked Caramel and Mallow Ring.

An honest worker queues up for his pud in the canteen and orders Manchester Tart. What is dumped on his plate is a wedge-shaped piece of thickish, warm cardboard lightly smeared with raspberry flavoured red lead. Hardly the sort of fodder to send him whistling back to Blast Furnace No. 2 replete and raring to go.

And then there's the Prime Minister. Flying to Moscow for a vital talk with the Soviet Premier. On the way they serve lunch. And what do they give him for pud on the plane? Half a tinned apricot resting on a bed of soggy rice. How can he stand up for us against the might of Russia with only that under his belt?

Ah, where are the puds of yesteryear? Spotted Dick; fine, crusty suet pudding studded with a galaxy of plump currants. Boiled Baby; heavy, densely textured pudding boiled in a cloth. A characteristic soft coating, known to aficionados as 'the slime' was scraped gently off the outside before the pudding was anointed with very hot golden syrup. Figgy Duff: the Prince of Suet Puddings, very popular in the Royal Navy, both as food and for pressing into service as keel ballast, emergency anchor, or ammunition for the cannons. An inch-and-a-half slice of a good Figgy Duff weighed about three and a quarter pounds.

But I suppose what we old Figgy Duff and Boiled Baby fanciers miss most of all is that unique physical sensation which set in when one had eaten that delicious little bit too much pudding. It was like a pain, except that it wasn't a pain. The tum, which before the pudding had been soft and flexible, became tight as a drum and firm enough to crack a flea on. And an odd, charming ache, halfway between a spasm of wind and an old-fashioned twinge, made its presence felt. The medical name for it was the 'winge'. And it was the most satisfying feeling in the world.

Coming home from a restaurant or a dinner-party nowadays my wife may say something like:

"Wasn't that Apple-peel and Ginger Mousse good? I feel absolutely full." Or, "Did you like the Marinated Passion-Fruit and Marshmallow Whip? I don't think I'll need another meal for a week!"

I agree with her, of course. But in my heart of hearts I know that at that moment I am missing something; something beautiful which has gone forever. And I think to myself:

"O, for the winge, for the winge of a duff!"

In the great right of an excessive wrong

Robert Browning
'The Ring and the Book'

THERE is little point in going into the reasons why Frank and I found ourselves running a Matrimonial Agency. It was, I suppose, a panic attempt to restore our finances after the failure of our first play, a sensitive social allegory about a black mermaid. But when, after eight months' trading, our Agency still only had two clients on its books, I was all for packing it in and turning the place into a massage parlour. ("Everyone likes to feel kneaded" was the argument I used.)

But Frank is made of more determined stuff. "All we have to do is show results," he said. "If we could just fix up the two we've got with *each other*. . . !" And he drew from his roll-top desk the well-thumbed dossiers of our only two supporters.

We gazed at their photographs with some gloom. The male client was named Jack Longland – no relation, just one of those happy coincidences. He was a slightly-built man, no more than five-foot-one in height. The lady was one Emma Williamson, six-foot-four and a good sixteen stone.

Surveying them side by side, even Frank's resolve wavered. "It's like trying to mate a pram and a furniture van," he said. I felt my own spirits droop like a wax banana in a heat wave. "I doubt whether Henry Kissinger could bring these two together."

"We have to try," said Frank firmly and picked up the telephone. In such circumstances, the first step is for each partner to be summoned to the Agency and there shown a photograph of the other. If, in both cases, the prospect pleases, then we arrange what is known in the trade as a 'meet'.

Emma presented us with no difficulties. In her early forties – her *late* early forties – she was far enough down the home-stretch to settle for practically anything with the right hormones. "Twelve years now I've been on the Pill," she confided. "And if I don't get talking to somebody soon. . . ."

It was Jack who proved to be the recalcitrant partner. Possessing, like most small men, an acute sense of personal dignity, he was immediately sensitive to the disparity in their respective square footages. "Great ugly fat lump," he said when I displayed Emma's picture. "Put her in a white dress, you could show films on her."

Fortunately Frank is the type who could sell bagels to the Arab League. "Looks aren't everything, Jack," he argued. "And, anyway, beauty fades. But a big plain girl, Jack – she stays big and plain forever." It took a deal of persuasion but Jack was finally talked into accepting Emma's invitation to a whirl round the Planetarium the following Saturday afternoon.

In this, as in their subsequent get-togethers, it was Emma who made the running. She it also was who phoned in progress reports after each meeting. The first few were bleak indeed. "We spent an evening at Battersea Fun Fair," was one of her early bulletins. "In the Tunnel Of Love, he insisted on separate carriages."

On the few occasions that Jack dropped in to pay his subs, we found ourselves committed to long sessions of reassurance and rebuttal. "But she's so enormous," he'd protest. "In that lurex dress, it's like being out with a giant Brillo pad."

"Don't keep dwelling on Emma's bad points," Frank would plead. "Think *benefits*! Warmth in the winter and shade in the summer!"

Finally, against all odds, it began to happen. The first hint was an excited message from Emma. "Last night," she exclaimed, "last night he hung up on me so gently, it was almost a caress."

When Jack came into the office next morning, the change in his demeanour was unmistakable. "Well," he said, "I never thought I would but I have."

"Emma?" I asked eagerly.

He nodded and smiled slightly. "I've fallen for that mountain of womanhood."

"Oh well done, Jack," Frank said warmly. "Accept our sincere condolences for your future happiness."

"Dunno about getting that far," Jack said. A muscle in his cheek twitched. "Did you know she's also a bit mutt-and-jeff?"

Well, we were aware that Emma had a slight hearing problem but it was not something we'd emphasised, any more than a car dealer will go out of his way to show the wear on the rear tyres. "Could well put a spoke in the whole shooting-match, that could," Jack went on unhappily. "I mean, how do I set about proposing to her? If I go down on the knee and ask her, it could well happen that due to the inordinate distance between my mouth and her ears she won't hear a blind word. And I'm not going to kneel there shouting it. I don't hold with small-built men shouting."

Behind his glasses his eyes blinked miserably, giving him the appearance of an evicted owl. Frank and I exchanged glances. We had come to respect the little man's sensitivity towards his lack of tall, so we saw the need to tread carefully.

Then Frank narrowed his eyes and tapped the side of his nose at me. It was a gesture which meant, I recalled from our Paul Newman/Robert Redford games, he'd had an idea.

"Jack," he said. "Let me show you what we use to clean that light-fitting up on the ceiling." He crossed the room and opened the broom cupboard. Withdrawing from it a folding ladder, he said. "We use this. Jack, go thou and do likewise."

"Do what?"

"Take the ladder away, Jack. Take it round to Emma's flat, stand it at her side and climb to its topmost rung. Then make your proposal from there."

Jack's blinking slowed momentarily then became even more agitated. "But a gentleman can't go clambering about ladders in a lady's drawing room. What if she asks *why* I'm climbing up it?"

"Tell her – because it's there."

Frank still avers that it could have worked and it should have worked. All I know is it didn't work. Immediately we received Emma's distraught phone-call, we sped round to her basement flat. There, in the fireplace, lay Jack's limp and broken form.

I deduced instantly what had happened. After taking the ladder and measuring it against Emma's length, my suspicions were confirmed. The ladder was too long.

Jack, in his joyous haste, had rushed up it so fast he'd gone one rung too many, shot clean over her head, and landed in the fireplace. Now he lay where he had fallen:

In the grate, right off an excessive rung.

Come into the garden, Maud

Alfred, Lord Tennyson
'Maud'

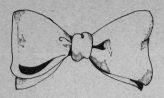

I must have been about nine at the time of the tragedy; a wiry, quiet lad, much given to solitary walks and Uncle William's Banana-Flavour Toffee.

They were long, hot summers at Broadstairs in those days. A military band played in the bandstand on the promenade, Uncle Mac performed his Minstrel Show on the beach twice daily, and the 'Perseverance', smelling excitingly of diesel oil fumes, took trippers for a sick round the bay.

All day was spent on the beach. I wore a bathing costume, bathing hat, and plimsolls from dawn to dusk, wet or fine. The costume was my pride; the acme of chic men's beachwear around the year 1929; the top half was like a vest, with horizontal hoops of maroon, and – a design featurette – large holes below the normal armholes. Then, working southwards, came an imitation belt with a rusty buckle, and a navy-blue lower half complete with a modesty skirt.

The bathing hat, which was worn at all times, was made of some intractable black rubber, possibly from old tractor inner-tubes, about a quarter of an inch thick. It had rubber ear-pieces welded on, into which the ears were supposed to repose snugly. Because I had found the hat on the beach my ears did not quite coincide and so not only was much agony endured but my ears are now about half an inch farther forward than is normal.

I found myself attracted more and more to the pier end of the beach, where the boats were moored. This now has a concrete slipway and a brass plate reading 'Edward Heath Slipped Here' but in those days there was just a lot of seaweed and a few moored dinghies gently banging into each other. What with the seaweed and the toffee papers and the Choc-Ice wrappers it was not so much messing about in boats as boating about in mess.

Very soon the Dinghy Set had accepted me as a sort of mascot and I spent all my time with them. Sometimes one of them would take me out for a sail and let me lower the centre-board and do a bit of bailing, and I would run all the way home, ten feet tall, freezing cold, with a soaking wet bottom.

They were all very much older than me. My particular hero was the group's acknowledged leader, Guy Beauchamp, a middle-aged man of about twenty-two. Most of the others shared a boat between them but Guy had his own, which he worked on all day, touching up varnish and tightening the stays. I spoke very little in those days. Not because I was timid but because I usually had a chunk of Uncle William's toffee in my mouth and as the toffee was broken off a block with a toffee-hammer and the pieces were usually large, pointed triangles which almost pierced the cheeks, any attempt at speech usually resulted in the listener being drenched with a fine spray of Banana-Flavour juice. But Guy spoke even less than I did. His conversation seemed to be entirely restricted to laconic, one-word instructions; 'Anchor', he would say. And perhaps an hour later, 'Oar'. He had fair hair, a cleft in his chin, and he wore khaki shorts which came just below the knee and a roll-neck sweater apparently knitted from spaghetti. He pottered about in the water all day getting his feet wet and never caught cold. A tremendously impressive chap.

His girl friend was Carmen Rowbottom, the ironmonger's daughter, although Mr Rowbottom called it 'Row-both-am' because he had married the gas manager's daughter and was a sidesman. I could never see much to Carmen at the time. She was quite elderly, pushing twenty, and wasn't very interesting to look at, having rather a lot of loose hair, like a carthorse's ankle, and huge bumps above her waist which got in the way when she rowed. But Guy was very keen on her, taking her for long, silent sails.

At the other end of the scale was Charlie Gordon who worked as a reporter on the *East Kent Messenger*. He was known as 'Toothy' because he hadn't got many, due to a cricket-ball. Toothy was small, bow-legged and ugly. He spent most of the time sitting on the edge of the pier, not helping, making rather funny comments.

Then it happened. There had been a week of bad weather and none of us had been on the beach. I was sitting on the pier wondering when the rain would ease up when I found Carmen standing there, eyes sparkling.

"I'm married!" she said.

For a while I couldn't speak. I'd swallowed my lump of toffee. When the pain in my chest had diminished I lifted one ear-piece of my bathing hat so as not to miss a word and wished her and Guy a lifetime of bliss.

"Not Guy," she said. "Toothy. I'm Mrs Gordon!"

"But . . ." I said, which wasn't much help but it was all I could think of to say in the stress of the moment.

"Be a sweet and tell Guy for me, will you? It'll be easier coming from you." And with a wifely peck on my cheek she was gone.

I found Guy in the sail-locker, darning a sail.

"Er, Guy, er," I said. "Er, Carmen's married. Asked me to tell you. Married Toothy. She's Mrs Gordon."

Guy stared at me with his unblinking, mariner's gaze.

"They're married," I repeated. "Married. Wed. Mr and Mrs Gordon."

Still no response.

"Miss Rowbotham has joined Mr Gordon in Holy Matrimony . . ."

As I ploughed on a horrifying truth dawned upon me. The splendid Guy, my idol, was as thick as a post. As dim as a nun's nightlight.

"Your ex-girl-friend and the man with few teeth are as one . . ."

But nothing was registering. As I sweated on, trying to get the message home to him, the scales dropping from my eyes like autumn leaves in a gale, I realised that My Hero was a man of few words because he only knew a few. In fact, apart from a few everyday phrases like 'Pass the marmalade', and 'Does this train stop at Faversham?' his entire vocabulary was nautical.

And so I translated my message into the language he knew.

"Mr Gordon and Miss Rowbotham," I said, "have sailed together into the harbour of matrimony. And are moored together for life."

Immediately he understood. His figure sagged. He seemed to be trying to say something.

I stood with him, but my words of comfort were of no use.

At dawn the following morning a longshoreman, out early to dig bait and nick things from the bathing huts, found Guy as I had left him; staring into space and muttering over and over again the harsh truth which he had, somehow, to accept:

"Carmen . . . Toothy Gordon . . . Moored!"

The game is not worth the candle

Proverb

CONTINUING our series, Cameos Of The Great Composers, the spotlight falls today on George Frederick Handel, the man who cleffed such great musicals as *Acis and Galatea*, both of which must be familiar to all lovers of the semi-classics.

Born in Germany, Handel acquired, according to the *Oxford Dictionary of Music*, 'a great reputation as a keyboard performer', a statement which we can only hope means he played the piano. After a spell as Kapellmeister to the Elector of Hanover, a dying craft nowadays, he came to England and took up residence just outside Edgeware in 1710. At least we believe that to have been his room-number but many pages of the parish-records were torn out in the Great Plague, there being no cleaning-tissues in those days.

However, the composer was immediately made welcome by the Edgeware gentry, for even in those days Handel was a name which opens all doors. As a young bachelor with several concerti grossi under his belt, to say nothing of his Harmonious Blacksmith, he was especially courted by parents of unmarried daughters and it was in this connection that he was accosted one day by Sir Tenleigh Knott.

Sir Tenleigh, a member of the old nobility, was the sixth son of the seventh Earl – or it may have been the seventh son of the sixth Earl, it was very difficult to tell with all those winding staircases – and he possessed an unmarried daughter, Arabella. She was a vivacious girl, not pretty by any accepted standards, if anything ugly by any accepted standards, but she could speak Latin and foot a quadrille and sometimes the two simultaneously if the tempo was right. So it was of her that Sir Tenleigh bethought himself when he espied Handel by the Long

Meadow, for in those days Edgeware was all fields even the agricultural land.

"Ah," said Sir Tenleigh, greeting him boisterously, "George Frederick Handel, isn't it?"

"Isn't it what?" said Handel, betraying his Teutonic meticulousness.

"Isn't it a shame that a nice young fellow like you should still be unmarried," said Sir Tenleigh, who never believed in shilly-shallying. "It's unnatural, that's what it is. I'll wager that since you arrived in this country, the only thing you've taken out is your naturalisation papers."

The remark contained enough truth to give Handel pause. Only too well did he know the torments of the flesh, having been up all the previous night with indigestion, a consequence of researching 'Alexander's Feast'. A wife who might be as adept at cooking as she was fair and slim of limb was a prospect which appealed to him strongly. So, "You have maybe somebody in mind?" he asked.

"My daughter Arabella," came the elder man's prompt reply. "An extremely vivacious girl. Gay, jolly, you might even say sporty."

"What does she look like?"

It was the age of 'arranged' marriages, as distinct from today's 'untidy' ones, so it was no unusual thing for two young people to be wed without ever having seen each other before the ceremony. Nevertheless, "What does she look like?," Handel asked.

"Foots a quadrille while speaking perfect Latin," said old Sir Tenleigh. "You have made a wise choice."

"What does she look like?"

"How's the *Messiah* going? Finished the Honolulu Chorus yet?"

"What does she look like?"

"Tell you what I'm prepared to do," Sir Tenleigh said. "I am willing to settle an estate on her." The truth was, Arabella had a shape it was perfectly possible to settle an estate on. Her main drawback had always been her resemblance to an early Georgian road-block but it was not a factor Sir Tenleigh felt like discussing.

"What does she look like?" enquired Handel again.

"You have made an old man very happy," said Sir Tenleigh, shaking his hand warmly. "Welcome to the Knott family."

"What does she look like?" Handel called after his departing figure, receiving in reply a cheery wave.

It was a troubled George Frederick who sat that night weighing up half a pound of toccatas. Somewhere deep within him he felt the vague unease that sometimes besets a man when he realises he's marrying a woman he's never laid eyes on. On impulse, he called in his man-servant, a devoted local rustic named Walter, to whom the composer later dedicated his chart-topping *Handel's Walter Music*. "I want you should run an errand for me," Handel said tossing him a florin, and we must remember that in those days a florin was worth – what? Two shillings, at least. "Go take a look at Miss Arabella Knott."

"'Ow will oi know 'er?" enquired Walter.

"She'll be the one footing a quadrille in Latin, very gay with it."

"What do 'ee want to know about 'er?" asked the rustic.

"What does she look like?"

When Walter returned, Handel could hardly wait to get the details, having by this time got himself worked up into a right state. "Tell me," he demanded eagerly, "Was she tall and fair, the vivacious Arabella? Was she a delicate wand of beauty? Was she straight as a yew-tree, slim as far-off violins?"

The rustic, in his slow way, sighed. What was the gentlest way he could break the news of Arabella's dimensions to this quivering Hun? Perhaps the only course was to be blunt. "Oi be sorry," he replied –

"The gay Miss Knott were thick, Handel."

There is no fire without some smoke

Proverb

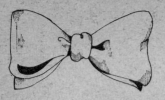

THERE has been a fatality in the village. The taped music in the Saloon Bar of the 'Red Lion' was switched off for twenty-four hours as a mark of respect, Mrs Dean removed the prop from her clothes-line and flew her washing at half-mast, Mrs Macnamara wore a black band on her sleeve but as her coat was also black nobody noticed, and the village schoolchildren, on a nature ramble, punched each other in a muted fashion, as though their hearts weren't in it.

Philomel, the donkey, has passed away, and the opening ceremony of the Thorpe Grand Autumn Fair Admission Free All Proceeds to Village Charities will never be the same. Never again will Mr Johns, the chairman, say "Ladies and gentleman, it gives me great pleasure to declare this year's Thorpe Grand Autumn Fair open . . ." only to be interrupted by a window-rattling bray and the entrance of Philomel. She would pause in front of the platform, paw the ground twice, roll an eye, and then sink onto her front elbows and waggle her tail at Mr Johns. One year she pawed the floor three times and forgot to roll her eye; several children burst into tears and there was a very stiff letter indeed in the following Thursday's local paper. Philomel's annual appearance had to be exactly the same each year. Young men would emigrate from Thorpe to Australia, marry, and return to Thorpe confident that their offspring would witness exactly the same ceremony that they had witnessed as ladlings. Philomel represented tradition, and continuity.

Mr Johns' eye was moist at the Parish Council meeting last night. "It wouldn't be a Thorpe Grand Autumn Fair without Philomel, me dears," he said. He was right, too.

It wasn't really much of a Grand Fair *with* Philomel. Thorpe Village

Hall is on the small side and only accommodates a few stalls. First came the games. There was the popular bucket-of-water-with-a-sixpence-in-the-bottom; the idea being to drop pennies into the water in the wistful hope that one would cover the sixpence and win a small prize. The trouble with that game was that since inflation and decimalisation one had to drop a 2p piece and attempt to cover a 10p piece, which is larger than a 2p piece.

Next came a game of rolling rubber balls down an inclined plane in an attempt to get them into holes. Unhappily the board had warped over the years and however you rolled the balls they all ended up in the bottom left-hand corner.

The most popular item came next; a stiff, wriggly wire along which you were supposed to pass a brass curtain-ring. The thing was wired up so that if your hand trembled a bell rang. The wires were still there but the old-fashioned battery had become obsolete fifteen years ago so the bell did not ring and everybody won a prize.

Then there was the cake stall. The home-made cakes were so popular that they were all bought by the other stall-holders before the Fair opened.

And finally there was the ever-popular Jumble stall. For the last twenty years this has consisted of a slightly rusty golf-club with the string unwinding from the handle, the sole survivor of a pair of book-ends, a pottery biscuit barrel with the knob missing from the lid and the brass showing through the chromium, a glass 'snow-storm' paper-weight with the Eiffel Tower inside which you turned upside down and nothing happened, a pianola roll of 'Marche Militaire', and four books: *Hiawatha, Rendered into Latin*, F. W. Newman, 1862; *Our Debt and Duty to the Soil, The Poetry and Philosophy of Sewage Utilisation*, E. D. Girdlestone, 1878; *Little Elsie's Book of Bible Animals*, 1878; and *Hindustani Self-Taught by the Natural Method*, E. Marlborough, 1908.

When I first came to the village I did not understand how these fêtes and fairs worked. I bought the biscuit barrel and kept it for tobacco. I was quietly corrected by the energetic lady who collected all the jumble for the various functions, Mrs Rumbold.

"If you don't mind me pointing out," she said, "these items are for buying and handing back, not for keeping. What you do is give the biscuit barrel back to me and it comes up at the Church Christmas Bazaar. I then collect it for the Scouts Hut Fund Jamboree. After that it goes to the Young Wives' Bring-and-Buy, the Annual Village Fête, the Darby and Joan White Elephant Night, the Thorpe Dramatic

Society Bargain Sale, and it then ends up again at the Thorpe Grand Autumn Fair. It brings in sixpence a time. If you hang on to it, Mr Muir, you are depriving village charities of three shillings and sixpence per annum."

My cheek mantling, I handed the biscuit barrel to Mrs Rumbold to be put back into circulation.

So you see the Grand Autumn Fair could hardly be described as a riveting, compulsive, not-to-be-missed-at-any-cost event. Except for Philomel.

"How did she . . . ?" I asked Mr Johns.

"Internal trouble." he said, quietly. "Sam is heartbroken."

Sam Thornton, the ancient old jobbing gardener, was not only Philomel's owner, he was also her front legs. Her back legs were occupied by Sam's brother Ron. Twenty years ago Ron had been lifting some leeks when his back clicked and he found that he had locked at right angles. He soon got used to walking about with his back at ninety degrees to his legs and Sam, being community minded, decided to make use of Ron's affliction for the good of charity and make him the back half of a pantomime donkey. Sam got the lady on the green who does bespoke loose covers for sofas to make the body out of canvas, Mr Hyde, the Egham saddler, made leather hooves and a papier-mâché head – and Philomel was born. Sam loved his moment of glory. Every first of September he would rub his hands and say, "Come on Ron, time to get the old moke working!" And they would practise for weeks.

"Last week," said Mr Johns. "Ron accidentally backed into a pitch-fork and straightened up for the first time in twenty years. Trouble was, though, he locked upright. Couldn't bend an inch. Sam had to find somebody else to work the back half. Do you know his great-nephew Fred?"

"City lad from Staines?" I said. "Bit thick? Keeps putting his skid-lid on back to front and riding into walls?"

"That's him. Well, Sam has been training him up to be the back legs. Last night Sam was giving him an extra hour's waggling practice when the lad suddenly went quiet. The next thing Sam knew was a terrible pain, a searing agony in his behind. He couldn't help leaping forward. The old, half-perished canvas ripped, and poor old Philomel was torn in half."

"But why the pain? What . . . ?"

"Fred had lit up a cigarette. The old boy couldn't bear to cope with

Philomel's remains so I took her to the road-sweeper, who was cleaning the drain by the bus-stop, and . . . I had her put down."

To break the long silence I said, "Well, I suppose we go ahead anyway with getting the jumble together and getting the cakes baked. . . ?"

"No," said Mr Johns. And he put into words what we, and the whole village, knew to be a sad but real truth:

"There is no Fair without Sam's moke."

"MR NORDEN," said this temporary shorthand-typist. "One more criticism about my spelling and I shall resign. You hear me? R-E-Z-Y-N, resign!"

Once again I silently maligned Brenda's husband. Brenda is my real secretary, the permanent one. A dear sweet girl, she's been with me for fifteen years, never a word of complaint, always unerringly efficient. Then, last year, she had the unmitigated gall to go and get married. And it was while she was away on her honeymoon – three whole days if you don't mind! – that I was forced to acquaint myself with that phenomenon of modern office life, the temporary secretary. Or, as they advertise themselves, 'Temps'.

For those of you who may be still unfamiliar with this consciousness-lowering group, let me explain their significance. You know how God dictated the Ten Commandments to Moses? Well if, instead of Moses, he had dictated them to a Temp – we would now all be working on only Four Commandments. Temps come in every size and shape but there are three characteristics shared by all of them: the first is a total unfamiliarity with the language the British use when communicating with each other, the second is the most tenuous acquaintanceship with the skills of shorthand and typing, the third is extremely little between the ear-rings.

I well remember the first one who came in to give a helping hand, at a hire-charge of 75p per hour per finger. Brenda was going off on another pleasure jaunt, some frivolity connected with a burst appendix, so I phoned the Agency to send over a temporary typist. What turned up was a lanky creature who, with her platform shoes and metal hair rollers, appeared to be about seven foot tall. Looking for all the world like a sexy radar-mast, she marched straight over to the typewriter, sat down and hit some keys. "Oh, look," she said. "It makes little letters."

When the next one arrived, I was somewhat cagier. "Before you start," I said, "could you tell me your speeds?"

"Well, I'm afraid I only do thirty words a minute," she said.

"Is that shorthand or typing?"

"No," she said, "reading."

To list all the agonies I have endured would be as boring for you as they were painful to me. On one occasion I went into Brenda's office to see how a short fat Temp was getting on with typing one of my letters, because when I'd dictated it to her she'd interrupted to ask how to spell comma. I found her sitting at the desk using two typewriters simultaneously; one with the left hand, the other with the right hand. Noticing my stupefaction, she gave a nervous smile. "I'm sorry," she said, "I couldn't find any carbon paper."

"How are you on the switchboard?" I asked one who'd pitched up looking like an explosion in a remnants factory. "Dunno," she replied. "I never done it on there." I remember the girl who arrived four hours late, having got out of the lift one floor down and spent the whole morning working for the wrong firm; the one who tried to look up telephone numbers in the *Oxford Dictionary*; the one who insisted on having a manual typewriter but an electric eraser. I had one girl who took snuff and another whose only previous commercial experience had been as a commère in a Dolphinarium.

I don't know what qualifications the Agencies require from a girl before they send her out. My private belief is that they show each applicant a washing-machine, a refrigerator and a typewriter. If she can identify the typewriter, she's on the books. What I know for certain is that ever since Brenda's perfidy forced me into availing myself of these creatures, I am become but a Xerox of my former self. Last week I asked one of them if she would fetch me a book of synonyms. "Oh, I love his books," she said. "Specially the Maigrets."

The breaking-point came this morning. A new Temp had arrived – the usual type, dolled up to the nines and trailing glories of cloudiness. After I had dictated my first letter to her, I said cautiously, "Do you think you could read it to me back, please?"

"Beg pardon?"

"Please read it to me back."

You won't believe this. That girl got up and started to *walk round behind me*. . . .

That's when I cried 'enough'. "No more temporary secretaries until further notice!" I screamed down the phone to the Agency.

It was only when the twitching ceased that it occurred to me that there might have been a more succinct way of putting the request. Musically. The way Peter Dawson used to sing it –

"Hold Further Temps!"

'Maybe It's Because I'm A Londoner'

Hubert Gregg
Title of Song

I'M retired now, of course. I retired about, oooh, no it was before that. I retired twice, as a matter of fact. For many years I worked for the General Post Office. I was employed at the Charing Cross Road, London, branch to stand behind a window and say, "I'm sorry but this window is closed, try the next one up". But when I retired from that my sister made me take another job for a week and retire again, because she didn't fancy having a brother who was a retired postal worker, in however responsible a position. That is the sister who was on the stage but is now in Dorking. She married, you know. Quite a few times. If my memory does not play me false, she is now married, or was at the time of her last Christmas card, to a gentleman who processes the films for a photographer attached to a local estate agency. She always refers to him as 'my husband the Property Developer'. So to please her I took a job at a garage for a week, coiling up the air-line used for inflating tyres, and then retired again. She always refers to me as 'my brother the retired Air-Line Executive'.

I am quite happy in my little room, not a stone's throw from Notting Hill. It is what is called a Bed–Sit. That is to say, if you want to sit you have to sit on the bed. I've lived in this same room for, it must be, oooh, or was it the year that, um. . . .

Until I found my little friend, my pet, I became rather lonely. I had my music, of course. I hum a great deal when I am on my own, sometimes accompanying myself on an old bongo drum which the previous tenant used for storing dried melon seeds. It is, I suppose, a humdrum existence, but there we are.

Ah. I was telling you of my pet. Well, I became lonely when I found it increasingly difficult to move about either swiftly or for any length of time. I am on the ninth floor and I soon found that although I could get down the stairs without difficulty I only had enough energy left to get back up again, with none to spare for going out. I had a friend, a Miss Winstanley, who lived in the basement. She was for many years Miss-On-Cash in a Mayfair butcher's shop until she retired some, oooh, it must now, let me see. . . . Well, we came to an arrangement whereby we met half-way down, or in her case half-way up, the stairs. There we would chat, d'you see, of the weather and similar topics, and we would return to our own rooms in fair condition, having divided the expenditure of energy between us.

But after a year or so we both began to feel less capable of tackling the stairs. It was all right when we each managed three flights, we could lean over the banisters and shout to each other. However, we soon could only manage two flights each and as neither of us could see or hear the other, with five flights of stairs in between, there seemed little point in continuing the arrangement.

That was when I began to feel lonely. Unhappily dogs and cats were strictly forbidden in the house. Rather surprising, really, because the landlord, Mr Carew-Entwistle-Carew, is clearly a dog-lover; he always arrives to collect the rent with two Doberman pinschers.

Then one day the problem was solved for me. I did not find myself a pet; a pet found me.

It was a bee. A handsome, brown bee. He was so plump and had such a rich fur coat that I christened him Diaghilev. I presume he must have fallen from a hive that was being transported through London on the back of a lorry because he was obviously lost and quite grateful to have somewhere to rest his head. I made him a little nest in the bongo drum and he took to staying with me all night and most of the day, buzzing off occasionally when he felt like it. He was free to come and go as he pleased; if the window was shut he could always fly out through the hole in the ceiling where the slate blew off in 1961, or through the aperture in the wall where I rather imagine a washbasin used to be.

Diaghilev and I got along splendidly for some weeks but then he began to lose weight. As the days sped past he became thinner and thinner until he no longer looked like a ballet impresario but more like the last half-inch of a used pipe-cleaner. I was in despair, as you might well imagine. And then I realised the problem was simply food. Bees eat nectar, and Diaghilev must have buzzed himself half silly trying to find nectar in Notting Hill.

I sprang, at my own pace, into action. I coerced my nice Health Visitor to bring me up a bucket of soil and a selection of honeysuckle plants. These I put into an old, oblong wooden box, which I had used for many years to hold my boot-cleaning things. This I fixed on my, albeit crumbling, window-ledge. I watered the plants with great care, and they flourished.

Oh, the joy of watching Diaghilev restore himself to health! I could not see the expression on his little face as he dipped, soared, buzzed, and then settled over the honeysuckle flowers – my eyes are not what they were – but I am sure that he wore a happy look. In a few days he filled out and became his old, sleek self again.

My cup of happiness became full a week later. He found himself a girl friend, a smaller, even sleeker bee, whom he brought home to show off his window-box. And quite suddenly one morning I noticed that Diaghilev was buzzing a different buzz, a high-pitched, interrupted buzz. He was engaged!

Every now and then somebody comes on the wireless and talks about bee-keeping, and they always say that you can't keep bees in a city, that to keep bees you need to own land so that they can have acres of fields and flowers to feed on. I just smile, and look at fat, happy Diaghilev buzzing round my window-box, and I hum a little hum to myself. I hum –

"My bee eats because I'm a landowner!"

A rose is a rose is a rose

Gertrude Stein
'Sacred Emily'

Hᴏᴡ strange! How really very strange! Do you know, that's the second time today I've come across that line. Isn't that a coincidence? No, really, sometimes I go for weeks without encountering 'a rose is a rose is a rose' but today – twice! Small world. This very morning I saw it written down on a note-pad at my psychiatrist's.

Did I tell you I've got this new psychiatrist now? Well, I never really had the confidence in that other fellow. I mean how much confidence can you have in a man who tries to cure a somatic anxiety-depressive psychosis with an ointment? Oh yes, very distinguished-looking, I admit, but that day I came in and heard him saying into the telephone, "Mummy, you'll just have to face up to it, I'm moving into my own flat" – well, that was it. "I'm sorry," I said, "but I must ask you for my symptoms back."

This new man now, what a difference! Don't go asking me whether he's the Jungian school or the Adlerian school because I can't tell you, all I know is it's the one that costs seven guineas a visit, but where the confidence-inspiring is concerned – chalk and cheese. And it's more than just the fact of no longer having to go through a barber's shop to get to him, it's his methods.

Dreams, you see. That's his thing. "I do tend to go a bundle on dreams," he told me when I signed on with him. So what I have to do now is, I have to keep some paper on the bedside-table and whenever I have a dream, get down a description of it the moment I wake up. Mind you, she leads off a bit about it, the Madam, because of the noise of the typewriter in the middle of the night. But the psychiatrist says take no mind of that, all women are troublemakers, he says, the Greeks had the right idea. Then twice a week I go along to him, lie down on his couch, a rexine one it is and he says the small change that slips down the sides, that's where the real money in psychiatry lies, and after I've read out my dreams to him he interprets them.

Which I must say is more than I could ever do. Just rubbish most of them seem to me, not to mention downright suggestive sometimes. Take the one I was telling him about this morning, the one where I was in a Cowboys and Indians scene. Now I agree that's one I do dream a lot but I've always put it down to childhood, because what with all those Randolph Scott pictures us kids used to go and see up the Regal, we were always playing Cowboys and Indians games. Not that I was ever allowed to be a Cowboy or an Indian in those games, that was always for the stronger boys. Me being so delicate, and like better dressed, I always used to be the lady having a baby in the end waggon.

But it stays in your unconscious, doesn't it, there's no denying it, so in this dream I was telling the psychiatrist about, I was in a waggon-train going along the prairie when suddenly thump-thump-thump, a storm of arrows on the roof. Comanches!

Up gallops the Waggon-master, and I remember something else now, should have told the psychiatrist this, in our games the Waggon-master was always the strongest fighter in the gang, so up gallops Alice, with arrows sticking out all over her, and she shouts, "Get the waggons in a circle."

Now you know how it is with dreams. Immediately she said the words "in a circle" there I was travelling on the Inner Circle. If you don't know what the Inner Circle is, it's part of the London Underground, a transport system which enables you to travel from say Liverpool Street to Blackfriars very much quicker than if you tried to get there crawling on your hands and knees. Anyway, there I was on the Inner Circle and I was stark naked.

"Symbolic," the psychiatrist said when I said that to him.

"All right," I said, "I was symbolic naked." Come to think of it, it's funny really how many of my dreams I do seem to wind up stark symbolic naked. When I'm not having a baby that is. But, as I say, I was travelling naked on the Inner Circle and while I was trying to remember where I could have put my ticket, suddenly the train stops at a station, I look out the window from idle curiosity and what do I see? It's Harrow.

And now it happens again. The moment I see the word 'Harrow', just as suddenly as last time – I'm the Headmaster of Harrow School. May I go blind, the Headmaster of Harrow School. Mortarboard, cane and full sidewhiskers. Otherwise stark naked, of course. And there, bending over in front of me, in a school cap and short trousers, is the psychiatrist. "Stop blubbing, boy," I hear myself saying, "you're down for six of the best."

Now when I got to this bit, the old psychiatrist perked up no end. He stopped shaving, put his electric razor down and came and sat down right there on the couch with me. "And did you cane me?" he says, nibbling his lip. "Talk slower."

Well, as it happens, I didn't cane him. Because, in the dream, just as I raise the cane, I notice he's got something knobbly tucked down the back of his trousers, so I stop. "Whatever you've got down there, boy," I say to him, "fetch it out." So he reaches behind into the seat of his trousers and know what he pulls out? A bust of Cicero. Now how I recognise it's a bust of Cicero is because he's got one himself in his surgery, the psychiatrist, and he showed me it one day. He's got lots of Greek statues round his walls come to think of it, though they're mainly of young fellows carrying wine-cups.

Anyway, in the dream, after he's pulled out the bust of Cicero, I say to him, "Sure there's nothing else down there, lad?" and he sobs "Yes, sir." And from the same place he pulls out another bust of Cicero. Then another one, then another one.

And from then on, the sort of nightmare-thing sets in, because he keeps on pulling them out. One bust of Cicero after another, thirty of them, forty of them. And just when the whole room is getting waist-deep in busts of Cicero – I wake up.

Now, I ask you, what would you have made of a dream like that? Going from a Comanche Indian Raid, to Harrow Station on the Inner Circle, to God knows how many busts of Cicero – wouldn't you say just a lot of old nonsense? No logic in it all?

Me too. But that's why I've got the confidence in this new man. With his college-training, what he deduced right away was that I was revolting. And what was I revolting against? Some old bird called Gertrude Stein. Because, showing me the three little notes he'd made on his note-pad, he said what they represented was my unconscious rejection of Gertrude Stein.

What he'd written, you see, was –

"Arrows . . . sees Harrow . . . Ciceros."

Allons, enfants de la patrie!

Rouget de Lisle
'La Marseillaise'

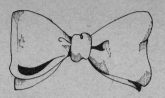

I had this nasty experience with a pair of trousers.
For years I bought my trousers from the same shop, a dimly lit,
mahogany-panelled oasis of calm in an alley off Bond Street. Mr
Herring, who was about a hundred and four, would creep forward,
fingering the tape measure round his neck, and ask my pleasure.
Having selected a likely pair of trousers I would be waved into the
Changing Cabinet to try them on. The Changing Cabinet was about
the size of an average hotel bedroom and it always contained Mr
Herring's partner, Mr Butterfield, furtively eating egg sandwiches. Mr
Butterfield, who was about a hundred and six, would mumble apolo-
gies and back out, shedding crumbs, and I would examine myself in a
spotted pier-glass while Mr Herring fussed round me ensuring that the
trousers fitted snugly under the arm-pits and that there was plenty of
room in the seat for sitting.

When I went back there a few months ago the shop had gone. In
its place was a shop selling Japanese cameras and coloured slides of the
Changing of the Guard, so I had, perforce, to find another seller of
trousers. It's all changed, hasn't it? Whereas I once dealt with Herring,
Butterfield and Nephew (Estd. 1901), I found myself entering a shop
called the Kensington Panty Boo-Teak.

And there was no Changing Cabinet. When it came to trying on the
trousers I was shown a row of booths up against the wall. These had
no door, as such, just a pair of extremely inadequate cowboy saloon
swing doors, about eighteen inches deep, hung half-way up.

I don't know what the height of the normal trouser tryer-onner is
but I don't think that it is six feet six inches, which is what I am. The
vulnerable area was in grave danger; indeed, had I been wearing unduly

thick socks I would probably have been arrested. But worse was to follow. It was impossible, I found, to remove one pair of trousers and encase the legs in a trendy new pair whilst standing bolt upright. A certain amount of knee-bending was unavoidable. It was while I was doubled over in a kind of foetal crouch trying to get my feet into the new trousers that I found myself gazing into the eyes of a lady sitting on a couch opposite. The full horror then dawned. Not only was any kind of privacy impossible but it was a mixed establishment open to both sexes. I shouted for an assistant, because the trousers, by an error of manufacture, appeared to have the zip at the back, to be faced by a ravishing Deb-of-the-Year who promptly burst into squeals of laughter and shrieked to the whole shop that I'd put my trousers on back to front.

I staggered out of the booth feeling very wobbly indeed. All I wanted was a sit-down for a few minutes. I sagged into a seat and closed my eyes. Almost immediately I heard a male voice say, "You look a bit ribby, squire. Permit me to do the laying on of the hands."

I opened my eyes to see an odd figure looming over me. He was wearing a wide, black sombrero, and a cloak of some dark material, underneath which was a bus conductor's uniform.

"Hold still, guv," he said. He put his fingers on my head, kneaded the scalp a bit, and hummed the opening bars of 'La Marseillaise'. "Ta-tum, ti-tum, tum, ta, ti, TA, ti-tum . . . Feeling better now?"

"No," I said. "Exactly as before."

"Blast!" he said. "It's no go, I'm afraid. Oh, well, it was worth trying."

He joined me on the seat and handed me a card. It read 'Alonzo Rathbone. Layer-On Of Hands. Cures While-U-Wait.'

"But," I said, "you're a bus conductor."

"Professionally I conduct buses, that is true." he said. "But by vocation, I am a Healer."

"Of people?"

"Well, no. That's the problem. So far, only plants. I was hoping for a breakthrough with you, but alas, it was not meant. My Granny's glad."

"What about?"

"No, no", he said. "Her glad. Her gladioli. That's how I discovered I had this gift. The gladioli were wilting and I was touching them, fondling them, and I began to hum the opening bars of the Marseillaise, and suddenly my finger-tips went all trembly and I could feel a kind of energy leaving me and entering into the glad. Next day the glad was so sprightly that Gran entered it in the Stoke Newington Darby and Joan flower show and won a linen tea-towel with a recipe for bouillabaisse printed on it. Sorry I couldn't help you, guv, but if you ever have trouble with wilting plants, fruit trees, leguminous veg, just get in touch with me. Remember the name, Alonzo Rathbone." And with a swing of his cloak he strode off to the bus depot.

I forgot all about Alonzo until a few days ago. I don't know about you but we have had a disastrous year in the garden. The front gate got Dutch Elm disease; the white paint turned yellow and the top bar crumbled away. The new rose bed was too near the oil central heating chimney and all the roses went down with flue. The lawn stopped growing, went brown, and still had a new mown look after seven weeks; a classic case of newmownia. But worst of all our Comice pear tree had a nervous breakdown.

"Look at it!" said my wife, her face twisted with grief. "Our oldest tree! Our delight! And now – brown leaves, bark flaking away. And look at the pears! They look more like spotty nutmegs!"

It certainly looked a goner.

"My favourite tree in the whole garden. The whole world," said my wife, plying the hanky. "Doomed. Nobody can save it now!"

"Alonzo!" I yelled, without warning.

"What?"

"There is just a chance in a million that I know a man who could restore it to health. With his 'fluence. He touches them up!"

I hurtled upstairs and found the trousers I had bought at the Boo-Teak. I had never worn them because when I got them home they seemed to have been designed for a seventeen-year-old, colour-blind neuter, but inside the hip pocket was the card I was looking for, reading 'Alonzo Rathbone. Layer-On Of Hands. Cures While-U-Wait'. But – oh, misery – no address.

But you never know your luck. Perhaps bus conductors read books like this to while away the time between rush hours. If so I have a message for a Mr Rathbone. More than a message, really, a plea to make two middle-aged fruit fanciers happy:

"Alonzo, fondle our pear tree!"

Sweet are the uses of adversity

William Shakespeare
'As You Like It'

IN a previous book of 'My Word!' stories ("*A finger on the pulse of our time . . .*" *F. Muir*), I made mention of Mrs Thora Tidmarsh, our local High Priestess where cultural matters are concerned. Mrs Tidmarsh is a strapping clear-eyed lady, well-built without being the slightest bit sexy, like a Junior Minister's wife. As is often the way with such ladies, her husband Arthur, although an extremely good credit-risk, is so totally devoid of personality he gives the impression he'd come out black and white even on colour TV. At Mrs Tidmarsh's Sunday Afternoon Musical Teas, the soirées which established her ascendancy as local arbiter on all questions artistic, he was little more than a plate-passer.

Those Sunday afternoons were occasions of absolutely teeth-aching refinement. They took place in her lovely dining room, a muted mixture of all the more expensive greens and browns but furnished with so many marble-top tables it was like eating in an indoor cemetery. While you munched hopelessly at unidentifiable squares of thin bread, Mrs Tidmarsh played – and thoroughly explained – records of what is called 'atonal' music. It is called that, I most sincerely hope, because somebody, sometime, is going to have to atone for it. Of the whole experience, what I remember most clearly is that peculiar ache in the neck one only gets from too much nodding appreciatively.

However, because the presence of every person invited was unfailingly reported in the local press, Mrs Tidmarsh's Musical Teas became a sort of social Access Card. If the Manager of the Supermarket had noticed your name among the list of those attending, his man at the check-out could be persuaded to help hump your shopping out to the car. For that reason no-one ever turned down an invite and Mrs Tidmarsh reigned unchallenged as cultural champ of N.W.11.

Unchallenged, that is, until the arrival in the neighbourhood of Alf and Rowena Hughes. The first hint that these two might qualify as contenders for the title came from the milkman, our quartier's acknowledged│Nigel Dempster. "Hey," he said, "know them new people who've taken Number Seventy-Four? They're installing one of them libidos in their bathroom."

It was – insofar as such an item can be so designated – a straw in the wind. Our suspicions that the Hugheses might prove persons of social consequence were strengthened when the local paper printed a story that Rowena intended to stage a Women's Liberation protest demonstration at the next Hampstead Heath Bank Holiday Fair. "I intend to lead a march," she was reported as saying, "demanding the abolition of Halfway For Ladies at the coconut-shy."

The actual gauntlet was thrown down in the form of a startling handwritten invitation stuffed into all our letter-boxes. Startling, I mean, by Tidmarsh literary standards. "Hi, new neighbours!" it read, in day-glo colours, "It's getting-to-know-ya time! Why not mosey up the trail│to the Hughes ranch 4│ p.m. this Sunday? Strong drink, light nosh and Poetry Reading!"

Poetry Reading! Well, I can tell you, the Washeteria that Saturday was a veritable buzz of indecision and in the Supermarket there was a five-cart pile-up. Was Sunday to be the Hugheses or the Tidmarshes? On the credit side, the milkman's last broadcast had stated that the Hughes's drawing room contained an ozone-spraying humidifier and inflatable Queen Anne chairs. On the debit side, might not the exchange of explained-music for spoken-poetry turn out to be a frying-pan and fire situation?

"Depends what kind of poetry it is," said the man from Number Sixteen, who runs a boutique called Mad Togs For Englishmen. "Like, T. S. Eliot like, he's quite catchy. My Mum had a record of him doing 'I used To Sigh For The Silvery Moon', you could get the hang of it practically first go off."

"Could we perhaps ring and *ask* them what kind of poetry?" offered Mr Twenty-Eight, who manufactures pregnant window-dummies for Mothercare. It was a bright suggestion so he was deputed to go and make the phone-call.

He came back wearing a rather dazed expression. "Guess what?" he said. "The Golden Treasury of Erotic Verse!"

So that's how Thora Tidmarsh's supremacy was broken, that's how a musical experience was exchanged for a literary experience, that's how wife-swapping got started in Hampstead Garden Suburb.

What often runs through my mind, though, is the phrase that Thora must have used to Arthur on the following Monday morning – after the milkman had arrived to tell her exactly *why* her Sunday afternoon audience had deserted her.

"Sweetheart," she must have said –

"Sweetheart, the Hugheses offer verse at tea."

If at first you don't succeed, try, try again

William Edward Hickson
'Try and Try Again'

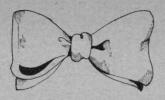

"IT is time," said my wife, "that you gave the puppy a bath."

A simple, friendly, wifely statement, spoken in a gentle, well-modulated tone, and yet my innards twisted into a knot. What was an undeniable truth was that Lady Ottoline Morrell – for that was our Afghan hound puppy's name – was, at the age of fifteen months, a bit old to be called a puppy, and was very long overdue for her first bath. As the condition of our house bore witness.

To begin with, the phrase 'giving the puppy a bath' conjures up a picture of gently dunking a scrap of fur in a pudding-basin of warm suds. It inadequately describes wrestling desperately with four and a half stone of powerfully-sinewed, wilful, furious doormat. I couldn't get her anywhere near the pudding-basin.

It might well be that high up in the hills of Afghanistan above Kabul a simple old shepherd had only to whistle once through blackened teeth for his obedient hound to round up a herd of alpaca, or cashmere goats, or whatever they rear up there to make those smelly coats out of, before leaping unbidden into a hot bath. But our puppy's mother came from Chelmsford, and the native skills seem to have been bred out of the strain in the soft life of the Home Counties.

If I whistled at Otty to summon her she would stop what she was doing and look at me with a mild surmise. If I whistled again with more authority she would smile gently to herself, tongue lolling out, then lope away before human behaviour became even more eccentric.

And it was hopeless to give chase. Otty could accelerate from rest to thirty mph in five yards and maintain that cruising speed indefinitely. She could go even faster out of doors.

I decided on a policy of stealth; Softly, Softly Wettee Otty. Squeezy tube of dog shampoo in left hand, water-bomb in right (as every schoolboy knows, along with 'who imprisoned Montezuma', a water-bomb is a large plastic bag full of water, which explodes on impact, deluging the victim).

This plan was not wholly successful. In retrospect I think that I was wrong to wear gumboots. These not only slow down the bomber's speed to well below thirty knots but the top of the gumboot acts as a funnel which receives the water when the lolloping action of running causes the plastic bag to rupture.

I changed out of gumboots, put on a dry right sock, and resolved that even though I had, at first, not succeeded I would try again. This time with the garden hose.

I shoved the nozzle of the hose down my shirt and strolled nonchalantly towards Otty, who was lying on the grass trying to hypnotise a sparrow into coming within paw range. She eyed me warily. I walked on right past her and waggled my hips, a sign to my wife in the garage to turn the water on. I removed the nozzle from my shirt and waited for the water to come through so that I could swing suddenly round and, to Otty's astonishment, drench her.

No water came. Not a trickle. I waggled my hips furiously. The hose remained dry. I turned to see what had gone wrong and there was Otty, tongue lolling happily, sitting on the hose.

"Off it!" I shouted. "Giddup! Nice Otty! Here girl! Up!" She made no move.

It was then that I made my mistake. In order to have both hands free to wave at Otty I shoved the nozzle of the hose down my trousers. At which moment Otty got off the hose.

How often can the human spirit try again before despair sets in? As I changed into dry trousers I was on the point of giving up when my eye alighted on a newspaper which had been pressed into service to line a drawer. Facing me was a photograph of a riot in Japan. And pictured there was my answer to the problem of how to give Otty a bath; a water-cannon. A device which could saturate a thousand aggrieved Japanese would surely be capable of dampening Otty.

The ironmongers in Egham did not stock water-cannons, I found, but I was able to borrow from Mrs Caddy a device which worked on exactly the same principle. Mrs Caddy called it a Grain Lifter and she used it on her farm to shift grain from a cart up to the top of her silo. It was a vast machine which plugged into the mains and consisted basically of a pipe which was thrust into the grain which needed to be lifted, an electric blower, and another pipe on top which squirted the grain, under great pressure, in whichever direction she wished it to be squirted.

I planned the operation most carefully. The Grain Lifter was towed in by tractor and parked on the lawn. I plugged it in to a 13 amp. plug in the house. The feed tube was inserted into a barrel of rainwater and the gun end was trained upon a spot, some twenty yards away, where I had assembled a little pile of goodies; old raincoats, telephone directories, chamois leathers, peppermints, elderly eggs, string from the Sunday joint – all Otty's favourite foods. We let Otty out of the house and she made immediately for the pile, reassured herself that there was nobody lurking within harmful range, and lay down contentedly for a good chew. I gave the signal to switch the current on.

What happened next can only be described as a blinding flash. The Grain Lifter burst into flames, the main fuses in the house blew, and the neon signs went dim outside every betting-shop within a ten-mile radius of Thorpe, Surrey.

The magistrates' court at Guildford took the view that I was entirely to blame. They went on and on about negligence and I must have known that the machine was not designed to be used with water and that the manufacturers had warned users that the machine would not work when dampness was present, and had I not seen the warning printed on the side of the machine?

I had seen the warning but, without my reading glasses, I had taken it for a motto encouraging perseverance. What was actually written across the thing, in humiliatingly large letters, was:

'IF AT FIRST YOU DON'T SUCK SEED, TRY DRIER GRAIN.'

Wonders will never cease

Sir Henry Bate Dudley
(*Letter to Garrick*, 1776)

A S I grow older – a practice I seem to be falling into more frequently these days – I find myself making increasing use of the expression 'mark my words'. Never was the utterance more bandied than in the argument about installing central heating.

I was against it, and eloquently. "When did our island people begin to decline as a world power?" I asked. "When they started living in warm rooms. Take the Victorians, whose homes were bone-achingly cold. Why was it they all went out and conquered tropical countries? Simply to have somewhere they could take their overcoats off. Mark my words, when we lost our goose-pimples, we lost our greatness. Moreover" – that's another word I've taken to, since the prematurely-greys – "moreover, when central heating came in, do you realise what went out? Chilblains! One of the greatest losses the hedonists of this country have ever suffered. Make what claims you will about your wife-swapping and your hard-core and your orgies, the permissive society has come up with no pleasure so purely ecstatic as scratching a chilblain."

I was, as usual, in a minority of one. Despite all my ingenious rearguard manoeuvres against installation – very strong peppermints, thermal underwear, letting the baby sleep in the airing-cupboard – I was eventually forced to yield to domestic pressures. What finally turned the tide against me was when the District Nurse halted at the bird-cage one December day. "Oh," she exclaimed, "what pretty bluebirds!" On learning they were canaries, she immediately finked to the Health Department.

So it was we began the whole dreary business of Heating Engineers and boilers and radiators and British Thermal Units and "you'll have to run the down-pipe through the master bedroom". One of the disadvantages of installing central heating in an aging house is that there is no way of hiding the piping. In consequence, every one of our living areas now gives the appearance of a ship's engine-room.

Let me point out another consequence of adding artificial warmth to a house that has managed to exist without it since before Crippen was apprehended. Everything warps. There is, apparently, a scientific law that heat makes things expand and cold makes things contract – the reason, I suppose, why days are longer in the summer and shorter in the winter. And when it comes to heating houses, this scientific law manifests itself by causing every bit of woodwork to swell, twist, curve and curl.

Doors, for example, jam in the half-open position. That is a peculiarly irritating phenomenon for me because I am a man given to dramatic gestures. In any argument, I have made an extremely satisfying practice of storming out of the room and slamming the door behind me. Now you try doing that with a door that jams in the half-open position. Your arm pulls half-way out of its socket.

Equally irritating, but more financially depressing, is what happens to windows. We have wooden sash-windows and when the central heating was put in, during the summer months, they were all open, in the 'up' position. Around November the wind started making BBC Sound Effects noises so I went round the house pulling down their lower halves. What did I come back with? Fourteen snapped sash-cords. The central heating's trial-run had corrugated every window-frame's edge, wedging each one fast within its groove.

"Not to worry," said the carpenter when he called to inspect them. "All it means is supplying and fitting fourteen new window-sections." Then he quoted me a price which could have kept a family of five in the Bahamas for three fun-packed months. "Not on your freelance-writing nelly," said the Bank Manager I went to for the money.

For the rest of the November-to-April period, our rooms, with every window jammed in the open position, presented some fascinatingly varied extremes of temperature. From the new radiators to the middle of the carpet we could have posed for one of those High Speed Gas commercials – everybody smilingly half-dressed and the baby tottering about naked. From the middle of the carpet to the window – Antarctica. On the radiator side of the room, daffodils bloomed. On the window side, edelweiss. The RSPCA said we had the only tortoise with schizophrenia.

I am not an obstinate man. I readily admit that a house without central heating does present certain snags. On a winter's morning it's not always convenient having to run four times round your bedroom before your fingers thaw enough to undo your pyjama buttons. But such a house does possess one important factor in its favour. Mark my words –

"Windows will never seize."

O for the touch of a vanish'd hand

Alfred, Lord Tennyson
'Break, Break, Break'

IT was frightful, standing there in the witness box of the North London Magistrates' Court, looking across at my dear old friend and comrade Denis Norden slumped in the dock.

He seemed drawn, as if by Felix Topolski; and his face looked – as indeed the whole of him had been – pinched. It was only a minor charge on which he stood arraigned, thanks be to merciful Providence; a matter of being caught whistling outside the Golders Green Scottish Presbyterian Church on a Sunday afternoon.

The magistrate was talking to me. "This sort of hooliganism has got to be stamped out. It's devil's work, d'ye ken?" he said. "But I'm prepared to give the laddie another wee chance. If I bind him over, will you stand surety for his good behaviour? To the tune of five pounds?"

I leapt at the chance of being the instrument of my colleague's freedom.

"Oh yes, sir!" I exclaimed. "Yes, yes! With all my heart! Indeed I will! Oh, yes and yes again!"

"Have you five pounds?"

"And to spare, sir!" I cried.

"Have you five pounds when all your debts are paid?"

A routine little question they always have to ask. Wasting the court's time. It's a wonder they don't do away with it.

"Yes, sir," I answered stoutly. "And I gladly pledge every. . . ."

I paused. I suddenly felt uneasy. Car not a debt – could be whipped back if instalments not paid. Owed Jim Knight the fishmonger for a pair of kippers – but he owed us for a dozen of our eggs so that was a credit rather than a debit. Why this unease?

The mists of memory cleared suddenly. All my debts were most certainly not paid. I had one outstanding debt, years old, and I had no idea how large the amount was.

It must have been about eleven years ago when the debt was incurred. At that time my wife and I had a canal boat, 'SAMANDA', in which we used to potter up and down the Inland Waterways when the summer wasn't too rigorous. I suppose that in a good year we spent about ten days actually afloat in her but we were privileged, as proud owners, to spend every spare hour from September to May scrubbing, derusting, painting and varnishing her so that she wouldn't disintegrate one day when we weren't looking; a trick that boats have.

That summer the drizzle was particularly warm so we decided to take 'SAMANDA' up the Oxford canal and round into the Grand Union, taking in the Blisworth tunnel, which is over a mile and a half long.

Halcyon days they were, with halcyons swooping over the water in a flash of glittering blue.

Occasionally we towed the boat along from the towpath in blissful silence, but we usually used the motor because the tow-rope chafed my wife's neck.

It was all so magical until we got halfway through Blisworth tunnel. Now canal tunnels are pitch dark, moist, and there is just room for two boats to pass. Just.

Half-way through the Blisworth we heard the sound that every Inland Waterway mariner dreads, the thump-thump-thump of an approaching narrow-boat's diesel engine. Narrow-boats are the old canal working boats, over seventy feet in length, made of steel, or elm planks about a foot thick, and one touch from them can stove in the hull of a fancy little cruiser like ours.

We switched off our engine and clung to the wall on our side of the tunnel, slightly alarmed by a regular series of dull thuds which got louder as the narrow-boat got nearer. When she came into our head-light beam the reason for the thuds became apparent. The narrow-boat was chugging up the tunnel towards us ricocheting from one wall to the other, clearly unmanned.

"It's the 'Flying Dutchman'!" I yelled.

"What, up the Grand Union canal?" replied my wife. "With nobody on board? No, be sensible. If anything it's the 'Marie Celeste'."

In fact it was the 'Alfred J. Crump'. We found out later that it had been hired by a couple of middle-aged ladies who didn't fancy going through the tunnel so left the engine in gear and hurried over the top to catch the boat at the other end.

By some miracle we were not sunk. The narrow-boat passed by in mid-bounce, but there was a board sticking out of its side which caught our craft a glancing blow at the bows.

"Thank Heavens!" my wife cried. "The only damage is a scratch on the 'AND' of 'SAMANDA'."

"But it's a deep scratch!" I said. "In my lovely varnishwork!"

As soon as we had moored up at the next village I went round asking where I could find a painter who would touch up our boat for us.

I should have known something was wrong when the painter arrived, a most distinguished-looking gentleman with a box of paints, an easel, and an umbrella. He seemed a little surprised when I explained what was wanted but he did a splendid job. It took him about two hours. He used best artist's quality varnish because I sneaked a look at the tin.

When he had finished I pumped his hand enthusiastically and congratulated him on his skill, commanding him to send his bill on to me. We exchanged names.

It was only later, when we were on the homeward leg of our journey, that I glanced at the card he had given me and found that the obliging painter who had touched up our name plate was the President of the Royal Academy.

And his bill has yet to arrive. The mind boggles as to how much two hours of the President of the Royal Academy's time costs. Hundreds? Thousands?

My reverie was broken by the magistrate.

"I asked you whether you have five pounds when your debts are paid!"

"I don't know, sir!" I blurted. "You see, sir, I've just remembered. I have one bill outstanding. So you'd better clap my friend in the clink, sir. You see, sir, I'm afraid I still . . . it's not my fault because he hasn't sent it, but I still . . ."

"You still what, man?"

"Owe for the touch of a varnished 'AND'."

Charity begins at home

Sir Thomas Browne
'Religio Medici'

"AMONG the contributors," read the third paragraph of the letter from the publishing firm, "will be Alexander Solzhenitsyn, Dr Christiaan Barnard, Lord Hailsham, Mother Teresa and other Television Personalities. The book's title will be *My Most Embarrassing Moment* and we would like its opening chapter to be contributed by you."

When I put the letter down, I could not disguise my pleasure. In addition to the natural gratification I felt at being included among such distinguished company, there was also the knowledge they had picked the right man for the right job. For if my life has been rich in no other ways, where moments of embarrassment are concerned shake hands with a millionaire. The trouble, if anything, was going to be that I had too many to choose from, an embarrassment of embarrassments.

I allowed my mind to wander over some of the more neck-reddening of the incidents. The occasion when a large dog followed me into a telephone box and I couldn't get the door open again? The backstage party given by The London Symphony Orchestra when I decided to slip away unobtrusively and walked right through a harp? The day I took a full-size cactus plant on a crowded Underground train? That moment during the Old Fashioned Waltz with the Lady Mayoress at the Huddersfield Press Ball when I realised that my left-hand contact lens had dropped into her cleavage? The time I spilled a whole cup of hot Bovril into my lap – at a nudist camp?

The mere remembrance of these and similar episodes gave me shudders sufficient to keep my automatic wrist-watch running for three days. However, were any of them, in these particular circumstances, really embarrassing *enough*? For an incident to deserve its place as the opening chapter of that book, surely it must identify itself immediately as an absolute nadir of experience, a true North Finchley of the soul.

Well, as with moments of sex, so with moments of embarrassment: it is often the most recent one that is remembered as the most significant. And as, at that time, my most recent one had happened no more than a month ago – moment of embarrassment, I mean – that was the one I decided to record and submit.

The story started with the fact that, when one of the new takeaway shops on the Parade went out of business – there just isn't the demand for organic beefburgers round here – a Japanese gentleman took over the premises and opened it as a Karate Academy. In no time at all he was raking in over a hundred quid a week teaching the neighbouring bourgeoisie how to break planks with their bare hands; to say nothing of the extra tenner or so he knocked up doing a sideline in firewood.

Why was I among the first to enrol? Many reasons, the main one being that having grown up on a cultural diet of those magazines with I Was a Seven Stone Weakling on the inside back cover, I hated acknowledging that, even today, if a bully were to kick sand in my girl's face on the beach I'd probably end up helping him.

The strange thing was, something within me responded to Karate. I was a natural. Within four weeks, Mr Sen informed me that I was probably the best fighting pupil he had, better even than old Mrs Willett. Straightaway I made a silent vow that I would never use my powers for evil, only for good.

I'm going to go into the Historic Present tense now, because it's necessary that the next sequence of events be related as graphically as possible. That night, I'm coming home from the Academy and what do I see? Under a lamp-post, two people are struggling. One is a well-built young man, the other a rather frail girl, and he's trying to wrest a handbag from her hands. She is kicking at his shins and struggling, but he's so much bigger than she is there can only be one outcome.

So – Karate-time, folks. In two rapid strides I step between them, raise my right arm and, with the heel of the hand – Hah! Ah! Ha-so! Three beautifully timed strikes, like a cobra, and there he lies – writhing on the ground! The girl gazes at me for a moment, then she seizes my hand and presses it to her soft cheek. Releasing it, she snatches up the handbag and runs off into the night.

Chest swelling, I give the big fellow a nudge with my toe. "On your feet, chummy," I say. "We're going down the nick." He stirs and looks up at me. I notice he has a strangely melting gaze. "Too jolly right we jolly are," he says.

"What do you mean?"

"That was *my* handbag."

Although *My Most Embarrassing Moment* has proved to be a voluminous tome, running to some eight hundred-odd pages, the Editorial Board have unanimously agreed that my contribution fully deserves its position as the opening chapter – a fact which their advertising boys were not slow to pick up. Indeed, it has become the subhead on most of the publicity releases:

'Karate Begins A Tome.'

What's the good of a home if you are never in it?

George and Weedon Grossmith
'The Diary of a Nobody'

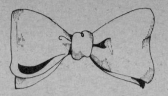

THE other morning at breakfast time I was sitting over a cup of hot coffee when I had a terrific idea. I wasn't even trying to think at the time; I was crouched over the cup trying to steam an egg stain out of the seat of my jeans. If I had a thought in my head at the time it was never again to put a tray with a soft-boiled egg on my chair, move forwards to switch on the television, then back gently and sit down on the egg. If I had been in a thinking mood I might have reflected further on the extraordinary amount of egg there is in an egg; enough in one small oval shell to besmear a cheek and a half of jeans.

But my mind was blank, and into it floated this idea. If pressed for a comparison in the world of nature I would say that it was not at all unlike a mushroom spoor alighting on a damp flannel.

Now every writer dreams about inventing a new character to write novels about. Think how excited Ian Fleming must have been when he dreamed up James Bond, or Galsworthy when he thought of Forsyte Saga. Once a writer has his hero, his Bond or his Saga, the rest is easy; best-sellers, major motion-pictures, television serials.

My idea was a totally original character – a criminal pixie. Or, to put it another way, a bent elf.

For the next three days I put everything else aside and worked like a madman on the plot of the book; I refused all offers of food – except at mealtimes, of course – and went without sleep all day, but at the end of it I had a synopsis roughed out.

There are four of them in the gang. Our hero, Norm the Gnome, is the leader. He is a criminal but we make it clear that he is not all that nasty. Nasty-ish but not revolting. He learned his bad habits when he did his National Service – two years in the National Elf Service – and has never since come to terms with society.

Norm's girl-friend is Mustard-Seed, hot stuff, still a bit green, although well past her salad-days. She earns her living as a dancer in the clubs, where she works under her professional name of 'Caustic Soda'. She is a stripper.

The heavy is Alf the Elf, a huge muscle-bound giant – a giant, that is, up against the elves – who gets all the dirty work to do. He is well known to the police because he unthinkingly allowed himself to be photographed in the nude, rippling his muscles, for the cover of the magazine *Elf and Strength*.

The last member of the group is Puck (real name Robin Badfellow), a layabout who spends most of his time filing his nails and passing remarks. His job with the gang is to act as contact-man and drive the getaway car when they can afford to buy one.

The gang always met on Tuesday evenings because it was a bad night on the telly and one Tuesday Norm strode in very purposefully with a Master Plan.

"Right," he said. "From tonight this gang stops being cat burglars. We've had a good year burgling cats but the market for hot cat-collars even with a bell attached, is satiated. We're going into the big time."

Consternation, as you might well imagine, reigned. The pros and cons were discussed with some heat, but Norm was adamant.

"I'm going to be Mr Big," he said. "Caesar of the Undergrowth. Drive round in an Elfa-Romeo. Take Mustard-Seed to the South of France, first-class on the Cross-Channel Fairy. So here's what we're gonna do. Next Saturday evening, after the Western on telly, we're going to rob a bank!"

"I know a bank whereon the wild thyme blows," said Puck, combing his hair with a thistle.

"That's the one we're going to do!" said Norm.

"I can't manage Saturday," said Puck. "I'll be in the middle of an ice-hockey match."

"Then Mustard-Seed can be look-out," said Norm. "We're going to nick all the thyme from that bank and then take it to a fence."

"Which fence?"

"The one at the bottom of my garden. We'll pin it out on the fence to dry, then put it into packets marked 'Dried Herbs' and flog it to Health Food addicts up the Goblin Market. There's a fortune in it."

"Hey boss," said Alf the Elf, to everybody's surprise as he didn't go in much for talking. "We'll get caught. That bank's floodlit!"

Norm silenced him with a look. "We are going to tunnel!" he announced. "I have recruited Mo the Mole and Harry Hedgehog for the job. We are going to go in underneath the plants and pull them up – *downwards!*"

Everything seemed to be going according to plan on the night. Mo the Mole burrowed a rough tunnel, then Harry the Hedgehog went in and scraped the tunnel smooth with his quills. The roots of the thyme dangled down. Norm dragged the thyme down by its roots and passed it to Alf, who staggered down the tunnel and deposited it in piles outside. And then something went wrong. Alf had disappeared with the last load when Norm had a gnomish feeling that all was not well. He ran down the tunnel to the entrance – and it was blocked. He was trapped by a large clod of turf, which had been rolled over the entrance.

"Somebody has grassed on me!" he groaned. And sat down to wait for the police.

The story ends with Norm the Gnome staring through his prison bars, while Mustard-Seed dances cheek to cheek with Puck in some thieves' hangout, humming to herself, "Thyme on my hands, you in my arms. . . ."

I really thought I had a winner in Norm, the delinquent Gnome. Original, dramatic, suitable for all age-groups. But I was wrong. He is useless to me, as I found out when I telephoned a publisher.

I telephoned the best publisher in London. I cannot, of course, mention his name but he was out so I spoke to his wife, Mrs Methuen.

"I've thought of this wonderful character for a book," I said. "He's a bent gnome called . . ."

That was as far as I got.

"A gnome?" she cried. "A *gnome?* You can't write books about a gnome! That's Enid Blyton's territory. You might be able to get away with writing about a gnome if you were another Enid Blyton, but that is what you will never be."

And so it has all been for nothing. I still have my beautiful little character, the crooked Norm, but I have to face facts:

'What's the good of a gnome if you're never Enid?'

Give your thoughts no tongue,
Nor any unproportion'd thought his act

Shakespeare
Hamlet Act I, sc. 3

ONE of the many profound experiences which people without children are deprived of is that of sitting through a small daughter's Dancing Class Concert. I was conscripted for this numbness one long-ago Christmas when my daughter was six years old.

The reason she had joined the class in the first place was because she had somehow got herself mixed-up with a boy there. By mixed-up, I'm not implying she was mistaken for him, I mean there was an emotional involvement. It was a relationship I frowned upon, not merely because the lad bore a striking facial resemblance to Joan Crawford – after all, so does Mick Jagger – but because he was going on for at least twelve and I never believe there's any future in those May and December things. Also, and perhaps unreasonably, I had a sneaking feeling that any boy who voluntarily joins a Dancing Class cannot be all good.

However even at six, my daughter had, as they say, a whim of iron, so I took her along to meet the Principal. That lady's name was Signora Estrellita Mariposa which I didn't believe for a second, especially as her husband's name was Ornstein. She took against my child on sight. The moment we entered the room, "Much too tall!" was her opening comment. I immediately bristled, thinking she was referring to me, but la Signora went on to aver that, for a member of a juvenile dancing troupe, the ideal specification is 'winsomely tiny'. Now while it is true that we are a lanky family and my daughter could have signed for the Harlem Globetrotters almost at birth, such a summary dismissal offended all my principles of equality in the arts. I therefore argued the case powerfully, and after a certain amount of wallet-waving Signora Mariposa consented to allow her assistant to take the child into the next room for an audition.

"This one is a natural mover," announced that lady on their return, rather giving the impression that some six-year-olds had been found to be battery operated. With bad grace and at an exorbitant fee, the Principal agreed to take the child aboard.

The ensuing months I remember mainly for the nightly thumps on the ceiling as practice took place upstairs but the high point was reached in mid-November. "I'm going to be a Snowball!" exulted my daughter when she returned from class one cold evening. Some narrow-eyed questioning elicited the explanation that in the forthcoming annual concert – 'Santa Claus's Workshop!, A Seasonal Extravaganza Of Song and Dance' – my daughter had won the coveted role over stiff opposition. "It's ninepence a ticket and everybody's got to come along and clap me," she ordered.

Everybody turned out to be me, all other blood-relations having had the foresight to develop Asian flu or go wintering in the Canary Isles. So, on that bleak December afternoon, I made my way to the concert's venue, the Cinema Café of the local Odeon.

All Cinema Cafés have a doomed air at the best of times, but on this occasion it was sheer Camus. And while we're on the literary references, you know that line of Sartre's about 'Hell is other people'? Well, it isn't. It's other people's *children*. There were sixty-seven pupils in that Dancing Class and every single one had a featured part in the two-and-a-half hour production. An unending parade of tidy winsomes, all of them bedaubed in lipstick and greasepaint and red dots in the corners of their eyes, like a procession of depraved midgets.

I did notice, though, that the entrance of each one was greeted by loud localised plaudits from whichever area of the auditorium his or her family group was located. This showed me where my own duty lay. "When my child comes on," I vowed, "I will make up in vociferousness what I lack in numbers."

So when the orchestra – Miss Larby on piano and tambourine – struck up 'Winter Wonderland', I was ready. From the months of overhead thumping I knew this to be the tune to which we did our bit, so I took a deep breath. And when that glittering white Snowball tittuped on from behind the papier-mâché icicles, I rose to my feet and let out the full Sammy Davis Jnr whoop. "Wah-hoo! Yowee! Great, great! The kid's a sensation! Let's hear it for a really wonderful performer! Encore, encore! A-one more time!"

It was when the Snowball burst into terrified tears that I realised two elements were amiss. One, her physique was of an unfamiliar tinyness; two, there were twenty-three other Snowballs entering behind her.

I had, as was explained to me afterwards, whooped it up for the wrong Snowball. My daughter was number sixteen in the Snowball line. At the time though, the father of the hysterical Snowball spun round and punched me in the throat. I kicked him in the elbow (no, I can't think how), the police were called, I was ejected and Signora Mariposa summarily withdrew my daughter from the Concert, not even allowing her to stay and wave in the Finale. "I shall never permit a tall tot on stage again," she snarled.

Next day she expelled her from the class completely, claiming that the whole ugly incident would never have taken place had it not been for the child's excessive height. My daughter, for her part, blamed the whole thing on me and left home as soon as she reached adolescence. She is now in North Cornwall living with an unemployed rifle-range attendant who bears a striking facial resemblance to Linda Darnell.

I can only hope that the sorry tale offers a guide-line to any other fathers who may have small daughters about to appear in Dancing Class Concerts. Unless they are of the requisite tinyness – keep your mouth shut when they make their entrance. As Polonius advised Laertes:

"Give your tots no tongue,
For any unproportion'd tot is sacked."

Half a loaf is better than no bread

Proverb

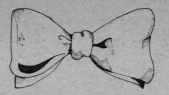

OH, believe me, it is not all glamour and laughter being Bimbo the Clown. Lots of you must have seen me when Potter and Ginsberg's Mammoth Imperial Circus visited your town. We usually pitched our big top in the car-park behind the pub.

I was the comic little chappie with baggy trousers and a ginger wig who ran on after the elephant. It was, from time to time, dangerous work.

Now no man is made of wood, not even Woden, The Wooden Man – he had a wooden leg but the rest of him was painted and grained to match it – and there came a time when I felt the urge to marry and settle down.

But who would marry Bimbo the Clown? What lady would be happy to say "That's my husband over there", pointing to a tiny, white-faced figure in enormous boots, with a red ping-pong ball nose, sitting in a bucket of whitewash? During most of my appearances I was deluged with whitewash. I had so much of it poured over me that my first thought when we arrived at a new town was to find a vet and get my distemper inoculation.

The first lady I approached with a view to courtship was Rumpo, the Fat Lady. Like many vast ladies she was a gentle, kindly person, always willing to help out when a lorry got stuck in the mud. One day the electricity in my caravan went off when I was in the middle of doing my ironing and Rumpo went down on all fours and turned the generator by hand. So I pressed my suit on her.

When I took her to Brighton on our day off everything seemed set fair. I had a little Mini at that time so I hired a van and away we went, as happy as two children let out of school. We even found a children's playground and played seesaw, Rumpo on one end and me and the van on the other. But tragedy struck later that night on the way home. I had stopped the van and helped Rumpo out of the back to give the springs a rest. As my arm went round part of her waist I suddenly blurted out my secret wish that I might one day make her Mrs Bimbo.

She burst into laughter. She howled with mirth that I could ever think she would marry a clown. As I worked the handle and jacked her up into the back of the van my heart was near breaking point.

Hath not a clown eyes? Hath not a clown hands, affections, passions? If you prick us, do not jets of water squirt out from our eyebrows? If you tickle us, doth not our ginger wig stand on end and the toes of our boots emit steam? If you poison us, doth not our bow-tie revolve?

Hurt and bruised, I scarcely spoke to another lady for some years. Then the side-show department of the circus acquired a new attraction, George-Ina, Half-Man Half-Woman. From delicate oval face to hairy legs, a vision of delight.

I was immediately attracted. There was a natural reticence there which appealed to me. Many circus-folk are over-friendly and are forever popping into your caravan but George-Ina, well – he kept himself to herself.

Perhaps the affair might have gone no further had not fate stepped in. One Sunday evening I returned late to the big top to hear screams and shouts. And George-Ina's unmistakable voice:

"HE-lp!"

A terrible scene greeted me as I rushed in. It seems that Flexo, the Indiarubber Man, had been on one of his benders. He was clutching George-Ina to him and, inflamed with cheap liquor, was threatening that unless she agreed to spend the night in his caravan he would release the lion from its cage to claw all and sundry.

Everybody from the circus was there, and they all turned to me.

"Flexo," I said levelly. "You're twisted."

He merely snarled.

An icy calm came over me. Putting on my ping-pong nose to give myself confidence I moved unobtrusively to the side of Madam Zaza, the Human Cannonball, and said to her, very quietly:

"Madam Zaza, will you do me the pleasure of inserting yourself up your cannon, fusing yourself where necessary?"

She slipped away like a shadow.

Affecting nonchalance, I sauntered towards the cannon, muttering to the others as I passed, "Hide behind something in case Madam Zaza ricochets."

Once at the cannon I swiftly swung it until the muzzle pointed straight at the Indiarubber Man's heart.

"All right, Flexo!" I shouted, a new authority in my voice. "Drop George-Ina and walk slowly forwards with your hands above your head. Make one false move and I'll fill you full of Madam Zaza!"

He knew he was beaten. He unhanded George-Ina and stumbled forward. At that moment the local police arrived and took him away. The Indiarubber Man is now in Wormwood Scrubs prison, doing a stretch.

George-Ina fell into my waiting arms, and suddenly we were alone under the big top.

"Dear sir/madam," I whispered, "will you be mine?"

"I wish I could make up my mind." George-Ina whispered back. "Half of me wants to, but the other half is not so sure. . . ."

"Then let me make your mind up for you!" I cried, and picking her up in my arms I ran with her to the sideshow marked See the Vicar Starving In A Barrel, where the vicar kindly interrupted his supper long enough to marry us.

People sometimes ask me whether I have not missed something, sharing my life with somebody who is half a gentleman and half a lady. Perhaps. But on a wintry evening, when we are snug in our caravan, me washing the whitewash out of my smalls, George-Ina varnishing her nails or lighting up her pipe, I think to myself – why cry for the moon when I have the stars?

Half a love is better than no bride.

THE most eloquent example of graffitti I can recall seeing was written on a road-sign. Under the notice 'Cul de Sac' someone had scrawled the words 'What isn't?'

Even if I had failed to recognise the handwriting, the sentiment would have identified the writer for me: Neville Pacefoot, the text-book example of what pop psychiatrists call 'a victim personality'. From early childhood, life treated him like the back wall of a squash court.

Neville's first brush with calamity came during his Boy Scout days. While he was helping an old lady across a street they both got run over. After a three-hour operation, he was taken off the danger-list and they allowed him to sit up and look at his Get Well cards. The first one was so amusing, he burst out laughing and broke eight stitches. Opening the next one he cut his finger and developed blood-poisoning.

Those were the earliest intimations that, in this supermarket we call Existence, Neville had grabbed the shopping-cart with the wonky wheel. At the outbreak of War he persuaded the RAF to accept him, despite the fact that two of his toes had been crushed shapeless. (By a falling First Aid Cabinet.) He immediately became the only serviceman to get wounded during his Preliminary Medical Examination. While the Medical Officer was sounding his chest, Neville noticed an Air Vice-Marshal entering the room, so he threw up a salute. It pulled the rubber tube of the stethoscope clean out of the M.O.'s head, and when the metal ear-pieces snapped back, that was the last of Neville's teeth. Nevertheless he persevered with the training and passed out as Sergeant Air Gunner.

The stripes did not survive his first mission. He spent that whole trip to and from Hamburg with his face pressed against the fuselage, the result of having slammed his handle-bar moustache in the plane door just before take-off. Invalided out with a disability pension a few months later, having been run over by an ambulance, he was directed to agricultural work and spent six months on a farm before a cow fell on him.

I lost touch with Neville for a while after the War, although I kept reading about him in such periodicals as the *Journal Of The Road Accident Research Centre*, whose cover he made four times. After he'd achieved national headlines as the first driver to break a leg by catching his foot in a car safety-belt, his insurance company wrote to ask for their calendar back. "It's like giving life cover to a lemming," the letter said.

It was round about this time that Neville's wife finally decided to leave him. For some time now she had found herself writing lipstick messages like "Enough's enough!" across the bedroom mirror, but when it was discovered that their daughter had been put in the family way by their son's Probation Officer, Mrs Pacefoot called it a day. She was given custody of the house, the furniture and the children, leaving Neville with only his savings, which had been safely invested in a pharmaceutical company making cyclamates.

From then on, things went steadily downhill. Fired from his job – his employer claimed that Neville's frequent trips to Intensive Care Units were inconsistent with being Manager of a Health Food Shop – he was obliged to seek whatever work he could. The day he was caught in the rain while carrying two thousand free samples of a new detergent, Neville gave way to despair and phoned the Samaritan organisation. The line was engaged.

How deeply his self-confidence had been shaken I did not realise till our next meeting. It took place as usual in a Casualty Ward, this time at St Mary's, where he had been rushed after swallowing a fishbone.

"Well, that's not unique," I said consolingly. "That happens to lots of people."

"Not when they're eating a chocolate mousse."

I discounted the strain in his tone at first, putting it down to the fact that he was also awaiting trial on a serious charge. While driving along the Bayswater Road, he'd put his hand out to indicate a right turn. His signal coincided with the arrival alongside of a motor-cycle policeman who had accelerated up to Neville's window to congratulate him on his courteous driving. Neville's hand smashed him right in the mouth.

"You must try and look on the bright side," I said. "Worse things happen at sea."

"I've been at sea," he said. "I was the only person on board to get lockjaw and seasickness at the same time. Know what I'm beginning to think? I'm coming round to the conclusion that perhaps life isn't a cabaret, old chum."

I must admit to some feeling of uneasiness when I bade him farewell and, in the event, my forebodings were justified. Neville left the hospital with every intention of making his quittance of life. The notion of throwing himself in front of a train seemed a fitting response to a world which had placed so many hazards in his own path.

He made his way swiftly to King's Cross but just outside the station he was halted by someone tugging his sleeve. It was an old woman. "Spare a silver piece, kind sir," she said. "Only a small silver piece."

"What for? he asked.

"A sprig of lucky white heather."

Despite the fact that fate had blunted most of Neville's physical features, his sense of irony remained keen. With a faint smile he handed her his last pound-note and thrust the sprig of heather into his buttonhole. There was something to be relished in the idea of casting himself in the path of a fast express while wearing a good-luck token.

Making his way to the platform where the 3.35 to Carlisle stood, he stationed himself in front of the engine. When the guard blew his whistle, he closed his eyes tightly, waited to hear the first turn of the mighty wheels, then flung himself forward.

Philosophical profundities are not really my speed but I will venture to offer you a small one: when you're a loser – it's no use even expecting to win. The train went out backwards.

A lady porter picked Neville up off the line and dusted him down. As she was due to go off duty in a few minutes anyway, she took him home with her and gave him a cup of tea, with some of her home-made ginger cake.

He's now living with her in quite blissful sin just outside Leatherhead, where they're running a small but thriving everything-shop.

Its name? Well, I suppose, in a wry kind of way, it's appropriate: THE WHITE HEATHER STORES.

'Goodbye, Mr Chips'

James Hilton
Title of Novel

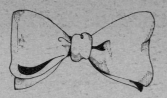

I am usually such a happy little chap, ever ready to dispel gloom with a merry quip or a saucy *bon mot*. I don't think that I would be breaking a confidence if I reveal that many years ago the lady with a mole who taught Sunday School at the Congregational Church referred to me as 'one of Nature's sunbeams'.

But a few months ago, I changed. Instead of dashing about the house wreathed in smiles and throwing off jolly epigrams I took to leaning silently against the wallpaper, scowling and plucking at the hem of my jacket.

The change came over me one day when I was lunching at the BBC canteen. I looked down at my tray, veal-loaf fritters and a waffle, and the awful realisation dawned that the meal epitomised my career; frittering my time away, and waffling on the radio. I had achieved nothing for which I would be remembered by posterity.

But what to do about it? What mark does one have to make so that when one is dead and gone one will be remembered long after one is forgotten?

The answer came to me on a bench in Hyde Park, where I was sitting brooding. A Japanese tourist beside me was fanning his face with a folded copy of the *Evening Standard* and a headline caught my eye: 'Paul Getty pays £15,000 for National Gallery's "Washerwoman"'. This seemed to me to be a stiff price to pay for recruiting domestic staff, even for a man reputedly not short of a bob, so my curiosity was aroused. I found that by getting on my knees in front of the man and synchronising my head with the oscillations of the newspaper I could read the whole piece. What emerged from the article was that Paul Getty had bought a terra-cotta portrait head from the National

Gallery. It was a study by Rodin of his washerwoman, Mme Gautier. She was a friendly, excitable woman, aged thirty-four, with two daughters, etc. etc.

Of course! The way to go down to posterity is to be sculptured! If the biography of an unknown washerwoman could, a hundred years after her death, still cool the brow of a Japanese tourist, surely the same fame would attend me? I can see the newspaper article now – 'A terra-cotta head changed hands for £15,000,000 today. It is reputedly the head of F. Muir, who lived a hundred years ago. Now famous, he was little known at the time being by trade a fritterer and waffler. A lady with a mole once called him "one of Nature's sunbeams", and certainly his noble brow betokens . . .' etc.

I set to at once to sculpt a terra-cotta head of myself to present to the National Gallery.

It seemed to me that the best way to ensure a likeness would be to work from photographs. So I persuaded the Egham Photographic Society to help. Eighty of them turned up one sunny Saturday. I formed them into a circle, stood in the middle, 'click', and a week later I had eighty photographs of my head, each taken from a slightly different angle.

The next problem was the terra-cotta. I always thought the word referred to beefy nursemaids who hurled the baby into its cot, but it turned out to be reddish clay. Happily our house is on gravel soil so I only had to dig down some five feet before striking clay. It was somewhat yellow so I mixed it with a tin of dark-brown boot-polish.

I had about enough terra-cotta to make two heads, each about the size of a grapefruit, so I decided to make a test run on one of the lumps first, just in case sculpting was more difficult than it looked.

I bashed the clay into shape with my fists and then pushed it about with a spoon and a toothpick until it began to look something like a human head. I was not attempting a likeness this time, which was a good thing because I had managed to get both ears on the same side. And three nostrils to the one nose.

Then into the oven it went, one hour at Regulo Mark 4.

When it came out – disaster. For some reason the whole head had slumped and spread. It still looked vaguely like a head but the head of a baboon.

"It's bound to sag when it's all in a lump," said my wife. "It's the same with pastry. What you want to do is treat it like we do a pie.

Make it hollow, fill it with dried peas so that it keeps its shape, then lay the top on, pinching the edges together as you do with pastry."

Which is what I did. It was a tricky operation with a tacky lump of clay-and-boot-polish, and it took nearly a pound of dried peas to fill it, but I managed it. Then I lined up my eighty photographs, took spoon in hand, and started.

Who can explain the workings of fate? Was it a fluke? Was it the awakening of latent genius? All I can say for sure is that after ten minutes with spoon and toothpick I had produced a startling likeness of myself, an amazing little portrait head which the National or any other gallery would be proud to shove in a glass case next to the postcard counter in the foyer. I shouted for my wife to come and see it.

"Incredible!" she breathed. "So lifelike, and exact. And, sort of, peaceful!"

"So it should be," I replied. "It's full of peas." (I was quite my old self again.)

With infinite care we carried the head through to the kitchen and slid it into the cooker. As my wife closed the oven door I drew a chair up to the oven and prepared for a long vigil.

"No you don't!" said my wife. "There's nothing more you can do until the clay is baked. Let's go to the pictures."

It was a Saturday, and on Saturdays my son often dropped in. He had finished at university and was working in the City. Down a hole in the City, digging up Roman remains before office blocks cemented them away for ever. It was his practice to nip home sometime over the weekend with his pockets full of clothes to be washed, stand up in the bath and scrape Thames mud and mediaeval effluent off his salient features, eat whatever he could find in the house as long as it was hot and preferably smothered in chips, and disappear, leaving a laconic note on the kitchen table.

We arrived home from the pictures. I made straight for the oven. As I had my hand on the oven door I heard my wife saying, "Hello, Jamie's been home. Funny. I don't remember leaving out a –"

At that moment I opened the oven door to look at my masterpiece. And the oven was empty.

I knew instinctively what had happened, of course. "Farewell posterity," I whispered to myself as I held my hand out for Jamie's note.

Yes, there it was in black and white. Just five words:

"Good pie. Missed the chips."

Take My
Word
For It

A snapper-up of unconsidered trifles

Shakespeare
The Winter's Tale, Act IV, Sc. 2

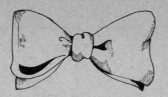

I never really liked Manby.

When he first came to the village I left a card, of course. Actually I got the cards mixed in my pocket and the one I pushed through his door was a Council card saying "Your cesspool has been emptied" but you know what I mean. I tried.

There was something about the man. Many well-to-do people have a touch of the cilious in their make-up but Manby was supercilious. Although a contemporary of mine, he had a bland, unwrinkled face with a delicate, pink complexion which tempted one to think that he ate babies. And he always seemed to wear those immensely thick tweed jackets with lumps in the tweed, as though it was woven from marmalade.

Matters rather came to a head when he invited me to dinner. He greeted me affably enough.

"What are you taking for it?" he asked.

I fingered the spot on my nose and said, "Well, actually I'm just keeping off fatty things and hoping it will go away."

He closed his eyes in a tiny expression of exasperation.

"That's a figure of speech. What do you want to *drink*?"

"Oh," I said. "I'll have the same as you're having. Pink gin, isn't it?"

"No. Actually it's gin-and-tonic but I cut my finger with the opener."

It was that sort of evening.

He had managed to get hold of some fresh salmon. This was followed by a reasonably decent Tournedos Rossini and a fine wedge of Stilton.

I had a poached egg.

Afterwards we settled down in his comfortable study, whose window, he pointed out to me, faced the sea. As the sea was forty-two miles away I thought this point irrelevant but nodded civilly. He helped himself to a brandy-and-soda from a bottle of brandy-and-soda on the desk while I drew on my cigar.

"What are you drawing on your cigar?" he suddenly asked.

I put down my ball-point guiltily.

"Just doodling," I mumbled. "A pin-man riding a bicycle."

He sighed. Reaching for a miniature score of Beethoven's Ninth Symphony he began to turn the pages, his damp lips moving as he silently hummed the first violin part.

After some ninety minutes of this he snapped the book closed, as though he had come to a decision, and looked straight at me.

"I have come to the conclusion, Muir," he said, "that you are something of a charlatan."

"Me?" I said. "A Chinese detective?"

"Not a Charlie Chan – a *charlatan*!" he said, the note of exasperation again creeping in. "A fake. Not what you purport to be. You are supposed to be quick-witted. When, I ask you man to man, were you last quick-witted in my presence. Eh? Eh?"

"Ah," I said, playing for time. Mind racing. "There was an occasion eight years ago when *you* said, 'My housekeeper is putting up fourteen pounds of gooseberry jam' and *I* said, without a moment's pause for thought, 'Up where?'."

His severe expression did not diminish. "I will go further," he said. "In that wireless programme 'My Word!' you pretend to know something of literature and you give the impression that you can play with words on the spur of the moment. It is my belief, after studying you for some years, that they are all written down for you beforehand, probably by some ghost-writing hack in your employ." He paused for effect. "It is my belief that you couldn't ad-lib pussy."

That stung. I rose to my feet, flinging away the ball-point and the remains of the cigar, which now looked like the over-tattooed forefinger of a Maori chieftain.

"Five pounds says I can!" I cried.

"Done," he said. He closed his eyes in thought for some minutes. "I will wager you five pounds that you cannot make a list of the contents of my greenhouse and turn it into a quotation from Shakespeare."

Five minutes later saw us in the greenhouse, he with a torch, me with a pad and pencil.

The first thing the torch lit up was a stuffed bird with a long beak.

"Right," I said. "Shove that old gin bottle next to it and I'm there. 'Now is the woodcock near the gin'. *Twelfth Night*."

"It isn't a woodcock," he said.

"A teal, perhaps?" I said. " 'The Winter's Teal'?"

"It's a snipe."

We moved on. The next object in the torch's beam was a frame thing with wires stretched across it.

"Got it," I said. "That thing is used for riddling top-soil. Lean a hoe against it and you have Goneril's famous line from *King Lear* 'Oh, ho, I know the riddle!'."

"I haven't got a hoe," he said, "and that isn't a riddle. It's a harp, a Welsh harp. I keep it here because it is warm and the thing won't warp."

"That thing next to it in a pot?" I asked, trying to ignore a slight feeling of desperation gripping my vitals, "Would it by any happy chance be a nut tree? Then when it begins to produce we will have 'Twelfth Nut'?"

"It's a maidenhead fern."

We moved on again. The beam lit up another potted something-or-other.

"Stop!" I said. "If that's a rose, and one of the branches comes from below the surface and is a sport, I'm home and dry – 'Out damned sport, out, out, I say!' *Macbeth*."

"It isn't a rose. I'll give you a clue. It's edible."

"Wheat!" I said. " 'A rose by any other name will smell as wheat'. *Romeo and Juliet*."

"It's corn-on-the-cob."

Defeat was staring me in the face. The fat, complacent Manby with his horrible greenhouse-cum-junkyard was going to get the better of me unless I had a bit of luck. And quickly.

I searched the gloom desperately for a bit of greenery that would fit a line of Shakespeare but it all looked the same to me.

I tried to work backwards from Shakespeare. Any pig-swill about so that I could claim 'All's Swill That Ends Swill'? Not one dollop.

Mustard and cress? 'Troilus and Cressida'? Not a leaf.

Green peppers for 'Curryolanus?' Nary a one.

Flowers? 'The Two Gentlemen of Veronica'? It was mid-winter.

A pair of pruning shears? 'Julius Scissor'?

Twine? 'The Rope of Lucrece'?

"Those seed trays!" I found myself shouting hysterically. It was my last chance. "Those trays are full of seed potatoes, aren't they? AREN'T THEY? And there you have it! Potatoes! 'Taters Andronicus'? Or, if you prefer, 'Masher for Masher'? I can even give you a line quotation, 'The quality of murphy is not strained'. I claim my five pounds, sir!"

He smiled a really nasty smile.

"They are lettuce seedlings."

I had lost. The unspeakable Manby had humbled me. But had he? As he turned to leave the greenhouse I happened to glance down at the list of items which I had jotted down and, by thunder, they *did* make up a quotation from Shakespeare!

A snipe.

A harp.

A fern.

Corn.

Seeded trayfuls.

'Take a Pair of Sparkling Eyes'

W. S. Gilbert
'The Gondoliers'

IT began when my son had one of his sore throats. While he was in the bathroom gargling I heard frantic feet thudding down the stairs, then in rushed Glinka, the au-pair girl. I use the word 'girl', but she was actually a middle-aged lady from Lapland who, prior to coming to live with us, had never left her little wooden hut in the northernmost part of Sweden. "The male child!" she shouted, yanking me to my feet, "Happen he's choking of hisself! Send for t'hospital sledge!"

Here I'd better explain that instead of learning her English at the Institute, Glinka was trying to pick it up by studying *Coronation Street*. "Coom quick!" she shouted. "The first-born! Likely he's snoofing it!"

I pelted up to the bathroom, Glinka yelping at my heels. There I found my son standing with his face up-tilted, noisily rolling salt-water round the back of this throat. "Hallo, Dad," he said. "Grrrrrr. . . ." Glinka clutched at me desperately. "Do summat!" she pleaded. "Fetch folk from 'Rover's Return'!"

"Oh, give over, Glinka," I said, "he's only gargling." There was a pause. "Doing what?" she said.

"Gargling," I said. "He's having a gargle."

She looked at me with absolute incomprehension. "Gargle?" she said. "What's yon?"

And then it was that a strange anthropological difference between our two cultures came to light. The people of Lapland do not gargle. Whether it's because the clean Arctic air protects them from sore throats or simply that seal-milk is too viscid for tracheal glugging, I don't know. All I can tell you is, Glinka had never before seen anybody performing this commonplace oral activity.

She was completely fascinated. "Show me again," she said to my son. Obediently he took another mouthful of warm salt-water. 'Grrrrr. . . .''

Her eyes shone with wonder. "Can anybody do it?" she said. "Or do you 'ave to belong to an industrialised society?"

"Have a go," I said, handing her the tumbler. She took a generous sip, tilted her head back and imitated my son's noises. Together we leapt at her, he thumping her back while I pushed her head over the washbasin. "Not quite, Glinka," he said. "Very nearly but not quite. The one essential thing to remember is – you must keep your mouth *open*."

Her next attempt was a success. And when she spat out, you should have seen the look on her face. Exhilarated isn't the word. Well, just imagine what it must feel like at the age of forty-three to discover that your body is capable of making a completely new noise! "Here, lad," she said, handing me the tumbler. "Giss a top-oop."

And from then on, there was no stopping her. Not a day passed that we didn't hear her up there in the bathroom emitting her throbbing "Grrrrr . . .", followed by chuckles of delight. No longer did she spend her time at wine and reindeer-cheese evenings at the Anglo-Lapland Club. Henceforth, every moment of leisure found her over the washbasin with our cruet and a pint tankard that the children bought her.

Well, it was such a harmless form of diversion and she derived so much inexpensive pleasure from it, it might well have continued for the rest of her sojourn with us. But six months later Britain was suddenly plunged, as seems to happen so frequently nowadays, into one of its periodic consumer crises. This time it was, of all things, a salt shortage. Overnight, every form of table-salt disappeared from the supermarket shelves and the Prime Minister found himself on yet another fast plane to Brussels. ('P.M. To Meet E.E.C. For Salt Talks.') What I was faced with, though, was the uncomfortable fact that if my household's fried chips were to retain any vestige of flavour, Glinka must sacrifice her uvula trilling.

I broke it to her as gently as I could. "I'm sorry, Glinka – but we just can't spare it any more. At a time like this, using salt for leisure-gargling is like people in wartime using petrol for inessential journeys."

I would not have thought it possible for a countenance whose component parts were so flattened to take on such a downcast expression. My son was so moved by it, he forgot to help himself to his sister's chips. "Dad," he said, "couldn't Glinka flavour her lukewarm water with something else? What about all that stuff in the spice-rack?"

Our kitchen featured a spice-rack which my daughter had purchased in Camden Market because she thought the jar labelled Cinnamon might have belonged to the author of the Maigret stories. In the jars were thyme, nutmeg, basil, oregano and something called Cumin Seed which always put me in mind of a Yorkshireman inviting you to enter his house.

After dipping a finger in each, Glinka opted for the nutmeg. "Right gradely," she said and took it upstairs. Moments later, the familiar outboard-motor noises were once more drifting down.

Now comes the peculiar bit. Over the next four weeks we became aware of a distressing change in Glinka. Not only did it manifest itself in the way she performed her duties – mashing the potatoes with the sink-plunger, scouring the saucepans with a left-over hamburger – but her whole demeanour took on aspects of the slatternly, not to say sluttish. Almost, at times – the leering. I thought at first she might just be going through the change-of-climate, but when we finally per- suaded her to see a doctor, another astonishing item of scientific infor- mation emerged.

Did you know that nutmeg is a mild intoxicant? Absolute fact – especially when taken in quantity. And having laced her gargle-water with it every day for the preceding month, quantity was certainly what Glinka had been taking it in. Not to mince words, she'd spent the whole of the past four weeks smashed out of her mind.

I know that when it's told as baldly as that, the story may arouse scepticism. But I do possess medical confirmation of it. Still available for inspection at any time during working hours is the doctor's curt note ordering us to prise Glinka away from the nutmeg. Just five words – six if hyphens don't count:

'Take au-pair off gargling spice.'

Where my caravan has rested

Edward Teschemacher

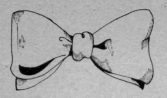

YESTERDAY afternoon, whilst gazing out of the window at the grass growing, I suddenly felt in urgent need of a walnut and a pair of braces. The ginger cat from next door was in amongst the dahlias.

The walnut was easy to find. There was one left over from Christmas, a perfect missile liable to explode with green dust on impact with the target. The firing mechanism, i.e. the pair of braces, was another matter. Where had I last seen a pair of braces about the house? For that matter, *when* had I last seen a pair of braces? As a *de rigueur* item of gents' outfittery they had gone out about the same time as sock-suspenders, long underwear and semi-stiff detachable collars.

The cat had by now trodden the dahlias flat and was eating a rhododendron. Swift action was called for.

It seemed to me that the likeliest place to find a pair of braces was the cupboard-under-the-stairs, if only because everything which became obsolete, unloved or broken ended up there.

I rushed into the cupboard and was suddenly overwhelmed by a feeling, a sensation difficult to describe, not at all unlike bashing the top of my head against the gas meter.

When I recovered consciousness I switched the light on, made sure the gas meter was still clicking away undamaged and settled down to a leisurely inspection of the contents of the cupboard. The diminution of any sense of urgency came about when I realised that I had closed the door behind me and cupboards-under-the-stairs can only ever be opened from the outside. And my wife was not due home for another three hours.

There were the usual household treasures stacked against the wall;

one left gumboot, a pile of *Radio Times* (circa 1948), a lidless tin of rock-hard green paint, a framed steel-engraving of Lord Roberts with the glass broken, a box containing nine dominoes, a gerbil cage (did we keep gerbils? Oh yes, when the children were children. The gerbils produced babies every fortnight which looked like baked beans), a hula hoop (not enough room in the cupboard to prove that my old skill had not left me), the frame of a deck-chair, two-and-a-half pairs of flippers covered with dried sand, an electric kettle of early design minus its element and cord, four Chianti bottles badly converted into reading lamps, a pile of old 78 rpm records (the only one unchipped was The Two Leslies singing 'Oh Monah'), approximately one-third of a bicycle, a school satchel (clearly labelled 'P. J. Muir, Form 1b. Touching this is punishable by death'), four home-made lampshades which should have gone on the Chanti bottles but didn't fit, a cushion which the dog had been sick on, a galvanised iron bucket with a hole in the bottom and an early edition of *Radiant Motherhood*.

By the time I had pored over and played with those relics of the past, which at today's inflated prices for items of nostalgia must represent capital of at least 80p, I had worked my way into the sharp end of the cupboard where the lower stairs and the floor came to point. Here I found an old suitcase wedged. I crawled forward on my knees, levered it free and opened it.

How the memories flooded back as I gazed down on the strange contents within! Here, carefully stored, were the inventions with which I had been going to make my fortune all those years ago. The brilliant devices I had made to fill the long-felt wants of society and make me stinking rich.

Reverently, I reached down and pulled out the top item. This was a round pad, about four inches in diameter, stuffed with feathers and covered in satin. Sewn to one edge of the pad was a six-inch circle of knicker elastic. On the opposite edge was sewn a fisherman's lead weight.

Its function was simplicity itself. The elastic was slipped around the head at forehead level and positioned so that the pad hung down and covered the left ear. The weight on the pad ensured that the pad did not flap up in a high wind. One was then fully protected against damage to the hearing whilst running for a taxi or a bus. The dilemma when catching a taxi or a bus in a hurry is, of course, whether to stay put and wait for one to come along or whether, as is usual, to hurry towards one's destination, glancing over one's right shoulder every two steps to see whether one is being overtaken by the vehicle. The next thing one knows one is lying on the pavement, semi-deaf, having crashed one's left ear into a lamp-post or a tree. The wearer of a Muir Ear-Wig (as I amusingly called it) would be immune. It seems incredible to me that no manufacturer expressed the slightest interest in the device, probably because of professional jealousy, even when I added a Continental model to the range (this fitted the right ear – for when vehicles drove on the other side of the road).

The next invention was more complicated, consisting of a black box with dials, switches and an aerial, and a pair of trousers. In essence it was a radio-operated, remote-control zip fastener, a boon for any man who feels the call of nature at the wrong moment, such as a boxer who is about to be called into the ring and has his boxing-gloves on.

I rooted round in the suitcase and found several minor inventions which never got off the ground; a tiny net for collecting goldfish bubbles to put into spirit-levels, a fine cambric moustache-snood for preventing the flotsam on the surface of minestrone soup from becoming entangled with the face hair, a silent alarm-clock for use at weekends, a rubber poker for prodding the artificial logs on electric fires . . .

I became aware of a rising mood of excitement, a feeling of expectancy. There had been one invention . . . what was it? . . . which I knew from the start was a winner. I thought hard. Of course! The Muir Patent All-Purpose Permanently Magnetised Wire! A seemingly ordinary coil of wire but, with its magnetic properties, capable of a thousand uses. Bent to the right shape it would pick up that nut which dropped off and fell into the engine of the car. Twisted straight it could be used to retrieve the house keys from behind the refrigerator. Sawn into little lengths and bent with pliers it would make a thousand magnetised staples. A piece balanced on the forefinger would point north . . .

But where was the wire? I bent over the suitcase but all I could see was a rusty old electric fan with lengths of rubber tubing and a packet of candles. What was *that* for? Ah, yes. Another brilliant idea which got nowhere. It was a device for bringing relief to dinner guests after one of my wife's curries.

You know how it is after a hot curry. Sweat breaks out on the forehead but the back of the neck goes cold and damp. My invention was designed to restore the back of the neck to its normal temperature by means of a controllable current of warm air. The fan would be connected to a socket, a row of candles would be lit and stood in front of the fan-blades and the lengths of rubber tubing would be fixed to a small gantry in front of the candle-flames and unrolled, the ends being handed to each of the curry-eating guests. When the fan was switched on the guests would point their rubber tubes at the backs of their necks and the hot air would do its work. If by any chance the curry worked the other way round and heated the back of the neck whilst the forehead went cold and clammy then the guest could direct his flexible hose towards his forehead. It was a foolproof system. But it had gone very rusty over the years.

I carefully picked the fan and all the other bits out of the suitcase and peered in. Yes, there was the coil of Muir Patent All-Purpose Permanently Magnetised Wire all right. But ruined. The rust from the fan had oxidised the wire, which was little more than a small pile of brown dust.

I was holding the small pile of brown dust in my hand, a tear of regret for lost hopes meandering down my cheek, when my wife opened the cupboard door.

"What's that mess you're holding?" she asked curiously.

"The end of a dream," I said.

"Yes, but what *is* it?"

Sadly, and slowly, I gave answer:

"Wire my curry-fan has rusted."

'I'm Dreaming of a White Christmas'

Irving Berlin
Title of song

WITH another Christmas at our throats in a mere ten days, the problem I confront is one that's been cropping up more and more these past few years. I've found out what I'm going to be given – and I don't want it.

I mention this predicament because I believe that somewhere within it lies the answer to the frequently asked question, 'What's gone wrong with the English Christmas?' To my mind, the deterioration dates back to whenever it was people stopped buying each other presents and began buying each other gifts.

Because there is a very real difference. A present is something given in the hope that it will fulfil a need or expectation. Gifts are things you buy from Gift Shops.

No High Street today is complete without its Gift Shop, usually standing where late there was a small bakery, or a cobbler's (how *did* the word for those eminently valuable tradesmen decline into its present expletive application?), or an ironmonger's where you could get a key cut while you waited, or a fruiterer who stayed open till midnight, or a drapers where the old lady would cash a cheque for you. A Gift Shop is staffed by a man who wears a brown pseud jacket and puts the word 'only' in front of every price ('Only £386'). Its heavily tarted-up front-window displays a small figurine of a shepherdess with a clock in her navel, magnetised backgammon boards, Moroccan drink-trays that have nothing to lift them up by, and things known as Executive Toys: these are designed to sit on a broad expanse of empty desk and either hit one part of themselves against another part, or flash a succession of tiny lights in so random a fashion that you begin to realise why so many stockbrokers are jumping out of windows.

Those are gifts, as distinct from presents. They are the new 'giving-objects', artefacts designed not for use or enjoyment but simply as currency for Christmas transactions. Within the shop's bedizened interior you can purchase loo-seats that shine in the dark, Mickey Mouse sundials, cans of spray-on dandruff, battery-operated tooth-picks, polythene snowmen and a frozen mushroom-pizza with 'Happy Xmas' spelt out in anchovies.

And, of all these non-felt wants, the one that makes my heart sink almost to knee-level is the gift for which, so I've discovered, my well-meaning sister paid out her good money this Yuletide – a Scandinavian Candle-Making Kit. The cinema in my skull is already screening its presentation ceremony: "Oh, it's a candle-making kit!... And *Scandinavian*!"

"You sure you haven't got one?"

"I'm practically certain."

Are you familiar with that particular kind of jaw-muscle ache that comes only from maintaining a grateful smile for six hours? The kind where you become convinced you're going to have to send for a doc-tor because your face has locked? I'll be down with it practically all Christmas Day. And I can also tell you the moment I fear most.

"Aren't you going to try it? Oh, go on. Make a candle for Auntie Rose."

My handedness at all manual endeavours is so invincibly cack, I can hardly bear thinking about all those lumps of wax and rolls of wick and plastic moulds – and *hot tallow*!

If any of you are curious to know which seasonal tune I'll be carolling Christmas Day after the relatives have departed, I can already hum it for you:

'I'm cleaning off a white grease mess.'

The more haste the less speed

Proverb

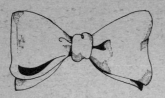

WHEN I was but a lad of some twelve summers (we only had summers when I was a lad) I was quiet and introspective, much given to leaning against the bandstand on the seafront at Broadstairs and undoing knots in string.

During one of my leans, when I was trying to perfect a technique of whistling 'Won't You Do, Do, Do What You Done, Done, Done Before, Baby' whilst at the same time undoing a knot in a piece of string, a disturbing thought struck me. I had made no plans for the future. I had formulated absolutely no ambitions whatever. And unless I came up with a few thoughts fairly quickly I would suddenly wake up to find myself aged forty-eight and still leaning up against the bandstand undoing knots in string.

Boys, unless they are the sons of clergymen, doctors or soldiers in which case they know from the age of two that they are either going to follow in father's footsteps or would rather drop dead than so do, rarely have firm ideas on what they want to do with their lives. The best most boys can rake up in the way of ambitions is to own a 1,000,000 cc. Japanese motorbike that will do 250 mph, or to have all their teeth pulled out so that they won't have to brush them any more, or to marry Raquel Welch. Only a few can hope to achieve any of these.

I proved to have been made of more thoughtful clay. After a mere eight leans I came up with not one ambition but *three*.

My three ambitions could be classified as (*a*) achieving a triumph of physical skill, (*b*) proving to myself that I possessed courage and initiative and (*c*) aiming high in the matter of a career.

More specifically these ambitions consisted of (*a*) managing to touch the tip of my nose with my tongue, (b) cycling at full speed along Broadstairs jetty with my eyes shut and completing eight turns of the pedals without opening them, and (c) becoming a recognised expert at something.

Alas, it seems that the loftier one raises the structure of one's aspirations the more likely – life being what it is – that it will descend about one's ears like cheap hair cream on a hot day.

After months of constant practice in school, at church, on buses, I finally had to admit to myself that there was an unbridgeable gap twixt the end of my tongue and the tip of my nose and never the twain were going to meet. The trouble was that I had an extra-long upper lip, as normally found on horses, so I decided I would be better employed on obscuring this by growing a moustache. I concentrated hard on forcing the moustache out and my singlemindedness worked – eight years later it emerged. I have it still.

My failure to cycle along the jetty with my eyes closed for eight turns of the pedals was a great disappointment to me at the time. But looking back I take great comfort in the fact that although it was high tide and the light was none too good on that cold February afternoon and there was a strong crosswind I did not lose my nerve and open my eyes. It was just that after six turns of the pedals I ran out of jetty.

My ambition to become recognised as an expert in something was, I admit, a little on the vague side. I took it for granted that it would be in some esoteric area like ferret-sexing, or comparative religion but I held no strong views on which; I just wanted to be an expert. Well, it has happened. A paltry forty-six years later my ambition has been fulfilled. It is fairly well recognised now by most civilised nations that I am the acknowledged expert on The Maintenance of Carpets in Households which include an Incontinent Afghan Hound Puppy.

My pre-eminence in the subject became undisputed when I began to write books for children about an Afghan puppy called What-a-mess. These were so successful, the sales soaring to double figures within months of publication, that hardly a week passes now without a postcard flooding in asking my advice in the matter of carpets and puppies. As postage rates are rising so high that it will soon be cheaper to send a letter by taxi this seems to be the moment to put into print my own experience of the puppy versus carpet problem and how I cope with it.

What-a-mess in the books is a fictional puppy based on our own small Afghan. He is a normal little chap, as well-behaved as any Afghan puppy. That is to say, he steals all food that is not under lock and key, chews chair legs, sits on top of the hedge and breaks it, jumps over the fence and disappears and digs holes four-feet deep in the lawn. Afghans are natural diggers. You will find no record of an Afghan Hound ever having been incarcerated in Colditz for the simple reason that no Kommandant could keep an Afghan in Colditz long enough to get its name and Kennel-Club number. I would give a fairly lazy Afghan eight minutes to dig its way out of Colditz. Ten if it was solid rock beneath.

And ours is as intelligent as any Afghan puppy. He knows perfectly well the difference between outdoors and indoors; he knows that in one he can streak about at full speed, dig and answer the calls of nature in peace and seclusion and in the other he can sleep. The trouble is that he gets them the wrong way round. He sleeps outside then comes into the house, tries to dig a hole in the parquet floor, leaps on to the dining-room table and sits in the mashed potatoes, gets up a speed of forty knots along the upstairs landing and then, when your back is turned, leaves a $9'' \times 5''$ damp map of Corsica sinking slowly into the pile of the carpet.

Further, once the $9'' \times 5''$ map of Corsica has been bestowed upon the carpet, the puppy has a compulsion to keep it fresh. To replenish it hourly. And then, to be on the safe side, to start a little reserve Sardinia by the radiator.

It was only by diligent observation and careful reasoning that I was able to make the breakthrough, to beat the Corsica problem and establish my reputation as the world's leading expert on the matter.

We have our Mrs Hayes who comes in twice a week and goes through the house like a tornado, elbows going like pistons, carrying all dirt and dust before her and leaving furniture and carpets like new. Mrs Hayes went away for three months to visit her son in Australia and I noticed that the maps of Corsica on the carpet increased ten-fold in her absence. I pondered why. Then I had a flash of inspiration. Dogs instinctively return to the scene of their crime. It's a matter of scent, or something, but the presence of a damp map of Corsica prompts the beast to re-anoint the same patch of carpet. Answer? Scrub out all traces of the first map of Corsica and the puppy is not tempted.

And so it proved. Mrs Hayes returned from Australia, went at the carpet with cleaner, brush and vacuum and the puppy soon lost interest.

From this experience I formulated a maxim which all carpet and Afghan puppy owners might well ponder. As far as *my* carpets are concerned:

The more Hayes'd the less peed.

Your money or your life!

Attr. Dick Turpin

IF people really do profit by their mistakes, by rights I should now be one of the richest men in the country. As just one example of what's happened to me in the rue-it-yourself area, let me tell you about the time I decided to avail myself of a Computer Dating Service.

Although that title may sound like a service for people desirous of dating a computer, it's actually a sort of electronic Match Factory. If you're a male, they give you a blue form on which you are asked to tick off your particular preferences and predilections in regard to the opposite sex. That form is then fed into an impressive machine which makes a whirring noise as it compares your blue form with a whole bunch of pink forms it has previously swallowed on behalf of various ladies who've signed on for the service. If the ticks on your blue one happen to coincide exactly with those on somebody's pink one, the ingenious mechanism utters the technological equivalent of 'snap!', ejects that pink one and there she is, the mate that fate had you created for.

What put me on to the service was hearing a chap in my office holding forth to an interested group about how he'd met his wife through Computer Dating. The reason he was going on with such fervour about it was that it had happened the previous day and they'd already been married eight years. So the point he was trying to impress on us was that although such accidents do occur, they only ever happen through pilot-error; in other words, careless or incorrect completion of the blue form.

So that became the part of the procedure over which I took the greatest pains. The first section of it, requesting my own personal history – all that 'where-were-you-born-and-what-did-you-do-before-that?' stuff – that presented no problems at all, unless you count having to ask the invigilator whether 'Freckles' ought to be written inside the box headed 'State any serious childhood ailments'.

It was when I came to Section Two, 'What type of opposite sex person are you seeking?', that I made myself stop and think hard. Mindful of the unhappy encounter resulting from my colleague's failure to supply adequate detail at this point, I set myself to writing what amounted to an in-depth profile of the woman my life had been spent in search of. So carefully did I outline the specifications for my ideal, so minutely did I describe the characteristics I'd always failed to find in a partner, my text over-ran the little boxes and I had to request four extra blue forms.

When they fed them into the machine it soon became obvious that no previous client had ever been this painstaking. Something inside the mechanism spluttered, the overhead lights dimmed, red bulbs blinked on and off and the sprinkler-system came on. "Please leave by the emergency exit," the machine's trainer said somewhat abruptly. "We'll have to send you your answer in the post." Sure enough, the letter arrived three days later, giving me a name, detailed arrangements for meeting under the clock at Waterloo Station and a description by which I would recognise her.

We had an unforgettable evening. It included a visit to 'Singa-longa-Max' where we even sunga-longa the intermission, a *table à deux* at the Curry House and an arm-in-arm stroll through the all-night Tesco's. It was there, in the Pickles And Spices aisle, that I said, "Your place or mine?"

When we entered her front door, she indicated that I should go on up while she put the chain on. When I entered the lounge, the first thing I saw was her husband.

"Hallo," he said. "Had a nice evening?"

"Yes thanks, Dad," I replied. He went up to bed, my mother put her apron on to make a cup of tea and I sat there brooding about computers and how they always take your requests so *literally*.

I didn't come to any real conclusions, except that although Computer Dating Services may be all right for some, if you're anything like me and the chap at the office all you're likely to end up with is what you might call Dick Turpin's choice:

Your mummy or your wife.

'Hello! Hello! Who's Your Lady Friend?'

Music Hall Song

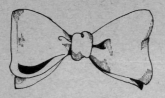

WE, the duly and democratically elected officers of the Thorpe Players Amateur Dramatic Society (tickets available at the door or from Nellie at the Thorpe Village Shop) are not easily panicked. We like to think, and audiences who miss the last bus home tend to agree with us, that we act slowly. We tend to weigh the pros and cons carefully before agreeing to do nothing rather than rush precipitously into action.

I refer you to the crisis of '63 (see the files of *Staines and Egham News* for full reportage) when, at the Annual General Meeting, a splinter group endeavoured to outvote the committee and accept the merger bid from the Egham Thespians. It was a nasty moment for us traditionalists. Egham Thespians had a reputation for going in for somewhat racier productions than was our wont; their staging of *Getting Gertie's Garter* caused many an Egham eyebrow to uplift, I can tell you. And the splinter group outnumbered us by five to four (it was an unusually high turnout for an AGM). But we did not panic. Just before the vote my vice-chairperson and prompter, Mrs Spink, rose to her feet and quietly reminded the meeting of the dramatic traditions which we had always cherished in the Players. After forty-five minutes of this I noticed that two of the splinter group – the old Dinwiddie brothers – were fast asleep so I quickly called a vote and we staved off the threat by four votes to three.

No, panic does not come easily to us fathers of Thorpe Players. But it came one black Thursday, just three days before the opening of our most ambitious production to date, a full musical comedy adapted by me from a work by Mr Sandy Wilson.

Most dramatic societies consist mainly of women and their problem is how to cast *The Importance of Being Earnest* with forty-two f's to select from but only two m's, the two m's consisting usually of a retired Civil Servant with an inaudible voice and no memory and an enthusiastic youth six feet seven in height with terminal acne. Our problem was the other way round – we had plenty of men but only one woman. This unusual circumstance came about when work began on the motorway near Thorpe and the village filled with sturdy, rather playful construction workers. For some reason the girls in our Society seemed to prefer their society to ours. The one lady we have, our leading and only lady, Miss Tozer, is so ample of build and homely of countenance that she has not as yet been offered temptation.

Finding it impossible to locate a play with a cast of 14 m : 1 f I decided to adapt Mr Wilson's musical comedy *The Boy Friend*. I twisted the story round so that it was not about a party of schoolgirls but of schoolboys. They go on an outing to Guildford and all fall in love with an adorable little French au-pair girl Antoinette (Miss Tozer). The songs adapted quite well ('Sur la Plage' became 'On the Towpath', 'A Room in Bloomsbury' became 'A Tent at Penton Hook', etc.). The title had to be changed from *The Boy Friend*, of course. I originally considered calling it *The Girl Friend* but I eventually decided on *The Lady Friend* as being more suitable for our audiences, some of whom come from Virginia Water and the superior end of Egham Hythe.

Rehearsals seemed to go swimmingly. Miss Tozer's frame may have been vast but, as so often is the case with enormous ladies, her voice was a high, light soprano and she was in fine condition. Mr Haddock, the organist, managed to repair the bellows of the harmonium with a bicycle puncture outfit and the musical accompaniment was strong and rich. We gaily bought a new bulb for our footlight.

Then, on the Thursday before our opening on the Monday, Mr Haddock turned up at my house, his face a mask of woe.

"Out with it, Haddock," I said instantly. "What has happened, man?"

Mutely he swung on his heel. I followed him out of the gate and along Coldharbour Lane towards our theatre, Thorpe Village Hall (originally a mediaeval tithe barn. Good brickwork but not as interesting as the church which is partly Saxon with fine modern stained glass windows). Entering the hall he flung out an arm and pointed towards where, below the stage, stood the harmonium.

"Great Heavens!" I breathed. The right-hand side of the keyboard had disappeared. From Middle C leftwards all was well but above

Middle C there was nothing. It was horrible, horrible. Like the grin of somebody who has had half his teeth removed. I was looking at a harmonium capable of accompanying bass singers and light baritones but not tenors or sopranos.

"And we open Monday," he said with a terrible calmness. "Who could have *done* this? Why? Why?" I comforted him as best I could.

"We of the governing body of the Thorpe Players do not yield easily to panic," I said. "It is clear that we must replace Miss Tozer with a lady baritone, and pretty damn' chop-chop. Let us to work."

Thorpe village ladies turned out to be a nest of singing birds. All of them sopranos. Few of them could get as low as Middle C, let alone sing 'I Could Be Happy With You' completely below it. Mrs Hayes made a valiant effort but only succeeded in bursting a – mercifully non-essential – button on her blouse.

Like most police work it demanded dogged patience and the skin of a rhinoceros. Late Friday afternoon I found myself addressing our last hope of finding a baritone leading lady, Mrs Knight of the fishshop.

"Nora," I said thickly, my eyes red with fatigue, "I need a special type of woman on Monday night. How low can you get?"

Looking back on it I am only glad that the fishshop was in Virginia Water and I was slapped on the face with a side of smoked salmon rather than a kipper.

It was a morose organist indeed who accompanied me on a sad stroll through the village on Saturday morning, all hope seemingly lost. "Are all Thorpe voices high?" I queried petulantly. "Are there no low? Is there not *one* low?"

At that moment we hove in sight of the allotments, those patches of ground on which a gracious Urban District Council allows grateful ratepayers to grow leeks and potatoes and so forth at a nominal rental.

"Look!" shouted Mr Haddock suddenly, grabbing my arm and then breaking for the first time since I had known him into swear words, "Great Handel, our most illustrious immigrant!" Following the line of his quivering finger I saw merely rows of lettuces and carrots and beans, each with a neat white label at its base.

"My bloody harmonium keys!"

And so it transpired. A tall lean figure straightened up from weeding and in a melodious bass-baritone voice explained all. He was Hugh Fimbo, a well-known local part-time gardener and full-time lover of ale.

"They be my plant labels," he said. "I done found 'em in the Village

Hall on Thursday afternoon, on an old harmonium. Nobody was using the said instrument so I took away a few of the keys. Lovely they be for plant labels. Shove the wooden bit in the earth and write the plant's name on the ivory bit. See?"

"Wait!" said Mr Haddock in a strangely choked voice. Then, turning to me, "Can you fit Hugh immediately with a size $10\frac{3}{4}$ wig, an outsize dress and size $10\frac{1}{2}$ high-heeled strap shoes?"

"What on earth for?" I riposted.

"Your search is over!" he countered. "Did you not hear his voice? You have found at last what you need after listening to a hundred high voices!"

"And what is that?" I asked, still mystified.

"A *low*! A *low*! *Hugh*'s your 'Lady Friend'!"

The mass of men lead lives of quiet desperation

Thoreau
'*Walden*'

NOT that long ago, I was conscripted for one of those po-faced television discussion-programmes which, when I'm at home viewing them, give me an intellectual sensation as of swimming through wet sand. It was around the subject of Marriage, I can't remember the precise theme – probably something on the lines of 'Do married women make the best wives?' – but, as expected, it turned out so boring that after about twenty minutes I'd got to the stage where I could actually *feel* my finger-nails growing.

Then came the big action scene. Just as I was beginning to think that *rigor mentis* had set in, I suddenly realised the rest of the panel were all looking at me. "I was asking you, Denis Norden," the chairman said patiently – as in Russian novels, chat-show participants are always addressed by both their names – "What would be your views on this delicate matter?"

"Oh, I'm for it," I said immediately. "Absolutely one hundred per cent for it!" The one thing I've learnt about TV debates is that when you have no idea what anyone's talking about – be *forceful*.

The faces of my fellow-panellists tightened and the chairman's eye-brows practically disappeared into his widow's peak. "You really believe that it's important for a young couple to sleep together before marriage?"

". . . Oh, that." Rapidly I put my brain into top. Then, drawing a deep breath, "Not only do I believe it important," I said, "I think it should be mandatory."

Now, because of the frantic ructions that this answer aroused – the BBC's switchboard practically ran molten from heated telephone-calls – I'd like to take this opportunity of explaining what I was actually advocating. In fact, it had nothing at all to do with Sex. I was thinking about Marriage.

The brutal point is that despite today's so-called open-ness of discussion regarding what goes on in a bedroom, there is one element of the action there that society still conceals from the adolescent male. It is the fact that women, as well as men, snore. In the face of all those Sex Education classes and all the instruction-pamphlets that come through the post when you get engaged, that truth still remains womanhood's best-kept secret. This very night, thousands of young men are going out for their first fumble in the profound conviction that the only gender that snorts in its sleep is the male.

To all those young men, let me say with all the urgency I can muster – not so. Yes, as Hemingway promises, yes, she may well make the earth move for you. But *after* the earth's moved – when she's turned over on her side and closed her eyes – she can also make the bedside-lamp rattle. By all means write poems to the honey that hides in those lips, sing songs to the promise that lurks in those eyes – but be mindful also of the power that resides in that nose. It can produce a sound like an approaching motor-boat.

And why is the possession of this knowledge so relevant to marriage? Because it's the one area of that sacred covenant nobody ever warns you about. Never mind the for-richer, for-poorer commitment – those aspects are tolerable because they are a *shared* experience. The one that is solitary, the one that has to be borne in loneliness, is staring up at the ceiling while you wait for the next rumble from the flaked-out figure at your side. Because, lad, the other grim truth is that in any bed where two people are gathered together, the one that snores is also the one that goes to sleep first.

What is more, the snores of a small woman are so much more burdensome than those of a large man. The bigger a man is, the burlier, the more heft he carries, the more even and regular his snore. Loud it may be, I'm not disputing that, but the main characteristic of the heavy male snore is its rhythm. And, as any scientist will tell you, a rhythmic sound is something a person can accustom herself to, adapt to – even, I venture, be lulled by. But when a woman snores . . . I tell you, son, the succession of sounds they emit is so unpredictably irregular, so alarmingly spasmodic, it can be heart-stopping. And what some of them go in for as well is a peculiarly urgent kind of gasp, like a diver who's got his air-lines crossed.

Now do you appreciate why I publicly advocated couples sleeping together before marriage? It was so that all those hulking youths who so often seem to favour diminutive girls won't discover, when it's too late, that they have taken unto themselves a partner who makes the night hideous with nasal obbligatos. As was once observed – more in Thoreau than in anger –

The massive men need wives of quiet respiration.

Between the devil and the deep blue sea

Proverbial saying

HOW splendid and Faust-like to be given the choice of yielding to Beelzebub or diving into the briny. And how seldom life offers up such dramatic alternatives. In most people's lives, i.e. mine, the hinges which determine one's destiny are hidden and the only decisions which one is given the chance to make are on a lesser scale, usually in the area of choosing between navel oranges at 10p each or a smaller, knobblier variety at 6p, or between the hard-wearing herring-bone tweed suit and the trendy beige.

But sometimes life gives a hiccup and presents one with a dilemma which is both dramatic and difficult to resolve.

My life, to date, has not been the stuff of which heroic autobiographies are made. Indeed it has been extremely difficult to whip up a paragraph calculated to get the turnstiles humming at the prospect of hearing me speak to the Thorpe Derby And Joan Club. Not for me those author's blurbs along the lines of: 'After leaving Eton under a cloud he served for some time in the Foreign Legion before escaping and helping to found a trout-farm in Chile. A spell as a lumberjack in Cheltenham was followed by being elected a fellow of All Souls from which he progressed to becoming the guttering-buyer of a departmental store in Atlanta, Georgia . . .' etc. My progress has been more like a Poohstick's carried along by a sluggish current from one patch of weeds to another.

And yet it happened. The Big Decision.

The four most emotionally satisfying events of my pale life have been (*a*) marrying, (*b*) buying my first boat, (*c*) getting rid of the boat, (*d*) being elected Rector of the University of St Andrews, Fife, Scotland. And it is the last of these of which I speak.

Rectorship is not only a peculiarly Scottish institution, it is also just plain peculiar. The Rector is elected solely by the students and his loyalty is entirely to the students and their welfare, yet by virtue of the high standing of his office he chairs the University Court, which meets once a month.

My first year in office was wholly delightful. I flew up to Edinburgh on British Airways Shuttle Service – an admirable service once you have swallowed the unpalatable fact that when the trolley comes up the gangway it is only to take your ticket: there are no drinks. Which is rather like realising at an accident that there is no hot, sweet tea. There were a couple of other slight complications that had to be got used to, e.g. on the drive from the airport to St Andrews the toll bridge does not take luncheon vouchers. And on the Motorway there is no Exit 7. As the route to St Andrews requires you to come off at Exit 8 this means that you overshoot and hurtle towards Perth unless you are vigilant. Why the Exits go from 6 to 8 seems to be a mystery locked in the bosom of the Kingdom of Fife.

Once in St Andrews I unpack in room fifteen of the Star Hotel. This is bang in the middle of this wholly delightful grey granite fishing village and room fifteen has advantages; it is, perhaps, two yards away from the church bell which tolls the hours, but it is large and warm.

One of the problems with paying a monthly visit to the east coast of Scotland is anticipating the weather. One leaves the decadent south-east of England in the hard-wearing herring-bone tweed and is projected into another clime. St Andrews, it seems to me, gets the best of whatever weather is hanging about Scotland, but this is somewhat unpredictable. So, with the connivance of the management of the hotel, I leave two garments in their broom-cupboard so that I will not be caught unprepared. For an onslaught of cold weather I have left a duffel coat; a vast, fawn tent which did service during the last war on the bridges of many of His Majesty's vessels, going down twice, and which has since served as a lying-in bed for the Afghan Hound to have her puppies on, a comforter for motor-car engines in frosty weather and a surrogate womb for seed potatoes. Should I run into a heat wave I have left a T-shirt. This cost me 15p at an auction in aid of a book-trade charity. It is a deeply unpleasant shade of bright blue and has across its front the words, 'Proof-readers Rule, O.J.?'

Members of the University Court were most kind to their ignorant and amateur chairman. Professors, lecturers, local council members and other Court participants leaned over backwards to put their chairman at ease and I was not at all worried until about the seventh meeting. Then I was aware of something rather strange. When I arrived for the meeting at 10 a.m. the whole assemblage was there as though to welcome me but although one face was glum the rest were smiling. As other meetings followed I became more aware of the pattern. At one meeting the University Architect would be downcast and the rest happy. A month later the Quaestor and Factor would look extremely miserable and the rest smiling.

The University, arguably the best university in the world, has a most efficient grapevine. What I learned from the grapevine was rather surprising. Apparently I had always turned up at the Court meeting wearing the hard-wearing herring-bone tweed. Members of the Court, racked with ennui after an hour of their chairman, had begun a sweepstake as to when I would turn up dressed differently. Hence the one unhappy face who had drawn that month only to see me turn up in the same old herring-bone tweed.

The grapevine also revealed that this month the one who stood to gain from my change of clothing was the University Secretary, David Devine. The sweepstake suddenly took on a new significance. It is Mr Devine who passes my claims for expenses and I am rather keen on upping my drive from Edinburgh airport to St Andrews from a bicycle to a moped. If I can cause him to win the sweepstake – which stands, the grapevine tells me, at a jackpot of 95p – I stand every chance of having my higher expenses passed by Devine intervention.

I swung into action immediately. I have a small wardrobe, and an even smaller collection of clothes within it. But I bundled the lot into a plastic bag for taking to the dry-cleaners so that I would have a selection of clothes with which to win Mr Devine his jackpot. It is a curious thing about laundries and dry-cleaners that once one has packed the stuff up to be taken one somehow assumes that the job is done and one forgets all about it. Suffice it to say that yesterday I suddenly found the plastic bag with all my clothes scrunched up in it and tomorrow I am off to St Andrews. Our local 24-Hour Cleaners are swifter than most but even they take three days.

I resolved to dry-clean the suits myself. All one needs, I reasoned, is a bucket of French chalk, a gallon of carbon tetrachloride and something to tumble the mixture and the clothes around in.

I found my something just along the road where they are building an extension to our local motorway – a nearly new, clean, bright cement-mixer. I tipped the bag of clothes in, poured in the fluid and the powder, started the motor and stood back to watch as the engine roared away and the drum spun merrily round. All was going well until I noticed, to my horror, a huge, revolving lorry backing remorselessly towards my mixer. I shouted out but all the machinery was making a shocking noise. As I watched helplessly the revolving bit of the lorry slowly tilted and about half a ton of wet cement poured into my mixer. My entire wardrobe is now half a yard of the M.25 (Sunbury to Basingstoke extension).

So if I am to wear something different tomorrow I will have to face the University Court wearing one of the two garments hanging up in in the Star Hotel's broom-cupboard. My choice is pathetically simple:

Between the duffel and the cheap, blue 'T'.

'Oh, Mr Porter, What Shall I Do?'

Music Hall Song

I had a profound and disturbing thought recently –
not that I don't have them quite often, of course – but this one really
brought me down. I was suddenly struck by the fact that, despite the
many years I've been on the entertainment scene, nobody has ever
tried to bribe or corrupt me.

I can't tell you how *small* that made me feel. I mean, every newspaper
you pick up nowadays seems to have a story about somebody in the
show-business receiving illicit offers of call-girls or Greek villas or
Swiss bank-deposits. But me – never. Nothing. Not even a book-token.

The more I thought about that, the lower my spirits sank. To such an
extent that the very next day I went round to my agent and put it to
him straight. "Are there any jobs going where a chap can get himself
tarnished?"

He's a nice fellow, my agent, very good-hearted, a warm and
wonderful friend, but anything that's the least bit out-of-the-way you
have to explain it as to a sleepy child. "What I would like you to find
me," I said, enunciating very slowly and with plenty of pauses so it
would sink in, "is a post of trust . . . which I can betray . . . for gain."

A small cloud of incomprehension settled about his face. "A position
of power," I went on doggedly, "that I can abuse. For my own
contemptible purposes. And when I say contemptible –"

"Before you go into that, Den," he broke in, "I had something come
up I meant to ring you about. Some holiday camp. They're enquiring
for somebody from the wireless to judge a Beauty Contest. The money's
not much but you get a cooked supper and . . ."

But I was no longer listening. It was perfect! Little though he
realised it, corruption-wise it could not have suited my purpose better.

Well, we've all read about what goes on at those Beauty Contests, haven't we? All those squalid behind-the-scenes episodes, where a desperate group of beautiful girls, all seeking the coveted First Prize, vie with each other to win the attention of a judge? Swiftly my mind ran through the scenario. "Really, Miss Orkneys And Shetlands, are you hinting that I should show you special favour? If that is so, we'd better sit down and discuss it. Tell me, child, are you not a little too warm in that sash . . .?"

Out loud, I said, "Book me on the next train."

Well, it wasn't what you'd call a large holiday camp. It wasn't even what you'd call a medium-size holiday camp. What you would call it, I think, was a dump. It had previously been an open prison, I was told, but the present owner – a certain Miss Dora Tapwater – had managed to convert it to holiday camp standards by sealing up a few more entrances and adding extra barbed wire. For what I had in mind, though, it could not have been more suitable. So, immediately on arrival, I presented Miss Tapwater with the text of an announcement to be put out over her loud-speaker system: 'The judge for the Beauty Contest is now available for consultation in Chalet Number Two.'

"You're not up to any funny business, are you?" she asked sharply. "Because I'm not running that kind of holiday camp here. This place is for parents and families, so I don't allow goings-on."

Throttling back the impulse to enquire how she thought parents managed to achieve families without resort to goings-on, I put on my most guileless face and assured her I was merely seeking background detail from the girls. Although remaining suspicious – "I scan every chalet door through a marine telescope after Lights Out!" – she finally consented to my veiled invitation being broadcast.

I had to sit in Chalet Two for nigh on three hours before I got a nibble. Then, just as my scented cachous were beginning to wear off, an envelope was pushed under my door. Leaping to my feet, I ripped it open and pulled out a sheet of perfumed notepaper and a photograph. I scanned the note first. 'Dear Judge, I would do anything to win First Prize.' The word 'anything' was underlined. Three times. In red! Pulses pounding, I read on. 'Soon as that old cow with the telescope nods off, I'll be back with an open mind and two bottles of milk stout. P.S. Hope the photo don't shock you. It shows me in the costume I wore when I won this same contest last year.'

As it happens, I didn't even get as far as looking at what she was wearing. When I turned to the photograph, the first thing that leapt to my eyes was the inscription on the trophy she was holding.

What I'd forgotten about holiday camps, you see, was that when they say they cater to every member of the family, they really do mean every member. Across the trophy, in bold capitals, were the triumphant words: 'First Prize, Most Glamorous Granny Contest.'

Thirty seconds after the words had sunk in, the camp's proprietor had her lonely vigil interrupted by an urgent telephone-call. The message, in as disguised a voice as its still uncorrupted owner could muster, must have sounded like the echo of an old song:

Oh, Miss Tapwater, Watch Chalet Two.

If you have tears, prepare to shed them now

Shakespeare
Julius Caesar, Act III, Sc. 2

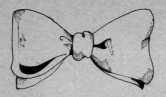

IT seems that in meteorological offices all over the country the seaweed has been dying in handfuls and not a corn has throbbed on a meteorological toe for months. The chaps held a meeting about it and issued an alarming statement. They say that the weather pattern is changing and we are due for a run of very hot summers.

This is bad news of the worst sort. If they had forecast a run of cold winters there would be no cause for dismay. As a nation we know how to cope with cold winters: at the first light fall of snow paraffin disappears off the market, the miners go on strike, all railway-line points freeze solid and doctors warn that Algerian 'flu is about to sweep the country and decimate the population. We just grit our teeth, force a smile and suffer on.

But hot summers are another dish of tea entirely. Look what happened when we had a bit of sun in the summer of '76; reservoirs dried to a puddle, lawns went brown, roads melted and doctors warned that Yugoslavian 'flu was about to sweep the country and slay one in eight. We all went about panting like retrievers, wearing too many clothes and longing for a cold bath which we couldn't have because there wasn't enough water.

It seems to me that if hot summers are going to be our lot from now on then we should prepare for them. Make a few plans.

Take clothes. I have given the matter some thought and it seems to me that we British are not going to go mad and dress like Hawaiian beachboys whatever the temperature. We will continue to wear our suits to work, perhaps leaving off our waistcoats when the thermometer rises above 100°F. So what we must do is provide our clothes with suitable ventilation.

Go to your nearest ironmonger and buy yourself what is called a leather punch. This is like a pair of pliers with a spiky thing on the end of one of the jaws. This spiky thing is really a collection of long holes of different widths. Select the widest hole, which is about a third of an inch, and systematically work your way over your suit, punching holes through the fabric at the rate of twelve to the foot. When you have completely perforated the suit do the same to your underwear.

Now you might think that all these holes in both your suit and your underwear will result in loss of modesty. Not so. Whilst wearing your ventilated clothes you keep gently on the move at all times, even when sitting down. Just a slight movement – a gentle shimmy as though moved by distant Latin American music – is enough to prevent the holes in underclothing and outer clothing from coinciding.

Keeping the home cool is a more complicated problem. An ideal method is to open the front door and the back door and to get an elephant to stand at the back door flapping its ears. This results in a pleasing through-draught.

Another procedure which gives good results is to save up odds and ends of household fluids like the washing-up water, unconsumed tea or milk which has gone sour, and fling the lot over the drawing-room wallpaper. This is known as 'cooling by evaporation'.

Getting to sleep at night can be a problem. One solution is to fling open the bedroom window, chuck a pillow out, follow it and sleep outside on the lawn.

A better method is to put your pyjamas into the refrigerator for an hour before retiring. Don't put them in the deep-freeze or severe lacerations can result.

Cars are a frightful problem during periods of heat. For one thing they tend to boil over if you stop at a traffic-light for more than four seconds. This is because of the anti-freeze in the radiator. Anti-freeze is a mixture of alcohol and water which has the property of not freezing in cold weather but, unhappily, boiling at the drop of a hat in hot weather. What you must do is to drain off the anti-freeze and refill the radiator with a mixture which is almost all water with hardly any alcohol in it at all. So park the car outside a pub, run a hose in from the radiator and ask the barman to fill her up with British keg bitter, the alcohol content of which is negligible.

Always carry a siphon of soda-water in the boot. When a car has been standing a few minutes in the sun you can fry eggs on the plastic upholstery. Before entering the car spray the seats generously with soda-water to cool them, then take your shirt off and mop the seats thoroughly. Put shirt back on (see above: 'cooling by evaporation').

The most grievous problem of all with cars is stopping the tyres from exploding. Air expands when warm and on a hot day in the South of France you can hear tyres popping off all around you like artillery fire.

The only hope is to keep the sun off the tyres as much as possible. A good idea is to hire a furniture van, get your wife to precede you along the road and when you need to park just drive up the ramp and into the back of the van. But this is rather too expensive for most people and there is a snag – the tyres of the van tend to explode.

The French sometimes drape little raffia mats over their tyres when parking in the sun but these mats blow off or slide down unless nailed firmly to the tyres – a stratagem which I found to be self-defeating.

The tyre problem seemed insoluble until I put my mind to it and came up with a complete answer. Here is what you do. Take a train or a plane to Edinburgh. Half-way up Princes Street there is a shop which sells tartans and knitting patterns. Buy a knitting pattern for a highland bonnet and half a hundredweight of knitting wool the same colour as your car.

When you get home take the knitting pattern and multiply all the numbers of stitches by ten. Start knitting. When you have finished you will have a giant highland bonnet. Knit another three giant highland bonnets. Carry them out to the car, jack up each wheel in turn and fit it with a bonnet, making sure that the rim of the bonnet fits snugly round the tread and the pom-pom is dead centre. Your tyres will now be permanently shaded from the sun for as long as you care to leave the car parked. To drive away simply jack the wheels up again and remove the bonnets.

To work! Don't let the next hot summer catch you unawares.

If you have tyres, prepare to shade them *now*.

Falstaff will die of a sweat

Shakespeare
King Henry V, Part 2, Epilogue

"IF you maintain your garden regularly," said the voice on the radio, "you can have something fresh-cut every day." I reached for my notebook. "The only something fresh-cut my garden gives me every day," I wrote, "is lawn-mower lead."

It was yet another telling point in the long list of indictments I was preparing against my garden lawn. My case against it, indeed against the whole institution of suburban back-lawns, had begun earlier that summer when, aching back bent over purpling knees, I suddenly let fall my copy of *Weeders Digest* and thought, "Something about all this is basically *unsound*. There's Nature growing weeds twenty-four hours a day and here's me pulling them out two hours a week."

That's when I started compiling my '*j'accuse*' notebook. Its next entry was a detailed breakdown of the iniquitous price of grass seed; plus, of course, the additional items required for nourishing it – mulch, fertiliser, nutrients and the like. Totting those up, I soon realised that my lawn was more expensively dressed than my children.

More pampered, too, One fertiliser on the list demanded to be applied every six hours. I defy anyone to find me a human activity more demeaning than getting up in the middle of the night to give a patch of grass its 2 a.m. feed.

What also has to be taken into account in estimating the financial burden of a lawn are the various decorative items you place upon it: things like gnomes, small windmills, bird-baths. Any one of those can cost enough to wipe you out in the bad times. For a small grey bird-bath, the chap in my Garden Suppliers was asking no less than £37! "You've gone beyond the limits of credibility," I told him. "Not even St Francis would pay £37 for a bird-bath."

And after you've spent all that money, what are you actually left with? In my case, despite all the outlay and the effort and the bending over it and trudging up and down it, that lawn still looked like it was written by Samuel Beckett. If you gazed down upon it from the bedroom window, its surface resembled nothing so much as one of those old-fashioned water biscuits, the kind that had little brown humps sticking up all over. The only time my grass could offer an onlooker the slightest vestige of aesthetic pleasure was when it was under three inches of snow.

The case the notebook finally presented was so unanswerable I took the only sensible course. Over the following weekend I had the whole lawn removed and a plastic one laid down.

Even at this distance, I can hear your gasps of revulsion. But bear with me. There is much to be said in favour of a plastic lawn. 'Synthetic turf' it's called – American, of course – and it comes in rolls. The one great thing about it, though, is that when you lay it down, it *stays* there – no brown humps, no weeds and no pathetic gasps for mulch or nutriment.

I'd go further. A summer evening offers few pleasures sweeter than settling back in a deckchair on your synthetic turf and listening contentedly to the man next door giving himself a coronary pushing his heavy mower. For that's another count against natural grass that I neglected to mention. They that live by the sward shall perish by the sward.

Mind you, I don't want to give the impression that the plastic version is completely free of drawbacks. It does possess one minor disadvantage – if it gets the slightest bit wet, it rots. However, all that amounts to in practical terms is that whenever there's a threat of rain, you just have to be careful to go outside, roll the lengths of turf up again, bring them all indoors and lean them against the walls of your dining room till the sun returns. A small price to pay I call it, especially as it also guarantees you'll hardly ever be able to invite people to dinner any more.

So it's a lifetime of ease and indolence that I'm now offering lawn-lovers. And all you have to do in return is bear in mind that one little warning which Shakespeare so presciently anticipated:

False turf will die if it's wet.

And thereby hangs a tale

Shakespeare
As You Like It, Act II, Sc. 7

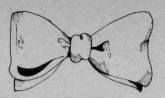

THE fact has to be admitted that I am to nature what Dame Margot Fonteyn is to non-ferrous sheet-metal welding. I know which end is which of Afghan hounds and Burmese cats, I can tell the difference between a daffodil and a horse, I can mow the lawn if the machine starts first time but beyond these I am as a child. Worse than a child, really, because most children, particularly girls, seem to know everything about animals from birth.

It was this lack of empathy with feathered and furry things which led to the tragic happening which occurred to the lamb Angus on the morning of Saturday, 10th April.

What I was doing half-way up a Highland mountain on a chilly April day can be explained in a trice. I was convalescing after a bout of virus pneumonia. Why I accepted that invitation from my friend who raised sheep on a hill-farm near Fort William rather than spend the time lolling on some warm beach in the sun is evidence that pneumonia weakens the brain as well as the body. It certainly weakens the body. For weeks after leaving hospital I had to use both hands to lift a potato crisp.

It was in this weak and emaciated state that I journeyed to Scotland. The train journey by sleeper was a nightmare. When I had finished playing with all the little folding shelves in the sleeper compartment and had worked out the purpose of the hook with the bit of chamois leather beneath it (it is for a gentleman to hang his pocket watch upon) and had taken a sip from the carafe of pond water and unrolled the paper drugget and tried the taps and switched the lighting to 'dim', I found that I had not enough strength to pull the bedclothes apart and get into the bunk and had, perforce, to wrap myself in the spare blanket and sleep on top of it.

It was a hollow-eyed, pale travesty of a guest who presented himself at the hill-farm in Ardgour, anxious to be no trouble and slip easily into the sheep-tending routine.

It was not easy. For one thing, my dear friend and host was an ex-Captain in the Navy, used to giving instructions briefly, crisply and once only. And hill-farming seems to have a vocabulary all its own. I never once understood a blind word I was told ('Up the scarp to the bothy . . . count the tups there . . . then go gathering . . .'). For another thing, life on a sheep farm is physical and I had hardly any physique left.

My first job was fairly harmless. It was to clear boulders from a meadow. This is a simple form of drudgery which was historically performed by convicts until Miss Fry or Mr Howard persuaded the government that it was utterly inhuman and convicts should be given more rewarding tasks like picking oakum or running up a tread-mill.

I squelched through the mud in my wellies and found the meadow, which was pock-marked with huge stones. I bent down and lifted a smallish specimen, managing to feel chill and break out in a sweat at the same time with the effort. As I stood there cradling the stone I was overwhelmed with a feeling that I was diminishing, as indeed I was; I was steadily sinking into the mud. When I had sunk to waist level my feet touched bedrock and I sank no more. Two hours later the tractor pulled me out – with the sound of a hippopotamus kissing its mate – and my host decided to put me onto lighter duties; getting the lambs into the Land-Rover trailer for taking to their new feeding pasture by the loch.

I staggered up a hill with Raymond, the shepherd, to sort out the beasts – we had to separate the ewes from the non-ewes – and urge them downhill towards the trailer. The trailer was rather cunningly adapted for this job, having a kind of platform which enabled two layers of sheep to be transported. Raymond grabbed the lambs by their wool and stuffed them into the lower compartment. He managed to get sixteen of them in and they stood placidly facing forward. He swung up the baseboard and locked them in.

"There's one left," he said. "It's Angus – always a wee bitty playful is Angus. You put him in the top compartment while I go and fetch the Land-Rover."

He left. I looked round and there was Angus right behind me, eyes innocent, baa-ing gently.

"Get in, Angus!" I said, without much hope. He gazed at me placidly. "If you take a running jump you'll make it," I pleaded. "Up, boy!" I coaxed.

I took hold of his wool and tried to lift him. A red mist swam before my eyes and the trembling began again. I tried running round him, barking like a sheepdog. He looked at me and went 'baa' vaguely. How on earth was I to get a sturdily built lamb onto the upper part of the trailer, some four feet off the ground?

I sat down in the mud and thought it over. Lifting was out of the question in my state of health. An inclined plane?

Into the house I rushed. There was an old Victorian sofa in the drawing room. In a flash I had whipped off its four casters. Up to the bathroom for a tin of sticking-plasters and then out to the workshop for an eight-foot plank.

Angus took it all very well, I must say. He stood perfectly still while I taped the casters to his feet. I propped the plank against the platform in the back of the trailer and coaxed Angus to walk forward until he was standing on the bottom of it. Then gently, oh so gently, I wheeled Angus up the plank and into the trailer. I had done it! I whipped the plank away and was about to slam down the top half of the trailer door when I heard a trundling noise.

Horror! The trailer was not on level ground. It was pointing slightly uphill and Angus was rolling backwards towards the open door.

I sprang forwards and managed to get my hands on his bottom before he rolled out and fell to the ground. I gave him a strong push as an experiment. He trundled forward until his nose was against the forward compartment and then began to roll back, accelerating as he went. I stopped him again and calculated that I would just have time to slam the hatch down on him if I gave him a good, strong push.

I pushed and reached up for the top of the door. But something went wrong. The top half of the door was held up by a catch and it took me that fatal second to disconnect the catch and slam down the door. In that second Angus had rolled back and – even now I find it painful to even think about it – this little tail – was trapped in the door and severed.

Small wonder that I have slept but fitfully since then. The thought of little Angus living out his life rudderless, imperfect, an object of scorn and mockery to his fellow lambs had haunted me. But what could I do? Nothing, I told myself. Tail-less he must remain.

But yesterday I was driving back from visiting a friend in the West

Country when, out of the corner of my eye, I saw a sign in a shop-window. I failed to register what sort of shop it was, a butcher's or a bookshop I fancy, but the sign said 'For Sale, Cheap. Lambs Tails. From Shakespeare'. (I take that to be the village of Shakespeare in Dorset.) So all is going to be all right after all. Tomorrow I am going to drive back along my route and locate that shop.

And there buy Angus a tail.

And is there honey still for tea?

Rupert Brooke
'The Old Vicarage, Grantchester'

THAT line, so evocative of the English countryside, never fails to bring back to me the year when, as a very bewildered, very frightened small boy, I was evacuated to the tiny village of Chiselbury.

Nestling like an Ovaltine advert within a grassy fold of the Mendips, Chiselbury represents even to this day the very heartbeat of rustic England. Just one street, one church, one pub, one everything-shop and one Chinese takeaway. But from the moment of my arrival there, the gentle-souled villagers took me to their hearts, despite the fact that I was the very first wartime evacuee they had seen. (This was because, thanks to a typically bureaucratic excess of caution, the year was only 1935.)

They billeted me in the cottage of Mr Bowman, whose trade was that most ancient and honourable of country crafts, wood-carving. And many were the spellbound hours I spent watching him as, using only a whittling-knife, his clever hands would fashion from some unpromising log a beautifully panelled door or spiral staircase, perhaps even an outside-privy with heart-shaped porthole. Sometimes, unable to restrain my childish curiosity, I would venture some question about his craft. "Mr Bowman," I'd say as the wood-chips flew, "wouldn't it be easier if you got out of bed to work?"

By way of answer, he would chuckle and playfully cuff my ear. Then, relenting, he'd take his knife and from a discarded off-cut he would whittle a little something especially for me; a wooden spoon, perhaps, or an exquisite catapult. Even, occasionally, if he had the time, something more elaborate – a fountain-pen or a pair of socks.

Mrs Bowman, his tiny and ever-smiling wife, the taste of whose cowslip-stew still comes back to me sometimes when the wind is off the Mendips, kept the village's everything-shop. And no everything-shop was ever more aptly named, for there was nothing a person could not purchase there. Milk, groceries, good country bread, ploughs, manicure sets, pianos, diving-suits, sports-cars – all the livelong day she'd be up and down the ladder fetching something or other off her many shelves. Because, besides all the other things, she also sold shelves. (And ladders.)

The third member of the Bowman household was their sixteen-year-old daughter, Annie; a strange withdrawn girl, with a great love for Nature's creatures and a forty-inch bust. So shy was she about this last attribute that she spent much of her time taking long solitary walks in the woods, accompanied only by her dog, an elderly Labrador with a matted, dank appearance like D. H. Lawrence. Sometimes, though, she would gesture me to accompany her and that, to a child of the London pavements, would indeed be a time of marvelling and wonderment.

"Oh, look, Annie!" I'd cry joyously. "Is that what they call wild honeysuckle?"

"Nay," she'd answer.

"Is it a climbing convolvulus?"

"Nay, lad."

"What is it then?"

"It's a goat." For she was wise in country-lore; sometimes we would stand motionless for whole hours at a stretch, simply so that she could observe the ways of the furred and feathered creatures that were her friends. "Sithee, lad," she'd mutter, plucking at a clump of grass, "A stoat have passed this way."

"How can you tell?" I would ask.

"Look what he done on your shoe."

Sadly, though, such was Annie's self-consciousness about her configuration, those enchanted excursions into the outer world gradually grew more and more infrequent. What finished them altogether was the morning when she washed her brassière. Having hung it out to dry on a rope between the tall trees, she came back to find two families of birds had built their nests in it. When she recognised what species of bird they were, the coincidence proved altogether too much for her.

But all that was, as the rural poet, Kern, has it, long ago and far away . . . To this day, though, there are moments when I still find myself wondering how the Bowmans are faring. Does Mr Bowman still whittle in his bed? Is Mrs Bowman still climbing up her ladder for a crêpe bandage or a two-stroke motorbike? And, perhaps the most heart-tugging question of all:

And is their Annie still forty?

There's a breathless hush in the close tonight

Sir Henry Newbolt
'Vitaï Lampada'

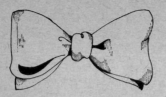

IF the poet Sir Henry Newbolt walked in on me at this moment, as the shades of night fall fast and the electric typewriter purrs like a contented cat, and asked me point blank "Are you sitting comfortably?" I would answer "Indeed I am, Sir Harry. For the first time for many a long year I am sitting without constriction, friction or loss of essential freedom."

Now any chap will confirm that this is a large claim to make. For some reason lost in antiquity the source of more discomfort and woe than anything else in a man's life is his underpant, knicker, short, brief, or whatever else you care to call his undercloth.

To begin with, why are they called 'a pair of'? We only wear one of them; the other is in the wash.

The whole history of the underpant is a harrowing story of faulty design, insufficient research and indifference to the consumer's requirements.

Why were they ever invented? Ladies went happily without the encumbrance well into the nineteenth century, taking the view that to do so would be to copy a totally masculine piece of stupidity, which would therefore be against the teachings of the Bible.

The Greeks and the Romans did not bother with underpants. On the continent of India the male underpant and the male overpant were – and often still are – the same garment.

Among the hardy Celts of North Europe the knicker was unknown. Even today your hardy Highlander disdains to wear anything beneath his kilt and suffers no vital damage, though in particularly icy weather groups of more elderly Scotsmen can be seen gathered together on the pavement grills above basement bakeries. But then the Highlanders were a warrior people, used to foraging for months high up in the glens with just their long, heavy kilts to keep their ankles warm, and their great plaid cloaks, which they would dip into the icy waters of a burn, wring out, and wrap themselves up in for a night's sleep.

No, the rot seemed to have set in during the Middle Ages in the more effete parts of Central Europe, at that time almost constantly at war. The first military, pike-and-gunpowder-proof underpant was invented by a brilliant young medical scientist who made the brief out of metal. His name, after which the protective device was named, was Coppernickers (sometimes spelt Copernicus). The new garment was celebrated by Shakespeare, you will remember, in his *All's Well That End's Well*, Act II, Sc. 3; when a London merchant won a contract to make them under licence:

> Good fortune and the favour of the king
> Smile upon this contract; whose ceremony
> Shall seem expedient on the now-born brief.

The idea for making the male undergarment out of cloth came from an eighteenth-century pirate, Silver, who was a martyr to cold and wanted the garment to reach down to his ankles. As he had only one leg and found it difficult to loop the other tube of copper out of the way he caused the thing to be made out of wool and thus invented the 'Long John'.

This long woollen garment was a great success in America where new industries were rapidly expanding, often in bleak, cold, frontier regions, and the American version had refinements like long sleeves, a vent in front and an escape-hatch at the back. These facilitated industrial action and the garment became known as a 'Union' suit.

During this century the underpant has shrunk considerably in size and now barely covers the salient features. The old idea of a passion-killing one-piece still lives on, however, amongst zealous young Mormon missionaries for whom it provides a useful bulwark against amorous housewives who thought the ring on the doorbell heralded an elderly meter-reader.

My main complaint against the twentieth-century brief is not its brevity but its inefficiency. And its lack of charm.

When I was a small boy the pant was still fashioned like a pair of trousers. It was loose and baggy and itchy and did not, I submit, answer the requirements of a pant. I was forever, like Samuel Pepys, leaping aboard vehicles and sitting down only to leap up again having done myself a small but painful injury. In Pepys' case it was because the coaches of his day were badly designed; in my case it was the pant which was ill-formed.

Then came 'boxer-shorts', frightfully baggy bunches of material with an elastic waistband which left the tummy crimped. And 'Y-Fronts', a breakthrough as regards industrial design but unsatisfactory as regards material – it was like being wrapped in an old vest.

In desperation I turned to the really brief 'briefs'. These came from the continent of Europe and bore names like 'Señor' and 'Hercule'. They arrived in three sizes: too small, too large, and medium. I wore 'medium', which were too small when I bought them and too large after two washes.

Why, oh why, I asked myself – as millions of chaps have asked themselves over the centuries – does our underwear have to be so *harsh*? The brief is the best of the bunch by a mile but is so unsympathetic. The elastic of the legs leaves weals on the upper thighs if it is to do its job and the cotton fabric rubs.

I resolved to solve the problem and begin from first principles. I went to Egham and bought a square yard of material which, clearly, lacked harshness; fine towelling. It had thousands of little cotton ears on it which made it soft. I bore it home and applied it to my nude person. I studied the geometry of the problem first, folded the square into a triangle and wrapped the hypotenuse round my waist. I then bent down and dragged the corner of the triangle forwards and upwards between my legs and fastened it, together with the ends of the hypotenuse, with a safety-pin. So far so good, but not far enough. The whole thing tended to swivel when I moved about. It was unstable. It needed anchorage. But to where?

The tummy-button is a much underestimated part of the human body. It is there, collecting fluff, but it is seldom put to use. Perhaps this is because of folklore. I believed – until humiliatingly recently – that if you unscrewed your tummy-button your bottom fell off. But the fact is that the tummy-button is there to be used if a use can be found.

I found the use. I nipped out into the garden and selected a tiny conker from beneath the horse-chestnut tree. I pierced the conker with a skewer and threaded a piece of string through it, tying the string to a safety-pin. Folding my non-harsh towelling about my person, I clasped the whole thing tightly about my waist and fastened the three corners with the conker-attached safety-pin, conker inwards.

You see the beauty – and truth – of my Creative Thinking? The conker nestled happily in my tummy-button like a ball in a socket; flexible, pliant, answering to my every movement yet anchoring the soft, towelling brief.

Which is why if Sir Henry Newbolt walked in and asked me "Are you sitting comfortably?" I would reply "Indeed I am, Sir Hal. It may not be immediately apparent as I am fully dressed, but beneath . . .?

"There's a brief, less harsh, in the clothes tonight."

You can't have your cake and eat it too

Proverb
Heywood

HAVE you noticed that although people who've
been pronounced innocent in court cases frequently proclaim the
verdict "a vindication of British Justice", you very rarely hear anyone
say that when he's been found guilty?

The reason that I didn't say it on the only occasion I was sent down
for a number of serious offences was not because the verdict was unfair
–which it was – but because I only had myself to blame. So convinced
had I been that the judge would immediately throw the whole series of
trumped-up charges out of court, I'd decided to conduct my own
defence.

Oh, I admit that the ridiculous accusations which the woman had
brought against me may have sounded bad – and, at the time of the
incident, they might even have looked pretty bad, too – but, as I tried
to explain to His Lordship, that kind of thing can so easily happen with
contact-lenses. Especially when you've only been wearing them for a
week, which is all I'd had them in for when my Lodge held their Ladies
Night Dinner & Dance.

Well, you're all reasonable people – having now heard my defence,
wouldn't you have dismissed all the charges against me and sent me
forth with no stain on my character and costs awarded for loss of
working time? I can only tell you – not him. Not that old poop sitting
up there in moth-eaten glory. He just pouted his lips and said,
"Mr Norden, I have not the faintest idea what you are talking
about."

So off we were obliged to launch into all the irrelevant details,
wasting the court's time and the taxpayers' money with a whole mass
of interminable argy-bargy. As patiently as I could I described how, on

the night in question, the woman and I had just finished dancing an Excuse-Me tango when I noticed that the right-hand side of the ballroom seemed to be in much clearer focus than the left-hand side.

Well, I twigged immediately what must have happened. Some time during the course of our dance, probably while I was moving her into one of my Valentino bend-overs, my left-hand contact-lens had dislodged itself and fallen. There being no sign of it on the highly polished floor, the only other landing-ground had to be my partner's dress. As the top of that garment featured what I believe is called a Boat Neck – in her case, of battleship proportions – that was obviously the first place to start searching.

All right, I concede that – arguably – I should perhaps have mentioned my intentions to the woman before attempting to retrieve the missing article. But, by the same token, I must disabuse you of any notion that I straightaway pulled up my sleeve, shoved an arm down and proceeded to grub around for the little sliver of plastic. On the contrary. In the most gentlemanly way possible, I simply positioned myself behind her, clasped both her shoulders, put a knee in her back and then – for no more than at most forty seconds – agitated her upper body in a rapid rotatory movement. Sure enough, my lost lens was shaken from its hiding-place and slid down to the floor.

That's really all there was to it. Be honest now, does it by any stretch of imagination constitute grounds for charging a person with grievous bodily harm, indecent assault and loss of conjugal benefit? That last enormity, by the way, was piled on by her husband, because – so he alleged – ever since the incident, not only did she throw a wobbly at the slightest murmur of tango rhythms, even the sight of a piano-accordion brought her out in hives. That being so, he averred, she was now rendered incapable of partnering him in their attempt on the forthcoming Southern Area Latin American Championships, so he was asking for punitive damages in the sum of £3,000, plus the cost of a wasted beehive wig.

Even to a layman, their entire case was so patently lacking in substance I had no hesitation at all in deciding to act as my own advocate. What's more, it soon became obvious that the barrister my opponents had hired – as foxy-looking a shyster as I've seen this side of Elisha Cook Jnr – was indulging in tactics that would have got him disbarred in a banana republic. After a few establishing questions to the wife, he had the usher put on a Victor Sylvester recording of *Jealousy* – then, to and fro across the well of the court, he and his client danced to it; his object being, of course, to demonstrate proof of the marked deterioration in her tango-ing faculties.

I let them do a full thirty-two bars before I released my shaft. Rising to my feet and pointing to the cavorting couple, "Your Lordship," I said, "I object."

"Why do you object?" said the judge.

"On the ground that Counsel is *leading* the witness."

The judge's response was to adjourn the court for lunch. Although, at the time, I viewed that as points to my side, it was actually the move which led to my downfall.

You see, in my ignorance of the law, what I'd failed to realise was that courtroom lunch-breaks only last from one o'clock till two. So instead of making for the canteen, I remained in my seat writing up some notes on the case with a view to getting them included in the BBC series 'Great Advocates Of Our Time'. It was only when I noticed the judge returning to his high-chair that I realised we were kicking off again and I hadn't had a thing to eat. All I could do was grab a hunk of cold bread-pudding I happened to be carrying in my brief-case and wolf it down.

Well, you've probably guessed the result. When I was called on to deliver my final masterly summing-up for the defence, I found myself overcome by such a grotesque attack of hiccups, I could only thump my chest wildly and shake my head. Taking this as a gesture of surrender, Your Lordship stopped the case and awarded judgment for the plaintiffs.

So, although I cannot in all fairness point an accusing finger at the workings of British Justice, I do have reservations about its mealtimes. Put it another way: if you ever decide to act as your own defence counsel, you must above all things make sure you get in the canteen-queue sharp at one.

Put it yet a third way:

You can't advocate and eat at two.

The game is up

Shakespeare
Cymbeline, Act III, Sc. 3

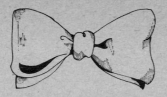

I propose to make a million pounds or so in the coming months by writing a best-seller, a romantic novel of the type known to hospital-library trolley-pushers and librarians as Light Love.

This will mean writing under a nom-de-plume, of course, but this is quite usual. It may come as something of a shock to you but Eleanor Papworthy (*Daddy Blue-Eyes, Sigh No More Stranger, Dimples,* etc.) is a retired accountant whose real name is Arthur Fosset. And Monica Lavender (*Beloved Rogue, For the Love of a King, The Passionate Quaker,* etc., etc.) is bearded and before striking it rich was a riveter in a Clyde shipyard. My romantic novel will be written under the pen-name of 'Deborah Horseland'. This should keep me just ahead of Barbara Cartland.

After studying a number of these novels and giving the matter a good deal of thought – I spent almost the whole of last Tuesday on it – I have come up with a winner of a plot. It has all the elements which are most successful in the genre; an historical setting, aristocracy, low life, dark doings in the past and a hero who is ideal for the heroine.

The heroine's mother is a ravishing Society beauty married to an elderly politician. I call her Lady Caroline Mutton because she is like a slightly older Lady Caroline Lamb. Lady Caroline had been a bit of a goer in her youth and had had a steamy ding-dong with an impoverished poet which resulted in the birth of our heroine. I call Lady Caroline's lover Thomas Tupper – a little joke for my sheep-farmer readers.

As was usual in those days our baby heroine is smuggled away and put out to a wet-nurse (whatever that is – I'll look it up). Lady Caroline disguises herself as a trollop (we all know what that is) and does the

239

rounds of the taverns to find foster-parents for the infant. This will give me the opportunity to indulge in some fine descriptive writing of Georgian London: squeaking inn-signs, "Won't you buy my sweet fresh lavender, kind lady?", one-legged beggars, stage-coaches setting off for Inverness (or somewhere. I'll check where they went), Bow-Street Runners, all that sort of rubbish.

In a tavern in Maiden Lane (singularly inappropriate Lane come to think of it – I'll change it later) over against a music shop ('over against' means 'next to': it is the sort of period phrase I will go in for strongly: they used 'over against' in the old days because most of the houses in Olde London fell over and rested against the house next door) Lady Caroline meets the owner of the shop, a kindly old retired musician named Jabez Harp. She strikes a bargain and for a guinea-and-a-half he undertakes to adopt the child and bring her up as his own. Lady Caroline then downs a swift port-and-lemon and disappears from his life and our story.

We then jump a few years and pick up where our heroine is sweet seventeen and a picture to behold and here I anticipate running into trouble. How do you describe a heroine except to state that she has an oval face? What alternative shape of face *could* she have? Rectangular? Square? And all heroines seem to have hazel eyes, i.e. eyes like a small nut (I'll work something out).

She has grown up into a happy young woman, always dashing about laughing and cheering people up. When the wind used to blow, and the house used to lean even further against the tavern next door, to the terror of Jabez and his good wife, the girl would laugh and cheer them up with a song. So they christened her Aeolian Harp.

With her merry laughter and her stunning good looks Aeolian becomes an actress. She joins the company of the celebrated actor, George Frederick Cooke, and goes with the company on a tour of the provinces (this is the origin of Cooke's Tours).

But all does not go well on tour. Aeolian's acting is not bad but her jollity becomes a little wearing on the nerves of the cast The first to crack is George Frederick Cooke himself. After a disastrous week in Scunthorpe he announces to the company that the total week's takings are three shillings and twopence.

"Never mind, love," cries Aeolian, bursting into a trill of laughter, "the play's the thing!"

He walks out, takes the drink and becomes one of the most spectacular drunks in the history of British theatre (quite true).

The next to crack is the saturnine, wild-eyed but exceedingly hand-some juvenile lead Jemmy Trotter (our hero). This is not his real name. He is really young Lord Battersea who has been temporarily diddled out of his stately home and inheritance by somebody-or-other for a reason I'll work out later and has taken to the stage incognito to earn his living.

He falls in love with Aeolian, and vice-versa, one afternoon when he blunders in while she is changing her costume. This will be a chance for a touch of 'her magnificent bare bosoms heaved as though his piercing eyes were exercising some spell upon them. With a faint cry she modestly covered her face with her hands as his breath, now so hot that the varnish on her dressing-room door began to bubble . . .' (they like a fair amount of this sort of stuff in Light Love as long as nobody actually *does* anything). But her unremitting jollity and stentorian laugh rapidly wear away his ardour and two days later he leaves and joins the Navy.

Aeolian, heartbroken, also leaves the stage and becomes a Kept Woman (it's all right; I'll make her protector an old merchant aged about a hundred and four who only wants her for a tax-loss, or some-thing like that). But one evening, when she is trying to cheer him up, her laugh shatters a priceless chandelier and she is flung out on her ear.

We next find her, destitute, hungry, being frog-marched out of a Revivalist Mission for laughing during Charles Wesley's sermon.

She decides to end it all by throwing herself over the Embankment into the cold, dark waters of the Thames (if there *was* an Embankment in those days. If not, over Chelsea Bridge. If that was not there either, off the top of the Tower of London).

Meanwhile our hero, Jemmy Trotter, has got on well in the Navy and is a captain. Unhappily he has a nasty accident and is invalided out. One day Nelson asks him to go and get the gunnery officer, Lieutenant Farr. Not knowing which gun the Lieutenant is working on, Jemmy shoves his head down the first gun-barrel he comes across and yells "Farr!!" The cannon-ball hits him on the head but misses anything vital so he lives. The only damage is to his hearing, which is per-manently impaired. But Fate smiles upon him. Whoever-it-was who had nicked his title and fortune comes to some sort of bad end and it is as wealthy Lord Battersea that he strolls that evening along the Embankment (or across Chelsea Bridge, or over the roof of the Tower of London) in time to stop his one true love from hurling herself into the waters.

"Aeolian!" he cries, clasping her to him, "I thank merciful Heaven that I found you in time. We will wed this very minute. There is an Off-Licence in Caxton Hall who will make us one!" (This ending is a bit like *Fanny Hill* but I think the readership of the two books will be sufficiently different for the rip-off to go unnoticed.)

"I am so happy!" she cries, and bursts into the loudest laughter she has ever laughed.

But the noise of her laughter does not bother him one bit. Theirs will be a truly happy marriage, however bright her merriment or cheerful her laughter, because, of course, her dear husband is stone deaf.

Good story, isn't it?

And I have found just the right title. Her name, with a description of her main characteristic, and a slight period flavour. I am going to call it:

The Gay Miss Harp.

Beggars can't be choosers

Proverb

AFTER Monsieur Lafarge had introduced me to his colleagues, he explained the problem which the Calais Chamber of Commerce had brought me over to solve. "What our town has become," he said gloomily, "is a sort of geographical revolving-door. A place many people pass through but no one ever thinks of staying inside."

I appreciated their predicament. For millions of British holiday-makers, the name Calais means little more than a port-of-entry for driving towards other Continental watering-places, or a port-of-departure for catching the car-ferry back to England. The truth, however, is that this pleasant seaside town has much to offer the English visitor, including attractive beaches, excellent local dishes, excursions to many places of interest and, in my case, a whacking down-payment on the fee, balance to be handed over in hundred-franc notes, no questions asked and blow the VAT. Provided, that is, provided I could dream up some novelty attraction that would induce my fellow-countrymen to linger round the dump for an extra few days. . . .

The first idea I put to the Chamber was the obvious one – capitalise on the town's well-established historical links with the U.K. After all, if there's one history lesson that every British school-child has dozed over, it's that episode about 'the burghers of Calais': those six old-timers Edward the Third threatened to string up with their own ropes. "So the thing to do," I instructed the assembled merchants, "is play-up your historical assets. The shop-keepers among you must stop present-ing yourselves to English visitors as retail-stockists or distributor-outlets. From now on, you've all got to be 'burghers'. That's where the money is. Is there a butcher here?" Monsieur Hippolyte raised his hand. "Right," I said. "You be the beef-burgher. The chap who runs the dairy can be the cheese-burgher. And if any of you are in the local Amateur Dramatic society –?" No less than four hands went up. "Fine," I said, "Ham-burghers."

I was really warming to it now. "Tell you what," I said, "you four can help push the history tie-up even further. For a really dead-cert tourist grabber, how about we put on a 'Son et Lumière' presentation in the Main Square, re-enacting the whole Edward the Third scenario throughout the holiday season?"

Everyone received the idea so enthusiastically it really should have worked, especially as it cost nearly as much as *A Bridge Too Far* to produce and I went to no end of trouble writing the script. What I neglected to bear in mind, however, was that a 'Son et Lumière' differs from a situation-comedy in two vital respects. First, it has to be done in the open air; second, you have to stage it in darkness, at night. As the road alongside the Main Square is the principal highway to the Côte d'Azur, the whole 'Son' part of the 'Son et Lumière' got drowned-out by a procession of GB-plate drivers putting their foot down so as to get to Lyons before breakfast. And as for the 'Lumière' – well, that blinked out for good when the only British vehicle that did pause to watch – a four-berth caravan – parked smack on the power cables.

Fortunately, I have never been one to let a mere disaster upset me. "Not to worry," I said, surveying the despondent faces at the next Chamber of Commerce meeting. "There's more than one way for a seaside resort to pull in passing trade. Know what lots of British places have been finding surefire? A Beauty Contest! 'Miss Bridlington', 'Miss Jaywick Sands' – that sort of thing. Just vote me a few hundred thousand francs more for publicity, and I promise you – this time next month you'll be worrying about a shortage of hotel rooms."

Well, the moment the money was okayed, I started working like a demon. By the following Monday morning, there wasn't one roadway leading out of the dock area that didn't bear an enormous placard that read 'All this week – MISS CALAIS!'

The trouble was, every English driver coming off the ferry read it as an *instruction*.

The next time I met with the city elders there were distinct signs of what my mother calls 'an atmosphere'. I couldn't help but notice every one of them was looking at me as though I was in direct line-of-descent from Edward the Third. Monsieur Lafarge set the pace. "Mr Norden," he said, "the feeling of the meeting is that we are just playing silly burghers."

"D'accord," Monsieur Duval said. "In spite of all the money we have spent and the exorbitant fee you have charged us, our beaches are still deserted."

"More to the point," said Monsieur Aznavour (I asked him but he said he wasn't), "all our town has left in its coffers now is thirty francs. And, Mr Norden, there is no possible way that anyone can suddenly throng an empty resort by an expenditure of thirty francs."

Well, if there's one thing calculated to bring out the best in me, it's a challenge. I tell you, I positively *felt* my nostrils flare. "Monsieur Racine," I said to the local printer, "would thirty francs buy me just one more road-sign? Just a little one?"

Grudgingly, he nodded. And that nod is the reason why, today, a gratifying 83 per cent of those British cars that used to roar straight through Calais now make a sudden left-hand turn when they reach the dock gateway and follow the road indicated by the arrow on my little sign. A sign that is nevertheless large enough for the seven words above the arrow to be read by an oncoming driver:

'This Way To The Nude Bathing Beaches'.

Months later, in the speech I made graciously turning down the Chamber of Commerce's offer of a statue in the Main Square, I pointed out that I had already received my sufficient reward. That came in the form of the *Calais Observateur*'s front-page photograph of Messieurs Hippolyte, Lafarge and Racine standing by the breakwater, all busily using pocket-calculators to try and estimate how many thousands of British holidaymakers were wandering the sands in search of uncovered skin.

The caption beneath it, though it loses a little in translation, had a simple eloquence:

BURGHERS COUNT BEACH-USERS.

It is better to travel hopefully than to arrive

Proverbial saying derived from a line
by Robert Louis Stevenson

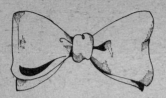

Amost extraordinary thing has happened to our household. After many years of being dog-people – first poodles and then Afghans – we have taken to cats. Once doggy we are now moggy. We have become transmogrified.

Our cats are Burmese which might explain a lot; Burmese cats tend to be individuals rather than members of the Cat Family. They have given us so much pleasure that I was tempted to do a rave about their beauty and companionship and sense of fun but I think a better picture will emerge of living with cats if I just drivel on about random incidents.

I first met a Burmese cat when we were having lunch at the home of a chap called Andrew Lloyd-Webber who writes music. After lunch we sat around discussing things like semi-quavers and royalties when a smallish, dark-brown cat strode in, summed up in a flash that I was not a cat-fancier, sprang lightly onto my lap, curled up and composed himself to slumber. It was like having a mink-covered hot-water bottle on one. When I rose to go he rose with me, transferring himself to my shoulder. When we left our host had to detach him from me by levering him off with a cello bow. Such affection was a rare experience.

My own Burmese kitten, Kettering (named after a town in Northants where lives a nice publisher) arrived on my birthday. I was in bed with a cold at the time. A cardboard box was presented to me by the family. Books? I wondered. Soap? A woolly garment? I opened the top of the box and a small, chocolate-coloured head emerged. Huge, round, yellow-Chartreuse eyes looked at me levelly. He skipped lightly out of the box and curled himself up round my Adam's apple for the day.

With two Afghan ladies of some age on the premises we had a

problem. The inborn instinct of a hound is to chase and kill small furry beasts. They could not believe their luck that they had been presented with a resident quarry. They hurled themselves at the bedroom door to get at Kettering. They tried to tunnel under the door. We resolved on a system of apartheid until we could solve the problem. The kitten lived during the day safely amid the springs of the bed. The dogs were kept downstairs.

On advice I telephoned the chief veterinary officer of one of our animal charities. He seemed a good bet as he owned Afghans himself.

"I wish to introduce a Burmese kitten into a household which includes two Afghans," I began.

"A *kitten*!" he said. "You've got two Afghans and now you've gone and got a kitten! Oh, my goodness! Oh deary, deary me! Oh, my goodness, you *have* got a problem! Oh, Gawd! . . ." That was the sum total of his professional advice.

I built a strong wire cage, like a huge rat-trap. We inserted a protesting Kettering into this every evening and took it downstairs so that the dogs would get used to him and realise that he had come to stay and was one of the family (we read that in a book). The dogs knocked us out of the way and tried to bite through the wire. Kettering was relatively unmoved. He sat and glared at them and if a nose was pushed through the bars he swatted it with a paw.

It took four nerve-wracked months but eventually the natural lethargy of living things took over and the dogs ceased to care all that much. A guarded form of peaceful co-existence came into being and it became accepted by all three that as long as there was no food about there would be no war. They walked warily past each other but there was no aggro.

At Christmas my wife's kitten arrived. Also in a cardboard box. He is called Monticello (after a village in Corsica) and is silver (i.e. grey) with a beautiful face, a raucous little voice and a fat tummy. His first meeting with an Afghan was interesting. He took one look at the great shaggy face looming over him, hauled off and let loose a right hook that would have felled an ox. The Afghan staggered away, gloomily contemplating the sad turn of world events.

It must be admitted that cats, unlike dogs, tend to shred the house a little. We have hessian wallpaper in the dining room and both cats like to show off when strangers are present and run up the wall. They also occasionally run up the curtains, stroll along the mantelpiece brushing the ornaments off the edge, hide in the kitchen cupboards and induce heart failure in somebody innocently reaching for a saucepan, and sit on one's paper when one is trying to write a letter.

Their need to unsheath their scimitars and lock onto one's clothing when being carried about means that threads are drawn. All my jackets are now covered in tiny fairy croquet-hoops.

Both cats sleep in our bed. This is quite indefensible on all grounds. It is not only unhygienic but downright dangerous. But how do you keep them out? They wait until you are asleep and then in they come, burrowing down to the bottom of the bed and then easing their way up until they find a warm nook or cranny. And they shift around during the night, unloosing the scimitars and having a good scratch at anything to hand. They rarely draw blood but they leave distinct weals in the flesh. When I had my first bath after the arrival of Kettering I saw my back in the mirror and I looked like a steel engraving from Foxe's *Book of Martyrs*.

I do not normally wear pyjamas and it seemed to me that now was the time to start, so, in self-protection, I wore a pair of pyjama bottoms. It was a grave error. There is nothing a kitten likes more than running up a tunnel.

What *is* it about cats that so intrigues? The French painter Méry wrote that cats were God's way of permitting man to caress a tiger. There is something in this but it does not stand up to close scrutiny. Caressing a tiger (or, at least, caressing a cheetah, which I have done) is like stroking a pig the wrong way. Caressing a Burmese cat is like stroking velvet. Cats walk in a beautiful, loping, tiger-like stride but when they run their bottoms seem to be trying to overtake them and they wobble from side to side in a most un-tigerlike fashion.

I suppose it comes down to trying to work out what cats are thinking about behind that shining, opaque stare. The theory is that cats know a hell of a lot but do not let on. I wonder. But perhaps wondering what goes on inside cats' noddles is what makes them seem not only beautiful and graceful but mysterious and enigmatic; a perpetual mystery.

Sorry this piece has not been more organised but as I said at the beginning I wanted to drivel on and, I hope, sketch in a picture of what living with cats means.

In a case like this I rather agree with Robert Louis Stevenson's thought:

It is better to drivel hopefully than do a rave.

Where are the snows of yesteryear?

François Villon

WHAT finally persuaded me I should have the operation was brandy-balloons; even though they represent only one of the embarrassments you encounter when you've got a big nose. A brandy-balloon is a drinking-glass with a large, voluptuously-shaped bowl that curves round to an extremely narrow rim – think of a fat avocado with the tip sliced off – but what happens when an extravagantly-beaked person drinks from such a goblet is that the moment his lips meet the near edge of the narrow rim, he finds his nose-tip is already jamming against the far edge. In consequence, it becomes quite impossible for him to get any kind of *tilt* on the balloon. When you remember that the brandy itself sits down at the bottom of it, that leaves a large-hootered person like myself only two options. I either have to ask my host if he'd please fill my glass right up to the brim or, failing that, bring out a straw. Both these alternatives get you talked about.

It was that kind of social discomfiture which led me to consider having what's called a 'nose-job'. What clinched it for me was reading in one of the Sunday supplements that this particular technique of cosmetic surgery has become such a doddle, you can now have your facial irregularity replaced by any shape or size of nose you fancy. I immediately contacted my secretary and asked her to send away for a Nose Catalogue.

Whether she was unfamiliar with medical procedures or whether she simply misheard me I don't know, but all I received by return of post was a highly-coloured brochure offering me a choice of standard, miniature, climbing or floribunda. So I got out the Yellow Pages, let my fingers do some jogging up the column marked Surgeons (Cosmetic), made a phone-call and fixed an appointment.

He was one of those black-jacket-and-striped-trouser types who probably looked like a boardroom portrait while still a child, but he was affable enough and after we'd agreed on a model that would blend with the rest of my facial environment, he said, "Fine. Now, when we've got you under, is there any other malformation you'd like corrected?" Somewhat on the principle, I thought, that a house-decorator will say, "While I'm up the ladder, want me to have a look at your guttering as well?"

"No thanks," I said. "Apart from the Cyrano, I think Nature has been reasonably kind." He inspected me searchingly. "Your ears are a bit sticking-out."

I'd forgotten about them. They do project somewhat; to an extent, in fact, that with my hair cut short, I bear a distinct face-on resemblance to the F.A. Cup. "All right then," I agreed, "perhaps you'd better give them just a slight pinning-back."

"Sure there's nothing else?"

I pondered. "Come to think of it," I said. "Every time I'm measured for a sports-jacket, they tell me my left shoulder is about an inch-and-a-half higher than the right." He made a note of it. "Oh, and another thing that's just come back to me. The chap in the shirt shop always says my right arm is a good three-quarters of an inch longer than the left."

He turned over a fresh page of his order-book. "That the lot?"

"Not quite," I said, warming to it now. "For some reason I take a size $10\frac{1}{2}$ shoe on one foot but an 11 on the other. And there was something else. What was it? . . . Oh yes. My inside-leg measurements."

"What about them?" he said.

"Well, I don't quite understand this, but for some reason they're longer than my outside-leg measurements."

He closed his book. "I think I'd better send you an estimate."

You'll never believe what he quoted me for the full service. £400! Naturally I queried it with him but he showed me a complete item-by-item breakdown of his costings and that does seem to be what this kind of job comes to nowadays. It's not the parts, you see, it's the labour.

But £400! I went straight home, sat down in front of the shaving mirror and made another long hard appraisal of the nose. Is it really all that awful? Well, not really. Certainly not by comparison with – no, I'd better not mention her name. Oh, admittedly it's looking a bit pointier and pinchier with every passing decade – but even so, there's still quite a bit of mileage there before it gets to be truly grotesque. All things considered, I'll stay with it.

So have I now completely discarded the idea of having a trumpet-trim? Not entirely. If I ever win the National Lottery, it would probably still be the first thing I'd lash out largesse on. But until then – well, at £400 a throw, my thinking has to be the same as François Villon's:

Wear out the shnozz of yesteryear.

He jests at scars that never felt a wound

Shakespeare
Romeo and Juliet, Act II, Sc. 2

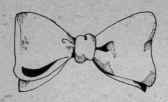

I was once very fond of Romeo and Juliet but they were too expensive for me and I changed to those little cigars that come five to a tin, like pilchards. They were not so nice to smoke but were probably nicer than smoking pilchards.

I became a cigar-smoker by chance some ten years ago. It was late in December and I remember wondering what I would get for Christmas. I had a shrewd idea that I would be getting either a street-map of the suburbs of Melbourne, an oboe reed or a jar of pickled walnuts. I am sometimes psychic in matters like these.

When Christmas came do you know what I got? Virus pneumonia. That was not all I got for Christmas, of course. I also got pleurisy.

It was not a very jolly Christmas for any of us. I ran a very high temperature and just lay flat, seeing faces in the wallpaper and steaming like a Christmas pudding. It was particularly arduous for my family. That Christmas was the coldest for years and it was a great labour for them to keep trundling me from room to room to warm the house up.

When it was all over I had an interview with my chest specialist in Harley Street.

"Do you want the bad news first?" he asked quietly.

I went suddenly cold. "Yes . . . yes, of course. Let me have it straight."

His eyes were full of compassion as, wordlessly, he passed me an envelope containing an account of his fees.

"And the good news?" I ventured.

"You are now perfectly healthy. Just give up smoking cigarettes from now on. O.K.?"

Give up smoking cigarettes? No problem to a person of my mental calibre and powers of self-discipline I assured myself. I turned over in my mind all the previous things I had managed to give up: ice-skating, the burnt currants in rice-pudding, Proust, Party Political Broadcasts, yoghourt, Charlie Chaplin films, striped toothpaste, pyjamas, hitch-hiking, sliced bread, waistcoats, Mrs Mary Whitehouse, toasted tea-cakes, turnups on trousers, weeding the garden, queueing, the novels of C. P. Snow, going for a bracing walk, fried onions, Y-Front pants, rice and 'Stars on Sunday'. But then a horrible truth made itself apparent; these were things I *wanted* to give up. I did not want to give up cigarettes.

What followed was a nightmare. As soon as the trembling hand reached for a packet of the forbidden weed I forced it back. I felt I was going mad, losing weight, falling apart. I kept telling myself that I *will* give up cigarettes, that as soon as I can begin to give them up then pride will strengthen my resolve. I went hot and cold alternately as I strove to break a deeply-entrenched habit. I developed a twitch. Was impatient, lost my knack of touching problems lightly and being a source of comfort to others. I developed a morbid conviction that my elbows were growing like weeds. That my fingernails itched. Finally I could take no more. I went back to the specialist and said, "I can't do it! I've tried! God knows I've tried! But I just can't give them up!"

He said, "You've only been as far as the front door and back. Give it a bit longer. If you want to you can smoke the occasional cigar."

I wrung his hand in gratitude and made my way home.

And so I began to smoke the occasional cigar. With immense difficulty.

The trouble with cigars is how to light them. There was no such trouble with cigarettes. One touched a flame to one end, sucked on the other and various chemicals ensured that the things stayed alight. The chemicals were more obvious in French cigarettes which fizzed away like sparklers, going 'snap', 'crackle' and 'pop'. A big cigar is another matter entirely. It rests in your hand like a deeply-bronzed banana. And unlike the humble cigarette, it is only open at one end. The end you shove in your mouth is closed up with folded leaves, like the blunt end of an onion.

In the Hollywood films of my youth Edward G. Robinson seemed to have no trouble in coping with this blunt end. As Betty Grable, bespangled, the famous legs clad in bullet-proof tights, took to the speakeasy stage to begin her hit number Edward G. bit into the end of his cigar, spat and applied match.

I think that you have to have the teeth for it. My front teeth do not quite match up in the middle. This means that I cannot easily eat corn on the cob. What I have to do is hold the cob and force each corn against the chisel surface of a specific tooth and lever away, one corn at a time. When I tried to bite the end off my cigar there was a crunching sound and I had a mouthful of what tasted like dead cabbage leaves.

I tried pushing a matchstick into the end to make a hole and sawing off the end with a penknife, but in each case I ended up with the thing unrolling itself and coming to rest in my palm rather like one of those bars of flaky chocolate.

I then tried moving away from big, real cigars into those tiny cigar-substitutes. The difficulty was keeping those alight. They lit readily but invariably went out half-way through. I found myself a victim of mid-whiffery.

Cigars are a mockery, I cried. Why cannot there be some system of smoking cigar tobacco as one smokes a pipe? Pipes do not unroll in one's palm, or need biting beforehand. They smoke evenly and placidly.

The answer to my prayers came to me in a Magic Shop. That is to say, a shop devoted to selling conjuring tricks and similar paraphernalia. I had gone into the shop to purchase a squirting carnation or, as the sign said, a 'Joke Button-Hole: Just Wait for The Laffs When Your Buddies Bend Down to Sniff Your Boutonniere!' I needed this to solve a small problem I found when travelling home by train from Waterloo station to Egham. I would nip into the station buffet and order a cup of coffee. When it arrived (if it arrived at all), it was usually steaming hot and undrinkable for eight minutes whereas my train was due to arrive in five minutes. I reckoned that if I had a Joke Squirting Buttonhole I could lean towards the hot coffee and, without bringing embarrass-ment upon myself, squirt the little rubber bulb and direct a stream of cold water into the coffee. Anyway, while I was in the Magic Shop I suddenly saw for sale an all-purpose Magic Wand. A thin wooden cylinder, painted black with white ends, into which the aspiring magician could stuff flags, silk handkerchiefs, fried eggs, in fact any-thing which he could then produce at will and amaze his friends. Inspiration struck. I bought four Magic Wands.

It was the work of but a few moments to carve a mouthpiece in the soft wood of the Wands. A cigar, unrolled, provided enough tobacco to fill three Wands. They lit beautifully, like a fine meerschaum pipe, and burnt steadily. I had found a perfect compromise between the efficiency of a pipe and the farce of trying to light a cigar.

I now no longer make mock of the dark-brown leaf. As Shakespeare almost said:

He jests at cigars who never filled a wand.

They make a desert and they call it peace

Tacitus
'Agricola'

YOU ready to hear something really chilling? Not long ago, a distinguished thinker hit upon the most profound philosophical statement ever revealed to mankind, then had to discard it because it wouldn't fit on a T-shirt.

I found that just one more piece of supporting evidence for my theory that if the nineteen-seventies do go down in history – and we're agreed, aren't we, that they are unlikely to go up – the decade will almost certainly be remembered as The T-shirt Years. Every person under the age of forty-five is taking on the appearance of an ambulant billboard. Wherever you turn, emblazoned singlets display multi-coloured full-face portaits of today's Culture Heroes – Solzhenitsyn, Kurt Vonnegut, Laurel and Hardy – or else they exhibit slogans embodying every kind of contemporary preoccupation. These range from the boldly partisan ('Boadicea Lives!'; 'Bring Back The Cod-Piece!') to the politically extreme ('Keep Foreigners Out Of The Common Market'; 'Put Betting Shops On The National Health'). From the ethically questionable ('Love Is A Many Gendered Thing'; 'Sex Leads To Housework') to the downright incomprehensible ('The Truth Lies Somewhere In-Between'; 'Keep On The Grass').

Until quite recently, though, this transformation of the population into human hoardings was something I viewed with little more than resigned tolerance. ("I may not agree with what your T-shirt says but I will fight to the death for your right to wear it.") Then something happened that changed my attitude significantly. One of the major networks made us a handsome offer to put the 'My Word!' series on television.

We could perform it, they promised, in exactly the same form as we were accustomed to doing it on radio, except – and here I quote from the eager-shirted young producer ('Social Consciousness Is Not Enough') they sent round – "except for one minor alteration". Apparently the average viewer is not what the young man kept calling "verbally orientated", so something would have to be done to give the televised version of the programme – and again I use quotation-marks to indicate his exact words – "more pace".

"Take those quotations you and Frank build your stories round," he argued. "Your average telly-addict would never be able to retain them in his mind all the while you're rabbiting. If we're going to hold his interest, maintain the pace he's got used to in *Starsky and Hutch*, we've really got to provide Joe Public with some sort of ongoing visual reference-point."

Thoughtfully, Frank took out his chased-silver snuff-box. "Such as like what?" he asked softly.

"Nothing you need worry yourself about, baby," the producer said, slapping him genially on the shoulder – never a wise thing to do while Frank is taking snuff. After we'd cleaned Frank's ears, the youth outlined his proposed revisions. During that portion of the programme in which the two stories are recounted, Dilys Powell, the lady who sits at Frank's side, would wear a T-shirt on which would be embroidered whatever quotation he was weaving his magic on; similarly, when it came to my turn, my partner Anne Scott-James would be seen in a T-shirt bearing the line I was working on.

"Get the visual impact?" he enquired eagerly. "All the time either of you is labouring his way through to the pay-off line, there – right next to you – is someone showing exactly what your target is. All kidding aside, fellers, it'll make that whole long-winded section go like a chase-sequence! . . . Do me a favour," he said as he noticed our faces, "at least think about it."

How can one think about the unthinkable? How is it possible to consider the inconceivable? Without getting too rhetorical, let me simply ask you to recall the Pepys quotation with which Frank was lumbered a scant few weeks back. In all honesty, can you really imagine Dilys Powell – our delicate, softly-spoken Dilys – can you imagine her clad in a white cotton singlet that reads 'And So To Bed'?

While Anne – the handsome, invincibly elegant Lady Scott-James – to put her in any kind of T-shirt can only be compared to draping bunting over the dome of St Paul's. As for embossing one of my questions across it – could anyone really want to see Anne Scott-James sitting with her noble upper-half covered in something that reads 'These Are A Few Of My Favourite Things'?

No, it's simply not on, is it? Typical though, I suppose. Typical both of the contemporary mania for communicating by means of an embroidered under-vest and Television's obsession with speeding-up everything it touches. Funny how nearly right old Tacitus got it:

They make a T-shirt and they call it 'pace'.

The workers have nothing to lose but their chains
Communist Manifesto

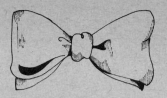

QUITE by accident I have stumbled upon a theory which could well turn the art world topsy-turvy and call for an entirely new approach to exhibitions, art histories and *catalogues raisonnés* (catalogues with raisins in them).

It all came about when I received a very flattering phone-call asking me to paint a picture for a local art exhibition to be put on by the Runnymede Art Society, of which I am president. The chap on the phone said that the theme of the exhibition was Florence Nightingale.

I had never painted a picture before so I had no canvases but I found an old tarpaulin in the garden which my aunty used to cover her motorbike. It was about eight feet by six feet, just the right size for an impressive oil painting, so I stretched it out and nailed it to the garage door. I sat down and had a think about what exactly I was going to paint. If I had heard the chap on the phone correctly the picture had to represent some aspect of Florence. At night. In a gale. No problem – only a few days previously I had received a picture postcard of Florence from my aunty who had gone to stay there for a couple of months while her hair returned to its natural colour. I went and fetched the postcard. It was a fine view of the cathedral, topped by Brunelleschi's mighty dome. Excitement mounting, I rang the ironmongers in Egham and said that I wanted some painting equipment.

"What do you want to paint?" asked a voice, patiently.

"A cathedral," I said. "At night. In a gale."

About an hour later a van backed up the drive and two men unloaded eight twenty-gallon drums of Exterior Brown and Exterior Black, a long ladder and a powerful torch. Also a collection of six-inch brushes and a set of oilskins.

I put on the oilskins, opened a drum of paint, stirred it with the torch and got cracking. It was surprising how short a time it took to paint an oil painting when I was using a six-inch brush. It was finished within the hour. I painted the dome in the pinky-brown paint and painted the sky black to show it was night. I then dabbed in the windows with some red paint I found in the garage and flicked some black here and there to give the illusion of a storm. I then strode away some ten feet, turned and had a good look at what I had got. It gave me quite a turn. It did not look like the Duomo in Florence at all. The dome looked for all the world like the head of a braw Scots laddie. The windows looked like his bloodshot eyes, the two smaller domes became his ears, the little spire in front was his nose and the great lantern on top of the dome just came out as a huge lump on his head. It was a bitterly disappointing moment.

What to do about it?

I decided to accept the inevitable and with small sigh and a rag soaked in turpentine I wiped off the title 'Florence: Night in Gale' and painted in 'The Laddie with the Lump'.

The picture was never exhibited, of course. Not only was the subject wrong but just after I had finished painting it I swung the up-and-over garage door up to get the car out and the top of the frame scraped all the paint off the tarpaulin.

It was only later that night, as I lay sleepless in bed wondering what to do with the remaining hundred and fifty-nine and a half gallons of Exterior Paint, that the great thought dawned: how many of the world's great works of art had, like 'The Laddie with the Lump', started out as something else entirely? How many of our masterpieces are, in fact, only masterpieces because of some accident?

If my theory was true it would revolutionise all our concepts of genius and the creative spirit. Anybody could have a go as long as they were either accident-prone or lucky.

The following morning, even though it was spitting with rain, I made my way to the Virginia Water Public Library and flung myself into research.

I reached down a book of Leonardo da Vinci's work and sat for an hour staring at a reproduction of 'Mona Lisa'. How had that picture started out, I asked myself? What was the real story that lay behind such an odd portrait? Suddenly the picture spoke out to me and yielded up its secret. Quite clearly Leonardo had set out to paint a picture entitled 'Model With a Slightly Green Face Spitting Water Through her Front Teeth'. He had found a model in the cabarets of Florence, a slightly green-faced singer named Lisa Minelli, and began painting furiously. But Lisa did not take well to modelling and complained loudly throughout the sittings; "Why do you paint-a like thees all day? Is no work for a man. Is sissy-work. Why you no getta job like a real Italiano. Be a waiter. I waste-a my time 'ere. I could-a be at 'ome enjoying my tagliatelli (Italian television)."

And so destiny took a hand and when the portrait was finished Leonardo decided not to call it 'Model With a Slightly Green Face Spitting Water Through her Front Teeth' – a hopeless title which would have doomed the picture to oblivion – and called it instead 'Moaner Lisa' ('Mona' in Italian) thus winning himself immortality and half a yard on the wall of the Louvre.

I then moved to sculpture. Rodin's famous statue of the embracing couple entitled 'The Kiss'. The more I stared at a picture of it the more I became convinced that Rodin had not set out to sculpt what he ended up with. No, I am of the firm opinion that Rodin began by sculpting two quite separate statues, one male and one female, in crouching positions with arms outstretched and bent, perhaps entitled 'Male and Female Nudes About to begin their Friday Evening Kung-Fu Exercises'. But when they were finished he loaded them into the back of a lorry and in his anxiety to get them swiftly to the Exhibition Hall rounded the Place de la Concorde in a tight turn and the two statues crashed together, became interlocked, and have stayed that way ever since.

Franz Hals' 'The Laughing Cavalier'? Originally painted clean-shaven? Would he have been exhibited clean-shaven had not Hals left the painting leaning up against the wall of the Underground station while he bought his ticket?

But the most striking example of my theory in action is my hypothesis of the creation of 'The Angelus' by the French painter Jean Millet. How on earth, I asked myself, did this drab masterpiece of two peasants leaning on their hoes come to be painted by the vivacious young artist who was even then known to his friends as Thoroughly Modern Millet?

My theory runs thus. Millet was on a walking tour with his two friends, Toulouse-Lautrec and Karl Marx when he saw these two peasants, clad in toil-worn French peasant-type blue jeans, leaning on their hoes while the distant church rang the Angelus.

"What a great idea for a masterpiece!" he exclaims boyishly. "Quick, my palette and plenty of paint, mainly Exterior Brown and Blue!" He rapidly begins to set up his portable easel.

"Un moment, mon brave," says Toulouse-Lautrec. "Not so vite. I have a better idea. Get the peasants to change into their best party clothes and paint a picture of them doing the Can-Can. That's what the Salon likes these days, frills, frou-frous and leg!"

"Right," says Millet. "You heard what Toulouse said, Karl. Would you mind asking the peasants to change into evening dress for me?"

Off goes Karl Marx. Chats with the peasants. Returns, face glum.

"No go, I'm afraid," he says. "They have nothing to change into." And then he adds the line which has gone into the history books and which gave Millet his masterpiece:

"The workers have nothing, Toulouse, but their jeans."

I think, therefore I am

René Descartes

ALTHOUGH that line launched René Descartes on his meteoric rise to stardom, what he actually wrote was something slightly different. So I can't tell you the pleasure it now gives me to put the record straight, if only for his sake.

I say that because life was not all roses for this seventeenth-century philosopher. In the first place, he'd been saddled with that unfortunate Christian name, and even though the French pronounce it 'Renay' it was still one hell of a liability for a growing lad in those rough times. Secondly, when he came to manhood he married this real granite-block of a wife. Although Mme Descartes brought some property to the marriage, the truth is she was several years his senior, had the disposition of an untipped taxi-driver and was an inveterate picture-straightener. Every time Descartes sat down to work on a crystalline aphorism in she'd come, still in her rollers, with – "I'm sorry, but I need this room for a social gathering." Or – "If you don't mind, kindly shift your philosophy kit to the shed."

It is hard to think of a way in which she could have been other than a millstone to any aspiring philosopher. Even in their more intimate moments, when he managed to steel himself for an attempt at love-making, her invariable response was the phrase which Gershwin was later to put to such melodious use – "Descartes, take that away from me."

You may wonder then, how was it, in such an unpromising work-environment, that René still managed to make Number One among philosophy's all-time chart-toppers? Well, as I've indicated, it's all down to the widespread misunderstanding about his line 'I think, therefore I am'. And to trace the *exact* origin of that I must take you back to the

New Year's Eve party which Madame Descartes threw to celebrate the advent of 1636.

As it was to be an informal affair, she'd decided to serve the guests 'buffet-style', which is a French expression meaning 'we've got more people than chairs'. As she also intended it to be a late do, with no one even arriving till around 11 p.m., she ran up an enormous bunch of that Gallic imitation of bacon-and-egg flan they call *quiches*. Not the large family-sized ones, but those small individual versions so affectionately celebrated by Yvette Guilbert. ('Just a leetle love, a leetle quiche.')

However – and you'll be glad to know we're now getting somewhere near the point of all this – Madame made it clear to René that although the quiches were all to be put out on the sideboard beforehand – "the one thing I *don't* want to see is people helping themselves in advance and treading their crumbs into the Aubusson. So I'm relying on you to see that nobody starts digging into them until at least one hour after we've seen the New Year in. Then they can take plates and eat properly."

Ironic, isn't it? The founder of the Cartesian school of philosophy relegated to the position of Securicor for bacon-and-egg flans. As he himself said to Father Dinet – I haven't mentioned him before, but he was the Jesuit priest who was just about the only real mate René had at that time – as he said to him "I can't think this is in any way advancing my career. Being sat down here at the sideboard till one o'clock in the morning, that's no way to get any philosophising done tomorrow, I'll be like a limp rag."

To which the good Father rejoined an extremely practical rejoinder. "Well, why don't you use *this* as working-time? Take a writing-instrument and, while you're sitting here, set your mind for lofty thoughts. Then, if any crop up, jot them down on a paper serviette."

"Nice thinking," said Descartes. "Give us a borrow of your quill then."

It worked extremely well. For the next hour or so the two friends sat quietly by the sideboard and Descartes was able to get off quite a few zingers relating to corporeal rationality. It was while he was fashioning an eternal verity on adventitious volition that he glanced up and, to his horror, saw what had happened. Father Dinet had helped himself to a quiche and was absently munching it.

Just as Descartes was about to exclaim, "Watch it, mate, they're not supposed to be eaten yet," he became aware of something else. There, well within earshot, stood his wife! There was only one thing to do.

Stealthily, Descartes took another serviette, scribbled his warning on it, then – equally furtively – pushed the serviette under the priest's nose.

Thus it was the whole three-hundred–year-old misunderstanding originated. That message, the one which Father Dinet was later to publish to the world as 'I think, therefore I am', was in fact only a reference to the time-ban on the bacon-and-egg flans.

All it actually said was:

"I think they're for 1 a.m."

'A Policeman's Lot is Not a Happy One'

W. S. Gilbert
Song from 'The Pirates of Penzance'

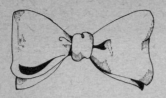

THE phone rang.

"Good morning," said the editor of my local paper *The Staines and Egham News*, "I badly need your help."

I had been waiting for just such a call for some years. It seemed incredible to me that the newspaper had not called upon my talents before to boost its circulation.

"It is yours to command," I riposted firmly. "I have in mind a satirical, hard-hitting yet compassionate column ripping the lid off the inefficiency and downright indifference of local council . . ."

I thought I detected a sigh at the other end of the phone.

"No," he said. "Could you take over our 'Advice to the Lovelorn' column just for this week? Estelle Laverne is indisposed."

"Nothing serious I trust?"

"Just routine. He drank too much after playing rugger and got his beard caught in the pub's glass-washing machine. I will bung on the letters as they come in."

I agreed. He bunged.

Hardly had I got over my sickening disappointment at finding that Estelle Laverne was a bearded, rugger-playing male – I had always enjoyed her lambent prose-style; she was particularly sensitive in advising schoolgirls embarrassed by enormous busts, and happily married solicitors who fancied the lady Parking-Meter Attendant – when I was further disappointed. Only one Lovelorn reader wrote in for Advice.

I shall call him Lafcadio Quilp to protect his anonymity, though that is not his real name (his mother is the dreadful Mrs Snaith who ruins the school dinners at a Staines educational establishment. I have met her son Ron a few times. A deeply thick lad. It surprised me that he was able to write his name let alone a request for Advice).

Ron's – that is to say Lafcadio's – problem was a simple one. Whilst skate-boarding to work along Thorpe Green Road he had glimpsed and become enamoured of the daughter of our new village constable. He had managed to find out her name, which was Lottie Leather-barrow. Should he take his chance in the lottery of life or should he first make enquiries and ensure that Lottie Leatherbarrow was kind in thought, word and deed and not a sharp-tongued, nagging harpy like his own dear mother?

My duty as the surrogate Estelle Laverne was clear. I must make discreet enquiries myself about Miss Leatherbarrow. Engage her in light banter. Observe how she reacted under pressure. I would then be in a strong position to give Ron Snaith the advice he sought.

As it happened I was distracted from doing anything further by a number of small domestic issues which engaged my time over the next few weeks, principally the choice of a Fancy-Dress costume to wear at a Ball in Norfolk I had agreed to attend. In the event it was a double function – my first and my last Fancy-Dress Ball. I will not weary you with details of the humiliations I suffered day after day as the staff of Nathans Theatrical Costumiers tried to stuff my bent six-feet-five frame into costumes which ranged from The Artful Dodger to Harlequin. Eventually, haggard, they flung an old red Father-Christmas cloak round me, thrust my head up through a paper doiley and said "That's it. Cardinal Richelieu!"

I did not enjoy the Ball.

And I did not enjoy the trip home. Something went wrong with the gear-box on my car and I had to do the whole journey in first gear, max speed 15 mph. Dawn broke round about Watford and it was nine o'clock on the Sunday morning when the car, which had been giving off steam like a kettle for miles, coughed, twanged and expired within sight of the transport café on the A.4 near Ascot.

"Good-morning, Father," said the café proprietor reverently as I went up to the counter. "And what would you be after having?"

I pulled my red robes closer against the cold of the morning.

"I need a lift," I said. "To Thorpe."

"Ah," he said, "It's lucky you are this morning, that it is, it is that. Those two lads there are doing overtime on the M.25 extension at Thorpe and it is there that they will be going, that they will, oh yes, Father."

And so it proved. But the vehicle they were driving was not entirely suitable for hitch-hikers. It was an hydraulic crane used for messing about with the motorway lamp-standards. It had a little cabin stuck onto a couple of hinged girders. When the driver pulled a lever the cabin rose up to the required height and whoever was crouched within the little cabin could get on with his work. As the inside of the vehicle was wholly occupied by the two lads, an enormous collie dog and a baby in a pram I had to grit my teeth and squat in the little cabin outside. But it was summer and not too windy and we bowled along happily.

It was as we were going along Thorpe Green that I suddenly realised that we were coming up to our village constable's house. The memory of my duty to Ron Snaith flooded back. The driver had given me the code they used – one thump on the floor to start the vehicle, two thumps to stop it. I thumped twice. The crane stopped.

"Yes?"

"Can you raise me so that I am level with that bedroom window there? There's somebody inside I have to talk to."

"Right."

The driver must have pulled a lever because my little cabin and I rose swiftly until we were level with the window and then moved forward until I was right up against the sill.

It was Lottie's bedroom, happily. And Lottie was combing her hair at her dressing-table. She seemed surprised to see me but opened the window affably.

"I speak on behalf of Ron Snaith," I said. "Could you join me in my little cabin for a minute. I want to engage you in banter and see how you react under pressure."

It was a bit of a shock when she climbed over the sill because she was wearing a very short nighty which appeared to be almost totally transparent. And her figure I can only describe as effeminate.

"Who is Ron Snaith?" she was about to say when she stumbled and fell with a thump on the floor of the cabin.

Taking this as the code signal the driver put the lorry into gear and roared away. Trying to help Lottie to her feet without actually looking at her or touching her I managed to thump twice on the floor and the crane came to a stop again.

"Take us back!" I shouted downwards. "Get us back, lads. please!"

"Right," came the reply. "We'll back up."

"We'd better kneel down," I said to Lottie, "Less chance of being seen."

The lorry backed and weaved and we in the cabin went up and down a few times and then came to rest against a window.

"Wait a minute," said Lottie suddenly, "This isn't my house!"

But it was too late. The window was flung up and glaring out in disbelief at us was the unlovely face of Mrs Gooch, village gossip, defender of morals and scourge of the wicked.

"What," she muttered between clenched teeth, "is the meaning of this?"

I knelt there, frozen with fear. I could see the headlines in the *Staines and Egham News*: 'SEX SCANDAL SHOCK HORROR REVELA-TION. FAKE CARDINAL AND POLICEMAN'S DAUGHTER CAUGHT IN CRANE'. I glanced fearfully at Lottie. Would she tear into the woman and give the old trout a piece of her mind, thus dooming us?

"Oh really," said Lottie, eyes modestly cast down. "Can't a girl go to mobile confessional on a Sunday morning?"

I can now state a fact:

Our policeman's Lottie's not a harpy, Ron.

Splendour in the grass

William Wordsworth
'*Intimations of Immortality*'

FIELD Marshals, Admirals Of The Fleet, Air Vice-Marshals and other distinguished members of the Imperial Staff College. ... While feeling extremely honoured at being asked to deliver this year's Kilroy Lecture, I must admit to some surprise at receiving the invitation; if only because the last time I was summoned to the presence of so many high-ranking officers was during the D-Day Landings when General Montgomery fell into a latrine-trench I had dug.

That sharply-etched memory, however, only spurred my determination to find a subject suitable to this annual lecture whose theme, by tradition, is always 'a neglected feat of military heroism'. To that end, I set myself the task of reading through the entire contents of my local library's 'Military History' section. If that turned out a less onerous undertaking than I'd feared, it was because all the shelf contained was a copy of *The Wooden Horse* and a bound volume of Vera Lynn hits.

Happily, though, the first of these – Mr Williams' excellent escape-story – did suggest to me an episode suitable to this occasion. Accordingly, the neglected feat of military heroism I would now like to recall is the one that took place inside that original and prototype Wooden Horse: the legendary decoy by which the Greeks gained final victory in their altercation with the Trojans. While this ingenious instrument-of-war has itself been frequently acclaimed in song and story, those to whom no tribute has ever been paid are the platoon of humble Greek soldiers whose duty it was to sit inside it for three days. Let me therefore, by drawing on memories of my own Service experiences as an L.A.C., endeavour to reconstruct their agonising ordeal.

It is likely to have begun, as all my agonising military ordeals began, with a briefing from a non-commissioned officer. Probably, I would venture, a sergeant with two long-service stripes.

"All right now, settle down and hold the jaw, let's have some quiet. And quiet means QUIET. That's better. Well now, you've probably all been wondering what this huge thing under the dust-sheets might be when it's at home. All right then, you are now going to be given the privilege of I'm showing you. Corporal, whip off them dust-sheets. . . . There you are, men. What about that then?"

"What is it, Sarge?"

"What do you mean 'What is it, Sarge?' Trust you, Epidoros, to ask what is it. If you wore your helmet on straight, my lad, you'd see what it is. It's an horse. That's what it is. A enormous dirty great wooden horse. And we're calling it The Horse Of Troy."

"You mean like the Mare of Blackpool?"

"No, I do not mean like the Mare of Blackpool, Epidoros. I mean it is an siege-breaking weapon what is going to be filled with something. And do you know what it is going to be filled with, Epidoros?"

". . . Toffees?"

"Toffees. Oh you disgust me sometimes, Epidoros. You really do. Great gormless Greek! How can toffees be used for siege-breaking purposes? No, what that horse is going to be filled with, me lucky lads, is you. All of you. Right then. On the command 'Enter Horse' I want to see this platoon file smartly inside the beast in Alpha Beta order. Entah – HOWSSE!"

"Through where, Sarge?"

"What do you mean, 'Through where'?"

"Where do we enter it? Do we go in through the mouth?"

"Course you do not go in through the mouth! Ordinary eighteen-pence should tell you you cannot enter an horse through the mouth!"

"Well, where then? . . . Hey, you're not getting me to –"

"Through the *trapdoor*! The special trapdoor what has been cut through its midriff! And one more word out of you, Epidoros, I'll have you up in front of the Colonel before you can say Agopemone!"

That then, gentlemen, was the start of their ordeal. What lay ahead was even worse. Try and imagine the torment it must have been for twenty men to sit, shoulder-to-shoulder, inside the confines of a wooden equine facsimile for three endless days.

"Sarge. . . ."

"Sh!"

"*Sarge!*"

"Will you keep your voice down! Want the bleeding Trojans to tumble us?"

"But it's Epidoros, Sarge."

"What about Epidoros?"

"He's got one of his tummies."

"Oh no. No! Not in *here*! Hang on, Epidoros! Attention everybody – can I have your attention, please? . . . Is there a doctor in the horse?"

Picture it, gentlemen. Discomfort, heat, hunger, thirst, enforced silence, no ablution facilities, no Naafi lady. But even those privations pale into insignificance beside the worst torture that gallant little band found itself subjected to. . . .

What every historian has neglected to take into account is that they were all citizens of Greece. In other words, the uniform they were wearing was that of the Greek Army. And we all know what that consists of – a short, flimsy *skirt*! Now, when you couple that skirt with the fact that the seats on which they were obliged to sit were of *wooden* construction – well, need I say more? If you can imagine your own practically bare hindquarters shifting about on rough, unpolished wood for a span of seventy-two hours – then, gentlemen, your personal and ever-present agony is not going to be Wordsworth's 'splendour in the *grass*' is it?

What it's much more likely to be is '*splinter* in . . . gentlemen-I-thank-you-for-your-attention'.

Chacun à son goût

French proverb

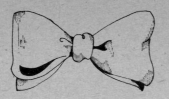

'EACH to his own taste' say the French and for once I agree with them. The French have quite a few philosophical sayings based on food, e.g. 'Sôle Bonne Femme et un oeuf' ('One good woman is enough'), 'Tarte à la Maison' ('The girl lives here'), 'Sauce Tartare' ('Bye-bye, Cheeky!'), but I am inclined to disbelieve most of them. It seems to me that the French nation has conned the rest of the world over a period of centuries into believing that only the French know how to cook food.

My own taste is for British food, cooked in the traditional British way. I speak of lunch, the only meal which I cook for myself. When my wife is out I drag myself away from the typewriter for exactly thirty minutes. During that time I prepare and consume a nicely balanced meal which sets me up for the afternoon's labours.

Until recently my nicely balanced lunch was the same every day: an inch and a half of cheddar and a banana.

Then I became more ambitious. I started to read some cookery book or other. The title escapes me. Was it something by John le Carrier called *The Pie Who Came in from the Cold*? No matter. The important thing is that it gave a recipe for what it called A Simple British Cooked Lunch. None of your Frenchified rubbish, you notice. Good plain food, simply cooked.

'Use butter for frying', said the recipe. I got a pound of butter out of the fridge, unwrapped it and slid it into a frying-pan.

'Melt the butter', said the recipe. I lit the gas and turned it full on. After about ten minutes an element of drama crept into the proceedings. The kitchen filled with smoke of a most subtle and delicate blue colour and about a quart of hot fluid bubbled away cheerfully in the pan.

'Now insert your rasher of bacon', said the recipe. It was a bit tricky getting near enough to the pan what with the smoke and the heat but I managed to lob the rasher into the pan at the third attempt and stood by to turn it when done.

Then a most extraordinary phenomenon occurred. The hot butter began spitting like an hysterical cat and there seemed to be about two hundred tiny, invisible wasps stinging the backs of my hands and forehead.

I retreated behind the door and appraised the situation coolly. It was clear that the spitting hot fat had an effective range of about five feet. If the rasher of bacon was to be turned, as per instructions, then I either had to turn it from six feet away with the aid of a long-handled tool like a garden rake, or protect myself from the wasps by hiding behind some sort of a shield.

The garden rake was useless. Its teeth were too far apart to pick up the bacon and all I succeeded in doing was splashing hot fat up the kitchen wall. The fork used for dung-spreading was a little better because its tines were sharp. I managed to spear the bacon after the fourth stab but in trying to turn it I dropped it down behind the fridge. While I was scooping it out with the rake and holding it under the tap to wash off some of the debris I came to the decision that a shield would be better.

And it was. For those of my readers about to venture into cooking A Simple British Cooked Lunch for the first time I have the perfect answer to the spitting fat problem. Borrow, hire or buy a motor-scooter. These vehicles have a huge, transparent plastic shield fitted on them to stop the rider being lacerated by rain. Wheel the scooter into the kitchen and park it facing the frying-pan, some three feet away. Crouch behind the screen. You will be protected from the flying fat yet be able to see the state of play of the bacon. Over your right arm you will have slipped a two-foot length of six-inch drainage pipe and a stout gardening-glove. When the bacon is due to be turned you merely reach round the screen with your armoured arm and turn the rasher by hand.

I got out two eggs, put them on the top of the refrigerator and consulted the cookery book. 'Now fry your eggs', the book said. I turned to the refrigerator and the eggs had disappeared. I got out two more and put them on the refrigerator. As I watched they gave a little shudder and, lemming-like, waddled over to the edge and committed suicide, joining their two shattered brothers on the floor below.

I got out two more eggs and rested them on the draining-board of the sink reckoning that the grooves in the draining-board would stop the eggs from rolling off. This they did satisfactorily but failed to stop the eggs from rolling *down*. In fact, as the draining-board sloped towards the sink the eggs fairly hurtled down.

I resolved to hold eggs numbers seven and eight in my hand and take advice as to my next move. The cookery book recommended cracking the eggs by tapping them gently against a sharp edge, such as the lip of a saucepan. I got out a saucepan and did as instructed. Half the shell fell into the saucepan and the other half – plus the egg – fell to the floor. I had better luck with the other egg. I managed to get half the egg as well as half the shell into the saucepan. I went back to the cookery book.

'Another method of cracking eggs,' it said, 'is to crack the shell lightly, urge both thumbs into the crack and pull steadily apart – this will enable the egg yolk to drop out undamaged.' Give credit where it is due. This method worked superbly although, looking back, I think I should have cracked the egg over a pan.

With eggs numbers ten and eleven I devised my own method which worked well and I have used it ever since. You simply stand over a receptacle with the egg held firmly in your hand and squeeze. The runny stuff, which is not all that runny, seeps between your fingers and the shell is retained. Or some of it is.

I cannot recall ever having enjoyed a meal as much as I enjoyed that Simple British Cooked Lunch.

The bacon was like no other I had ever eaten. It was a unique culinary sensation. Tiny, like a fragile, twisted, dead oak-leaf, it tasted like a fragment of salty charcoal.

And the fried eggs, though they looked a little like a pair of buttons clad in frilly black lace petticoats, were tender and sliced easily with the help of a serrated carving-knife.

Such a meal of good, honest ingredients and traditional cooking methods is quite beyond the French, of course. They must always over-do everything, like pouring liqueur over the food and setting fire to it.

I had a go at cooking à la française once and believe me it just does not work. At the back of my cookery book it gave a recipe for a typically French bit of 'haute cuisine' (which I always thought meant 'how to cook porridge'). The recipe required me to make a thin omelet, chuck half a pint of brandy over it while it was still hot and 'flambé' it, i.e. set it on fire.

My omelet turned out quite well. I used eighteen eggs – my aim wasn't too good that evening – and we were out of brandy so I chucked on half a litre of methylated spirits and lit it. Well! The French may like to cook like that but it is hardly to the British taste. As the match touched the meths there was a loud 'whooosh', a sheet of flame leaped up and set the kitchen curtains on fire and the omelet turned into a wet, soggy mess.

So as far as I am concerned the French taste for 'haute cuisine' can be summed up in an old English proverbial phrase which I have just made up:

Chuck on . . . arson . . . goo.

'Where the Blue of the Night Meets the Gold of the
Day'

Popular song
Fred E. Ahler, Roy Turk and Bing Crosby

LAST July, about half-past eleven one morning, I
received a telephone-call from my wife. "Do not, on any account,
have a big lunch today."

"Why not?"

"Because for dinner tonight I'm cooking you a leg of lamb, roast
chicken, veal cutlets, braised tongue, shepherd's pie and meat loaf."

I said, "I'll never eat all that lot."

"You'd better try," she said. "The deep-freeze has gone wrong."

Even before the 'ong' in her 'wrong' had died away, I was on the
other line to our local service-engineer, a chap we used to call 'that
little man in the electrical shop' but who's nowadays referred to as 'the
gentleman who owns that big house with two Aston Martins in the
drive'. When he came to the phone, I hailed him by the friendly nickname by which he prefers us to address him, "Sir," I said. "Our deep-
freeze is on the blink."

"Must be a short-circuit," he said.

"In that case, sir," I said, "Could you possibly come over and
lengthen it?"

He gave one of those deep satisfied chuckles you only hear from a
technical person who's just confirmed he's talking to a mug. "Be round
within the month."

When the bill for his services arrived, I glanced at its total and
without a word of a lie I thought it was an offer for the house. After
I'd cancelled our summer holiday and paid it, I made a solemn vow.
The next time any kind of domestic electrical fault developed, I
would repair it myself.

There are two grounds on which that pledge could be considered foolhardy. The first is that where anything to do with electrical matters is concerned I work from a basis of almost Neanderthal ignorance. (Asked by small son how it is that the same electricity which makes the deep-freeze cold is also able to make the toaster hot, I explained it's because the toaster is on the opposite side of the kitchen.) The second is that whenever you permit yourself to make an avowal of that kind, fate always takes you up on it.

Sure enough, little more than a week later, I arrived home to find that something had gone amiss with the interior illumination of our refrigerator. When you opened the fridge door, instead of that little light coming on and floodlighting the food on display, it was all sort of dark and crepuscular in there, which is not only inconvenient but it doesn't half make a two-day-old pizza look cruddy. Well, as technical problems go, it was a challenging one but now and again I do get these delusions of adequacy so I borrowed the screwdriver from small son's laser-beam kit and set to. The first problem was, I couldn't even find where the light-source was located. After searching the entire interior from yoghourts to orange juice, I admitted myself defeated and decided to tackle the job a different way.

Instead of repairing that light-source I would fit an entirely new one. By installing an ordinary twenty-five-watt bulb under the compartment that holds the ice-trays, not only would it give all the illumination necessary but if I also covered the bulb with one of those red-velvet lamp-shades, the whole interior of the fridge would look downright sexy.

I gained an enormous sense of satisfaction when it all worked out as I'd planned, especially as the entire job took no longer than three hours. Mind you, when I say three hours, I suppose it was nearer eleven really, if you count the periods when I had to come out of the fridge to thaw. Well, it had been decided I'd better work squatting inside it with the door closed, because of the three pieces of haddock we were keeping for Tuesday. You know how quickly haddock goes off if the fridge door's left open. Even at that, my candle frizzled the edges of the two bacon rashers for Wednesday. But, that apart – and discounting the fact that my overcoat and woolly gloves still niff slightly of haddock – all that aside, my new interior light works every bit as well as the former one and the fridge is as good as ever.

Well no. To be completely honest, not quite as good as ever. Screwing that light-bulb under the ice-tray compartment did have one side-effect. The ice-cubes are not really as cold as they were. As a matter of fact, they're inclined to be rather warm. Well, to come right out with it, our ice-cubes *boil*.

Now, I suppose all you electrical experts out there have already twigged the technical reason for it. I say that because, when I rang Sir to ask where all this unprecedented heat could be coming from, the phrase he used to indicate its location seemed a fairly familiar one:

Where the screw of the light meets the cold of the tray.

One penny plain and twopence coloured

Robert Louis Stevenson
'Travels With a Donkey'

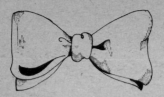

B<small>UT</small> for that one fatal slip I might have got away
with it. As it is I have no recourse but to face the full majesty of the law
and pay my debt to society.

The events which led to my downfall, I now see, followed one upon
the other inexorably, with the inevitability of Greek tragedy, beginning
when I tried to drag the cat down from a kitchen cupboard and tipped
a two-pound jar of home-made marmalade over my wife.

There is a surprising quantity of marmalade in a two-pound jar.
Sticky dollops of the stuff shot all over the place, up the wall, under
the refrigerator, across the cooker, but most of it landed on my wife's
head. And we had no shampoo in the house.

Accepting that I was partly to blame for what had happened I
volunteered to drive to a shop and buy shampoo.

"With lanolin," said my wife. "Any shampoo as long as it contains
lanolin."

"Lanolin?" I replied, puzzled. "Where does that come from?"

"It comes from Wool. Everybody knows that lanolin comes from
Wool."

"Then from Wool it shall come!" I retorted assuringly, grabbing
the AA *Book of the Road* and making for the car.

Wool turned out to be a small town, or large village, in Dorset,
about half-way between Bournemouth and Weymouth, and a fine old
drive from Thorpe, Surrey. It was dark by the time I arrived at Wool
but I found a shop open and bought a shampoo guaranteed by the
proprietor, hand on heart, to contain lanolin.

Things began to go awry from then on. I picked up a hitch-hiker, a
student, who told me all about the trouble with his girl-friend. It seems

that she had taken up a form of Yoga which resulted in her spending most evenings upside down on the carpet resting upon her head. His objections to this were not on religious or moral but aesthetic grounds. Apparently she lost her looks when reversed. Her bottom and bust assumed gross proportions like, he said, a primitive wood-carving, and her eyes became malevolent. I persuaded him to start anew with her. To adopt an inverted posture on the carpet next to her whereupon she should once again appear normal in his eyes. He thanked me warmly and persuaded me to drive him home to Birmingham.

It was four o'clock in the morning when I found myself in Lyne Lane, only a mile from home but the fog thickening. I don't know whether you know Lyne Lane but I usually only approach it from the Thorpe direction and I know full well that there is the Runnymede Council Rubbish tip on the right and the sewage disposal plant on the left. I decided to check my position in the fog by getting out of the car and locating with my hands the huge chain-link gates of the rubbish tip. But I had forgotten that I was facing the other way. I walked through the fog searching with my hands for the gates but could not find them. I walked on and on and eventually fell into a pit of something. I was soaked through, head to foot, in the something and it stank to high heaven.

It was clear that I could not go home in that condition, wet, reeking and totally unacceptable socially. But what could be done about it? Ah. I remembered that Virginia Water, but a mile up the road, had in its esplanade of shops a 24-hour, coin-operated dry-cleaners. I got back in the car and crept gently to Virginia Water. Yes, there was the dry-cleaners, lights a-blaze, empty.

In a flash I nipped into the shop, switched the lights out, stripped naked, stuffed everything into the machine, banged the door shut, thumbed in the appropriate coins and sat down to wait.

It then occurred to me that my car headlights were full on outside, just asking for the police, or some busybody, to investigate what was going on.

Like a shadow I crept out of the door, switched my lights off and went back to the shop. But the door would not open. From force of habit I had slipped the catch on leaving and had now locked myself out.

A car suddenly came through the fog, headlights on. I crouched in a heap, making a sound like a small hawthorn bush, and watched the car stop at the far end of the row of shops.

I considered my position. My chances of driving home unobserved, stark naked, were slim. My best plan would be to find somewhere warm to spend the hours until daylight and then formulate a plan to retrieve my clothes from the dry-cleaners.

The car that went past! Yes, of course, it was the baker going on duty at the bakery, the last shop on the esplanade. Bakers always begin work before dawn.

I made my way stealthily through the night past the dead shopfronts. Yes, the bakery was lit up. The door was unlocked. I slipped into the warmth and hid beneath a shelf of unsold assorted French pastries.

". . . ooooh give ME that night divine, let my arms INto yours entwine . . ." sang the baker, switching on this and that, and banging about in the bakery behind the shop. I heard his footsteps approaching and pressed my bare body into a rack of meringues.

". . . the Desert Song is caLLING . . ." he sang, switching out the lights, and exiting, locking the shop door behind him.

I reconsidered my position. I was locked in but I was at least locked into somewhere most agreeably warm. I had no clothes on. The baker had presumably lit his oven and was returning home for breakfast or a cup of tea or something while it heated up. There was every chance that he would return within half an hour when, if I could find some sort of clothing, I could make my escape.

I looked about me. Hanging up behind the door were some pinafores which the ladies who served in the shop wore. They were plain blue. The same as worn by the girls who bashed the tills at the supermarket four doors up. A plan began to form in my head. If I put on one of the plain pinnies and scraped my hair into a bouffant style I could make a dash for my car and, if stopped, pretend to be a girl-cashier who had worked late. I tried on a pinny. It fitted fairly well except that it did not meet at the back, which was worrying. I pulled my hair forward and messed it about to make it look feminine. I dipped a finger into a raspberry tartlet and reddened my lips. But there was still something wrong. Of course! My figure! Happily the fog was beginning to clear and a fitful moon gave enough light for me to see the shelves. I selected a pair of sticky buns; large buns covered with sticky stuff of a particularly revolting pink colour. Holding them pink sticky stuff inwards I rammed them against my chest. They adhered. I then pulled my plain blue pinny over them and I had the indications of femininity that I needed. Well satisfied, I curled up beneath the counter for a short rest before the baker returned.

Perhaps it was the long drive to Wool and back via Birmingham, perhaps the warmth of the bakery, but when I awoke it was twelve o'clock on Saturday morning and the shop was full of ladies buying bread.

It was one of the nastiest moments of my life but I did not panic. I resolved to make a dash for it. I got to my feet.

"Must get back to my till," I lisped, and minced out through the gaping ladies, clutching the fissure at the back where the pinny did not meet. Once outside I broke into a shambling trot, dived into my car and drove home, confident that I had got away with it.

But I had made one fatal slip. I had broken the law of the land in making my escape from the bakery and must answer to the magistrates' court for the offence, which is, according to the summons – that I did steal, appropriate, or convert to my own use property belonging to the Virginia Water Bakery as under:

One pinny – plain, and two buns – coloured.

A triumph of mind over matter

G. Paley
Natural Theology, 1819

I T'S always a saddening moment, unexpectedly meeting one of your boyhood sweethearts again. But to run across her in Soho, leaning boldly against a lamp-post –! That was heart-wrenching. The funny thing was, I recognised her immediately. A sudden coldness clutching at my heart, I said, "It's – it's Sandy, isn't it?"

"Isn't what, darling?"

"Your name." Then I remembered it wasn't. Her real name was Muriel. Sandy was only what I used to call her, because of the colour of her hair. In those days it was all golden and sparkling, like Sugar Frosties on a clear morning.

She stared at me without interest. Then her expression changed. "Stone me," she whispered. "Soppy."

That had been her pet-name for me; coined, I think, because my other pre-occupation at that time was constructing models of Sopwith aircraft. But just hearing her utter the word brought that whole portion of my life back again. The summer of '38 . . . Munich, Little Audrey jokes, trolley-buses, The Lambeth Walk, Joan Crawford and Clark Gable in *Forsaking All Others*. (Yes, I know that went out on General Release in 1934, but it didn't reach Stamford Hill till 1938.) And, through all those troubled days, Sandy and I roaming the wind-swept uplands of Clissold Park together, little fingers linked, an arm around each other's shoulders, sharing between us an Eldorado choc-ice. No easy task, I remember ruefully, when neither of you has a hand free.

"Oh, Sandy," I said. "Do you ever think about – the Curiously Strong Peppermints?" A flicker crossed her face. Curiously Strong Peppermints had been another of our 'shared' things. They dated from an evening in her father's air-raid shelter when she whispered "I'm narf cold" and moved closer to me. It was an invitation to which I responded with that surge of physical impulse only youth can muster. Jumping on my Raleigh, I pedalled full-pelt to the sweet-shop and brought her back a tin of those mints. Thereafter we never went anywhere without them and it was also from that evening she took to addressing me by that pet-name.

As I looked at her now, something within me ached at what the years do to us. Time had treated her looks kindly enough – her hair shone with the same golden hue I remembered and the shiny black stockings she wore still disturbed my senses – but my soul raged at the cruel fate that had reduced her to her present circumstances. Walking the streets!

"Oh, Sandy," I found myself saying. "What was it? What forced you into this kind of life?"

She shrugged. "The money."

"But to let yourself become a – a . . ." I swallowed, shook my head.

"A what?" she said, tauntingly. "Can't even say the word? You haven't changed much, Soppy."

Her mockery stung me. "All right, I will say it. Did you have to become a Traffic Warden?"

Her eyes blazed. "If it wasn't for men like you," she said, "there would be no need for women like me."

"Sandy," I said. "Listen to me. For old time's sake, won't you let me take you away from –" I gestured helplessly "– this?"

"This what?"

"This BMW. It's mine. And I'm only four minutes over the time. Please," I implored, "for the sake of what we once had together, couldn't you just wander up the road a bit further? Only for a minute or so. Just long enough for me to shove another 5p in."

Stubbornly, she shook her head. Despite my anguish, I could recognise the irony of the situation. What a world it's become when a man finds himself pleading with a woman because *he*'s overdue! My mind was churning like a tumble-dryer. Then suddenly, it calmed. I knew what I had to do. "Look, Sandy," I said. "Look, my dear." And from the recesses of my executive shoulder-bag I drew forth a tin of Curiously Strong Peppermints.

I have never seen female features soften so instantly. I think I even detected a glint of moisture in her eyes. "You – you still carry them?" she faltered. "Still?"

"Everywhere," I said. "And I think I always will."

Those even white teeth clamped down on her lower lip. With a broken word I didn't quite catch, she turned on her smartly polished heel and strode off towards Shaftesbury Avenue.

And that's all there was to the reunion except, as always, for the things that were left unsaid. In this case, I have to confess they amounted to only one thing. The reason I always carry a tin of that particular confectionery about my person is because, for parking-meter purposes, a Curiously Strong Peppermint is exactly the same size and weight as a 5p piece.

And that's why the encounter still retains a certain fragrance for me. Because even if it didn't exactly reach the status of a recaptured might-have-been, it did go part of the way towards achieving Mr Paley's ideal:

A triumph of mint over meter.

Oh,
My Word!

Beware of Greeks bearing gifts

Virgil
'Aeneid'

W H O can you turn to when you've just spent six weeks in the throes of a living nightmare and now that it's over, your so-called nearest and dearest refuse to believe a word of it? Not that I want to give the impression that I'm angry about their strange reaction, because I'm not. Just terribly, terribly hurt.

Let me calm down and give you the background to my appalling ordeal. It began with nothing more sinister than a Dundee cake. I'd had the happy idea of presenting it, as a souvenir of Britain, to a young Californian lady who'd once acted as my secretary when I was working in Los Angeles and who was now enjoying a free two-week stay at a top Mayfair hotel as part of her prize for winning the Miss Nude America Contest. A contest she had only entered, as I tried to explain to the frozen faces that gathered round me when I gift-wrapped the cake, because her heart was set on becoming a librarian and she hoped the prize-money would finance her studies.

Conscious that I'd left behind an atmosphere which would have been considered unseasonable even in Greenland, I made my way to the Mayfair hotel and entered the lift. There were already a few people inside it, one of whom I immediately recognised. He was an Arab potentate I shall only refer to as Haroun Al Raschid, because his riches and power are such that were I even to hint at his real name it could precipitate an international crisis.

One of his entourage pressed the button and, as we proceeded upwards, I couldn't help noticing that Haroun was smiling at me. Well, I didn't say anything to acknowledge it because, after all, what kind of small-talk can one enter into with a strange Arab sheikh? ("Crept into any good tents lately?") But, to my surprise, it was he who addressed me. "May I ask," he said, "are you Denis ben Norden, the wandering story-teller of the broadcasting caravans?"

It was when I nodded modest assent that the reign of terror began. He made a sign to one of his bodyguards, a great bearded fellow who looked as if he could open parking-meters with his teeth. As a result, there was a movement behind me, something suddenly hit me on the back of my skull and everything went black.

When I woke up, it was with a headache that must have shown up on the Richter Scale. I was in one of the hotel's luxury suites – all splashing fountains and Maria Montez baroque – and I was lying on a pile of silken cushions, with the Arabs grouped round looking down at me with gloating fascination.

"What do you want of me?" I said, clutching my hands protectively round my Dundee Cake.

Immediately, a jewelled dagger was at my throat. "One ill-advised move," said the bearded man, "and your Adam's apple will be on the other side of your neck."

"I will tell you what you are here for," said Haroun; and as he proceeded to do so I felt my knuckles whiten. Apparently, ever since the days of a bygone slave girl called Scheherazade, the ultimate status symbol among Arabian rulers has been to have your own live-in story-teller. A sort of human tranquilliser, to provide distraction when you get home exhausted from a heavy OPEC meeting. Haroun himself had been scouring the world to find a suitable candidate for his own household, and he'd only come to London because an agent of his – a former Armenian fig-packer now working as a BBC Light Entertainment producer – had sent word about two chaps who performed exactly that function on an obscure radio panel-game.

I don't have to tell you, when I realised what he had in mind for me, my heart chilled. The prospect of spending the rest of my life doing a nightly turn for a desert despot . . .! Drawing a deep breath – "I refuse," I said resolutely.

In a flash, a gleaming scimitar was nudging me. "How would you like to be turned into a soprano?" said the bearded man.

Faltering, I said, "This should really have been arranged through my agent."

"I will let you remain alive," Haroun said, "only as long as your stories amuse me."

And so it proved. Every night for the next six weeks, the moment Haroun returned from a tough day putting up world petrol prices, he would seat himself expectantly before me and I'd launch into a typical 'My Word!' story. Only when I saw that stern mouth relax could I feel reassured that, for another day at least, the pun had proved mightier than the sword.

It was an incarceration that might well have ended tragically had I not had the good fortune to attract the favour of one of the female members of Haroun's retinue. In deference to the world's need to conserve energy, he had only brought a small assortment of his wives with him – about a six-pack – but I soon noticed that one of them was eyeing me with what can only be described as a hungry look. Realising that women have the same urges the world over, I promised that if she'd help me effect an escape, I'd oblige with what she so obviously had in mind: the Dundee cake. She proved as good as her word and I sped home.

As I've mentioned, the thing I still can't reconcile myself to is the attitude my dear ones have adopted towards the terrifying ordeal I have now related. What makes it especially trying is that they were the ones who kept *demanding* a reasonable explanation of how I could go off to a Miss Nude America's hotel and not come back for six weeks.

All I can now hope is that at least my experience will provide a moral for anyone else who makes his living from hastily improvised fiction. As that old Latin tag forewarned:

Beware of sheikhs sharing lifts.

The female of the species is more deadly
than the male

Rudyard Kipling
'*The Female of the Species*'

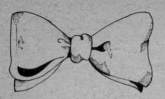

"GO, little book ..." wrote Chaucer, drawing
Troilus and Criseyde to its conclusion. Like a paper boat, the little
volume was launched on the waters and wished well.

Robert Louis Stevenson sent *Envoy* on its way with a powerful
suggestion that buying the book would radically improve the pur-
chaser's lifestyle. He wrote:

> Go, little book,
> And wish to all,
> Flowers in the garden, meat in the hall,
> A bit of wine, a spice of wit,
> A house with lawns enclosing it,
> A living river by the door,
> A nightingale in the sycamore.

It seems that nowadays, in the fierce competition of the book world,
sending a book on its way with a gentle prayer and a pat on the spine
is about as efficient a method of distribution as hurling a boomerang.
The method now in vogue is not to market the book at all but to market the author.

An author nowadays may still write, "Go, little book ...", but in
all honesty he should add, "... but hang on, I am coming with you."

My first Author Tour was a year or two ago but I still wake up at
night shivering and twitching at the thought of it. I propose here and
now to recount a few details of that trip so as to give a kind of Survival
Guide to those of you proposing to burst into print.

My book was first published in the USA and my Author Tour

started there. It was not so much a question of being sent out on circuit as being shot out of a cannon. I was given a pile of airline tickets, an itinerary, and away I went, unaccompanied, across the Middle West.

The first thing you have to get to grips with is the problem of taxis. In New York all taxis are yellow and dented. They are ex-saloon cars and most of the space formally given over to the passengers is taken up by a malefactor-proof steel grille. This means that anybody over four feet six inches in height – which I am – has to bend into a kind of foetal crouch on the back seat. While he can. The trouble is that New York cabbies are chatty. I had one whose greatest experience was once having driven the bandleader Geraldo. We careered across New York late at night singing – in harmony – 'You Stepped Out of a Dream'. The difficulty was that I had to get on my knees and talk to him through a small aperture in the steel grille. It was like travelling in a weird mobile confessional.

And then there was the problem of laundry on the tour. The itinerary called for one night only in every town so there was no question of handing the laundry in. I had to do it myself. For those of you who may have to face the same problem, here is my method.

N.B. American hotel washbasins do not have rubber plugs but those lever arrangements whereby you press a knob and the plug leaps out and when you pull it the plug leaps back into its hole. But the plug does not seat properly. *Ever*. So if you try to do your washing in the basin the suds disappear before you have got to the collar. But do not despair. Every American bathroom has a white waterproof wastepaper basket. Always use this.

On arriving in your hotel room at six-thirty p.m. (it always is six-thirty p.m. when you arrive; all American flights take fifty-five minutes, incidentally), ring Room Service and order a Club Sandwich. The girl will say, "Right away, sir," which will give you forty-five minutes to do your laundry before your supper arrives.

Strip off everything *except your socks* (for some reason to do with the shape of socks they cannot be washed in the hand). Shove your shirt, pants, hanky and whatever else you want to wash into the wastepaper basket, add detergent, hold it under the shower – on 'hot' – swill it round a bit and leave it. Take a shower – soaping your socks well *whilst still on your feet* – then dry yourself. Remove socks and hang on shower rail to dry.

Pound the garments in the wastepaper basket. Pour off the water and refill. Pound them again. Repeat until the water you pour away is reasonably transparent, then hang them on the shower rail to dry. *Except for the handkerchiefs*.

Dangle your hankies in water until they are sopping wet and then squeegee them with the edge of your hand on to the bathroom tiles. When you peel them off in the morning they will come away *ironed*.

The problems of an Author Tour in England, which came next, are different but just as grievous.

Trying to cram the ancient frame into a British Rail sleeping berth designed to accommodate nobody taller or wider than Beryl Bainbridge . . .

It was the night sleeper to Manchester, first class (the publishers insisted, rather as Torquemada always gave the subject of his Inquisition a rose). Sleeping compartments, I found, are not spacious but by sitting on the basin I could get my trousers off. I spent a happy hour playing with the little folding shelves and the lights and adjusting the paper drugget, and trying to work out what the piece of bent wire hanging from the door was for (I still do not know) and then I got into bed and tried to sleep. Sleep was not possible. The heating was on and would not turn off and the temperature was something like 140 degrees Fahrenheit. I stuffed a sock in the vent but the smell of hot sock soon became insupportable. I removed the charred sock, lay on top of the bedclothes and hoped for the best. Every time the train pulled up at a station, which it did eighteen times between London and Manchester, I fell off the bed.

Bone tired, shaken and bruised, I made a tour of Manchester bookshops and then presented myself at the . . . Hotel (name suppressed on legal advice) where I was to attend a Literary Luncheon.

It was the worst meal I have ever eaten.

It began with what is called 'Leak Soup'. This tasted like rusty water which had somehow leaked through the ceiling on to the plates.

The main course was supposed to be steak and kidney pie and vegetables. It had been hanging around for many hours and the steak and kidney pie tasted of Brussels sprouts, and the Brussels sprouts tasted of peas, and the peas had no taste at all.

Lastly there was apple pie. This was a kind of dim frogspawn with a bit of cardboard on top.

The lunch was a truly deadly experience but worse was to come. The speeches. The first two were tolerable. A poet spoke briefly and quite inaudibly about a poet who died three hundred years ago of whom nobody had ever heard. He was followed by a large jolly man with a mottled face who wrote books about badgers and stoats and earwigs who talked like humans. He had clearly avoided the food and concentrated on knocking back the hock (which tasted like water that daffodils had stood in for a week). His speech was a string of racial jokes, some obscene but all offensive, which cheered us up a little.

The came the star turn. A lady novelist. She read from a sheaf of notes the thickness of *Decline and Fall of the Roman Empire*, Vol. I, in a loud and hectoring voice which rattled the coffee cups. It also caused the microphone to go eeeeeeeeEEEE*EEEE*! which went through the head like an assegai. It was difficult to follow the drift of her argument as she dropped her notes through nerves after a minute and scooped them up again in the wrong order but it seemed to be a minute-by-minute description of her working day. As this consisted almost wholly of staring at a blank sheet of paper, chewing a biro and wallowing in self-pity, it did not make for merry listening. After thirty minutes half the guests were asleep. After forty-five minutes the other half had left. She finished, after fifty-eight minutes on her feet, to a patter of applause from the committee and two ladies who were staying in the hotel and had joined the lunch by mistake.

So I conclude my Author's Survival Guide with an apt quotation from Rudyard Kipling, who had suffered and knew what he was talking about.

Avoid Literary Lunches if possible. If they are anything like mine the food is awful. But that is not all:

The female of the speeches is more deadly than the meal.

You can lead a horse to water
but you cannot make him drink

Proverb

IT'S probably due to some kind of personality defect, but I just don't seem to have the knack of bribing people effectively. Perhaps I don't put out the correct feelers, perhaps I don't phrase the proposition properly, perhaps the inducements I dangle just aren't suitable – whatever the reason, I simply don't appear to be blessed with any kind of talent for corruption.

And that's a shame. Because where Frank and the editor of *The Guinness Book of Records* were concerned I really wanted to succeed. Strange about Frank, that. Did you know – and not many people know this – despite all the honours and tokens of public acclaim that have been showered upon Frank Muir, many of them from a great height, the one honour he most avidly craves still eludes him? I'm talking about seeing his name in *The Guinness Book of Records*.

No, I didn't believe it either when he first confessed it to me. But after I discovered it to be true, I found myself – well, I dunno – moved. Big tall fellow like that, all the poise in the world, pink bow tie, and yet going on deep down inside him, there's something quite different from what gnaws away at us ordinary folk. Nothing to do with Elsie Tanner or the second Nolan Sister or Olga Korbut. His most burning secret desire is to have his name recorded in that brewery book.

I don't mind telling you, that made such an impression on me that I went out and bought a copy. After a prolonged study of it, I came back and reported to Frank. "Seems to me," I said, "that there's two ways most of 'em in there qualified for entry. Either by doing something nobody else had done before; or by doing something people had done before but doing it faster, longer, or more often. Which of these alternatives appeals to you?"

"The first one," he said unhesitatingly.

Do you know – and here's something else not many people know – it's awfully difficult to think of something nobody else has ever done before? I toyed with all sorts of possibilities; going over Niagara Falls on roller-skates; jogging nude round and round inside the Dorchester revolving-door; pushing an ice-cube across Richmond Common with your nose; being shot across Lake Windermere by a giant catapult suspended between two trees. All of them Frank rejected as either impossible, inconvenient or undignified. So we were forced to settle for the second alternative.

Leafing through the book, I came up with a couple of record-breakers Frank might try going one better than – "Chap named Fyodor Vassilet of Moscow," I said. "He fathered sixty-nine children. Or Don Carter of Michigan who, by using quite different skills, balanced on one foot for eight hours forty-six minutes."

In that pipe-smoking way of his, Frank pondered. "How many children did you say that Russian fellow had?" he asked finally.

"Sixty-nine," I said, "but remember you start with the advantage of already having two. Cuts your target all the way down to sixty-eight."

"True," he said, and puffed away a bit more. Then – "Trouble is," he said, "what I really had in mind was getting into next year's edition."

"Lessens your chances," I warned. "Unless you're prepared to spread yourself round a bit." He shook his head. I drew a line through Fyodor Vassilet's name and, after a moment's reflection, drew another through that of Don Carter. Knowing Frank as I do, I doubt whether he could balance for eight hours forty-six minutes even lying down.

Out came the book again and I searched for other feats of skill or endurance. The one that seemed to offer Frank the best opportunity of making the record book was that set up by a Mr Crosby of Harrogate, who earned his immortality by spitting a cherry-stone forty-two feet five and a half inches from a sitting position.

There and then I went out and bought two pounds of cooking cherries – well, it seemed needless extravagance to get the eating ones just for spitting purposes – and brought them to Frank. He settled himself in a comfortable armchair while I stood by with a tape measure.

As it turned out, long-distance cherry-stone spitting is by no means as easy as it sounds. For one thing, it now appears that Frank shouldn't even have considered making his attempt on the spitting record from within the Savile Club. (Or so, at any rate, would seem to be the opinion of the current Membership Committee.) Secondly, it could be that this particular activity is not one that should be even attempted by anyone with a bridgework problem. (The number of times I had to dash out into Brook Street and retrieve it from under passing taxis!) Thirdly, did you know – and here's yet another thing not many people know – did you know there even *was* such an ailment as Dislocation of the Tongue?

Nevertheless, the moment the orthodontist had signed Frank off, there I was – Old Faithful – waiting with another record for him to better. This time, it was the one set up by Lindsay R. Dodd who walked backwards from Leeds, Yorkshire to Kendal, Cumbria.

Experience had taught us by now that before any record-breaking attempt, it was as well to estimate one's chances by having a practice go. So, after I'd worked a route out on the map, Frank set out from his home in Thorpe, Surrey, walking backwards in what I'd estimated would take him in a dead straight line to where I was waiting with a stopwatch in Marble Arch, London. It was only when he arrived eighteen hours late and wet from head to foot that I realised my map-reading had failed to take into account Staines Reservoir.

To give you all the details of what happened with the other records he set himself to break could well take a lifetime, and as we obviously haven't got a lifetime let me simply enumerate some of them in such a way that it may seem like one. Among the record-breakers my colleague went on to try to displace was Bob Blackmore who ate three lemons in twenty-four seconds – it took four of us three hours to get Frank's lips to unpucker; a man in Wolverhampton who jumped a twelve-foot billiard table lengthways – I *told* Frank to let go the cue; and Bill White, who was buried alive for 134 days. (It was after just fifteen seconds that we began hearing the muffled screams.)

"We'll have to try again with the first option," I said finally. "Doing something nobody has ever done before."

"Like what?" said Frank.

"Like bribing the editor of *The Guinness Book of Records*," I said. "Leave it to me."

Norris McWhirter has been editing the volumes since 1955 and whatever other faults he may have, he is at least approachable. When I invited him to a slap-up lunch at the Savoy Grill, he agreed readily. It was over the coffee that I made my move. "See here, Mr McWhirter," I said, "I could make arrangements for you to eat this kind of meal regularly, providing you could bend a few rules to the extent of including in next year's edition the name of a man who has established what you could justify as a *sort* of record."

He looked at me expressionlessly. "What does 'a sort of record' mean?"

"Well," I said, "isn't it in itself a record to have made more unsuccessful attempts to get into *The Guinness Book of Records* than anyone else on record?"

By way of answer, he picked up the jug of iced water, poured it carefully into my lap and left. See what I mean by my incompetence at bribery? Despite all the expensive food and drink I'd stuffed down that man, he refused to compromise his principles by one jot.

Perhaps I should have listened to the old proverb:

You can feed a Norris McWhirter but you cannot make him fink.

It is a riddle wrapped in a mystery
inside an enigma

Winston Churchill
Description of Russian foreign policy

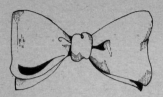

KNOWING that my old friend Sherlock Holmes
was partial to a newly baked loaf, I stopped off at his bakers in Chamber
Street before going on to his chambers in Baker Street.

But Holmes was not there.

This hardly surprised me. One day he might be in Marrakech removing secret papers from the safe of the Bosnian consulate in the guise of a
Japanese wrestler, the next foiling an attempt to sabotage an assault on
the Matterhorn in the guise of an Egyptian channel swimmer. There
was no telling.

I settled myself in a comfortable old leather chair to await his return.
The loaf looked delicious. I took a bite of the crust. It splintered with
the noise of a small-calibre pistol shot and I was deluged with crumbs.

Quite a large part of my time was spent waiting for Holmes but this
was no matter. I had no dependants to consider: I just sat there, a crusty
old bachelor.

He, on the other hand, was the world's greatest criminologist; the
ideal man to call upon when the Empire stood in jeopardy. I mused
upon an idea I had had for some time of mounting an exhibition of
relics of some of his greater triumphs: the odd hat-band, spy, dead dog
and so forth. I would call it the Ideal Holmes Exhibition.

It was a quarter to five the following afternoon that I was interrupted
from my reverie by a distant but unmistakable sound: the oath of a
cabby who has been under-tipped. Moments later I heard footsteps on
the stairs and Holmes appeared in the doorway. He flung his deer-
stalker hat away from him distractedly. It circled the room twice,
clearly seeking a suitable landing site, before settling gently upon the
beak of a stuffed ptarmigan. And then he saw me and his eyes lit up.

"Lillie Langry!" he cried, taking my hand. "By all that's delightful!"

"It's me – Watson!" I said.

"Then what are you doing there in a dress covered with beige spots?" he demanded fiercely.

"They are breadcrumbs, old friend," I said, brushing them off. I could see that he had something on his mind.

After a moment of restless pacing he suddenly said, "I have just been given tea by Her Majesty's Foreign Secretary –"

"Earl Grey?"

"No," he said. "A fairly ordinary Darjeeling. Grown, I rather fancy, on that south-facing hill just above the handbag factory. He gave me very worrying news."

Holmes paced the room again. The cat was sitting asleep on his chair and Holmes bent to tickle it behind an ear.

"Watson, my violin if you please."

I handed it to him and with a forehand drive worthy of the great Dr Grace himself, he batted the cat out of the chair and on to the floor. He settled himself comfortably into the chair.

"I am informed, Watson, that there is in this country an important Balkan princeling, here under the protection of Her Britannic Majesty. He has travelled from his own squalid little country to Britain in order to undergo an operation at which our British surgeons lead the world. The removal of an in-growing toe-nail."

"Just so. What we medical men call a 'piggyectomy'."

"Would you mind shutting up while I'm talking?"

I nodded assent.

"The Foreign Office believe that an attempt is going to be made on the prince's life. Tonight."

"But by whom? Holmes. By whom? – if you will pardon the understandable interruption."

"There is a secret sect in Russia whose members are trained in all techniques of assassination. Their job is to spread out over Europe and foment revolution. They are fanatics and will stop at nothing – not even road-signs saying 'Major Road Ahead'."

"Good grief," I whispered.

"When a member is fully trained there is a strange Russian indoctrination ceremony. Their leader, a mysterious lady known as Sister Anna, kisses him on both cheeks twice and he is then known by a special name."

"What name?"

"He is thereafter known as an – Anarchist."

My blood went cold.

"Our information is that they are in London and have their orders to poison the prince tonight, thus provoking a diplomatic incident which might lead to a major conflagration among the leading nations of Europe."

Holmes had already taken every precaution. A police constable was on duty by the side of every bed in the Charing Cross Hospital where the prince lay. Eight men were on permanent duty round the prince's bed. No visitors were to be allowed in. The prince was to eat nothing and drink nothing until it was all over.

"Wait a minute, Holmes. The prince will be under an anaesthetic. Can they not get him *then* and make him swallow something?"

"He will not lose consciousness at any time. A local anaesthetic will be applied to his foot, which will go to sleep."

"Ah yes. A condition we doctors call comatose."

"What is worrying me, Watson, is that these fiends are masters of disguise. I am sure that they are already within the hospital disguised as porters, or matrons or bunches of grapes. But how – how, man – will they strike? How will they force the poison *down* him? They must force the poison *down* him in some manner or . . ." He paused, then continued softly, "I've got it! I think I've got it! Why should we assume that they will attempt to force the poison *down* him? I must get to Charing Cross Hospital immediately, if not before . . ."

"But, Holmes, you have nothing to go on!"

"Then I will borrow your bike."

I waited for two hours, fortifying myself with eating the remains of the loaf, which I found lodged within my waistcoat.

He strode into the room with a look of quiet triumph on his hawk-like face.

"The assassination will not take place," he said. "I found the murder device and the fiends have been apprehended, lurking within the hospital walls disguised as light diets. This is what they proposed to use to introduce the poison into the prince!"

He flung on to the table an object I knew well from my medical practice. It was a long rubber tube with a bulb at one end. Near the end of the tube was an odd bulge.

"There is the proof that the villains were Russian anarchists," he cried.

"But how did they suppose to use this to poison the prince?" I faltered. "By what system?"

"Alimentary, my dear Watson. If you will do me the goodness to take the device apart I will deduce what you will find therein."

I did so.

"I think you will find," said Holmes, "that you have in your hand a wee doll, made of wood, with 'Made in the Ukraine' stamped on its base."

"Correct, Holmes."

"It is, of course, the smallest of a nest of eight, which are popular with Russian children. Be careful how you handle it, Watson. Inside the doll will be a poison which is tasteless, odourless, colourless and for which even our music-halls have no known anecdote."

"There seems to be a piece of paper wrapped around the doll, Holmes."

"I think you will find that it is a page ripped at random from some cheap edition of a mystery novel. It is there to hold the doll firmly within the tube."

"Correct. It is a page from Wilkie Collins's famous mystery, *The Woman in White*. Amazing, Holmes! But how did you deduce from this device that it spelled Russia?"

Holmes lit his pipe, injected himself with a snort of cocaine and played a swift chorus of Monti's *Czardas* on the violin before saying, quietly: "See what it is man –?

"It is a wee doll wrapped in a mystery inside an enema."

Speak of one who loved not wisely, but too
well

Shakespeare
Othello Act, V sc. 2

BECAUSE the publication of the collected corres-
pondence of the Duke of Wellington was one of the most talked-about
literary events of the past few years, you can imagine my excitement
when I recently came into possession of one of his unpublished letters.
What's more, it is dated 1811, which means he wrote it before he was
even made a duke; while, in fact, he was still plain Sir Arthur Wellesley. The postmark on the letter's envelope is Spain, it is addressed
to his father's sister, a Miss H. Wellesley, and its content reads as
follows:

Dear Auntie Hilda,
  Thank you for the knitted things. We are presently encamped before
Salamanca and the tent they have given me is very nice, if a bit on the
small side, especially when I am on my horse. As you advised, I have
taken the precaution, while encamped with the rough and licentious
soldiery, to keep all my valuables in a safe place, even though this does
tend to make me walk oddly.
  But the purpose of this missive relates to something more important;
namely, your constant urgings that I should find myself a nice girl for
the purpose of getting married and perpetuating the Wellesley name.
In that respect, I am moved to recount a strange occurrence which
occurred soon after we made camp.
  Late one evening, there came a knock at my tent-flap and when I
bade whoever was without to make his way within, it turned out to be
faithful Colour Sergeant Parker. When he spoke, I could not help but
notice it was in a strangely hesitant tone, because his more customary
method of reporting is at a pitch of voice to make your ears water.

Accordingly – "You seem to be labouring under the stress of some emotion, Colour Sergeant," I remarked.

"Trouble in B Lines, sir," he replied, one mutton-chop twitching noticeably.

Such tidings constitute no unusual occurrence among the sweepings I command. In fact, I can confide to you, dear Aunt – knowing that your discretion will never allow the comment to go further – that my troops may not frighten the enemy but, by G——, they frighten me. So I evinced no surprise, merely nodded him to proceed.

"I have reason to believe, sir," he said, with even more difficulty, "I have reason to believe that a certain fusilier in the fourth tent is – a female!"

Here, indeed, *was* an unusual occurrence. Need I say that the intelligence left me so put about, I removed the epaulettes from my pyjamas, replaced them upon my uniform and, bidding the Colour Sergeant bring the soldier hither immediately, redonned full military order. Within moments, what appeared to be a slim boyish fusilier was standing before me.

"At ease, soldier," I said. "Now what is this I hear? An accusation has been made that, contrary to Army Regulations, you have undertaken Active Service while knowingly being other than of the male gender. How do you answer this charge?"

By way of response, the young soldier removed his forage-cap and tossed his head. Then, dear Aunt, did I behold a sight that for one suffocating moment had me neglecting the inherent reflex of breathing. For, from the lad's shoulders, a cascade of golden hair shook itself loose and fell down behind him, descending to almost as far as where the back changes its name. At the spectacle, the Colour Sergeant gave such a sharp intake of breath, his side-whiskers were sucked down his throat and it became necessary for me to pound his shoulders to prevent him choking.

The fusilier was indeed a girl!

Endeavouring to regain my composure, I said to her, "What can have induced you, a female, to join the colours?"

Her answer was immediate and confident, " 'Twas, sir, for a pair of laughing brown eyes."

Further interrogation elicited that the said eyes, brown, laughing, two, were the property of her betrothed, who had been pressed into service with the Limehouse Blues. "And after he'd been taken away, sir," she said, "I found I couldn't do without him."

"Couldn't do what without him?" I asked.

She coloured prettily. "I joined the Army to find him and be at his side, sir." Then she went on to explain the manner in which she had effected this difficult undertaking. Her first step had been to seek out a Recruiting Station with a near-sighted Medical Officer. Luck being with her, she was duly sworn in and posted to a regiment where, by reason of her boyish form and deepness of voice, she was able to maintain the deception for nearly twenty minutes.

The Colour Sergeant muttered an oath. "So that's it," he said. "That's why B Troop have put in no applications for leave since 1809."

But, suddenly aware that something within my heart was throbbing like a stubbed toe, I motioned him to silence. "Tell me, child," I said, "What is your name?"

"Kitty," she said. "But they do call me Kit."

Kit! My soul leaped. It was the name of my favourite inspection! Conscious of a certain dryness of throat, I pressed on. "And the name of your betrothed? He of the laughing brown eyes?"

"If you please, sir," she said. "Fred Pacefoot."

My lips tightened. Well did I remember Pacefoot – a slovenly, poltroonish malcontent. One of the few soldiers in the Peninsula to be demoted from Private to Semi-Private.

A sudden resolve stirred within me. Dismissing the Colour Sergeant, I addressed the girl urgently. "Miss Kit," I said. "For some years now, my Auntie Hilda has been urging me to take a wife. Can I not now persuade you – moved as I am by the devoted gallantry you have exhibited – to forget this Pacefoot and think rather of exchanging your maiden name for that of Wellesley? For I can promise you much. Not only am I in prospect of being granted an Iron Dukedom, but there is every chance of having a popular boot named after me. What can a Fred Pacefoot offer to match that?"

Her answer was immediate. "Sir – a pair of laughing brown eyes." To which, dear Aunt, I had no answer but to allow her to leave my tent and continue her search.

Having already called upon your discretion once, I must seek it again. Because the initials of that girl will be carved forever on my ridge-pole, I must now ask you not to allow the tale I have told you about her to become the common tittle-tattle of your tea-time cronies.

Or if, perforce, you find yourself in some wise obliged to bandy about the story of that devoted girl, then do me this favour –

Speak of one who loved not Wellesley, but two eyes.

There are fairies at the bottom of our garden

Rose Fyleman
'Fairies'

"**G**r-r-r – you swine!"

A bit strong, mayhap, for a literary work of this sensitivity? Not a bit of it. I merely quote Browning: *Soliloquy of the Spanish Cloister.*

When I am feeling as grim as I am now I frequently growl that line to people I meet. If they faint, or try to beat my skull in with a broken lump of concrete, I am able to recover my poise by murmuring, "Don't you know your Browning?" They are then wrong-footed and usually apologise. Unless they are, at the time, sun-bathing.

What I am really suffering from is Progressive Melancholia brought on by the breakfast I had this morning. 'Progressive Melancholia' is an age-old malady which I have just invented. It is a good name because it works in both senses of the word 'progressive'. The melancholy gets progressively worse. And it is induced by what some misguided idiots – Gr-r-r – you swine – call progress.

Items we are supposed to regard as progress include:

(a) advertising a very good bar of chocolate not by the excellence of its ingredients, or its taste, or the nourishment it provides, but by the loudness of the noise it makes when you break it in half;

(b) printing telephone directories by computer so that the names are not *quite* in alphabetical order;

(c) putting up a notice which says 'For your convenience, all lifts are out of use for servicing';

(d) packing biscuits on airlines in such impenetrable plastic envelopes that, wrench or bite as you may, you end up with a handful of biscuit-dust;

(e) replacing room service in hotels with an electric kettle whose lead is too short to reach the table so you have to grovel on your knees to mix together a plastic envelope containing too much sugar, a small plastic pot of something which is not milk but has curdled anyway, and a thin brown packet seemingly containing the ashes of a cremated mole.

Small grievances, you may think, amid the greater lunacies of our century. But I remind you that it is the tiny things, not the large, which irritate. A flea within the ear is unbearable. An elephant cannot get in.

My flea this morning was breakfast.

Do you remember breakfast? What happened to it?

Do you remember porridge? Hot goo which filled you up and made the ends of your fingers tingle?

For centuries porridge nourished the entire Scottish nation. Athletes trained on it and such was its energy-giving property that, during the Highland Games, cabers – entire pine-trees – were tossed high in the air as easily as if they were 2B lead pencils.

A good bowl of porridge could grow hair on a haggis.

It was made on a Saturday night, poured into the kitchen drawer, and allowed to cool all Sunday while the family sat around repenting and refraining from whistling. At dawn on Monday the honest crofter would saw off a lump, stuff it into his sporran and set off up the hills for a week's sheep-gathering, confident that he would be well sustained by an occasional gnaw of the grey/beige oaten manna.

All gone now, with the arrival of progress. Porridge has now been improved and is what is known as 'instant porridge'. A food which is called 'instant' superficially resembles the original but has been dealt with chemically so that it takes slightly less time to prepare in return for losing ninety per cent of its flavour and all its nourishment.

Bacon is no longer bacon. It emerges, sweating heavily, from its plastic envelope and resists all efforts to fry it to crispness. The only hope is to continue frying for hours, hand on the gas tap. The slice of bacon will first shrivel, then shrink. At the very moment it is about to disappear, entirely switch off the gas. The minute crumb of bacon you are left with will not be *crisp* – as we used to know and love crisp bacon – but it will be the best you can do these days.

And fried eggs. A fried egg should be sluttish. It should be irregular in shape and its petticoats should be frayed and none too clean.

In a hotel or a restaurant nowadays progress has decreed that fried eggs should be neat, clean and hygienic. The yolk is anaemic and the white is hospital white and slimy with oil. If you try to fork a piece when having breakfast in bed it slides off the fork and slithers down your chest, ending up in your tummy-button.

What we are given to eat for breakfast nowadays is called a 'cereal'. These products were invented by an American vegetarian called Post. He had the bright idea of providing vegetarians with an alternative to bacon and eggs. His method was to take an ear of corn, hit it with a smallish toffee-hammer until it was flat, then roast it in the oven and serve it with milk and sugar. As the world was going through one of its periodic fits of lunacy and deciding that anything new was better, these flakes of corn became hugely popular for breakfast. Other manufacturers got busy and hammered away at all sorts of other things like grains of rice and oats and wheat and bran. And they made them into all sorts of shapes so that they could claim them as 'new', i.e. better.

My wife has lately been breaking her fast with something called 'muesli'. It seems that some manufacturer decided that hitting a grain of cereal with a toffee-hammer was too painful on the finger and thumb of the left hand and there must be an easier way of earning a fortune. So he hit upon the simple notion of emptying out the leavings of cart-horses' nosebags, adding a few other things like unconsumed portions of chicken layers' mash and the sweepings of racing stables, packaging the mixture in little bags and selling them to health food shops. I cannot be *sure* that this is what happened, of course. It is merely a hypothesis based on what the stuff looks like.

My wife actually likes it. But so do the cats and every breakfast sees a running battle between my wife and the beasts as to who gets most of her bowl of carthorses' delight. A week ago I had to put my foot down. I got used to the noise of the battle but the cats kept crashing through my newspaper from the other side, an unnerving surprise which had me soaring a foot in the air from a sitting position.

This morning my wife produced a huge carton of some new stuff for us to try as a substitute. It is called 'Huskies'. It looks, and I must say tastes, like roughly chopped-up corrugated cardboard, but the blurb on the packet says that it is made from cereal husks, which the company scientists have discovered contain everything the body needs.

I was crunching away at my first spoonful this morning when something horrible lodged itself in my throat. Something small, thick and hairy, like a dead bee. I did not panic. I took a deep breath through my nose and tried to dislodge it by screaming. My wife thought she might be able to hook it out with a wire coat-hanger and ran to find one. I had a more scientific thought which I put into practice. We have a roller towel on the back of the kitchen door. I draped myself through the roller towel and balanced myself in it with my legs dangling out one side and my head and shoulders out the other. I then knocked the top of my head rhythmically on the floor.

Out of my throat dropped a tiny plastic caveman. He was short and fat and was clad in a skin of plastic imitation fur.

As I climbed out of the towel my eye caught the back of the carton. In large letters it proclaimed "See Inside – Free Caveman! Collect the Set! Found Your Own Fine Family of Furries!"

Do join us at breakfast one morning down here in Thorpe, Surrey. Help yourself to a brimming bowl of cereal.

But be warned. Progress has been made in breakfast foods:

There are Furries at the bottom of our carton.

One man's meat is another man's poison

Proverb

THERE was only one occasion in my life when I put myself on a strict diet and I can tell you, hand on heart, it was the most miserable afternoon I've ever spent. A Sunday it was, and I didn't even get up till going on quarter-to-two. This was because I'd been sleeping with Lady Pamela that Saturday night and when you're in bed with her you don't get much chance for any shut-eye.

Lady Pamela, I should explain, was a bitch. A Doberman Pinscher bitch, to be precise, belonging to the couple at Number 64 who'd asked us to look after her while they made one of their weekend visits to Scotland. (They always go up there once a year; nobody knows why, but the neighbourhood rumour, judging from the contents of their dustbin, is that it's to lay a wreath on the grave of Johnny Walker.) Well, I don't know how much you've had to do with Doberman Pinschers – it can't be less than I have – but this one, for all her enormous size, was of such surpassing cowardliness that she wouldn't sleep by herself. We had a try at leaving her down in the kitchen, but every time the fridge motor switched on, she went into moans of hysteria so wracking we had to feed her Good Boys dipped in brandy. So she wound up on our bed; though even there she had an attack of the quivering yelps when the Teasmaid went off.

So when I got up at midday, I was already suffering from the Redeye Headthuds and what made me feel even more irritable was that when Lady Pamela followed me into the bathroom I discovered in myself an uncharacteristic modesty about undressing in front of a strange dog. However, I couldn't very well shove her out because someone three doors away had just started up a vacuum cleaner and she was already carrying on as though it was *The Invasion of the Body Snatchers*.

So I let her hang around, had my bath, dried myself on the non-guest towel then, as is my weekend wont, stood on the bathroom-scales. And that's where I received this wellnigh heart-stopping shock . . . Since the previous Sunday I'd put on sixteen pounds!

Now I must explain I'd been very fortunate in that never in my life had I ever needed to worry about any kind of weight problem. While most of my contemporaries were now lunching on those diet biscuits that taste like tongue-depressors, then spending the rest of the hour wandering from shop to shop in search of shirts that taper outwards, I was still able to eat whatever I fancied and still get into a stock-size slim-fitting. Nevertheless I'd always nursed a secret fear that one day this happy state of metabolism would leave me; that, overnight, my body would suddenly develop some kind of immunity to being thin. So the moment I saw that dial-reading my immediate thought was "It's happened!" Grabbing a bathrobe, I hurried down the stairs, shouting "Here it *is*! The spread has come upon me! Overweight has arrived! Action stations!"

The announcement aroused a certain mild interest among the loved ones seating themselves for Sunday lunch, but nothing like the wild consternation I had anticipated. "Don't you understand?" I screamed. "This is the onset! My metabolic rate has upped itself to sixteen pounds in one week! By Christmas I'll be getting approaches from fairgrounds."

"Do close that bathrobe," my wife said, with a motion of her head indicating her mother's presence.

Was this to be their only reaction to the thunderbolt I had unleashed? "If you think," I said deliberately, "that I'm just tamely going to allow it to happen, I must inform you that is not my way. From now on, gang – it's Diet Time!" With which, I grasped the trolley that held the Sunday lunch, ran it through to the kitchen, out the back door and tipped the whole lot neatly into a dustbin.

That succeeded in focusing their attention on the problem. "What the flaming hell are you playing at?" said my daughter. She was, if I remember correctly, three at the time.

So I sat down and told them about the one firm conclusion I have come to with regard to dieting. Contrary to popular opinion, the most uncomfortable aspect of it is not the continual need to watch what you eat. To my mind, the really difficult part is having to watch what other people are eating. "Therefore," I explained, "if I'm to be obliged to cut out meals, so must everyone else. That way you will subject me neither to envy nor temptation. In other words, what I'm now calling upon you to display is that precious quality of family life called supportiveness."

You know all that stuff you keep hearing on *Woman's Hour* about the British still deriving their strength from the intangible bonds which unite individual families? That Sunday I learned it's a theory to be taken with more salt than you'll find in a Cerebos warehouse. By four o'clock, my daughter had already been in touch with three different adoption societies. As for my son, my only male progeny, my posterity . . . frankly, it's something I still don't like talking about. You work your fingers to send them to a good school, give them all the advantages – and where do they end up? Out at the dustbin, using their bare hands . . .!

I'm still not sure whether I'd ever have regained my faith in the family as a viable unit, had it not been for my mother-in-law. Somewhere round half-past five, just after the couple from Number 64 had arrived, beaming and swaying, to collect Lady Pamela, she came over to me and whispered, "I've been thinking."

"Not as bitterly as I have," I said.

"Please do something for me. Go upstairs and see what you weigh now."

"Going without my lunch can't have made much difference."

"You can never tell," she insisted. Unwillingly, muttering savagely, I climbed the stairs again, threw off the robe and sceptically placed myself back on the fateful machine.

How many calories are there in humble pie? What I read on the dial sent me hurtling downstairs in elation. Throwing my arms round my mother-in-law, I cried, "How did you *know*? It's gone! The whole sixteen pounds! What did it? What got rid of it? Was it merely doing without one load of roast potatoes and treacle tart? Or was it" – I swallowed hard – "was it the energy-force that's only generated by the love of a close-knit family?"

"Neither," she said. "This time that animal didn't have its foot on the scales."

I still say the manufacturers of those bathroom-scales were the ones to blame. What kind of technology is it which allows its evaluation of human body-weight to be influenced by the intrusion of a great stupid dog? There is something very much to be deplored in a household machine where, as the old proverb hinted:

One man's meat is a Doberman's paws on.

'Tess of the D'Urbervilles'

Thomas Hardy
Title of novel

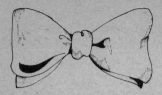

Iʼm worried about Fred.

You know. *Fred.* Of course you do. Fred Selmes? Comes and rearranges nature in our garden a couple of afternoons a week? Shortish? Widish? Can work for hours planting things with his legs straight and his forehead brushing the ground?

When I say I'm worried – I'm not really all *that* worried. I mean, nobody sleeps all that well at this time of the year and I don't really need much sleep. It's really a matter of face. Or rather, face: potential loss of.

He hasn't said anything, of course. But then he doesn't need to. The other morning, for instance, he asked me to give him a hand by brushing the leaves off the lawn preparatory to mowing. I immediately sprang into action with a brisk "Can do, Skipper", nipped into the house, located the dustpan and brush in the cupboard-under-the-stairs and in a trice was down on my hands and knees on the lawn flicking the leaves into the pan like billy-oh. I looked up and there was Fred. Not saying anything. Just sort of staring at me. He was breathing a little strangely, I thought, and shaking his head slightly from side to side. I found it most unnerving.

When things are going well, i.e. when Fred has the garden to himself and I am not helping, he is the soul of fun, regaling us with stories of old village characters, chuckling away to himself. But when I take it upon myself to do a bit of gardening a change seems to come over him. He becomes markedly terse.

Like the *affaire* of the potatoes. I think that was the beginning of my loss of face with Fred. My wife needed some potatoes dug up. Fred was busy planting out (whatever that means). "Taters," he said to me. "Would you mind?"

I selected a fork with which to dig and strolled through the kitchen garden, determined to locate the ripest bunch of potatoes available, two or three pounds of the little darlings at point of lay, each in its prime. I couldn't find any at all. I searched the ground, peered in the fruit-cage, inspected the trees. Not a spud to be seen. The kitchen garden was to all intents and purposes murphyless.

I was about to report the state of affairs to Fred when some sixth sense held me back. Instead, I slipped upstairs to consult my daughter, who was in bed with 'flu. With a few graphic phrases I sketched in my predicament.

"They grow underground," said my daughter.

"Ah," I said. "That explains much."

Back I went and peered round the kitchen garden. There was a bewildering choice of green vegetation to choose from. I experimented by digging up a random selection and harvested some onions, a carrot, an albino carrot which, with hindsight, I think must have been a parsnip, and a croquet hoop.

I returned to the bedroom and persuaded my daughter to wrap herself in the eiderdown and totter outside to point out to me exactly where the potatoes were. They lay below such nondescript foliage that I was not at all surprised that I had overlooked them. I plunged the fork downwards, heaved upwards and found the spikes covered with impaled potatoes. The fork looked like a weird four-decker vegetarian kebab. I removed the pierced potatoes with the edge of my boot and had another go. Same thing happened.

I sat down and had a big think. Clearly the potatoes had to be approached differently. By the side of the row of potatoes was some disused earth with bits of fern straggling over it. I took a spade and dug a long trench in it, about two feet wide and three feet deep. I then crouched down inside the trench and tunnelled sideways in the direction of the potato plants. I used a trowel for this so as not to pierce any more of the precious fruit. Sure enough, after a fair bit of tunnelling and scraping, I exposed a number of potatoes, hanging downwards from the roots. These I carefully pulled up – as it were, downwards. When I had finished, Fred appeared. He just stood there, looking at my trench, silent; but his Adam's apple was going up and down like a yoyo.

"New way of gathering spuds," I said, breaking the silence after what seemed about an hour. "Dug up this bit of waste here – nothing on it but fern . . ."

Fred spoke. With some difficulty. And quite quietly.

"That . . . was the asparagus bed," he said.

After that he went terse for a month and life became unbearable.

It was the same after the *affaire* of the hose. Which, I still maintain, was not my fault. Fred wanted to do a bit of watering amongst the shrubs. This needed a fine spray which he first had to clip on to a gadget which then clipped on to the end of the hose. The hose was at its fullest stretch and the tap was round the corner of the house, out of sight of the shrubbery. Naturally I offered to switch the water on for Fred to save him marching back and forth. I asked him to call out when he was ready. The rose with the fine spray does not clip easily on to the gadget so Fred parked the end of the hose inside the waistband of his trousers while he struggled with it. He eventually got it on and let out a shout of triumph.

Put yourself in my position. I was out of sight, standing by the water-tap, and I suddenly heard Fred shout "YES!" I turned the tap on.

No permanent damage was done, of course. All that really happened was that, as Fred's trouser bottoms were tucked into his wellies, his trousers filled with water and bulged out until he looked like a Dutchman. In a flash I plunged a pruning knife into the seat and he quickly deflated. And that was that.

Another month of terseness before he returned to normal.

Now perhaps you can understand why, after nearly three months of the happy, chatty side of Fred I am desperately anxious not to slip up on a little commission which he has asked me to undertake.

It was yesterday. He was sorting out plants and suddenly said to me, "Dibber."

Thinking he was giving me the old Boy Scout greeting, I replied suitably, "And dib, dib, dib to you!"

He closed his eyes for a moment and then went on, "I need a dibber. By Friday if possible."

I said, "I know what a dibber is, of course. Who doesn't, ho-ho! But – what precisely do you want it for? If you know what I mean . . ."

"To put seeds in, of course. And bulbs."

"Righty-ho!" I said. "You shall have your dibber. By Friday."

I rushed to the dictionary. Do you know what a dibber is? According to my dictionary a 'dibber' is a kind of fishing-rod used when you fish by trailing the bait across the surface of the water. Well, if that's what he wants. I rushed into Egham and bought a long, whippy bamboo pole, about eight feet long.

If he was going to use it, as he said he was, to put seeds in, then presumably he would stick it in the earth so as to have his seeds near at hand. And he would need containers for the seeds. I rushed back to Egham and bought a dozen little plastic bags. These I nailed to the pole at intervals, labelling them, for his convenience, Potato Seeds, Mushroom Seeds, Daffodil Seeds, etc.

What was the other thing he needed the dibber for? Ah yes – bulbs. Presumably so that he could garden by night. I rushed back to Egham, bought half a dozen hundred-watt bulbs, half a dozen sockets and fifty yards of flex. I screwed a cross-bar to the pole and wired up the bulbs along it. To finish the whole thing off I painted it red and tied a pink bow to the tip.

It is undeniably a fine dibber. I would go further and say it is a beautiful dibber. But the point is, will it at last convince Fred that I know quite a bit about gardening and am not just a poop with a nincom? All will be revealed tomorrow when I give it to him. Which is why I am so worried.

He will be his old, happy self for the next three months if the dibber succeeds. But . . .

Terse if the dibber fails.

He who hesitates is lost

Proverb

WHEN I was sixteen, going on seventeen, if you'd have asked me what my greatest immediate ambition was, I'd have said, "To write a large exclamation-mark in my diary." What made such an objective even more remarkable was that, for a large part of that period, I had no idea what the exclamation-mark was supposed to signify.

All I knew was, one Monday morning soon after that school term began, a friend of mine called Snitch Herman entered the classroom, beckoned some of us to him and, looking around to make sure we were unobserved, exhibited his diary. There, on the page for the Saturday just past, he'd written a large red exclamation-mark. It was followed by the words, "Approx 10.45 p.m. In shed on her father's allotment."

"Cor!" Weedy Forbes said, in a hushed voice. (We called him Weedy because he was so painfully skinny it was claimed he could climb into a polo-neck sweater from either end.) "Cor!" said Weedy, "that makes you the first one in the class!" Snitch's only response to that was a smirk, but I noticed that as he went to his desk, his walk had acquired a definite swagger.

By that dinner-hour the news was buzzing round the whole school. "Did you hear about Snitch on Saturday night? Cor!" Caught up in the general excitement, I even began retailing it myself. "Did you hear about Snitch?" I said, grabbing another friend of mine called Wally Beckman. "Last Saturday night at 10.45. Cor!"

"Not an exclamation-mark?" said Wally hoarsely. I nodded. "Cor!" he said, and it was clear from the admiration in his eyes that I had acquired kudos by merely conveying the information. This even though I still had not the faintest idea what I was talking about.

The following Monday it was Puffy Layton's turn. "I'm the second in the class!" he shouted as he entered. And, sure enough, there in his Hobbies diary, flanked by the words, "9.17p.m. – inside Out Of Order telephone-box" was another large, triumphant exclamation-mark. Over the next few weeks one after another of my fellow students came into school brandishing their various diaries. By half-term no less than fifteen out of my class of thirty had uttered their cries of "I'm twelfth!", "I'm fourteenth!" then flushed and grinned at the congratulatory whoops it evoked.

It was obvious that some kind of race was in progress.

Equally obvious was the status one attained by reaching its mysterious finishing-line. So if I was ever to share that status, it looked like I'd have to file my own qualifying round pretty soon. But what sort of race was it? And what did you have to *do* to qualify?

My ignorance was only dispelled when I was allowed to read the considerably more specific details added in tiny writing beside the exclamation-mark which Wally Beckman ("I'm seventeenth!") had awarded himself. It was all to do with – oh, no! – persuading *girls*! In effect our diaries needed to become what would nowadays be known as score-boards. What's more, at the rate at which the ones belonging to my peer-group were achieving that conversion, unless I started exercising persuasion on someone within the next two weeks, end-of-term would see Weedy Forbes and me dead-heating for last place.

My heart sank. When it came to exerting power over the opposite sex, I'd already discovered that I had neither the silver-tongued quick-wittedness of a Snitch Herman – his exclamation-mark had been achieved by convincing a girl in Form V that the captain of a cricket-team could perform marriages – nor the uncaring brutality of a Puffy Layton. ("You might as well. I'll tell everyone you did anyway.") In fact, I had long ago resigned myself to the probability that in the same way that a hero of those days had become known as The Man Who Never Was, I would probably end my life as The Man Who Never Did.

My one source of hope looked to be Bessie Arkwright. She was the only girl I'd ever met who seemed to prefer being in my company to going home and helping her mother unblock the sink. The reason I hadn't yet responded to the unspoken invitation in her eyes was because – how can I put this kindly? – she had the configuration of a born ice-hockey goalkeeper. To phrase it more bluntly, she was built in the way they used to build cars at that time – all the weight at the back. Nevertheless, I had taken her out a few times, mainly because she was the only girl I could get with the kind of suits my parents had bought me that summer. Besides that, though, not only was she enthusiastically disposed towards me, but her father owned the local cinema, so she was cheap to run.

One could therefore sum up our relationship so far by saying that although it had the right chemistry, up to this time there had been no signs of biology. Now, however, with no more than a fortnight to go before the end of term, Bessie suddenly became my only exclamation-mark hope.

That's why the very next Saturday night found us in the back row of her father's cinema, with me making ardently unsuccessful attempts to practise what might be called 'slide of hand'. Immediately after the big film, which she hadn't actually seen that much of, owing to some trouble getting her glasses on over newly acquired false eyelashes, I set in motion the next step of my carefully prepared plan. Hurrying her to the milk bar, I plied her with double-strength strawberry shakes. The moment she began gazing at me with that familiar misty look, I called for the bill and rushed her back to her house.

Once installed on her couch, I went to action-stations, "Bessie," I said, "come and sit on my lap."

"Why?" she said, lost in some romantic dream.

Drawing in a deep breath, I gave it to her straight across the bows. "Because," I murmured with painstakingly rehearsed fervour, "you and I could make beautiful exclamation-marks together."

She rose from her chair. "All right then," she said – and dropped into my lap.

Now, one belief that was unquestioningly accepted by all pubescent youths of those days was that girls judged your machismo by the number of keys you had on your key-ring. So bearing in mind what I've already told you about the way Bessie's body-weight was distributed, do you really need a detailed description of what happens when a girl of that build drops into the lap of a lad carrying a bunch of twenty-two keys in his trouser-pocket?

I'll content myself with saying that as far as the Exclamation-Mark Stakes were concerned, I was forced to retire hurt. To such an extent, in fact, that two kids from the Lower Third got their diaries marked before I did.

But even more humiliating, perhaps, was the jeering message I received from Weedy ("I'm twenty-ninth!") Forbes. Scrawled across the front of his get-well card were the words:

"He who Bessie dates is last."

One good turn deserves another

English proverb

Hello, children!
Are you all sitting comfortably? If you are, shuffle about a bit other-wise you might go to sleep. That's better. If you are all sitting reason-ably uncomfortably, but alert, I will begin.

It is a story of unrequited love in the depths of a fairy wood. A nature story of the Great Outdoors. It has to be an outdoor story because that is where nature is, on the whole. In fact, apart from a few Chicago Ivy plants and an onion-like hyacinth bulb dying in a jam-jar on the kitchen windowsill, I cannot think of much nature going on indoors.

The scene of our story is a forest clearing by the banks of a river; an enchanted spot which the animals called 'Never-Never Land'. No-body knew why it was called Never-Never Land but the wise old owl thought it was because the little ducklings in the water kept warm by a little down every week. And the parrots lived on higher perches.

Some of the birds and the beasts and the fish and the insects and the – whatever else hangs about forest glades – were very happy living in their little homes by the river and as the sun went down at twilight, the glade would ring with merry laughter and the sharp cries of wild things greeting each other.

Trout shouted "Toodle-pip!"
The carp (which cheers but not inebriates) cried "Cheerio!"
Molluscs murmured "Morning!"
And salmon chanted "Evening!"

But all was not peace and beauty in that lovely dell. Oh, my good-ness, no. As the poet wrote (but forgot to rhyme) "nature in the raw is seldom mild". Several small, furry and finny things were not at all happy. For instance, Beatrice the Bunny was madly in love with Vincent the Vole. All day long they mooned about in the long grass holding paws and sighing and gazing into each other's eyes – a complicated business as their eyes were on either side of their heads rather than in front so they had to keep dashing round each other to gaze into the loved one's other eye, only to find that the loved one was on the way round to do the same.

But worse than that, they had to do their courting in full view of all the other animals. This was because the woods were full of evil hunters with guns who were on the lookout for game to make into potted meat to sell to West Germany. And Vincent and Beatrice were prime targets. In the words of the wise old owl, "A vole and his bunny are soon pâtéd."

And there was Terence the tadpole who was so looking forward to growing up and turning into a butterfly that nobody had the heart to tell him that he had got it wrong.

And there was the other little water creature who lost all his money playing poker with a group of leopards (one of them turned out to be a cheetah) and spent every evening singing to himself and falling into the river. He was Titus, a newt.

However, the saddest of all the animals in the clearing was Starkers the otter. He was not always called Starkers. His real name was Tarka, but he moulted. Now say what you will, I maintain that there is no more unhappy a sight in outdoors nature than a bald otter. Starkers looked dreadful without his sleek, mink-like coat. It just did not look right for him to go around clad only in his pink skin. It was a shock to the system, like suddenly coming face to face with a policeman in a ballet skirt, or Miss Barbara Cartland in jeans and a T-shirt.

All the other animals were kindness itself to Starkers, never mentioning his affliction in case it gave him pain, always the soul of tact, ever seeking to cheer him up. "Hey, Baldy!" one would shout. "Coming to the pub tonight?" Or "Care to come as my guest to the Fancy-Dress Dance? Don't bother to change – just come as a skinned rabbit."

But for all their efforts, Starkers sank deeper and deeper into gloom. He began to avoid the company of the other animals, even refusing to go with them into the forest on the annual orang outing. He would spend all day up a lonely creek of the river blowing his cheeks out until his eyes popped, trying to force his hair to grow.

Now Starkers had a friend. It was his cousin Geezer, a water-otter. Geezer became so upset at his friend's unhappiness that he went to consult the wise old owl. This he did not decide to do lightly, as besides being wise, the old owl was a crashing bore, but something had to be done.

"Why, wise old owl, is Starkers starkers? There must be a reason his coat fell off. Did he grow too fast and burst through it? Could he have run under a lawn-mower without noticing? Has he contracted otter-rot?"

The wise old owl held up a wing for silence and nearly bored the tail off Geezer for an hour, chuntering on about the need to keep the forest tidy and not to drop toffee-papers on the grass and there's far too much larking about in the tree-tops after dark and always leave the waterhole as you would wish to find it. Then he went on, "I'm surprised you haven't asked me about your friend Starkers. Haven't you ever wondered why he's bald?"

"Yes, you stupid fowl," muttered Geezer under his breath, "I've just asked you!"

"Interesting case," went on the owl. "Quite simple, really. He's lonely. Needs a mate. So all his hair has fallen out. There is just one thing he needs to do and his hair will grow in again."

"Just one thing he needs to do?"

"Just one thing," said the owl. "To wit – to woo."

He was right, too. And here our story takes a happy turn before its sad ending. A few days after Geezer had seen the wise, boring old owl, Starkers fell in love.

She was not only, to his eyes, an otter of beauty. She was also as bald as he was. Entranced by her quiet, nay silent, charms he spent all day, every day, alone with her up his remote little creek of the river. And the more he wooed her the more his hair grew until – and this is the happy bit – his coat was once more as sleek and glossy as it ever was.

We now come to the sad bit. Misty eyed with love, poor Starkers had not seen things too clearly. What he took to be a beautiful, bald lady otter drifting downstream into his arms was not an otter at all. It was not even a live animal.

A few days previously a band of hunters had made camp upstream, feasting and carousing as was their wont. At one point in their proceedings they found that the gourd in which they kept their wine had a tear in it and was leaking so they flung it into the river. Vaguely animal-shaped, and completely bald, it had drifted downstream . . .

The whole tragic occurrence was summed up in the following morning's newspaper headline:

Wine-Gourd, Torn, Deceives an Otter.

Here today, gone tomorrow

Proverb

MOST of the items in my collection of show-business memorabilia are of minor historical interest – a custard pie once worn by Buster Keaton; the black wig that Betty Hutton put on to make Sonny Tufts think she was Rosemary Lane in *Here Comes The Waves*; a flower from the bouquet Dana Andrews gave Anne Baxter in *Crash Dive* (little realising she was already in love with Tyrone Power). But one item that does offer a modicum of sociological value is a collection of reports sent back to England by the ringmaster of a small travelling circus while it was touring Europe in the early fifties. They are all addressed to the circus's owner, who appears to have exercised his proprietorial role from a small suite of rooms at the surgical appliances end of Charing Cross Road. I append a selection herewith:

15 November, Northern Spain. Another exhausting overnight journey, this time from Mannheim, West Germany, where I'm afraid business was not as brisk as expected. Our box-office takings, like the breezes that unexpectedly blew our Big Top down, were light and variable. As a consequence of the tent's collapse, we were obliged to give the rest of the week's performances in the open air, a circumstance which played havoc with several of our star acts, particularly Supremo, The Human Cannon Ball. Unaccustomed to adjusting his trajectory for wind-deflection, Supremo had the misfortune to crash into a low-flying aircraft.

We had to leave him in Mannheim General Hospital and although I am advertising in the Pamplona papers for a man to take over his act, I fear it will be difficult to find a performer of his calibre.

22 November, Central Italy. I really must register my misgivings about the zig-zag manner in which you appear to have routed this year's venues. We had the utmost difficulty making the journey from Pamplona on Saturday night in time to open here in Assissi by five p.m. on Monday. For any circus which includes a travelling menagerie, such non-stop dashes through the night on minor European roads present a multitude of problems, particularly in the matter of low bridges. We arrived here minus yet another giraffe – a tragedy which, I can assure you, has not made for good relations with the Assissi Chamber of Commerce.

Takings at Pamplona were up somewhat on the preceding week, thanks mainly to the resourcefulness displayed by Ram Das Jamshid, Mystic Eastern Snake-Charmer. In an endeavour to liven up business, he advertised that, Second House Saturday, he would perform his snake-charming routine with – for the first time in any ring – no less than three poisonous cobras, all of whom were absolutely stone-deaf. Such showmanship reflects nothing but credit on Mr Jamshid, who would have been thirty-eight next Tuesday.

29 November, Southern Norway. If the journey from Assissi to Stavanger proved less hectic than had been anticipated, put that down to the unfortunate fact that we were unable to play out the full week there, being obliged to depart first thing Wednesday morning. This was because certain sharp-eyed members of Tuesday night's audience spotted that one of Madame Zorba's Team of Magnificent Arabian Liberty Horses was, in fact, stuffed.

You will recall that when I phoned you last September from Lisbon to convey the news of the animal's demise, you made the suggestion that rather than go to the expense of a replacement I should come to a discreet arrangement with a good local taxidermist. As I later reported, he turned out to be an expatriate Englishman called Nigel Deames who, apart from a tendency to make distasteful remarks about "taking a dead Liberty", performed his duties so admirably that until last week no spectator had commented.

However, Tuesday First House, even though we maintained our usual precaution of bringing the inanimate animal into the ring while the tent was darkened, murmurs were heard when the spotlights came on again. When, a little later, Madame Z's splendid pretence of feeding it a lump of sugar after leaping off its back brought a group of Assissi priests surging over the barrier, I thought it best to de-rig and start north.

In this same connection, I have been asked to relay a request from another of our attractions, Buffalo Cyril Cody – the stellar half of

Cody & Bessie, Western Knife Throwers Extraordinaire. Having had the misfortune to suffer a sudden power blackout right at the most dramatic moment of their act, Mr Cody would now like to know whether, instead of wasting time auditioning for a new Bessie, you would prefer him to get in touch with Mr Nigel Deames again?

6 December, Austria. May I once again touch on the matter of inconvenient routing? Our journey from Stavanger to our present location in Graz meant travelling, according to my pedometer, more than 800 miles. That really does seem an inordinate distance to come for a one-night stand, especially as we are booked to appear in the South of France tomorrow night.

If my reports seem to harp unduly on this point, it is because one effect of such arduous and prolonged journeys is that more and more pieces of equipment vital to artists' performances are getting either damaged or mislaid. It cannot but detract from the glamour of a circus when, as happened tonight, an audience sees a daredevil tight-rope walker walking a high wire which has had to be tied in the middle with an improvised granny knot.

There were equally disillusioning consequences when the special-sized swords used by Largo, our Midget Sword Swallower, were found to have disappeared somewhere in transit. As a result, the poor little fellow was obliged to give his performance tonight using hastily borrowed substitutes from the Stavanger Museum of Viking History. Although the very smallest of these was over four feet in length, not only did Largo succeed in getting it down as far as the embossed handle, he might have gone on to complete his act had not the applause induced him to try to take a bow.

However, trouper that he is, he insists on coming along with us to the South of France date tomorrow, claiming that we can still make use of him in some capacity, if only as a tent-peg.

13 December, the South of France. This really is the last straw! When we arrived at our site this morning, after a journey across the Alps of such nightmare dimensions that Elasta, the Amazing Lady Contortionist, still cannot be persuaded from the caravan where she lies sprawled across a bunk sobbing hysterically into the small of her back, what did I find? A letter from you, addressed Post Restante, Hyères, informing me that you have donated our services to a charity gala to be held tomorrow afternoon in central Belgium!

I regret having to tell you this, but when I conveyed that information to our artists and roustabouts, their unanimous reaction was "We

Shall Not Be Moved!" Pamplona to Assissi they could understand; Assissi to Stavanger they were ready to accept; Stavanger to Graz was complied with and they even agreed to the overnight safari from Graz to Hyères.

But if there is one journey which even the great warm heart of circus folk will balk at, it is the itinerary with which we are presently confronted:

Hyères today, Ghent tomorrow.

> Dirty British coaster with a salt-caked smoke stack
>
> *John Masefield*
> 'Cargoes'

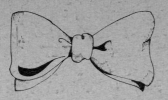

To my generation, that line of Masefield's must be the best-known line of poetry in the English language. In Broadstairs we grew up with it ringing in our ears. If we were nabbed by a constable riding away from school on a bicycle with a wobbly saddle we were required to recite 'Dirty British coaster with a salt-caked smoke stack' faultlessly or were booked for not only riding a bicycle with a wobbly saddle but also for being drunk in charge of a bicycle with a wobbly saddle.

In those careless, carefree years of the nineteen-twenties and thirties we flung ourselves recklessly into the business of living. Our life seemed to be one continuous round of beach parties, some of them going on far into the night until half-past ten or a quarter-to-eleven. And one of our favourite games was a kind of Russian Roulette. We all ate three Jacob's Cream Crackers and then tried to say 'Dirty British coaster with a salt-caked smoke stack'. The first one to spit crumbs was whacked with a rolled-up copy of *Razzle*.

By what strange metaphysical alchemy did Masefield conceive that one line, so powerful that it shaped a generation? So versatile that it was readily pressed into service as a breathalyser and as an activator of crumb-spitting?

These are not easy questions.

To find the answers we have to delve deep into Masefield's past and the psychological and physical background to the poem.

The first significant fact we find is that Masefield was married when he wrote the poem. But far more interesting to us is the fact that, in spite of the social attitudes prevalent at the turn of the century, Masefield's was a mixed marriage. He was a man and his wife was a woman.

As we follow the progress of the marriage it becomes clear that his wife was a great inspiration to him in his work.

One Tuesday morning we find him in the breakfast room contemplating his breakfast without much enthusiasm. He has a slight cold. This may not be of importance to us but it was to him because it meant he could not smell his porridge and he liked the smell of porridge better than its taste. Without the smell it always seemed to him to be like warm, sodden confetti. What does concern us is that he lacked one poem to finish a new book and was not getting far with it. Deep in unproductive thought, he filleted a kipper, ate the bones and piled the fish at the side of his plate.

In zoomed Mrs Masefield, bright as a button, carrying a pork pie and a flagon of rum for her friends Mr and Mrs C—, who were unwell (*Note:* Humbert Clitheroe and his wife Tetty. They lived at the foot of the hill and were old friends of the Masefields).

"Sorry to leave you alone, dear," she said, "But it can't be helped. I must go down the C—s again."

Masefield's eyes flickered. "Make that 'seas'," he thought to himself. "I must go down to the seas again." He pondered. "Could be something there but not a winner, I fancy," He looked up.

"You can't go," he said. "Car won't start."

"It will for me!" she riposted, with a wave of her basket.

Sure enough, she had only to adjust the advance lever on the steering wheel, turn the petrol on and give the handle a quick upward pull and the Austin Seven twitched into life. Mrs Masefield went back to the house, put her head through the (open) window of the breakfast room and announced, "Car goes!"

"*That's* the title I've been searching for!" he cried. "Cargoes!"

Absently peeling a boiled egg, he ate the shell with a spoon and piled the egg neatly at the side of his plate, his fertile poet's imagination busy fertilising. "Cargoes. Three different sorts of boats and cargoes, I think."

He began to make notes on a piece of toast.

"Piglead, ivory, peacocks – what else do ships carry? – apes, firewood . . ."

But somehow the poem would not come together. He made one false start after another.

"A dirty old ship with one funnel,
Was laden with apes to the gunwale,
Plus Palestine wine,

Cheap coal from the Tyne . . . No, too ordinary a metre. I need something more tumty-tumty-tumty-tumty-tum-tum-tum-tum."

All day he worked but the one magic line which would set the metre of the poem eluded him.

His wife did not return until the early evening. With a woman's intuition she sensed, from the fact that he was still in his pyjamas and the room was knee-deep in rolled up bits of paper, that he was working so she sat down quietly to read the evening paper. Not really aware that she was speaking aloud, she read out the headline.

"That's *it*!" shouted Masefield. "That's the line I have been searching for all day! The key line of the poem! Read it again!"

Mrs Masefield looked at the headline. And the picture beneath it. Deeply interested by now, she read the whole story.

The year was 1930 and the British film industry had started to shoot the first British musical, to the excitement of the press and the British public.

The film was to be called *Mayfair Lady*. It told the story of a little flowergirl in Covent Garden who is taken up by an Italian Mafia boss. He teaches her to speak with an Italian accent with the intention of setting her up in Mayfair as a high-class foreign tart. But he falls in love with her instead. He takes her to Ascot races to test her accent but accidentally falls in front of the king's horse and the film ends with her marrying the young man who has been in love with her all along, George Bernard Shaw.

The star of the film was the great Italian tenor Beniamino Gigli. He had most of the big songs, like 'Why Can't a Woman Be More Like a Horse', 'I've Thrown a Custard in Her Face' and 'Get Me to the Judge on Time'.

His co-star was the vivacious British *ingénue*, Lottie Lucas, known to film fans as the Gin-and-It Girl. Lottie, if not actually certifiable as off her chump, was distinctly dotty. She had been divorced at the age of seventeen by her first husband, an earl, who had cited forty-two co-respondents, including five footballers (mostly Third Division), a gondolier and the front-of-house manager of the Electric Kinema, Dalston Junction. One of her little peccadilloes was, when bored, to break into an extremely rapid Charleston dance, wherever she happened to be, e.g. at her first husband's funeral.

It seems that the film company had been shooting a key scene that day on the jetty at Broadstairs. It was the scene where Eliza Dottle (Lottie Lucas), unable to master the Italian language and at her lowest ebb, had decided to run for it. She has disguised herself as a peasant by donning a heavy Breton smock and is just about to hitch a lift in a fishing-boat to France when after her, along the jetty, belts Gigli.

All had gone well with the shooting until after lunch when Lottie, stiff with Gin-and-Its, became bored with hanging around the jetty waiting for her next shot and broke into a fierce and swift Charleston. Her left foot caught in a coil of rope and the next moment she was wallowing in the water, yelling for help.

There was no real danger. There was a little donkey-engine near with a basket which was lowered into the fishing-boats to land their catch. It was started up and Lottie managed to scramble into the basket. The donkey-engine chuffed away and Lottie rose slowly out of the sea. And then, eight feet up in the air, pouring out sea-water and swaying slightly, the basket – and Lottie – stuck.

The trouble was that it was only a very tiny donkey-engine, designed to lift fish. A heavy Breton smock full of sea-water and Lottie was another matter. The donkey-engine wheezed and died. And Lottie dangled.

And that was the scene which a photographer snapped and which the evening paper published.

Her husband's voice broke into Mrs Masefield's reveries.

"What was that headline, again?" His poetry-writing pencil hovered over paper.

Obediently she read it out:

"Dotty British Co-Star with a Salt-Caked Smock Stuck."

'Luck, Be a Lady Tonight'

Frank Loesser
Popular song

"**D**OCTOR, you've got to find a way to help me." The speaker was a shortish, middle-aged man with a look of uneasy jauntiness, like those minor relatives who swarm on at the end of *This Is Your Life*.

I surveyed him joylessly. Although this was only my second evening on Casualty Ward, I'd already made up my mind to jack in being a doctor. Whatever the practice of medicine may have done to provide Somerset Maugham with short-story material, it obviously wasn't going to be much help with my literary career. How can anyone jot down significant human insights when he's heaving and fainting all the time?

The little man broke into my reverie. "Fact is, doctor . . ." His voice faltered, then dropped to a confidential whisper. "It's my Prue."

Automatically, my trained mind performed a rapid flip-through of *Gray's Anatomy*. Was it above or below the waist? Or was it – yet again – one of those parts of the body which, despite seven years of lectures, my brain still resolutely rejected the very idea of?

He solved the problem by going to the door and ushering someone in. "My daughter," he said.

Prue turned out to be the sort of docile heavily-built girl you could imagine being shared out among an undistinguished Hell's Angels chapter. She had a skin whose colours and texture resembled that of a baked rice pudding and everything below her neck was so unconfined that when her feet came to a halt, the rest of her took perceptibly longer to settle down.

Standing in front of me, she stared into my face. Not only was her gaze devoid of all expression but her lips were in continuous motion without any sound emerging. I took a step back, preferring to put a little more distance between us.

"Bloody Radio One," her father said.

It took me some moments to establish the relevance of that comment to his daughter's condition. Then I noticed the thin white lead which was dangling from her right ear down to a bulky transistor set she was clutching to her stomach. "She's listening to the radio?"

"Has been for three days and nights non-stop," he replied gloomily. "Earpiece won't come out. It's got stuck in."

Moving to her side, I reached forward and gave the lead a tentative tug. Although nothing emerged from within the thicket of brandy-snap curls that insulated her ear, the movement turned her face back towards me. Again that empty stare.

Glancing at his watch, her father consulted a crumpled *Radio Times* he was carrying and shook his head despondently. "It's *Your All-Time Top Forty*," he said. He tossed the *Radio Times* on to my instrument trolley. "Be no getting through to her now till News on the hour."

He sighed. "Point is, you see, she doesn't *mind* it being jammed in there. Doesn't want it out. She *likes* having continuous rock music, as it were, plumbed-in."

Could that fact be a significant human insight? Just in case, I decided to essay the Maugham role of detached observer. "I don't really think . . ." I began in as ironic a tone as I could manage.

Unfortunately he interrupted me. "Say what you like, it's unnatural for a girl every time she undresses she's got to take her jumper off over her transistor. What I had in mind, you see, what I was hoping, was perhaps you could administer a swift anaesthetic, then prise it free while she's sparkers."

My spirits fell again. Of all the parts of the human body a doctor is obliged to go grubbing around in, ears are among the least pleasant, especially after you've just washed your hands. Besides which, it would mean having to place that metal band with a light in it round my forehead, and I'd not yet managed to do that without it falling over my eyes.

I decided to seek a second opinion. "Would you excuse me a moment?"

Stethoscope swinging, I hastened over to the Orthopaedic Ward, hoping to find the man who knew more about surgical procedures than anyone in the hospital. Luckily he was still in his Porter's cubicle. "Tom," I panted. "Emergency. Narrow passage-way. Small object wedged in top of aperture. How to extract?"

He pondered. "When we had it happen with the Nurses Home wastepipe, some bloke came and squirted water up from underneath."

Good old Tom. But as I hurried back to Casualty I found myself assailed by doubts which, by the time I was facing Prue again, had hardened into certainty. Surely such a remedy was physiologically contraindicated?

So how to free this prisoner of pop? She was now swaying slightly, eyes closed, small moaning sounds audible. "It's *The Clash In Concert*," explained her father wearily, indicating the *Radio Times* he'd retrieved.

I ransacked my mind. Then, on a sudden impulse – or it could even have been a significant human insight – I took the magazine from him and flicked back a few pages. Luck was with me!

Uttering a few words of silent prayer, I picked up my No. 4 forceps and, grasping them firmly, reached forward to Prue. Seizing hold, I performed one deft, sideways movement.

Abruptly her swaying ceased. There was about ten seconds of silence. Then from her lips came the most anguished wail of desolation I have ever heard a human emit. Clapping a hand to the side of her head, she wrenched out the earpiece, flung it from her and collapsed into her father's arms. "That was awful, Dad," she sobbed. "It was *agony!*"

Clasping her to him, her father looked at me accusingly. "What did you do to my girl?"

Sometimes it is best to tell the patient the truth. I broke it to him as gently as I could. "I switched her over to Radio Three."

His jaw dropped. "*Classical* music?"

"A performance of *Iphigenia in Tauris*."

There was a moment's pause, then he reached forward and wrung my hand. "Thank you, doctor."

"Don't thank me," I said. "Thank the composer of that opera for answering my silent prayer."

For, indeed, it was he to whom I'd addressed my words when, noticing his work billed for that hour in the *Radio Times*, I had offered up that mute entreaty:

Gluck, free a lady tonight.

I am monarch of all I survey

William Cowper
Verses supposed to have been written by
Alexander Selkirk

THE last three weeks have been a nightmare. The house is awash with maps, dictionaries of quotations, dictionaries of biography; vicars have been hurried in, consulted and hurried out again; telephone directories have been studied; bibles have been sent for . . .

We are trying to find a name for our new kitten.

Constant readers of these reminiscences will know that this household already supports an ageing Afghan hound named Casanis (after a Corsican drink seemingly blended from liquorice and torpedo fluid) and two Burmese cats, Monticello (after a small Corsican village) and Kettering (after a large Northamptonshire town where a nice publisher lives), and naming them took a month apiece.

Then my daughter acquired this new kitten.

Cuddles? Yuk. Fred? Nooooo. Bardolph? Gnaah. Millamant? Urrrr. Spot? Bah. Gwen? Owwwww . . . far into the night we argued and suggested and made noises of disgust at each other's suggestions. Tempers frayed. A vase narrowly missed my ear when I put up 'Tweedles'. Over breakfast I came up with what I thought was a winner.

"Listen everybody!" I cried. "It came to me in the night – Wolverhampton!"

I am not sure quite why the name was unacceptable to my family because I did not hear much of the subsequent discussion – I was at the sink washing home-made marmalade out of my hair – but it was clear to me that I had soon to make a political initiative if the family unit was to survive.

"The kitten will stay with me in my study for a week," I said quietly but firmly. "During which time I will observe it closely; its manner-isms, its personality, its physical appearance From this data I will produce an apt and fitting name. This will be accepted by you all without demur, discussion or heaving jars of marmalade at me."

All began to shout at once.

I held up my hand.

"I have spoken," I said, with dignity. And ran for it.

It was a funny old week, looking back on it. The kitten and I got on well, on the whole, although I did not see much of her; she spent most of the working day up the back of my sweater. Not *all* day, of course, or she might have become bored. She usually spent the first half hour looking out of the window from her vantage point on top of my head. Quite why she took to sitting on top of my head escapes me. One would have thought that a shoulder would have been more comfort-able but kittens – if I may be forgiven a generality – do not think logically. It was all right when I was typing because there was very little head movement and she could sit up there like a yellow sphinx, beadily eyeing the pigeons. It was more unsettling when the phone rang. To answer I had to swing my head round which meant that the kitten had to unleash her scimitars and get a purchase on my skull. Most phone-calls that week were answered by me with a brisk, "Hello – six two seven five AAAAH!"

After half an hour the kitten would leap lightly down on to the key-board of my typewriter – which meant that the beautiful prose which I was composing would then go $1\frac{3}{8}2 = ns\frac{13}{24}\$ + \&b\%hr@$ – and make her way up the back of the inside of my sweater. There she would anchor herself firmly with four claws in my shirt and go to sleep indefinitely, leaving me with a profile like the late King Richard III or the French part-time bellringer, Quasimodo.

The kitten was clearly shy and hated to be moved from her nest and brought out to face the world, even for her lunch. It was all right when my wife was at home at midday, but on those days when she was away I had to trudge down to the gate and persuade a passing cat-lover to wrench the kitten out.

I had a girlfriend once who was as shy as the kitten. I was about fourteen at the time and a bit shy myself. Monica Willoughby, my lady love at that time, was of sturdy build. She too was fourteen and weighed in at twelve stone, including about a pound and a half of Everton toffee which she habitually carried on her person. Monica's shyness took the form of a change of colour in her face when addressed by somebody not of her immediate family. Her normally sallow, olive complexion would change to a shiny shade of beige with embarrassment, and then turn bright scarlet. It was like having a traffic-light for a girlfriend.

When the kitten was awake she talked all the time. "Waaaah," she went, "Waaah, WAAAAAAAAAAH!" She reminded me irresistibly of another girl I knew in my youth, Val Valentine. Val chattered away happily every moment of her waking day. She never said anything; just talked. I took her to see Charles Laughton in *Mutiny on the Bounty* and she chuntered in a low voice throughout: "–I had a coloured shirt like Fletcher Christian's once – my aunt Bet gave it to me – I gave it away eventually – oh, look at that pretty beach! – ever been to Bognor? – I'd love to go to wassisname, the Barbados – I heard that Franchot Tone's mother was a French countess – would you like to finish my choc-ice? It's gone runny –" etc. We parted eventually. Not because of her chattering but because I felt she took too light a view of the charms of Clara Bow.

The kitten had a beautiful head of hair, a blonde mixture of apricots and cream. It reminded me irresistibly of the many happy hours I spent during the war cuddling Sergeant Baxter. Sergeant Lisa Baxter was a physiotherapist WAAF who gave me post-natal contraction exercises in the hospital where I had my appendix out. Lisa had striking blonde locks, much like the kitten's in hue, with a bit of black showing at the roots, which reminded me of the old French saying: 'At each parting we dye a little'. Our wartime romance was to be short-lived. I was posted away to convalesce at Blackpool and sent Lisa a sad little postcard, saying "Those blue lagoons, and tropic moons are nowhere near Blackpool, H. de Vere Stackpoole". She did not reply.

Perhaps the most remarkable thing I observed about the kitten during that week was how clumsy she was. Most kittens race for an apple tree and run up it. My kitten ran at the apple tree but her head hit it with a sickening thud and she staggered away, semi-conscious. Again, ordinary kittens love leaping four feet into the air with *joie de vivre*. My kitten attempted this when under the kitchen table. She was only temporarily concussed but I can still hear that awful crunch of tiny skull on wood The kitten's clumsiness brought to mind another girlfriend of my past, Fay Furness. Fay was not fat but she was, undeniably, a big girl. And beefy. She was hockey captain of her school when we met, but she was not allowed to bully-off because of the number of hockey sticks which she had snapped in two. When I went to Sunday tea at her home her mother would say "Hand the cakes round, Fay. There's a good girl." Fay would pick up the plate and swing it round. The plate would hit a small occasional table, demolishing it, and the cakes would fly across the room and thud into the wallpaper. Our romance came to an end when I went one day to Sunday lunch. I staggered away with crackling in my hair, an earful of apple sauce and a pint of gravy down my pullover.

Musing over the kitten's characteristics, it dawned on me that the problem of naming the kitten was solved. I would call it after the ex-girlfriend it most reminded me of. But which of the four was that? The shy one? The talkative one? The blonde-haired one? Or the clumsy one? Why not – I thought with a sudden flash of inspiration – all four?

I convened a family conference.

"I have a name," I announced. "A name which perfectly fits the kitten's general bearing and character. I will have a collar made for her, with a name tab. And, when she next runs up the drawing-room curtains and looks down on us with her usual expression of disdain, the name tab on her collar will proclaim:

"I am Monica Val Lisa Fay."

N.B. The kitten turned out not to be a girl but a boy and my daughter has named him Lumio (after a Corsican village).

Do not try to bite off more than you can chew

Proverb

THE whole rotten experience began when I received a notably terse letter from the manager of my bank, asking me to call in and see him with regard to my personal finances. I pitched up at his office sharp on the hour he'd designated and found him frowning over what I recognised as my bank pass-sheets.

After about four minutes of disapproving silence, he looked up from the documents. Narrowing his eyes, he said, "Mr Norden, is this the very first time a bank manager has called you in for an interview?"

"Yes," I said. "How did you know?"

He said, "Because it's not necessary to undress."

While I was buttoning-up again, he leaned back and put the tips of his fingers together. "Well, now," he said, "your overdraft seems to have reached alarming proportions. Have you any explanation for that?"

I said, "Well, not off-hand, no. It could have been this inflation all the chat-shows are on about. Or perhaps I diversified when I should have conglomerated. Who can say? You know how quickly money goes when you're enjoying yourself. No good worrying about it though, is it?"

His eyebrows shot up so fast I distinctly felt the air stir. He said, "I'm afraid we are obliged to worry about it, Mr Norden. From the evidence of these accounts, what you seem to have been doing, if I may express it in a homely analogy, is earning money in Centigrade and spending it in Fahrenheit. Far from being able to afford your present life-style, you can't even run to the VAT on it."

I must admit that up to that moment I hadn't even been aware that I had a life-style. I thought I'd just been living. But brushing aside my attempts to raise this interesting semantic point, he went on. "There are some unpleasant consequences up to which we must now face." Then he launched forth into a lengthy speech about "credit-balance shortfall" and "fixed term repayments" and "secured interest arrangements". Only when he began using terms like "eviction order" and "bankruptcy proceedings" did I begin to realise what he was suggesting.

Aware that he'd attained the goal of alarm and despondency towards which he'd been striving, he leaned forward again with a little smile. "In short," he said, "unless you effect sufficient domestic economies to write-off that overdraft within six months, you're down the tubes."

To such an extent did that warning succeed in giving me the wind up, I couldn't wait to rush home and relay the news to my family. "From now on," I informed the dismayed faces gathered about me, "your *vita* becomes a whole lot less *dolce*. Henceforth, it's goodbye the Nordens – hallo, the Waltons. This is Economies Time. As of today, the TV goes off sharp at ten, the car will only be used for going to places that are downhill, and for Sunday lunch the butcher will supply the cut of meat known as ankle of lamb."

The next few months would have been grim indeed had it not been for the fact that, by one of those coincidences without which most of these stories would never even achieve lift-off, a leading women's magazine came out that week with a leading article called 'How We Can All Cut Down the Weekly Household Bills'. (You'll know the magazine I mean – it's the one that put its price up 10p the following issue.) And the main thrust of that important article was that in order to reduce household expenses, it is not necessary to deprive yourself of anything. "Simply purchase *wisely*," it said. "Start going in for bulk-buying or mail order, or keep your eyes open for goods reduced in price because they're marked 'Slightly Imperfect'."

Well, no one can say I didn't follow these three pieces of advice to the letter; but nor can it be said that any of them proved as cost-effective as was anticipated. There weren't many items being offered for bulk-buying round our way at that particular time and of those that were, I perhaps made the wrong choice. It could be that black pepper is not something the average family really needs to buy in bulk. Apart from the problem of where to store the sacks, my son has calculated it will take another four generations to work through the whole hundred-weight. Neither have we yet found any really practical use for the twenty dozen used bicycle saddles and the four gross of condolence cards.

Something else I only learned by trial-and-error was that in the case of goods which are advertised at reduced prices because they are 'slightly flawed', it is advisable before purchasing to enquire as to the nature of the imperfection. Had I done that, it is unlikely that my wife would have had to find room in the attic for two dozen pillowcases with no openings in them, and six made-in-Paris bras, all of them cross-your-heart styling but each containing three cups. She also had stinging things to say about the twenty-five pairs of sheer stockings whose reason for being reduced to only 25p a pair was that they had the seams at the front. ("For that price," I said when she pointed out the draw-back, "surely you can walk backwards.")

The matter of mail order purchasing led to another conflict of opinion. Although my family has still not allowed me to leave the house wearing the £18 suit I sent off for – made in Taiwan, and advertised as 'virtually indistinguishable from Savile Row tailoring' – I still believe that passers-by would have to be sharp-eyed indeed to notice that the fly is on the hip.

I don't want to give the impression that all our attempts at retrench-ment were unsuccessful. I can wholly recommend using the mangle to squeeze the last drop of toothpaste out of the tube and, though it may appear to reach some new low in penny-pinching, affixing a rev-counter on the toilet-roll holder does achieve quantifiable results. (Strangely enough, cheese-paring didn't. Perhaps it just doesn't work on Camembert, but what we saved on cheese we had to spend on buying new razor-blades.)

So, you're probably now asking, what was the nett financial result of all this thrift? Well, I think it only goes to confirm what a car-dealer once told me – "If you want economy, guv, you've got to pay for it." When I went back to the bank manager after six months of the most determined and ingenious frugality, he had figures to prove that I was £600 deeper into the red than when I started.

The lesson, according to him, is that it's a waste of time trying to get your overdraft written-off unless you are prepared to deprive yourself and family of such unnecessary luxuries as food, clothing and shelter.

Or, if I may express it in another of his homely analogies –

Do not try to write-off more than you can eschew.

'The Miner's Dream of Home'

Music-hall song

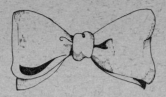

> I saw the old homestead and faces I love,
> I saw England's valleys and dells.
> I listened with joy
> As I did when a boy
> To the sound of the old village bells.
> The fire was burning brightly . . .

It was when I set fire to our house that I realised how true the words of that beautiful old song were. And how inaccurate was the advice given in *The Householder's Vade-Mecum: A Thousand Hints, Tips and Wrinkles for the Home-Owner* (1928. 14th edn. Cover detached. Some spotting. Lacks Chap. 8. 1/9d.).

The older I grow – which I do annually, almost as a matter of routine – the more the scales drop from my eyes and I find that not only do the horses of instruction, which were the lodestones of my youth, turn out to be men of straw with feet of clay, but metaphors are not what they used to be either.

One after another of the old adages which I was brought up to believe have turned out to be false when put to the test. For example: 'Least said, soonest mended'. I took my car in for servicing recently. The clock needed mending. Nothing drastic, just an adjustment. On the way to the garage I remembered the old adage, which clearly indicated that the less I spoke, the quicker the clock would be mended, and resolved to be terse. I handed the keys to the service chap. "150,000-mile service, please," I muttered briefly. "And one other thing. Slow. Running too slow. Adjust, please." When I returned the following day I found the car in pieces. The engine had been dismantled and the entire garage staff was trying to find out why it was malfunctioning. Had I spoken in full and said that there was a small problem with the clock . . .

I grew up in the belief, handed on to me by the wise men of my tribe, that if you drop a slice of bread it always falls on to the carpet butter side down. A few years ago I tested the adage scientifically. I spread ten slices of bread thickly. I proceeded into the drawing room and balanced them on the up-turned palm of my right hand. With a powerful thrust of my right arm I hurled the slices into the air and observed the result. The real, true, figures were:

> 10 per cent hit me in the eye.
>
> 10 per cent hit the ceiling and stuck to it.
>
> 10 per cent hit the cat and stuck to it.
>
> 60 per cent dropped to the carpet butter side down.
>
> 10 per cent disappeared completely. Years later I found it in the springs underneath the sofa. How it got there is still a scientific enigma, as baffling in its way as the Bermuda Triangle.

Small wonder, then, that riffling through *The Householder's Vade-Mecum: A Thousand Hints, Tips and Wrinkles* a couple of years ago I noted, with some scepticism, advice therein that when you have a household fire, the greatest amount of damage is done not by the fire but by the major jet of water poured over your goods and chattels by the Fire Brigade. This hint, tip or wrinkle stuck in my mind because I was at the time experimenting with the truth of another adage remembered from my youth that there is no smoke without fire.

I had discovered that afternoon that there *is* smoke without fire. At least there is if you buy a small, conical, firework-like thing called a greenhouse fumigator and light the blue touchpaper. A few sparks appear, true, and creep down the blue touchpaper but they soon disappear and the thing begins to belch smoke. Acrid, nasty smoke which stings your eyes and makes you cough and drop it and have difficulty finding it again and then you cannot think where to put it.

At two o'clock the following morning I suddenly found myself wide awake. There was a smell in the house. I woke my wife and said, "Can you smell something peculiar or is it just me?" She sniffed. "Smoke! I can smell smoke!"

I rushed along the corridor and woke the children. "Sorry to disturb you," I said, "but the house is on fire. Proceed in an orderly manner to a place of safety," and rushed back.

"Don't keep rushing backwards and forwards," said my wife. "Ring for the Fire Brigade."

"Never!" I shouted back. "Did you not know that according to *The Householder's Vade-Mecum: A Thousand Hints, Tips and Wrinkles* the worst damage is not done by the fire itself but by the mighty jets of water poured over belongings by the Fire Brigade's hoses? The book says that the best treatment for household blazes is to stifle the heart of the fire with foam."

"But we haven't got any foam," said my wife, climbing wearily into dressing-gown and gumboots.

This was true and a bit of a poser.

I climbed reflectively into my own gumboots, brain ice-cold and racing.

"We'll make some!" I cried, in a flash of inspiration.

It is surprising how long it takes to find and gather together a few simple household requisites when your family is not in the mood to co-operate fully and cheerfully.

I found my daughter leaning up against the front door, fast asleep. I shook her awake and set her to work.

I found my son in the kitchen, eating cold roast potatoes from the refrigerator. I spoke to him warmly about rallying in a family emergency and sent him to find a bucket.

The smoke was getting very thick, and thickening, but we all assembled outside while I mixed my foam.

For what it is worth here is the recipe:

Three partly used tins of bubble fluid, without bubble-blowing wire rings.

A plastic bottle of dish-washing fluid.

Half a cake of toilet soap.

A sachet of something labelled 'Hollywood Stars Bubble-Bath – Free with *Over 21* Magazine'. We could not open the sachet so bunged it in whole.

A packet of washing-machine powder.

Half a bucket of water from the greenhouse water-butt.

I swirled the whole lot round in the bucket and it foamed happily, if a bit glutinously, and sought the heart of the fire. I could not find this so decided to hurl the foam through the back door. I had just done this when my wife suddenly said, "The house isn't on fire."

I said, "What? *What?*"

She said, "There is no flame. And the smoke is smelly. What did you do with that greenhouse fumigator you were mucking about with this afternoon?"

"*Experimenting* with," I corrected, with dignity. "It went out so I put it in the larder. At least, I *think* it went out. Come to think of it, there might have been just a *wisp* of smoke still curling from it . . ."

I left her thumbing through *The Householder's Vade-Mecum* under D for Divorce and stepped forward resolutely to retrieve the fumigator and hurl it somewhere out of harm's way.

I do not know whether you have ever stepped, in gumboots, on to a sea of foam over plastic tiles but I can assure you that the effect is instantaneous.

My gumboots seemed to shoot up so that for a split second I was horizontal, like an illusionist's assistant being levitated, then my head went down. There was a sharp 'crack' as my skull hit the floor, a blinding flash in my head, and I saw the old homestead and faces I love, and I saw England's valleys and dells, and I listened with joy, as I did when a boy, to the sound of the old village bells.

Which is why I maintain that the advice given for dealing with a fire in *The Householder's Vade-Mecum* is hopelessly wrong and that the old song is dead right.

It is not the great jet of water from the firemen's hoses which does the damage. It is something quite different:

The minor stream of foam.

'See What the Boys in the Back Room Will Have'

F. Hollander/Frank Loesser
Popular song

MOST people are aware that Johann Sebastian Bach wrote more than a thousand musical compositions, but something I only found out recently was that he also produced no less than twenty children.

I must say, it increased my respect for him no end. Speaking as someone who also dabbles in writing stuff for Radio Four's off-peak hours, I have some experience of how difficult it is to create work of an enduring nature when you've got progeny exchanging hammer-blows in an adjoining room, even though there's only two of them in my case. How Bach managed to turn out all those immortal toccatas and capriccios with twenty of them belting each other about I can't begin to imagine.

What's more, as all of us striving to produce art of lasting importance are only too aware, nothing impinges on your working hours like the minor distractions of parenthood. Contrary to what sociologists would have us believe, the most time-consuming interruptions are not provoked by such issues as 'sibling-rivalry' or 'viable social inter-reacting'. No, what parts you from your desk for really protracted periods are questions like "Who had the scissors last?" Just imagine how long it must have taken to sort that one out when there were twenty-two denials to be cross-examined.

As to that other daily problem, the regular morning set-to regarding who should have the bathroom next, think of how complex that becomes when you're twenty-two in family. One musicologist I consulted maintains that the only way Johann Sebastian was able to solve it was by adopting the system that some launderettes use now – the issue of numbered tokens. He lent weight to the theory by pointing out that it would also explain why there's been so much argument regarding the sequential cataloguing of Bach's works. At some point the opus numbers obviously got mixed up with the bathroom rota.

What's more, that was by no means the only creative drain which Bach's fertility imposed on his genius. Has anyone ever considered the precious mental resources he must have expended simply in finding names for all those children? Although I've only had to do it for a mere two, I can vouch for the number of wasted working hours that are spent crouching over a dictionary of Christian names, muttering things like "Well, Edwin means 'Happy Conqueror'." "Yes, but Robert means 'Famous In Counsel'." So what must it have been like for someone who not only had twenty of them to label, but also a Mass in B Flat Minor to knock into shape before Christmas? In response to that question, my friendly musicologist could only offer me some inconclusive evidence that after the eleventh one Bach resorted to picking names out of the Yellow Pages.

But the major question I found myself asking was the financial one. How could this unique man, a father who probably had the bite put on him for more Smarties each Saturday than you and I shell out for over the course of a whole summer term, how could he afford to have no regular job and simply remain at home thinking up fugues and motets and the occasional Magnificat? Admittedly, he must have done very well from the Social Services – with that amount of progeny, they probably delivered the Family Allowance by Securicor – but just the same, there must have been quite a strain on the Bach finances. So how did he manage?

Well, that's where my musicologist directed me to the history books. According to most of the official biographies, the way in which this one-man population explosion assured himself of a steady growth in his current account was by hiring each of his children out to a member of the local aristocracy as either personal organist, Kappelmeister or Concert Master in Ordinary. (I didn't have time to look up exactly what the last post means, but I presume the holder of it must differ in some way from a Concert Master in Extraordinary, if only in certain personal habits.) What Johann Sebastian had been shrewd enough to realise was that the moment he had one solid chart-topper behind him – in the event, the Brandenburg Concerto – then for one of the local dukes or princelings to boast of having his own personal Bach in the drawing room would be, in status symbol terms, the eighteenth-century equivalent of possessing an eight-track stereo.

That the results must have exceeded even his own expectations can be seen by what happened when Prince Leopold of Anhalt summoned him with the news that he was about to move into a new schloss. When he asked whether there was any chance of hiring a spare young Bach as family music tutor, Johann could afford to be quite cavalier. "Sorry," he said. "They're all spoken for now. I've just promised the last one to the Duke of Weiner."

Prince Leopold's face fell. "I see . . . Any possibility you might have another one on the way?"

Johann shrugged. "I really can't say. I haven't been home since this morning."

There was no disguising the Prince's disappointment but your Hun does not give up that easily. "Tell you what I'm prepared to do," he said. "Whatever the Duke has offered you for a lad, I'll not only match it pfennig for pfennig, I'll also commission two partitas and a suite."

Bach reflected. Besides his having trouble with the Goldberg Variations, contrapuntal forms were passing out of style, Telemann's star was in the ascendant and that tailor was pushing for payment on the baroque overcoat. Prince Leopold, noting this indecision, was quick to press home his advantage. "Why don't we talk further about it?" he said. "How about lunch next Thursday? Tell you what – why not bring the family?"

And it was at this lunch that the Prince produced the remark which finally assured Bach's immortality. They all met at one of Saxony's most exclusive restaurants, where the head waiter conducted them to a table for twenty-three. "Right then," said the Prince as they sat down. "What would everyone like to drink? . . . Frau Bach?"

"Nothing for me, thanks," Bach's wife said. "Not in my condition." Johann Sebastian's knuckles whitened. "That being the case," he said, "make mine a double scotch."

"How about the children?" asked the Prince. "Herr Oberst, please go round and see what each of them would like.' 'Obediently the head waiter circled the table, taking orders for nine lemonades, seven fizzy oranges, two blackcurrant juices and one apfel-strudel. (That was Wilhelm Friedeman, the oldest but by no means the brightest; later died in poverty.)

Totalling up the children's requests, the head waiter said, "That only comes to nineteen. Is one child missing?"

Johann Sebastian sighed. "It always happens," he said to the Prince apologetically. "I *told* them to go before we left."

"No matter," said the Prince expansively. "I'll have the waiter go in there and ask him."

And, pointing an imperious finger at the door marked *Herren*, he gave the waiter the order which has resounded in musical history ever since:

"See What the Bach in the Boy's Room will have."

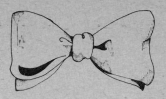

HEREWITH absolutely everything there is to know about Scotland, its rainfall, exports, geographical features and history.

If you look at a map of Great Britain and take Britain as a chap in a very large hat riding a pig westward, then Scotland is his head down to his Adam's apple. Then you get Cumbria.

Rain certainly falls in Scotland (there are no recorded instances of it rising) but it also has a trick of hanging about in the air at about ear level. This phenomenon of white-coloured water suspended in the air around your face is known on the east coast as a 'haar'. This can be a trap to foreigners, e.g. the English, as it closely resembles the word 'ha' which is a 'hall'. Or it might be mistaken as part of the English word 'ha-ha' and taken to refer to half a sunken fence. In the Highlands it is referred to as a 'Scotch mist' but they usually try to pretend that it never happens so the word 'Scotch mist' is now applied to something which does not exist.

The traditional exports of Scotland are, in order of importance, whisky, whisky and whisky. Traditional minor exports have included such useful everyday items as oats; jam; jute; journalism; ships' engineers; doctors; James Boswell; shortcake biscuits; the populations of Canada and New Zealand; the Presbyterian religion; kilts; Burns Nicht (popular in Canada and New Zealand); Andrew Carnegie; golf; Angus bulls; marmalade; television programmes on New Year's Eve; Labour politicians with pale faces, forelocks and fierce convictions; white heather; swingeing literary criticism; smoked salmon; bits chipped off the Cairngorm Mountains and made into cuff-links; broth; putting the shot (a gentle game played by fat men all by themselves);

shinty (an exceedingly rough game, a murderous form of hockey); curling (a game like bowls-on-ice played by sliding forward small anti-personnel mines with a handle); venison; oil; and even more whisky.

The geographical features need not detain us too long as they are there for all to see. Most of the geography of Scotland consists of mountains, grass, heather and Edinburgh. As there is a steady rainfall, particularly during the Edinburgh Festival, there are a number of lakes. As these are land-locked they have been given the Scottish name of 'lochs'. One of these, Loch Ness, has not got a monster in it but the locals are keeping the fact quiet. The word 'loch' is pronounced like the word 'lock' except that you clear your throat rather noisily at the end. There is a lot of throat-clearing when speaking Scottish words.

And so we come to the history of Scotland – about as well known to foreigners as the history of Fernando Po. Scotland is very ancient but little is heard of it before religion arrived. This is not surprising as only the religious could write things down. And, come to think of it, read what was written down. There must have been lots of lads dashing about the glens and washing their things in the burns and having bairns and so forth but what they got up to was not recorded and is beyond our ken ('beyond our ken' is a Scottish phrase meaning, roughly, not known to Kenneth McKellar – a high tenor who sings of the River Clyde).

Religion came to North Britain when a load of Irish monks sailed round the coast and tried to establish a monastery on the island of Lindisfarne, just south of Berwick-upon-Tweed (or, as the Romans called it, St Albans). The monastery was not a success. It just did not take. The Danes levelled it. It tried to keep going making wine, honey, cork table-mats, opening the kitchen gardens as an animal park, but it languished. When last heard of it was a pop group.

Meanwhile another batch of monks had landed in East Fife and founded the cathedral, town and university of St Andrews – arguably the most beautiful little town in the whole of Scotland.

Infant mortality was so high in those primitive days and so few people managed to survive into old age that the period is known to historians as the Middle Ages. During the Middle Ages religion and literacy spread out from St Andrews until the whole country was opened up to learning. This meant that records were kept and we now know what life was like in the remoter areas.

Life in the Highlands was always much grimmer than it was in the fertile Lowlands. The ancient Highland blessing of 'lang may yeer lum reek' is an indication of this, meaning 'long may your chimney smoke' that is to say, long may you be able to keep warm by having in your possession something to toss on the fire, like a faggot, or a Campbell. It is unwise to use this expression when talking to a non-Scottish stranger as it sounds to untutored ears like an Old Testament curse to do with boils and private parts.

The Highlanders traditionally wore the kilt. There is some interest as to what a Highlander wore below his kilt. The answer is simple: below his kilt a self-respecting Highlander wore – and still wears – shoes and socks.

Over their shoulders the Highlanders wore a rolled up piece of woollen cloth which they called a 'plaid'. At night, up the mountains, when the snow lay on the heather and the air was below freezing point, the Highlander would find a 'burn' (a small poetic stream), dip his plaid into the icy water, wring it out and then roll himself up in it to keep warm. This practice produced men so tough that they formed the nucleus of what is now the famous Coldstream Guards.

This hardiness was expressed annually in the Highland Games, a series of contests in which beefy Scotsmen, clad in vests and the kilt, blood-lust aroused by skirling bagpipes, competed against one another in front of royalty and American tourists. The height of the Highland Games was reached when they were mounted in front of Queen Victoria and her entire Cabinet. A new item was introduced to mark the occasion, 'throwing the hammer'. In this the participating Scotsmen picked up a fourteen-pound weight on the end of a length of chain, whirled it round and round, gathering momentum, and then launched it in the air, the object being to drop it on the head of the Englishman who was Secretary of State for Scotland.

Perhaps the greatest contribution which Scotland has made to inter-national affairs has been to develop the game of golf. This takes us back to the beautiful little grey stone fishing town of St Andrews, for its links – the Old Course – is the home of golf. It is there that the rules were formulated: that the game should be scored like a man waiting to be sentenced for a crime, or waiting for news of a wife having given multiple birth – the lower the number the better. That any player whose ball hits a seagull shall be said to have scored a 'birdie'. Or, if the bird is much vaster and rarer, an 'eagle'. That the ball shall be dimpled like a bishop's knees. That the hired assistant who prepares the 'tee' should be called a 'caddy'. Recognition of the St Andrews Golf Club's enormous contribution to the game came when, during the last years of the frail Queen Victoria's life, the name of the club was changed in her honour to the 'Royal and Ancient'.

St Andrews has many claims to fame, of course – the discovery of a sea salt in local seaweed which proved to have a beneficial effect on the liver and became famous as 'St Andrews Liver Salts', the extraordinary way in which students always seem to elect as their Rector men of enormous wit, charm and modesty. But to the ordinary visitor to Scotland St Andrews is not only the cradle of Scottish culture but also, perhaps more importantly, its most beautiful town.

This claim does not go uncontested. Many people claim that other coastal towns in East Fife and further north are even prettier. Arbroath, for instance, where the 'smokies' (small fish cured over smouldering fag-ends) come from.

I cannot agree.

The fact is that St Andrews, once the head of religion in Scotland, escaped the various evangelical movements of the last century, whereas almost every street corner in Arbroath has a 'kirk' built on it; a Wee Free, or a Seventh-Day Evangelist Mission, or a Presbyterian.

To my mind there is no doubt that St Andrews wins the contest for Scotland's most beautiful town, if only for one fact:

Too many kirks spoil Arbroath.

Watchman, what of the night?

Book of Isaiah, xiv:ii

IF I were asked to enumerate the Seven Deadly Virtues, the one I'd put right at the top of my list – even above A Sense of Humour and Speaking Frankly – is Female Tidiness. It is my belief that a houseproud wife can undermine the male ego infinitely more destructively than can any so-called 'liberated' housewife. In my opinion – which I respect – it is not the orgasm-seekers who have made contemporary men insecure about their masculinity, it's the cushion-plumpers and picture-straighteners.

The most heartbreaking proof of that I can offer you is the case of Dolly and Gerald. (As is customary when citing case-histories, I am only identifying them by their Christian names because to reveal their surnames would be grossly unethical.) (I am opening this additional bracket just in case when you saw those Christian names your first thought was, "I bet I know the couple he's talking about; they're the Dolly and Gerald who live in that road just past the traffic-lights, he drives a Lancia, she's got her own pasta-maker." Because they are not *that* Dolly and Gerald, honestly they're not. Word of honour.) (Don't go mentioning what you just thought, though.)

In many respects, Dolly was an ideal wife – attractive, caring, intelligent, stinking rich – but in matters relating to keeping her home neat and tidy her finickiness reached the height of fanaticism. There can't be another woman in north-west London who sets aside an hour every Friday afternoon for boiling wire coat-hangers. And that was only one symptom of an obsessiveness you could discern the moment you entered their house. 'Gleaming' didn't do justice to what met your eyes. The floor of their front hall was polished to such a high degree of gloss, it was like coming into a bowling lane.

"It helps preserve the parquet," Dolly would explain – and, to be fair, I suppose it sometimes did. So smoothly had that hall floor been waxed, I've seen an unwary visitor enter the front door, take one step forward, and the next time he stopped he was in the back garden.

There were many other respects in which spending an evening with Dolly and Gerald became Urban Stress at its most exquisite. "Try not to leave footprints on the carpet," she'd trill from upstairs while you wandered about the front room looking for somewhere to sit. This search was made necessary because all her armchairs and sofas were encased in slipcovers of protective transparent plastic. These are not only peculiarly unwelcoming – it's like sitting on a shower-curtain – but, in an odd way, slightly eerie. (If you spill a drink on one, it *stays* there.)

There was never any point in trying to relieve one's tension by lighting a furtive cigarette because where these were concerned, Dolly's early warning system was remarkable. One sniff of smoke and in she'd charge like Cochise leading a war-party. "What are you doing with your ash?"

"I'm thinking of swallowing it," I once said, hoping the implied rebuke might disconcert her.

Fat chance. "You know we have a special room for anyone who wants to smoke," was her smiling reply as she led me out to the toolshed.

Eating in that house was another aspect of her hospitality which demanded nerves of steel. By consequence of such unavoidable dining-table hazards as crumbs, soup-spill or spongecake splatter, it was impossible not to be made aware that Dolly would far rather have fed us all intravenously. As it was, not only did we have to endure her refusal to serve any plate of spaghetti until she'd taken a fork and combed each strand into a mathematically straight line, but her recipes for any kind of dessert always included the addition of a pinch of detergent powder. "It puts such a gleam on the plates when I wash them up," she'd murmur dreamily.

Of course, the one all our hearts went out to was Gerald. It is difficult enough to withhold compassion from a man who has elected to spend his life with a woman who polishes ice-cubes, but the more we found out about his domestic circumstances, the harder it became to remain unmoved. Imagine a wife who not only insists that her husband parks his car so that the name on the hubcap is always exactly parallel with the kerb, she also makes him put away all his clothing in strict alphabetical order. (Have you the remotest idea how much it costs to have a wardrobe that's fitted with twenty-six drawers?)

Opinions differ as to exactly what it was that finally drove Gerald to do what he did. Some say his breaking-point was reached when she hoovered his stamp-collection; others claim it was after she'd had him standing for two hours trying to straighten a watercolour of the Leaning Tower of Pisa. All we know for certain is that one morning Dolly came into their living room to find him hanging from a ceiling-fitting. (I dismiss as malicious gossip the rumour that her immediate reaction was to moan, "Oh, Gerald – you'd look so much better in the other corner.")

Although it could be said that Gerald's final act did, in some way, redeem his dignity – they found a will stipulating that he be cremated and his ashes scattered all over her best dining-room rug – I still think there's a place in those books about Feminine Ailments for a condition called Terminal Neatness.

There is, I repeat, a lot of it about – and anyone belonging to the male sex must be alert to the syndrome. Should any female betray her feelings for you by such typical early symptoms as 'straightening the tie', or 'flicking a speck off the lapel', then my advice is – repel her advances immediately!

Or, to make use of Isaiah's succinct warning –

"Watch, men – ward off the neat!"

Shall I compare thee to a summer's day?

William Shakespeare

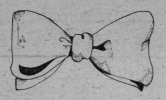

LITTLE in history turns out to be quite what we were told at school. Keats wrote in his "On First Looking Into Chapman's Homer" that the stout explorer and conqueror Cortez stood 'silent, upon a peak in Darien'. We now know that at the time he was, in fact, putting Mexico to the sword and, far from being silent upon a peak, was being very noisy in Chihuahua. The lad who stared at the Pacific and who exchanged glances of wild surmise with his fellow sailors was another explorer entirely, a slightly furtive, thinner explorer called Bilbao.

One is left with the impression that most of history is an exercise in sleight-of-hand; or, in the case of the wrong explorer standing in the right place, sleight-of-foot.

One after another the old beliefs are shattered. 'Purcell's Trumpet Voluntary' – you know, "Dadiddleiddleiddleiddleiddleiddle-Da-Di-Da-Da-*Dah*-di-da-didi-da-da" – was not written by Purcell but by another composer, Jeremiah Clarke. The screen tough-guy John Wayne's real name was not John but Marion. Dick Turpin was a small-time, violent crook who did not ride to York (somebody else did but I forget his name). 'Birdseye Peas' are not so called because the word 'birdseye' conjures up visions of something small, bright and wholesome but because the principle of deep-freezing was developed by an American explorer named Clarence Birdseye (explorers seem to get everywhere). Mrs Beeton did not write, 'First catch your hare'. Students are referred to the eighteenth-century writer on cookery, Hannah Glasse. She did not write it either.

And now another myth is exposed.

I am able to reveal that Shakespeare did not write the opening line of one of the loveliest of his romantic sonnets, i.e. 'Shall I compare thee to a summer's day?' It was written by Bacon.

It is important to explain at this juncture that the Bacon in question was not Francis Bacon, the essayist and statesman, but T. Harcourt Bacon, an actor in Shakespeare's company.

Throughout the history of drama it has been the misfortune of almost every company of actors to have a colleague such as T. Harcourt Bacon in their midst. That is to say, a decrepit old bore who had been with the company too long to be got rid of easily and who was almost un-castable as an actor.

Shakespeare's particular cross-to-bear was not only ancient but was incapable of remembering lines and those few which he did remember were delivered in a deep, resonant, incomprehensible mumble.

He was also a religious maniac, being a member of an eccentric sect known as the Eighth-Day Brethren of the Pentecost (Southwark Chapel) who made their point every alternate Friday afternoon by stripping naked and running through the City of London with a brazier of live coals on their heads calling "Repent or Burn!" Most of them did both before getting back to base. These sorties earned T. Harcourt Bacon the nickname of 'Streaky'.

It was a damp Friday afternoon in a backroom of the Boar's Head tavern, the meeting place of actors and poets, on 23 October 1608. Shakespeare sat at a table by the window, quill in hand, trying to think of something to write about. In truth he was a bit short of money for the furnishing of New Place, Stratford. The trouble was that plays brought him prestige but not much cash and there were chairs to buy, candles, a second-best bed ... the list seemed endless. Shakespeare finished nibbling his quill, spat out the feathers and sharpened up another, ready for inspiration.

"Masques!" Ben Jonson had said. "The king loves 'em! Hardly any dialogue. Just write 'Enter eight ladies-in-waiting from the ceiling on swans' and Inigo Jones does the rest. It's a doddle!"

"What are the fees like?" Shakespeare had asked.

"Dunno," Ben Jonson had answered. "All I've received so far from the king is a terce of canary."

"What sort of canary is a tersoff? Does it sing?"

"No. Canary *wine*. A terce is a barrel."

"How much does it hold?"

"Dunno. It's in the new Continental measure."

But Shakespeare did not reckon that there was a future for him in masques. No, the new thing was books. Write a book of poetry. Dedicate it to somebody important who would take an interest in it. Get it published and sit back and count the takings. That was where the steady money lay.

Shakespeare had already worked out to whom he was going to dedicate his book. In those days books were printed, published and sold from the printer's shop. A few were sold at a discount to booksellers and pedlars but there was no system of distributing them widely. Then a bright young man, seeing that passengers on stage-coaches needed reading material, decided to open up booths at coaching inns. The bright young man was named W. H. Smith. Soon every coaching inn in the country had a little stall close to where the passengers embarked which sold books, journals, nuts, etc. and each had Mr Smith's name above it. Shakespeare decided to flatter Mr Smith and thereby get his book sold throughout the land. He had already composed the dedication.

It read "To the onlie begetter of these ensuing sonnets, Mr W.H.".

All he had to do now was write the sonnets themselves, but it was not proving easy. First of all he had been interrupted by Streaky Bacon stripping off for his Friday afternoon trot through Eastcheap and then failing to light his brazier. Shakespeare had to stand on a chair and try to light the coal with a candle but the hot wax kept dropping on Streaky's bare flesh. And then there was trouble with his actors who were rehearsing for their autumn provincial tour.

Each autumn the company went on tour with a revue. This consisted of funny bits from the plays and scenes set to music, for instance the Portia scene in *Merchant of Venice* where the cast went into a dance and sang "A-tisket, a-tasket, don't choose the golden casket". All very light-hearted. The revue was compèred by Dai Llewellyn, a comedian who took Welsh parts and did a nimble hornpipe as well. Unhappily Dai Llewellyn had more theatrical sense than he had common sense and the night before, at a performance in front of Queen Elizabeth, he had done an impression of Sir Walter Raleigh, who was in the Tower for treason, which had so upset the Queen that Llewellyn was sent to join him. So the tour was due to take to the road the following day without a compère.

Just as Shakespeare was finishing eating his fourth quill, the door opened and Streaky Bacon staggered in, soaking wet, with his brazier hissing and making smoke.

"You look put out," said Shakespeare, always a great believer in a little comic relief.

"Too bloody wet for saving souls," mumbled the evangelist, wrapping himself in the curtain and drying himself vigorously. "Laddie –" he began cautiously. "I think that I should go on tour with the rest of the thespians. My experience will be of great use and I am up on the words of all the major roles, Richard the whatsisname, Henry the thingummy, that fellow with the gut . . ."

"Falstaff?"

"Who?"

"Sorry, Streaky, all the parts have been allocated."

"Ah. Shall I superintend the lighting, my dear fellow?"

"We haven't got any lights."

Streaky towelled away for a minute in silence. Then:

"The excellent woman who keeps my lodging-house is being a mite awkward about the rent. And I owe the coal-merchant a fair bit for brazier fodder. Shall I stage-manage the trip?"

"Sorry, Streaky. Burbage has put in his brother-in-law."

"Young Llewellyn has blotted his copybook and there is nobody to introduce the items . . ."

"Streaky, *please*. I am trying to start a poem and I need peace."

There was silence for quite a few minutes while both men struggled with their thoughts. Then, from Bacon: "May I put a wee idea into your fertile head, laddie? You would do well to think on't."

"Any idea would be better than this awful nothing."

It was then that Streaky Bacon said:

"Shall I compère the tour, same as Dai?"

'I'll Gladly Go from Rags to Riches'

Richard Adler and Jerry Ross
Popular song

THIS is by way of being my Auto Biography; in other words, a chronicle of the hate–hate relationship which has blossomed between me and the second-hand dealers from whom I've bought the automobiles in my life. If your first reaction is to ask why I've never chosen to buy new cars, the answer to that lies in my firm belief that those feelings of anguished resentment which so quickly follow the purchase of any kind of car today are somehow less keenly experienced when the car is a second-hand one; possibly because the discovery that you've been gypped doesn't come as so much of a surprise.

In any case, there are two reasons why that lack of surprise is now more or less total. Firstly, I've learned that second-hand car dealers, like cats, can sense when someone is afraid of them. Secondly, since I'm what might be termed technologically retarded, by the time I've driven any car for longer than twelve months, it's in such a clapped-out condition that whatever substitute a dealer offers me in exchange can always be represented as an improvement.

As an example of that, let me take you through what happened on my last transaction. The car I'd been driving for the previous three years had developed disabilities of such magnitude that had it been a horse you would have been obliged to shoot it. Like the course of true love, it never had run smooth but by now the only part of it that didn't make a noise when in motion was the hooter. Even disregarding some of the minor frailties to which it had become subject – if you kicked a tyre, the wing-mirror fell off; whenever you turned the radio on, the windscreen wiper slowed down – something in the nature of a major defect had begun afflicting the braking system. You've read about those supertankers which have to travel ten miles before they can come to a halt? A similar tardiness of response was observable whenever I applied brake-pressure. If I wanted to pull up in Park Lane, I had to begin putting my foot on the pedal half-way down the Edgware Road. And even when I did manage to stop the vehicle within a stone's throw of its intended resting place, after I'd switched off the ignition the whole inside of the bonnet would go on shaking for about three minutes, like a dog coming out of water.

It was a motor which, as I was the first to acknowledge when I finally took it to a dealer for exchange, was not one he could honestly describe as being in showroom condition.

"What exactly is the matter with it?" he asked, fondling the dead carnation in his buttonhole.

"I think it's beginning to self-destruct," I acknowledged. "What can you show me?"

He cast a professional eye over the car's general appearance. "Everything bar respect," he said. "But we'll find you something." He drew my attention to a large American car which had what looked like a cousin of his asleep on the back seat. "Fancy one of those? Lovely job."

He switched on the engine, which coughed a little, then emitted an impressive vroom. "Beautiful, isn't it. Only thing that'll pass you in this is a plane."

"Why is white smoke coming up from it?" I ventured to ask.

He drew me closer. "It was previously owned by a Pope."

"I really had in mind something a little smaller."

"Something smaller? Ah, now." He took me over to a bright red saloon, lifted its bonnet and motioned me to look inside. "Cast your eyes over this, squire. Who's a lucky boy then?"

As I've mentioned, when it comes to mechanical assemblies, anything more complex than a door-knocker and I'm banjaxed. However, not wishing to refuse his invitation in case it might confirm me as being easier meat than he'd supposed, I bent low over the engine and, assuming what I hoped was an expression of eagle-eyed expertise, plucked at what looked to be an efficient metal bar. The bonnet fell down on my neck. Lifting it off me, he said, "You've got a little beauty there, Sir Percy."

"How many miles has it done?" I asked.

They never answer a question directly. He said, "One owner. That's all it's had. Just one careful owner."

"Have you got his name?" I asked.

"You wouldn't know him," he assured me. "A fellow called Herz."

I hesitate to use the expression 'rip-off'. One does not wish to malign a whole profession when the majority of its members are probably every bit as transparently honest as they look. However, I am impelled to confess that my subsequent association with that bright red saloon has turned out to be just another Action Replay of the doomed affair between me and the internal combustion engine. We've been together now for eighteen months and the last time I took it for an MOT test, they warned me that the only parts of it which could be considered roadworthy were the sun-visor and one ashtray. Not only does it suffer from a condition that is technically known as 'oversteer' – in layman's terms, this means that if you blink hard while driving the whole car turns left – but it's so chronically underpowered that if I'm going past a schoolboy with a magnet in his pocket, I have to fight for control of the wheel.

Which means two things have now become inevitable. One, the car has reached the condition where I have to begin arrangements for exchanging it for another and two, whatever dealer I take it to will offer me an alternative which will simply set the whole sorry cycle in motion yet again. Without wishing to appear paranoid on the subject, I do get the distinct impression that, as far as the cars in my life are concerned, it was Tony Bennett who sang what is almost my theme song:

"I'll Sadly Go from Wrecks to Rip-offs."

A source of innocent merriment

W. S. Gilbert
Line from 'I've Got a Little List'
'The Mikado'

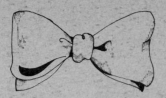

EACH year at about this time it is my practice to take a large foolscap notebook and a used bus ticket. I enter into the former a list of my failures for the year and on the back of the latter I note my achievements.

I very nearly filled the notebook this year. What sorry reading it made. What a monument to the vanity of human hopes: page 5, item 9, "Try to entice cat down from apple tree. Fall off ladder and break collar-bone (the small plastic stiffener in my shirt-collar) which I then cannot get out of its little tunnel. Try using pliers and tear collar right across. Throw pliers on floor in exasperation. This disturbs dog who wakes up in terror and is slightly, but tellingly, sick."

Or page 3, item 14, "Decide to try jogging as an aid to health. Soon break out in heavy sweat – hot on forehead, cold on back of neck. Difficulty with what to do with arms, which keep flying about like those of rag doll. Finally ram hands into trouser-pockets. Find this puts me off balance and I keep banging into things with my shoulders. Left ankle goes. No pain but ankle does not respond to instructions and foot dangles uselessly at end of it like broken golf club. Hop on. Breathing becomes difficult and cannot see clearly as red mist has descended over landscape. Heart worrying as pounding so loudly that the noise might frighten passing cars and induce accident. Decide that I will never make it as far as the front gate so have a rest and walk back up the drive."

Or page 15, item 6, "Collect wife's dress from cleaners as going out that evening to dinner party. Am standing holding the dress over my arm when lorry passes v. close to me. Hook of wire coat-hanger catches in rope securing lorry's load of iron rods and dress is snatched out of my arms. As lorry disappears round bend with dress, note that it says on the backboard 'Thos. Greenhough Ltd. The Ironworks. Hudders-field'."

Or page 38, item 12, "After wife has been trying unsuccessfully for twenty minutes to start lawn-mower, offer to do it for her by dint of superior strength, etc. Take firm hold of toggle and give a long mighty pull. Pull is longer than the cord. Cord snaps. Mower falls on to its side. Petrol and oil leak out killing grass. I, released from strain, hurtle backwards, trip over wheelbarrow and fall heavily, breaking comb in rear trouser-pocket and demolishing tiny dogwood tree just planted to commemorate thirty years of marital bliss."

And so on. Perhaps the most poignant entries were on the last page, page 54, items 16 and 17: "Once again note, with heavy heart, that the Nobel Prize for Literature has gone elsewhere. Nothing for yet another year from the judges, not even a book token."

In marked contrast, I could not think of one thing to write on the back of the bus ticket. The only achievements that sprang to mind, after an hour's deep thought, were that I managed to cut my toe-nails without also cutting a toe, and I glimpsed Esther Rantzen in the Oxford Street Woolworths. Neither of these seemed to be achievements of a high enough calibre to merit being recorded so I tore up the bus ticket and sank into melancholy.

"Had it always been thus?" I mused, miserably. "Have I never achieved *anything* memorable? Has not only this year been unfertile but the whole of my life?"

Then I remembered. I *had* achieved things when young. I had received prizes and awards. And, what is more, I had kept them.

There they were still. Up in the loft, between a dead deckchair and a hand-propelled sewing machine with angels all over it, in a cardboard suitcase marked "F. Muir. Trophies. Do not disturb or a curse will fall upon you." I dusted off the case, took it downstairs and, unmindful of the curse in my excitement, opened it up.

There they all were, lovingly wrapped in pre-war copies of the *East Kent Messenger*. The very first prize I ever won – a cup and saucer with 'God Bless the Prince of Wales' printed in large red letters. I have total recall of the occasion. Broadstairs sands. Uncle Mac's Minstrel Show Amateur Talent Contest (held every Wednesday morning to stiffen the takings). I was aged seven and decided that in spite of having no front teeth I would regale them with a song. There was a sensational film 'White Cargo' doing the rounds at that time which featured a torrid love-affair between a tea-planter and a tempestuous jungle beauty named Tondelayo. I sang the theme song, which went "Tell me, Tondelayo, wild jungle flower . . ." In the absence of any other competitors I was awarded first prize. This was so exciting that I fell off the platform and broke the cup.

I unwrapped another trophy. Yes, yes, the prize for selling most programmes for the Annual Water Sports! How I laboured. I used to run up and down the promenade pestering visitors, waving the programmes in their faces, until they bought one to get rid of me. On the day before the sports I skipped school and got a head start on the other programme sellers and won the prize, a quarter of a bottle of red stuff which said on the label 'Vino. Product of Italy'. My father said it was horse liniment and I was not to take it internally so I put it away.

A tiny little bottle came next, about the size of a third of a thermometer. Yes, of course, the scent I won at the first dance I ever went to! I sniffed it. It still gave off the unforgettable, heady fragrance of Phūl-Nana. Looking back, I rather think that it was a sample because it only held one drop which would not come out. I had to take the tiny stopper out and shove the bottle up my nose to get a god whiff. We had all been shuffling vaguely round the floor to the strains of 'Won't You Do, Do, Do What You Done, Done, Done Before, Baby' when there was a roll on the drums and Mr Potter said, "Stay where you are, everybody! Now we come to the moment you have all been waiting for – the Spot Prize!" I won it easily, having at least half again as many spots as the boy who was runner-up (acne was disallowed).

The next item was much larger. A hand-mirror inscribed 'Mackeson's Milk Stout'. Who on earth . . .? Oh, yes! Vicar! Mr Dinwiddie, who pumped the organ, was getting a little old for it and when Mr Firth, the organist, decided to end his voluntary with a tremendous crescendo of sound so that his wife up the street would know the service was nearly over and put the greens on, Mr Dinwiddie had to pump so vigorously that he put his back out. And I volunteered to pump for the evening service and the vicar gave me the mirror as a gift for, as he expressed it, "doing him a service".

My last trophy was a Curiously Strong Peppermint (without a hole in the middle. This was before confectioners caught on that customers would happily buy a hole if it had a bit of mint round it). The headmaster had announced that he would give a gold sovereign to the first boy to score a century in the annual cricket match against our deadly rivals, Chatham House. The first ball bowled at me was wide so I took a mighty sweep at it. Unhappily the top strap of my pad had come undone. As I swung round, the pad drooped out at right angles and demolished my wicket. The Booby Prize for the match was a Curiously Strong Peppermint.

Five fine trophies of past glories! And there was I thinking I had achieved nothing in life!

I reconstituted my torn-up bus ticket with Sellotape and began writing.

"No achievements indeed," I murmured to myself. "On the contrary, I've got a little list! –"

A saucer
Vino
Scent
Mirror
Mint.

Peter Piper picked a peck of pickled pepper

Proverb

QUITE the oddest item to arrive in my post of late was an envelope bearing the name of one of London's most expensive and exclusive hotels. All it contained was a cassette, on which a soft male voice, speaking in a tone of confidential servility, had recorded the following message:

You won't know me, Mr Norden, but after listening regularly to your programme I realise how badly you could do with an interesting story. Well, on account of me being a night porter at this place, I come into contact with all sorts of human dramas of every kind, so I have had ample experience of the tragic and heartbreaking events what get enacted within the confines of an opulent international hotel, especially as I also do a lot of looking through keyholes. And the tale I would like to enfold to you now is the strangest one whereof I was ever involved in.

It took place no more than a month ago in our Renaissance Penthouse, a suite of rooms so vast and luxurious it makes the Taj Mahal look like a hostel. Orders came that it was to be reserved for an elderly American millionaire of whom it had been learned that his Who's Who was twelve inches long. When he arrived on December 6th I found him to be an insignificant little old man, but that he was accustomed to having his whims obeyed became plain when he rammed me in the groin with a Bernini bronze for failing to draw the Persian lamb shower-curtains. Having thus chastised me, he then brought out a bunch of fivers the size of a cauliflower and behested me to purchase him the very finest pair of night-vision binoculars available.

It was only when I returned with these that he divulged me the bizarre purpose for which they were to be put to. Mr Norden, to say I was flabbergasted by it would be understating. So taken aback was I, I very nearly gave him the right change.

What it derived from was the fact that, although he was now rich beyond dreams of aviaries, his millions had only been acquired at the expense of the poor, the lowly, the under-privileged and the dis-advantaged. In fact, that whole class of person obliged to buy at recommended retail prices. But now, in the twilight of his life, his conscience was smoting him. He wanted to make a gesture of recompense.

"Just one magnificent gesture," he said. "With these binoculars, I will spend the next few weeks looking down from this plush eyrie, scanning the shivering down-and-outs and tramps who are obliged to spend their nights on the Embankment benches below. Then, like some Caliph of old, I will select one single unfortunate, bring him up to this palace of opulence – and bestow upon him a night of such pleasures as he has never even imagined."

My response was immediate. "Why go to strangers?" I said. "There's poor people all around."

He gazed at me with contempt. "Have you ever really known what it's like to be without in the midst of plenty?"

"Indeed I have," I said. "Wasn't I once caretaker in a girls' school?"

The backhander with the Bernini sent me clear into the bidet.

"I want a true pauper," he said. "The man my binoculars will be searching for must be starving, penniless, no home, no possessions, no hopes. And when they light on him, it is you who will pluck him from his degradation and bring him up here to the most unforgettable New Year's Eve of his squalid life. Not merely the finest food and wine money can buy, not merely the gift of marble bathrooms and satin bed-sheets – but also a night of almost unendurable ecstasy with the most desirable girl to be found in this great metropolis!"

I will freely confess to you, Mr Norden, that over the next few weeks I was in a mood I can only describe as moody. The idea that all these benefits would go to some unwashed bum who probably wouldn't even appreciate them – it shuddered me even thinking about it. But every night the Caliph was there at the window, his binoculars peering down into the blackness in search of the last of the big-time losers. As the nights passed and no suitable candidate was found, my hopes rose a little. Perhaps he'd be unable to find anybody capable of living down to his expectations? Then, right at the very last moment – in fact, at seven o'clock on the night of December 31st itself – my hopes were shattered. Buzz went the indicator for the Renaissance Penthouse and when I got up there, the old boy was in a state of high excitement. "Down there!" he said, pointing out the window and handing me the binoculars. "The one curled up in the litter bin!"

I looked down and saw – well, how can I describe him? Filthy, unshaved, unkempt, ragged, bleary-eyed – and those were his more attractive aspects. "Fetch him," said Mr Millionaire. "The rest is up to you. While I depart in my private plane for my private château on the Côte d'Azur in the Riviera of the South of France, conduct him hither and lay before him oysters, lobsters, pheasant, Charlotte Russe and the finest champagne in your cellars. Then, when a certain Miss McGinty arrives at five minutes past midnight, dim the lights, put on the Mantovani and withdraw."

My heart sank. So it was to be Florence McGinty. Though the name is probably not known in the world you inhabit, Mr Norden, there isn't a red-blooded member of the free-spending, high-flying jet set who wouldn't pawn his Piaget for one hour with her. Besides being one of the few girls who could get into the hotel lift and press the Up button just by breathing, she was someone for whom I'd harboured wriggling-about longings for so many years, I could now only moan and whimper.

But what could I do but obey instructions? Gritting my teeth, I collected the strong-smelling person from his disgraceful place of rest, conveyed him, blinking and muttering, to the silken splendours at the top of the hotel, set before him his unaccustomed and undeserved luxury fare, and departed.

It could have been the most disgruntling night of my life had it not been for a most unusual error on the part of Mr Ali Patel, our world-renowned French wine waiter. On his champagne order, instead of writing "Four bottles of the '47", he'd put down "Forty-seven bottles of the '4".

The consequence was that when, at one minute past midnight, I made my accustomed round of the keyholes, what do I see through the aperture of the Renaissance Suite? There's Mr Unsavoury lying sprawled across the Charlotte Russe, dead to the wide. It was obvious what had happened. Because of the inordinate quantity of champers he had poured into a system grown unaccustomed to it – he and the old year had passed out together.

My mind raced. When the exquisite Florence came tapping at his door in less than five minutes time, about the only thing she could now expect in the way of fleshly delight was the Scottish Dancing belting out on BBC 2. Well, Mr Norden, if there's one thing in this world I hate, it's waste. So, in less time than it takes to tell, I'd opened that door with my master-key, bundled our friend down the laundry-chute, whipped-off my porter's jacket, slipped on a silk dressing-gown that had been supplied – and by the time that soft tap arrived, I was on the chaise longue in an attitude of negligent welcome.

Mr Norden, in expressing the doubt that you'll ever enjoy a New Year one-tenth as happy as mine, may I also hope that you can put this story to some good use. It occurs to me that the tale of how an eye-balling hotel servant appropriated a perquisite intended for an in-ebriated indigent might be covered by that old adagio:

"Peeping porter nicked a perk of pickled pauper."

The better part of valour is discretion

Shakespeare
Falstaff in King Henry IV, Part 1 Act V, sc. 4.

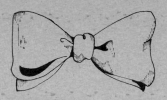

THIS is the love story of three girls. It is a sad story, particularly at the end if you can get that far.

The three girls went to boarding school together in the superior part of Surrey and they were inseparable friends. They all came from the same sort of background. They all lived in houses backing on to golf-courses and all boasted to friends who lived more simply, "There are fairways at the bottom of our garden." Their fathers were driven to the City in polished cars. The fathers never looked out of the windows but read balance-sheets in the back seat. At night they read with the help of a little light on an arm, and smoked a small cigar. The girls' mothers were all very thin from eating a lot of avocado salad and smoking a great number of low-tar cigarettes in a patent holder which was supposed to cure them of smoking.

All three girls were named after rich aunts in Great Expectation and their names were Leonora, Samantha and Deirdre. One evening, sitting in Deirdre's room, swapping Polaroids of their ponies, they swore a solemn swear that when they grew up they would all marry very rich men. They were eating a jar of caviare at the time which Samantha's mother had sent her as it was left over from the Golf-Club Fête's White-Elephant Stall. The three girls spread the rest of it on a chocolate digestive biscuit and each ate a piece to seal their vow.

The rest of the girls in the school were not at all surprised when they heard about the vow. Leonora, Samantha and Deirdre were so totally absorbed in the pursuit of luxury and the acquisition and disposal of pounds, shillings and pence that they were known to the school as L., S. and D.

Physically they were an ill-assorted trio and the general feeling in the

Prefects' Room was that they had a one-in-three chance of marrying wealth. The one-in-three with the chance was D. (Deirdre) who even at that age was a great beauty and had a figure that would start the windmill turning on a Dutch landscape painting at forty paces.

S. (Samantha) was another matter. For one thing she was abominably thin. Rumour had it that when Miss Proctor (Geography and Personal Hygiene) first supervised the juniors' baths, she made S. clench a coat-hanger between her teeth when she pulled out the plug so that she would not be swept down the plughole. She also had much too much hair for a girl of that lack of width, and it hung dankly down, getting into everything.

L. (Leonora) on the other hand was vast and rectangular. She had shoulders like those of an American full-back and only tapered slightly down to unfortunate ankles. No bosom, no waist. When permitted to wear Own Clothes she favoured ankle-length black dresses. This, and the fact that her hair was a mop of frizzy beige, meant that from a distance she closely resembled a recently poured glass of Guinness.

After leaving school the girls were set up in a tiny, but suitably expensive, flat in a square in West Kensington and the parents began making vague plans for massive weddings for the three of them. Meanwhile the girls were installed by their fathers in approved jobs. D. was learning the Montessori Method of teaching kindergarten. L. had taken a Cordon Bleu course and was cooking directors' lunches, and S. was mucking out stables for a lightly titled cousin of her Mummy.

Their problem was that they were not meeting eligible, i.e. rich, young men. L. and D. were certainly meeting very rich men in the course of their careers but L.'s men were old and heavily married and D.'s were between four and six years of age. S.'s clients were aristocratic enough but were horses.

So the three decided to take out their savings, pop their pony brooches, sell their Hermes scarves and have a month's holiday at the most fashionable and chic hotel they could find in the Greek Islands. There they would hope, nay expect, to meet their Mr Right. Or rather, Prince Right. Or Sheikh Right. Or, better still, Lord Right of the Bank of England.

The weather was perfect. The sun bronzed them, they swam and played tennis and lay about in their bikinis. And all three fell deeply in love.

It was the Tuesday afternoon. S. and L., who had not won a single admiring glance from the rich young men in the hotel, went for a stroll along the beach and found that just round the corner was a group of chalets filled with a package tour of Britishers. No sooner had they sat on the sand when they were joined by two likely lads. Next to slim talkative S. sat vast silent Reg. Reg, it transpired, worked in a pet shop in Woking and loved all living things including, after three minutes, S. Next to vast bovine L. sat weasely wise-cracking Sid, a computer programmer from Slough. L. had never met anybody so wonderful in her life, so amusing and intelligent and worldly. She felt she could sit and listen to him for hours. Which is just what she did.

In a pink haze of happiness S. and L. floated back to their hotel as the sun began to sink. The first thing they saw was D. lying on the beach very close indeed to a bronzed figure. The girls shouted. The figure looked up, muttered something to D., waved and strolled away. He was young, dark, muscular and was very beautiful; a combination of Omar Sharif and Robert Redford, with a hint of Nureyev about the loins.

D. looked as though she had been hit on the head with a hammer.

Over dinner they came down to earth a little and exchanged stories. D. was absolutely appalled at what L. and S. had to tell. "A shop-assistant! And an office clerk!" she screamed in her rather loud voice which sounded like a seagull with its foot caught. "Oh, my dears, how *ghastly*!"

L. and S. stared at her in amazement. "But Reg is *lovely*!" said S.

"Sid is *heaven*!" said L.

"But they are not *rich*!" screamed D. "My Aristotle is *stinking* rich! He is a nephew of Niarchos. Poor lamb has had *the* most *frightful* row with his uncle – something about a dozen supertankers his father gave him which uncle is trying to get off him – and he is lying low here for a few weeks. I shall comfort him, poor sweetie. Isn't he the absolutely, hyper most? Like a Grecian god!"

For the first time since they first met at school a rift grew between them. That evening L. and S. trotted down the beach for an Olde Tyme Dance at the chalet restaurant with their beloveds. They arrived back at their hotel at half past eleven. D. did not turn up at all. She staggered in at ten o'clock the following morn.

"He seems rather keen," she said, and went to bed.

And that was the pattern for the rest of the holidays.

Aristotle, it appears, remained keen and L. and S. saw very little indeed of D.

When they got back to London they realised that their lives had changed irrevocably. S. took a job at a supermarket in Woking to be near her Reg. L. moved out too and became a waitress in Slough so that she could see her Sid at lunchtime as well as in the evenings. D. waited for her rich Greek to come and take her to her new life of unimaginable luxury. He had promised to collect her by helicopter as soon as the feud with his uncle was settled.

The three girls agreed to meet in London on the anniversary of their holiday and exchange news.

Which they did.

S. had inherited money from her aunt and she and Reg were going to open a stables and cattery in an animally bit of Sussex. They were getting married the following week. Sid, the computer programmer, had been promoted and was going to be the firm's Far East chief. He and L. were going to be married and were clearly going to do great things together on behalf of the company.

And beautiful D.? She spent most of her days looking up in the sky for the helicopter and bashing into lamp-posts.

The three old friends walked along the Edgware Road, looking vaguely for somewhere to eat and chatting away. D. was a bit ahead, eyes up to the sky, when they passed the Athens Kebab and Takeaway House. It was a hot day, the door was open and inside S. could make out two waiters in greasy vests. One was setting tables and the other was slapping butter into little pots and patting it flat.

"There's a restaurant!" said L. "Kebabs, too. How suitable!"

"No!" said S. urgently. "Quick – move on!"

"But, why?"

"See inside?"

"Yes. Just a couple of fellers working."

"Look again . . .

"The butter-patter feller is D.'s Grecian."

'Try a Little Tenderness'

Harry Woods/James Campbell/Reg Connelly
Popular song

IN an earlier episode of these readings, I happened to remark that the countryside bores me boneless. As far as I'm concerned, all it represents is an area where the trees may be more crowded but people are further apart. In fact, so incurably urban am I by temperament, were I forced to live within an unspoilt rural environment for any length of time, I am quite certain I'd wind up in one of those places where they take the laces out of your shoes. I can't help it, but prolonged exposure to clean country air leaves me in a state of such melancholy, they can only restore me to health by holding me near the exhaust of a bus.

It would be very difficult to exaggerate the storm of outrage which those off-hand remarks called forth from listeners. But I'll try. Perhaps the best exemplar was the letter that arrived from a Mrs O.W. of Surrey, because that one expressed hurt even in its form of address. Instead of starting "Dear Denis", it began "Poor Denis . . ."

"Poor, *poor* Denis," it went on. "If only you could be made aware of all the beauty you are depriving yourself of by this distrust you exhibit towards our most precious heritage. I pity you, poor Denis, I do really, I really pity you." After continuing in this compassionate vein for a few more lines, it went on. "May I make a suggestion to you, poor Denis? Soon it will be spring again, the time of year when Mother Nature calls to all her growing things, 'Come on now – one more time.' Denis, why don't you allow yourself to become *part* of that perennial miracle? Find some verdant pasture and, from the vantage point of a small tent, let yourself *experience* the lyrical marvel of earth's awakening. Do that but once, poor Denis, and I guarantee you that never more will you use the public airwaves to proclaim that all

Nature means to you is the unseen force which lets birds know when you've just washed your car."

Well, I'll admit it – Mrs O.W.'s letter got to me. I mean, somewhere deep inside. Although the argument sometimes expressed as "If you've never tried it, don't knock it" is one that's advanced today in relation to everything from muesli to incest, it still has a certain force behind it. So much, in fact, that I resolved to take up the lady's suggestion. What follows, therefore, is by way of being a report to Mrs O.W., written in the first person rural, regarding my attempt at a reconciliation with natural phenomena.

Faithful to her instructions, on the very first weekend of spring – which arrived somewhere round the middle of July – I jumped in the car, betook myself to the nearest verdant pasture and struggled across it till I found a suitable site for pitching my small tent. I am glad to acknowledge, Mrs O.W., that even in that short journey I learned something about the countryside which I'd never realised before. Although I had often listened to that well-loved old spiritual 'Carry Me Back To Green, Green Pastures', it was only the experience of walking across one on which several cows had been grazing that taught me why its lyric insists so strongly on being *carried*.

My next lesson came when I was presented with the challenge of my tent. I have come round to the view, dear Mrs O.W., that you may have placed too much emphasis on its being a small one. As I measure some six-foot-three in length, I spent most of that night with everything below my knee-cap protruding from its entrance. Admittedly, this meant that the flap had to be left open, allowing me a different view of the night sky from the one I generally get between the chimney-tops – all those glittering stars stretching above like some huge connect-the-dots game – but whatever majestic thoughts that sight aroused in me were dispelled next morning when I awoke to find myself devoid of all sensation in my lower legs. I won't make too much of a sob-story of that because, on inspection, all it proved to be was the natural result of leaving them extended all night on damp grass; combined with certain after-effects from a cow sitting on them.

What I'll readily grant you, Mrs O.W., is that, to a born and bred city-dweller like myself, there really is something about waking up in a meadow. Not only are you conscious of a scent you've never encountered before – as though the whole world had been suddenly sprayed with Room Freshener – but there's nothing to beat that pure clean country air for improving the taste of your first cigarette.

In fact, as I stood by my small tent, drinking in all the rustic sights and sounds, I found myself thinking, "This might yet turn out to be a really enjoyable weekend. Providing, of course, I can get out of this damn sleeping bag." You see, Mrs O.W., owing to some difficulty with the zip, I'd woken up to find myself imprisoned within it. Apparently, it was a lady's model, and therefore fitted with some kind of chastity lock.

Sadly, even when I did finally succeed in cutting my way out of it, the day failed to brighten much because the floral pattern on my pyjamas attracted a swarm of bees, so that I had to return inside the tent till nearly midday. "This is hardly getting up with the lark," I remember musing when the swarm finally departed – presumably because it was now opening time for real flowers – but, determined to make the best of the time left to me, I slipped off my p.j.s and reached for my clothes. If I tell you it was only at that moment I noticed that some species of furry beetle had taken up residence inside my Y-Fronts, perhaps you will understand why I was back in London just after one-thirty.

As you will appreciate from the foregoing, Mrs O.W. – I did try. But I think you'll have to live with the fact that there are some people for whom Nature just doesn't ackle. We are not all made the same, Mrs O.W. So what I suggest is that until such time as I can equip myself with a three-bedroom tent with underfloor heating and double garage, we cool it. You take the great outdoors and I'll stay with the grate, indoors. Once we agree on that, something I'd also advise is that next time you feel impelled to urge a certain unnatural course of action on a complete stranger, think for a little while first. I don't mean for long. Just, say, a decade.

And you'll know, of course, the unnatural course of action I'm referring to:

Try a little tent, Denis.

Messing about in boats

Kenneth Grahame
'The Wind in the Willows'

IT is a strange tale I tell. A tale of the bygone past. Of men and women long dead, of noble and of common birth both. There is danger in the tale, too. A very real danger of the whole thing becoming deadly boring before I have even started. So my story begins.

I happened upon my literary discovery quite by chance whilst browsing through the non-fiction section of Egham Public Library last Tuesday. Well, actually the Mobile Van which calls at our village on Tuesday afternoon. I did not mean to browse but Sonia does the non-fiction and as Mrs Spottiswode (Light Love, Crime and van-driver) is getting suspicious, I thought I had better pretend that I was in the van to pore over the books. With a hasty whisper to Sonia that I would meet her on Saturday morning at the supermarket as usual between cat food and fruit yoghourts, I picked up the first book to hand and buried my nose in it.

It turned out to be a very old book called *Curiosities of Literature* by the Rev. T. Thurlingwold Plackett (a name new to me). It was published in 1901 and in the front, in ink, was written "To Captain Trumper – who kindly overcame my *idée fixe* that I could never love a man with a tattoo on his bottom – Lady Anne Plover, March 2nd (and a little bit of March 3rd), 1902." I turned to the main text and was instantly enthralled. I was in for a few surprises, I can tell you.

Like me, you have probably always thought that national advertising first began in this country in the early years of the last century and that the world's first nationwide ads were for Warren's Blacking, Pear's Soap and Rowlands Macassar Oil. Not so, it seems. The first nationally advertised product was something very different.

Further. You have probably lived all your life under the delusion that

Lord Byron was the first famous writer to write advertisements and that he wrote solely for Mrs Warren, of Warren's Blacking, who paid him £600 a year, a fortune in those days. You cling to the fact that the *Edinburgh Review* wrote: "The praises of blacking were sung in strains which would have done no discredit to Childe Harold himself, even in his own opinion – for when accused of receiving £600 a year for his services to Mrs Warren – of being, in short, the actual personage alluded to in her famous boast, 'We keeps a poet' – he showed no anxiety to repudiate the charge." But I now know better. Three years before writing verse for Mrs Warren, Byron had written a fine piece of copy extolling the praises of a make of boot.

Wedging myself in the corner between Juvenile and Reference as Mrs Spottiswode took roundabouts at speed on the way back to Egham, and ignoring Sonia who was bent on nibbling my ear, I read on and on. What a story unfolded.

It all began one Tuesday morning in Wilton House, the Wiltshire home of the Earls of Pembroke, in the year 1583, when a son was born to Mrs Massinger, the wife of one of the family retainers. He was steward to either the fourth son of the second Earl or the second son of the fourth Earl – it was difficult to tell with all those winding staircases – and a trusted employee, so the little lad, whom the doting parents christened Philip, was allowed the run of the house.

Young Philip Massinger grew up to be a veal-faced lad, much given to solitary walks and book reading. He spent a great deal of time in his Lordship's library with his nose stuck in a book. This was an indication not only of the boy's love of literature but also of the fact that books were so strongly bound in those days that if your nose got in the way when you closed a book it was the devil's own job to wrench it free.

In the year 1603, when Philip was twenty years old, his parents died of a surfeit of Lampreys. Mr and Mrs Lamprey were deadly dull at the best of times and their coming to stay with the Massingers proved fatal to the old couple. The fourth Earl was most sympathetic to the young Philip, gave him five shillings (a miserable sum in those days) and sent him out into the world.

Within a year Philip Massinger had made his name as one of the brightest of the new wave of Jacobean playwrights. As the years passed his reputation grew. He wrote plays with the famed duo Beaumont and Fletcher; he became a friend of hit poet and playwright Ben Jonson; he married, had a son and, inspired, wrote the play he is best known by and which is still produced by the National Theatre when they want to bung on a cheap revival – *A New Way to Pay Old Debts*.

In 1640 Philip Massinger died. As far as the world was concerned that was the last that was to be heard of the Massinger family; the line disappeared without trace. Disappeared, that is, until the Rev. T. Thurlingwold Plackett started sniffing into the archives. The truth is stranger than fiction.

The old Earl took the Widow Massinger and her son back to Wilton House and let them live there. Now Wilton House is very, very old – parts of it go back as far as the A30 – and very, very large. The rooms he allotted the Widow Massinger were in the West Wing, which was in Hampshire, and the corridors were so long and winding that she never did manage to find her way out again. And so the Massinger son grew up within the maze-like confines of Wilton House. This was no hardship because a busy life went on back there. Gipsies arrived to sell clothes-pegs and could not find the exit. Burglars broke in and could not break out again. Curates arrived to solicit funds for repairing the organ and found themselves trapped for life. Young people fell in love, were married, started families. Life went on.

In the year 1781 the tenth Earl, a notable explorer, assembled a group of like-minded intrepid sportsmen and mounted an expedition into the interior of Wilton House. After three weeks of dangerous progress, bivouacking where they could, they reached the West Wing and discovered the tribe living there. The tenth Earl was particularly taken with young Thaddeus Massinger, an ingenious lad who was trying to make a water clock which ran on quarts of beer (it was history's first quarts timepiece).

Realising that the boy had a future, the Earl had him wrapped in a stout sheet of brown paper and posted to London to be apprenticed to a bootmaker.

By 1790 Thaddeus owned his own bootmaking business in St James's and was on his way to becoming very rich indeed. (His subsequent career is beyond the scope of this work but it might be noted that he ended up a peer, Lord Last, the sole purveyor of unifoot boots to Queen Victoria's army. 'Unifoot' boots were army boots which fitted either the left or the right foot. Or, to be more accurate, did *not* fit either the left or the right foot.)

Thaddeus's success came from his brilliant inventions in footwear. Until he came upon the scene all footwear was either a shoe which buckled or a tall, loose, floppy boot. When farm workers walked through mud their loose boots stuck and they had to walk on in their socks. Thaddeus invented what he called 'gumboots'. The farm workers paraded in front of him and he poured a bucket of gum inside the boots. This stuck the boots on to the workers. For life. Not wholly satisfied with his gumboots, he turned his attention to light shoes and invented a white shoe which could be worn to play tennis in. It was made of canvas and soaked in whitewash. These proved so comfortable that the gentry took to wearing them as bedroom slippers. The trouble with them, though, was that they left trails of white powder on the landing carpet and next morning the hostess could tell from them where everybody had spent the night. They became known as 'sneakers'.

Thaddeus Massinger's breakthrough came with his invention of boots which did up at the side with buttons. For the first time in history the gentry could wear slim, close-fitting boots, tailored to their ankles. They swept through London society like wildfire until everybody who was anybody had a dozen pairs. And Thaddeus's sales fell off drastically.

It was then that he had his great idea, and the world's first national advertising campaign was born. Thaddeus decided to put an advertisement in every newspaper in the kingdom. He hired the great cartoonist Cruikshank to make an engraving showing an elegant pair of the boots, buttons prominently displayed. And he hired a noble but poor young poet, Lord Byron, to write the copy.

And this was what Byron wrote. At the top of the advertisement were the words "There is nothing, absolutely nothing, quite so worthwhile as –" Then came Cruikshank's engraving. Then the world's first advertising phrase:

"Massinger Button Boots".

'I Left My Heart in San Francisco'

Cross/Cory
Popular song

THANKS to a radio series called *My Music!*, it is now a matter of public knowledge that my singing voice is to melody roughly what bubble-gum is to gourmet cuisine. As the format of the programme requires each of its participants to perform a song every week, my constitutional inability to carry a tune, together with a certain nervous tendency to change key every fourth bar, have both become the subject of widespread comment, particularly from Frank Muir. Employing the privileged candour of an old friend, he frequently draws the attention of listening audiences to my vocal inadequacies with such telling phrases as "sounds like a wounded moose recorded at the wrong speed"; or, "I've experienced better harmonies from a leaking balloon"; or even once, in a spontaneously Shakespearian moment of eloquence:

> Oh what is so rare as a day in June?
> A song which Denis sings in tune.

It was therefore all the more surprising – I'm tempted to say touching – when I received a telephone-call from him one afternoon suggesting I come along and sing a few songs of my own choice at a charity cabaret he was arranging that weekend. Even though I knew him to be one of the few people aware of the secret fantasy I've always nursed – namely, that some night, given the right conditions, my vocal shortcomings would miraculously disappear and I'd suddenly astonish an audience by displaying all the arts of a Sinatra or a Bennett – I still found myself deeply moved by his invitation. Controlling my emotions, I questioned him as to 'the venue of the gig' as we singers call it.

It was to take place in the grounds of his own home. He'd donated his spacious garden to a local charitable organisation for a Saturday afternoon fête, which would be followed in the evening by a Disco to be held inside a large marquee on his paddock. Around 10 p.m. the dancing would be halted and Frank would announce an All Star Cabaret. Me. I would then go on and sing a selection of popular favourites, accompanied by the local church organist at the piano.

"But why me?" I couldn't help asking. It was a little ungracious, perhaps, but I was only too aware that Frank's wide circle of acquaintances included such luminaries of popular song as Jack Jones, Paul McCartney, even Vince Hill.

There was a pause. "Because you're my friend," he said gruffly.

Say what you like about this heartbreak world of showbusiness, I found myself thinking, but there are still nuggets of pure gold to be found among the dross. Without further ado I set about ordering a Lurex jacket and selecting my repertoire. After days of agonising I came up with what was undeniably a shrewdly balanced programme. A driving up-tempo version of 'I Met Her on the Beach At Bali-Bali' to open, straight into a medley from *Gold-diggers Of 1929*, then – for my big crowd-pleasing finish – a really belting version of 'When It's Springtime in the Rockies'. As I said to Frank when I met him in the marquee that Saturday night, "Something there to please all ages."

His answering grunt seemed a little perfunctory, but it didn't disturb me. Discos aren't really my scene, either. What with all those flashing lights and whirling audio-visual effects, it's a bit like dancing inside a pin-table. Nor was I particularly worried when 10 p.m. came and went without that roll on the drums which is the prelude to a cabaret announcement.

However, when midnight arrived and there was still no sign of a halt in the frantic bopping, some slight agitation did begin setting in. Noticing that Frank was now boogeying with a neighbour who breeds Sealyhams – she's married to someone called Edward Sealyham – I approached him again. "Excuse me, guv," I said, "shouldn't I go on and do my turn before the beer runs out?"

"Not yet," he said. "Not till it becomes necessary." And with a whirl of his kaftan he was off back into the merry throng.

It was that word 'necessary' which sowed the seeds of suspicion. Noticing the church organist sprawled across the piano, I shook him awake and, while he was still bemused, put some questions to him.

Then it was that the whole sorry truth of the matter emerged. Apparently, after Frank had erected the marquee, he made application to the Council to approve its use as a place of dancing and entertainment. They'd sent along an inspector who looked round it, then shook his head regretfully. "Sorry," he said, "I am afraid I can't allow this to be used as a disco."

"Why not?"

"Fire regulations, Mr Muir. We can't have two hundred people crowding in here unless you can provide some means by which, if an emergency arises, you can get all of them out of the place within twenty seconds."

Whereupon Frank had pondered for a moment, then snapped his fingers. "No problem," he said. "I know exactly how I can do that."

"How?" said the Inspector.

"At the first sign of smoke, I'll get Denis Norden to *sing*."

Do I need to describe my feelings on discovering such a betrayal? Without even stopping to think, I ran over to the group who'd been playing for the dancing, waved them to silence and requested a drum-roll. Then, before anyone could stop me, I stepped to the microphone. "Ladies and gentlemen," I called. "It's Cabaret Time!" A hush fell over the audience. "By arrangement with Frank Muir, we now present – SingalongaDen!" A nod to my accompanist and we were into 'Bali-Bali'.

Very seldom in a man's life does a futile gesture become a memory to treasure. But, without a word of a lie, my singing *paralysed* that audience. They were *spellbound*! Breathless with excitement and poor ventilation, they sat there and cheered my every song to the echo! Seventeen encores!

Mind, you, it wasn't until the following day I learned that the people making up the audience were all beneficiaries of the charity for whom the evening had been organised; in other words, the National Association for the Hard of Hearing.

But even that knowledge doesn't diminish the thrill that flushes over me whenever I recall that performance. Nothing will ever erase the memory of the night when, against all odds –

I let my art entrance Frank's disco.

Many are called, but few are chosen

New Testament

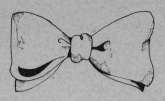

SHOULD you ever have the pleasure of staying with my lady wife and me at our lovely home in Thorpe, Surrey (and you are more than welcome), you will sleep in what we are pleased to refer to as our 'New Testament Spare Bedroom'.

The reason we call it that might well be of interest to those of you of a scientific bent – or even those who are scientific but not bent – so here is the story, in all its strange and subtle beauty.

A while ago my wife and I watched a science programme on television. This was unusual for us as we are not in the habit of watching science programmes. In fact we are not in the habit of watching *any* type of programme. We believe that watching television is destroying the art of conversation so we ration ourselves to looking at one programme per year. We normally choose a programme which is concerned with something we are interested in, like the cheeses of Iceland or Arnold Bennett, but we happened to switch on when this science programme was in progress and we did not want to switch off in case we upset the man who was on the screen. It was one of those very serious investigative programmes in which young interviewers in dreadful little overcoats stopped people in the street and asked them things. And frightfully important scientists, looking like unemployed cellists, told us things in regional accents. And politicians, sleek and pale, kept saying "Let us be quite clear about one thing . . ." and "I have said before and I will say again . . ." and "In a situation like the situation we are in . . ." and "As I said recently to the Home Secker-tree . . ."

The burden of the programme, which came as something as a shock to my lady wife and me, was that very shortly, either in fifty years' time or next Tuesday – the sound went wobbly and we are not certain which – all the oil in the world is going to dry up. One need not stress what repercussions this will have. The Arabs will have nothing valuable to sell to the West and will be reduced to penury and going round pubs with cardboard suitcases trying to flog sand to put into egg-timers. One will have to fry one's aubergines in dripping.

Worse than that, the programme pointed out, there will be no electricity. We will have no television once a year. We will have to drill little holes in our electric light bulbs and put nightlights in them. The pop-up toaster will remain cold and inert. Oil lamps which were expensively converted to electricity will have to be reconverted to oil and then, because there will not be any oil, thrown away.

But there is hope. It seems that we shall be all right – or all right for a week or two longer – if, instead of squandering our oil and coal and electricity, we eke it out. Chaps are now studying how best we can eke out absolutely everything – eke out trees, eke out food, eke out wildlife – in a new science which they called 'ekeology'. An ekeologist then came on the screen – he looked about fourteen, with staring eyes and hair like a Brillo pad – and told us to eke like mad; not to waste a drop of oil or a volt of electricity. Then there was a power-cut and all the lights went out.

I swung into action immediately. I switched off the central heating thereby ekeing electricity and gas in one go.

Then came the problem of how to keep warm during the winter. It was not too bad during the day. We burned unekeable rubbish in the fireplace, like potato peelings and tea leaves, which gave off a bit of heat. Also the thick smoke which filled the house was not only acrid but also faintly warm. We developed a technique of dashing about the house all day at the double and eating our meals standing up and running-on-the-spot. The trouble came at night. The house is old, and winds creep in all over the place and find many cracks to creep out of, so in cold weather there is a constant icy gale blowing through the bedrooms.

I solved the problem of our own bedroom with beautiful simplicity. I bought a pair of baggy clown costumes from a theatrical costumier. When night fell and we retired (to save candles), we each donned our clown costume. These did up tightly at the ankles but were very loose about the body and had a wide neck. When my wife was safely within hers she stood still and I carefully poured buckets of sawdust down inside her collar and into her costume until she filled out and could accept no more. I then wedged rolled-up newspaper into her collar to prevent the sawdust escaping, sealed it with sticky tape and she was four feet wide but snug and warm. She then did the same to me and we rolled each other into bed.

My problem was the spare bedroom. I bought another pair of clown costumes but our guests did not take to them kindly. Nor were they all that efficient on some of our friends: the Bishop, for instance, who was so portly that the costume fitted him like a glove, leaving no room for sawdust to be poured in. It was a poser.

Then one day, musing on the theme of solar heating, I noticed my wife's greenhouse. Although cold in the garden, the interior of the greenhouse was snug and warm. And it was just large enough to take a double bed.

The next few days were busy ones. I began by buying a quantity of oak beams. These I installed in the dining room to prop up the ceiling, which was the floor of the spare bedroom and had to bear a great deal of extra weight.

Next task was to dismantle the greenhouse, number each part, cart it up to the spare bedroom and reconstitute it in the middle of the floor. There was a nasty moment when the double bed would not go through the greenhouse door. We overcame that by dismantling the greenhouse again and re-erecting it over the bed.

That night my wife and I slept in it to give it a trial run. It was not a success. We had left a quantity of vegetables still growing in the greenhouse and the night was so cold that we woke up frozen to the marrow.

It was my wife who spotted the design fault. The greenhouse was not getting any sun to warm it, now that it was in the bedroom.

I removed the tiles from the roof over the spare bedroom, hacked away the ceiling above the greenhouse and had the satisfaction of seeing sunshine – albeit thin and watery winter sun – pour on to the glass. I took the temperature inside at 4 p.m. and it stood at 84 degrees Fahrenheit. We had another trial run that night. Another disaster. At 4 a.m. the temperature dropped to minus two and in the greenhouse it was cold enough to freeze the wheels off a Douglas DC3.

"But . . ." I said.

"Well," said my wife. "You see, when it was in the garden the sun warmed it during the day and at night a little electric heater came on."

Pretty infuriating, you must admit. There was I, patriotically ekeing like fury, and all the time the potted plants were being kept happy on watts galore. I put my foot down, of course. No consumption of energy would take place in the spare bedroom of any sort whatwhomsoever. Somehow I had to think of a way of providing gentle, natural warmth within the greenhouse without using coal, wood, electricity, gas, oil . . .

In the garden next day I gave a great shout. "D-U-N-G!!!"

"Is it one o'clock already?" said my wife, straightening up from her hoe.

"That was not the church clock striking," I exclaimed, "it was me! What is dung used to make? A – wait for it – a HOT-BED! If we fill the spare mattress with dung it will give off a constant natural heat, twenty-four hours a day! Quick, I will hold the mattress cover open while you fork the stuff in – Lady Muckberth!"

With a smile she got to work. We filled the mattress with dung, laid it on the bed in the greenhouse upstairs and in a moment it had begun giving off its gentle warmth. Nothing dramatic, of course, but the temperature never dropped below freezing point again.

"A good job jobbed, I think," I said, putting an arm round my wife. "Now all that remains is for you to cover a pair of clothes-pegs with padded cretonne for our guests' noses when in bed . . ."

Now, when we have guests to stay at our lovely home (and they are more than welcome), we can, without worry, put them to bed in our Old Testament Spare Bedroom.

Many are cold, but few are frozen.

'The Stars and Stripes Forever'

J. P. Sousa

I don't know how you feel about going to parties in fancy dress, but as a source of pleasure I have always ranked it somewhere on a level with cleaning the oven. That's why, when I received an invitation last August from a certain rather florid magazine publisher inviting us to an opulent costume party to be held at his legendary country home, my overwhelming impulse was to weasel out. "Make some plausible excuse," I pleaded to my wife. "I've been carried off by a UFO. The Welsh Nationalists are holding me hostage. I'm having labour pains. Think of *something*!"

She gave that sigh of patient tolerance with which those closest to me seem to greet so many of my most passionate utterances these days. "I'm well aware how much you hate having to think up something you can go as," she said. "But this should be an easy one for you. The invitation asks guests to dress up as 'The Title of One of Your Favourite Films', and you *love* films. So you should be able to think of *hundreds* you can design a costume for."

Because my enthusiasm for indulging in any kind of dressing up cannot be understressed, I refused to rise even to that bait. Consequently, when we went to get the car out on the night of the party I was attired in my usual clothes. If reproached, I had decided to claim I was representing the title of a 1950s Gregory Peck vehicle, *The Man in the Grey Flannel Suit*. By contrast, however, my partner had really entered into the spirit of the thing. She'd found herself a fairly *dégagé* chiffon nightie, cut it even lower at the neck, and was going as *In the Heat of the Night*.

The trouble started when I suggested that an alternative title for her might be *Room at the Top*. She didn't take it very well. But it was when

I went on to weave an engaging fantasy round the theme of *The Odd Couple* that her lips pursed to the size of a penny jam-tart. She jumped into the car and sped off into the night, leaving me alone in the garage.

It was apparent that I had gone too far. I also realised, from long experience of such moments, that the only chance I now had of restoring even a semblance of harmony would be to return to the house and penitently don something in the nature of real fancy dress.

It was at this point that I realised something else. Not only had she gone off with the car, but she'd also taken the house keys with her. In other words, whatever costume I might manage to dream up, it could only be assembled from the materials available in the garage.

A glance around showed these to be both few and unpromising. Hanging from a hook on a side wall were two old raincoats the kids used to wear for school. If I were to try climbing into those, could I get away with *The Blue Macs*? A moment's consideration and I rejected the idea, if only because it was never a film I could support as being among my favourites.

What else was to hand? (I silently cursed the uncharacteristic attack of neatness that had prompted me to clean out the garage the previous week.) Leaning against the back wall was an old perspex windscreen. Ah . . .! Suppose I cut a neat rectangle out of the seat of my trousers, then covered the hole with an oblong of the transparent perspex? Could I then pass myself off as the Hitchcock masterpiece, *Rear Window*? Or even, possibly, *Smiling Through*?

Neither possibility satisfied the complete transformation of dress I had to achieve if I were to be granted a parole from the doghouse. Then my eye lighted on something which fulfilled all the requirements – two chamois washleathers! By joining them together with a staple-gun they could be pressed into service as an unexceptionable facsimile of a jungle loin-cloth. It was the work of a moment to strip off, fasten the leathers around me, and there I was – the undeniable title of one of my all-time favourite motion-pictures, *Tarzan of the Apes*.

I still believe my personal Jane would be talking to me today if the taxi I called to transport me to the party hadn't broken down half a mile from the publisher's country house. As it was, I was obliged to make the last section of the journey on foot and, not wishing to court undue attention by walking along the road in such an exiguous garment, I set off across the dark fields.

This, as has now been dinned into me, was my major mistake. I hadn't gone a hundred yards when there was a pounding of hooves behind me. Looking over my shoulder, I saw the most wicked looking bull I've ever set eyes on making towards me.

I don't know how many of you have ever tried running at speed in a tight leather loin-cloth? For those who haven't, let me explain that the faster you move, the tighter the loin-cloth constricts the area it covers. (In fact, I now take that to be the reason why the real Tarzan used to emit so many of those peculiarly high-pitched cries.) In the end, the garment became such an impediment that I realised the only way I'd keep ahead of the bull was to cast it off.

Which was why, when I finally burst through the hedge on to the lawn where the publisher's fashionable gathering was assembled, I was panting, sweating and stark naked. They, of course, took my nudity to be the costume I'd chosen to arrive in and immediately began exchanging guesses as to which film I was representing.

Some of those guesses were, I will admit, quite flattering. I was as taken by one gentleman's venture at *Splendour in the Grass* as I was by a certain lady's *The Greatest Show on Earth*. Other speculations, though, were as ill-mannered as they were inapposite. While I was somewhat affronted by my host's stab at *The Incredible Shrinking Man* the suggestion I really took exception to came from his daughter who, after one brief glance, proposed a film I didn't even think she looked old enough to remember: *Wee Willie Winkie*.

But it was a keen-eyed local farmer who brought me to the depths of humiliation. To justify his confident declaration that the only possible film title for me had to be *Midnight Cowboy*, he proceeded to point out that the animal from which I'd been fleeing hadn't actually been a bull at all.

It was that explanation which prompted the caption the local newspaper printed under a quarter-page picture their enterprising photographer had managed to snap of me while I was running across the field. Taken just at the moment when I was divesting myself of my loin-cloth in an attempt to escape from what could now clearly be seen as a young cow, it bore the words:

"This Tarzan strips for heifer".

'Pickwick Papers'

Charles Dickens
Title of novel

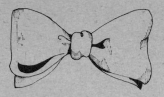

I give you – and I am in no hurry to have it back – the Muir Method of Throwing a Successful Party.

One has only to think of famous hosts and hostesses of the past – the names of Signora Borgia, Count Dracula, Lady Macbeth spring instantly to mind – to realise that the failure rate of parties has always been high. In our modern world it has never been higher and it is, in my view, due to a basic misconception of what constitutes a good party.

The golden rule is simple and obvious but so important that every hostess should have it tattooed on her thigh – *people do not go to parties to enjoy themselves.*

People accept invitations to parties for a variety of reasons but the prospect of having a good time is seldom one of them. My researches indicate that 81 per cent accept because they are the victims of a mild form of moral blackmail and will lose face if they refuse. Eight per cent accept because they fail to read the invitation properly and think it is for something else. Six per cent do not know that they *have* accepted because their spouse has accepted for them. Four per cent accept because there is only a play about dying and a Party Political Broadcast on television. And 1 per cent have no choice.

The 1 per cent I met who had no choice was a lecturer in philosophy and linguistics at an emergent university on the east coast. Rigid with boredom, he had given up picking bits of the flock wallpaper off with his thumbnail and had begun hitting the wine-cup. I got to him just as his forehead went shiny and walked him round the block.

"What a boring party," he mumbled to the stars. "*Boringly* boring, to boot. And boring *with* it . . ."

"Then why did you accept the invitation?" I asked, notebook at the ready.

"Had to," he mumbled. "I'm the wassisname . . . the host."

Once you accept that none of your guests are there to enjoy themselves the whole philosophy falls into place. Clearly to give them an enjoyable time would be letting them down. They would forget the whole thing in an hour. But give them a subtly awful party and they will be able to pick it over and wallow in it in retrospect for months. A grievance shared is a grievance doubled. Your aim must be to send them home happily grumbling about all aspects of the evening.

To achieve this success needs careful planning and vigilant attention to detail. Nothing must be left to chance if everything is to go with a thud.

Guests can help a little in making the party fail to go with a swing. Quite a good idea is to grip your host by the hand when he opens the door to you and embark upon an immensely obscure and lengthy anecdote. If your timing is good you should be able to pile up other arriving guests behind you until a sizeable queue is waiting and grumbling. Making guests bellow with laughter when their mouths are stuffed with flaky *vol-au-vent* is an effective ploy, as is pressing a cup of coffee on a guest when she is already clutching a drink and her handbag in one hand and a plate of cheese and half a metre of French bread in the other.

But making a party ghastly/successful is mostly the responsibility of the hostess. She must be always alert for pockets of resistance, e.g. couples who are enjoying talking to each other (disgracefully antisocial behaviour). She must move instantly, take one of the malefactors firmly by the elbow and cry shrilly, "I'm going to break you two things up! There's someone here absolutely *dying* to meet you . . .!"

Happy laughter anywhere in the room, unless it has an edge of hysteria to it, is a bad sign. An experienced hostess immediately bangs on the table for attention and screams, "Food everybody!"

The food and drink which you serve are a vital element in making your party the most talked-about of the year. A successfully awful party is one where the hostess has clearly gone to immense trouble to provide fine, interesting food and drink and has, even more clearly, failed miserably.

The wine should be red (cheap red wine is much fouler than cheap white wine). As poor wine improves enormously on being served slightly warm you should serve yours straight from the fridge. It is important that the wine should not be instantly detectable as rubbish. The guests must be able to retain a slight doubt as to whether it is the wine which is at fault or their palates, so choose one of those extremely cheap plonks which have a homely label with a simple, seemingly honest inscription which just says 'Sound French Table Wine' or, even better, 'Red'.

Always have plenty of pretty bowls around filled with elderly potato crisps. Open the packets a few days before the party and give the crisps a good airing. They are ready when they look and taste like autumn leaves. Olives are always popular but make sure that they are not the stuffed variety but those which consist of a stone covered with immovable green skin. An optional extra is to provide oriental rice crackers. These are spotty little biscuits so hard that you will hear your guests' fillings crack like small-arms' fire. They are very expensive, taste like earth and, before they had the bright idea of exporting them, were what Japanese peasants ate when they could not afford food.

For the more ambitious hostess, here is a list of prepared dishes. Next to the recipe I have given a name; this is in case one of your guests is drunk enough, or fawning enough, to exclaim "This is delicious! – do tell me what it is!"

(1) Fine slices of brown plastic which stay in the mouth undiminished even after five long hours of chewing.   PARMA HAM
(2) A bowl of shaving cream from an aerosol sprinkled with grated cheese rind.   GARLIC WHIP
(3) Half a pint of white impact glue warming over a nightlight.   SWISS FONDUE
(4) Small squares of old toast smeared with bacon rind, cleansing cream, dripping, sardine tails or anything.   CANAPÉS
(5) Thin slices of stale Hovis spread with butter into which a drop of cochineal has been dropped to make it pink, rolled up and rubbed on a kipper.   SMOKED SALMON FINGERS
(6) A failed omelet into which bits of ham have been thumbed, served on a piece of cardboard.   QUICHE

My wife and I have operated the Muir Method of Throwing a Successful Party for some years now with only one failure that I can remember. It was a Burns Night Party and it went so well, according to plan, that after twenty minutes guests were looking at their watches and stifling yawns.

My big mistake was piping in the haggis. The haggis itself was perfect – my wife had made a shepherd's pie, with porridge instead of meat, and stuffed an old football bladder with it – but I had misguidedly engaged four members of the London-Scottish Rugby Club to play the bagpipes. I put the steaming haggis on a silver tray and carried it from the kitchen out into the corridor to lead the pipers into the dining room. What a shock when I saw the pipers. They were all about nine feet tall and built like brick oast-houses. Below their kilts their calf muscles stuck out like water-melons. We formed up. I opened the dining-room door and marched in. Behind me four right arms clamped down on their bagpipe bags like legs of mutton clamping on grapes, and they blew. And there came forth noise.

Several things then happened at once. The Afghan hound rose in the air as if by levitation, hung for a moment on the curtain-rail and then pulled the whole thing out of the wall. They raised Tower Bridge. Two lady guests had hysterics and disappeared backwards over the rear of the sofa. The mirror cracked in two. The fire brigade arrived.

It was three in the morning before the last guest departed, wringing our hands and saying how much he had enjoyed himself – the whole evening was a total disaster. They had had *fun*.

Do by all means use the Muir Method for your next party but make sure that you do not make that one mistake that we made. If you have a Burns Night Party, pipe in the haggis – but, in the words of Charles Dickens –

Pick weak pipers.